OLGA DE LEBEDEFF

A LIFE
ACROSS EMPIRES

A Scholar's Quest from Tsarist
Russia to the Bosphorus & Beyond

Carina Hamilton

With Contributions by Marilyn Booth

Dedicated to Veronica, Michael, Jamie, Luke & Daniel

Pomegranate Star Publishing

First Printing in 2024

Copyright © Carina Hamilton, 2024
All Rights Reserved.

The moral right of the author has been asserted.

Every reasonable effort has been made to trace copyright holders of material in this book, but if any have been inadvertently overlooked, the publishers would be glad to hear from them. For legal purposes the Sources and Acknowledgements constitute an extension of this copyright page.

No part of this publication may be reproduced, distributed, or transmitted in any form or by any means, including photocopying, recording, or other electronic or mechanical methods, without the prior written permission of the publisher, except in the case of brief quotations embodied in a book review and certain other non-commercial uses permitted by copyright law. No reproduction by any means may be made of the images from the De Gubernatis correspondence authorised for this volume by the Minister of Culture / Biblioteca Nazionale Centrale, Firenze.

ISBN 978-1-7394294-1-6

Contact us by email: pomegranatestar@icloud.com
Or connect on:
Facebook.com/PomegranateStarPublishing
Instagram: @publishingpomegranatestar

Coat of Arms: Barstchoff / Borshov

Coat of Arms: Kutaissoff / Kutaisov

Coat of Arms: Lebedeff / Lebedev

Olga de Lebedeff's pseudonym, Gülnar, printed in golden Arabic script

Contents

Preface ix

Introduction x

Book One ....

1 Origins at St Petersburg 1
    Olga's paternal line in the nineteenth century   2
    Grandmother Elizaveta and the Grand Duchess Elena Pavlovna   4
    Serge and the Lancers Lifeguards Regiment   5
    Olga's maternal line: the countess bride and her upbringing   6
    Cornet to Cavalry Captain: The Crimean War   8
    On the reform Emancipation of the Serfs   9

2 A Thousand Gracious Thoughts 11
    Godfather - The Heir Apparent   11
    Life in St Petersburg   12
    The Chancellor – Uncle Alexander Gorchakov   15
    The memoirs of Cassius Clay, US envoy to St Petersburg   17

3 Letters from the Grand Tour: Down the Rhine 19
    To dear Serge   21
    Basel – Geneva – St Jean-de Maurienne – Turin   23
    A month on the Ligurian riviera at Genoa   27
    Dear Papa   30

4 Your Obedient Daughter: Paris 34
    Four languages   38

	Count Charles Lambert	42
	Sighting of Napoleon III	45
	Summer – happy as a lark	46
	Years later and a photograph from Sicily	51
5	**The New Family: Dlotovsky**	**53**
	The arranged marriage	55
	About Olga's betrothed, Volodya	59
	Family life in Kovno and public charity	63
	A new posting to Kazan	68
6	**The Mayor of Kazan**	**72**
	The diaries of Alexandra Bogdanovich	74
	About Alexander Alexandrovich Lebedeff	76
	The countryside estate at Lubiana, Viatka	79
	In winter and summer	84
7	**Gülnar and the Jadids**	**90**
	Pen name of Gülnar	91
	Professor Gottwald	93
	Madame Gülnar's early 'sharqi' folk songs	94
	The Society of Archaeology, History and Ethnography (O.A.I.E.)	97
	The Jadids	98
	Three Tatar Educationalists	101
8	**The Invitation to Constantinople**	**106**
	Introducing the publisher Ahmed Midhat Efendi	107
	At the Stockholm Congress in 1889	109
	The journey across Europe to Paris	112
	Olga's arrival in Constantinople, 1890	118
9	**First Translations from Princes to Pushkin**	**125**
	First publication – The Qabus Nameh – or Book of Cavus	126
	Refuting the French Orientalist, Ernest Renan	128
	The Poet Pushkin: His Life, Art, Works	130
	On the literary circle: The Souls of Arzamas	132
	To elicit sympathy through fiction	134

10	**A Wedding and the World of Harems**	137
	Secretaire de S.M.I. Le Sultan Abd-Ul-Hamid Khan II	140
	To Ahmed Midhat's mansion on the Bosphorus	143
11	**On Skilful Women Writers**	149
	Fatma Aliye and Gülnar as a role model	150
	Representation at Chicago's World Fair in 1893	152
	The concept of a 'New Woman'	153
	Friendship and misunderstanding	155
	Olga's departure from Constantinople	158
12	**Islamic Revival of Volga Tatars**	161
	Pilgrimages and transnational networks	163
	Missionaries	165
	Influential madrasas	166
	Gilman Karimov	168
13	**Censorship and Discontent**	170
	Interview with a St Petersburg journalist	172
	Pre-1905 censorship of Muslim teaching & Tatar discontent	173
	On Tatar Schooling and Government Attitudes	175
	Education for women and girls	179
	Stories of famous women from Bulgar, Sarai and Kazan	181
	A new Tatar poem for Madame Gülnar	182
14	**An Account of the Conquest of Kazan, 1899**	185
	References and Sources	186
	An outline translation of Abrégé de l'Histoire de Kazan	187
	Reflections on the text	196
	On the 'civilising' of Asia	198
15	**Letters to Tolstoy & on the Unity of Religion**	203
	Dear Sir, Count Lev Nikolayevich!	203
	Fears about hostility towards Christians	205
	Parallel text on the unity of religion (1894)	206
	Babis and Baha'i	208
16	**The Draw of Cairo**	212
	The Italian Count de Gubernatis	212

	First impressions of Cairo (1898)	215
	Famous women: Princess Nazli and Zaynab Fawwaz	220
	A history of heroines: Young Woman of the East	221
17	The Call for Women's Emancipation	223
	On the Emancipation of Muslim Women 1900	225
	The Russian copy	229
	The international women's movement in 1900	231
	An advocate in E. Groult: 1899 & 1901	232
	Ideologist of the Young Turks	237
18	At the International Congress of Orientalists 1889-1899 ...	240
	Stockholm VIII Congress: 3- 12 September 1889	242
	Geneva X Congress: 1894	243
	Between the congresses: 1895 -1897 & The Spirit of Islam	243
	Rome XII Congress: 4 to 15 October 1899	245
19	Society of Oriental Studies: St Petersburg 1900	249
	Key questions facing Russia: A Unified Empire	250
	Aims of the Society of Oriental Studies	252
	International recognition	258
	Academicians and women in the field	259
	Building bridges	260
20	At the Congress: Hamburg to Athens (1902 -1912)	262
	Hamburg XIII Congress: 8 September 1902	262
	Algiers XIV Congress: 6 - 19 April 1905	265
	Copenhagen XV Congress 14 -20 August 1908	266
	Athens XVI Congress: 6-14 April 1912	267
21	Old Wisdom - Theosophy in Cairo	269
	Other Russian Theosophists	271
	Influence of Theosophy on Olga de Lebedeff	272
	Olga's choice of translations	273
22	Arco, Austro-Hungarian Empire	276
	The death of Prascovia	280
	Villa Lubiana and its guests	280

		A million rubles and personal loss	*282*
23		**Russian biography, Revolution and Revelation**	284
		At the Revolution	*285*
		Destination Arco	*286*
		The Pearl of France	*288*
		A revelation in Sacha's confiscated letters	*290*

Epilogue 292

Book Two 299
    Translations   *299*

The Poet Pushkin (1891) 300

Muslim Women at the Time of the Caliphs (1899) 327

On the Emancipation of Muslim Women (1900) 329

On The New Rights of Muslim Women (1902) 341

Speech at the Algiers Congress (1905) 348

An Appreciation: On The Conversion of the Georgians to Christianity by the Patriarch Macaire 350

Famous Women: Gülnar Hanım, or Mme Olga de Lébédef (1907, Cairo) 354

Appendix: A Short History of Ivan Kutaisov (Koutaissoff) 362
    The Favourite   *363*
    The Unopened Letter   *366*
    Olga's Great Grandparents   *367*
    The last Kutaisovs   *370*

Author's Notes 372
    Calendar Dates   *372*
    Variations in Spelling of Names & Places   *372*
    Olga de Lebedeff or Olga Lebedeva?   *374*
    Patronymics   *375*
    Questions and Debates of the Period   *376*

Orientalist and Orientologist 377

Sources and Acknowledgements 383

Bibliography 388

Endnotes 395

Preface

Ten years ago, I began to make a study of a collection of sepia-coloured photographs and family documents. The majority of these had been transported to England from Argentina in a series of brown envelopes, sent by my cousin Nina. What history lay behind these treasured antique pictures?

A photograph of Olga de Lebedeff was one of these, and it caught my eye because the surname of Lebedeff inscribed on the back did not appear to match any other surnames in the family tree. When people are no longer a memory and just a name, this is still a place to start.

Amongst the papers were timeworn original manuscripts, some dating back to the eighteenth century from Tsarist Russia. As I was the only descendant to have learned any Russian, it was down to me to decipher the scrawling hand-written Cyrillic words, and though this was not going to be an easy job, there was something compelling about it.

Carina Hamilton
Farnham, UK
July 2024

INTRODUCTION

This book centres around the life and works of Olga de Lebedeff (1852-1933), whose life began in St Petersburg just before the Crimean War and ended in the turmoil of 1930s Europe. She is also known as Olga Sergeevna Lebedeva, or by her Turkic sounding pen name: *Gülnar*.

Women in St Petersburg of Olga's generation and social standing were often educated by foreign governesses or at elite girls' boarding schools and then married to someone of their parents' choosing. If they could produce children to continue the family name, someone else would nurse and educate them. A wife would principally occupy the drawing room engaged in private pursuits or social engagements, unless drawn into helping some charitable cause. It was a time in Russia when such women began to desire and seek out higher educational opportunities and how to help those less fortunate than themselves, because they saw service to society as a personal moral duty.

In tracing Olga's family background and discovering her early life from newly translated letters, we meet a visionary who was inspired to travel and study independently, and whose achievements bent the rules of tradition. Despite having eight children which was not uncommon for the time, she broke other domestic and social stereotypes.

By the turn of the twentieth century, emerging from a period when the very idea of a well-educated woman was ridiculed, Olga de Lebedeff was renowned as a Turcologist and an Orientalist. It was a field dominated by male academics, but she managed to forge a place amongst them. She was one of the first translators of Russian literature into Ottoman Turkish, including works by Leo Tolstoy and Alexander

INTRODUCTION

Pushkin. In this book, her contribution within Russian Orientalism is explored, framed within the Russian and European concepts of 'the Orient' of that era.

Olga is important to European history in her work, through her intimate knowledge of the Ottoman empire and her engagement with the Islamic world. With her knowledge of Ottoman Turkish and Tatar languages and her role as a translator of Russian works, she ploughed a unique furrow between East and West, interpreting the cultures of each for the other. She was taught and influenced by reformist Muslim teachers in the Russian Empire called Jadids. Many times she countered misperceptions about the Muslim world, including amongst European Orientalists.

Olga promoted the cause of Muslim women both in Russia and abroad, an activist for their education and rights. As a woman, she had an almost unique exposure to the life of the harem. Both Russian and Tatar historians have previously recognised her as the first woman Oriental scholar and advocate for Muslim women.

An author of intellectual repute and a foreigner, she was viewed for a time by some elite Ottomans as an example or prototype of a 'new woman.'[1] This meant a woman with broader horizons and capabilities, whose attainments were perceived to merit an expanded domain of autonomy. The ideal of a new woman was one of lasting importance. The concept of women high achievers would enter nationalist discourse in Turkey decades later.

At a time of great political rivalry between Imperial Russia and the Ottoman Empire, one of Olga's key aims was to improve relations between these neighbouring peoples of different cultures and religions. In 1900, she founded a Society of Oriental Studies in St Petersburg, with support of government officials and the royal household. The society comprised a practical academy for trade and cultural exchange within and outside Russia, and a language school, which over the years taught languages from the Middle East, Central Asia and the Far East.

With her interest in religion and the spiritual life, in her mid-fifties Olga de Lebedeff founded the first Theosophical lodge in Cairo in 1908, a lodge that continued its existence into the 1930's.

She is still fondly remembered in Tatarstan, which in her day was named Kazan Governorate, for defending the rights of Kazan's Tatars.

OLGA DE LEBEDEFF – A LIFE ACROSS EMPIRES

Olga de Lebedeff ended life as a refugee in the tumult of the twentieth century, one of the displaced peoples of Russian origin who became a diaspora. Descendants tended to hold onto nostalgic memories of a place and culture that after the Russian Revolution and Civil War changed unrecognisably.

A Personal Connection

Olga de Lebedeff is my great-great-grandmother. Her story is brought to light here through newly found archive materials, memoirs and press articles, as well as by her own unique photographs preserved by her daughter and granddaughter. Olga's life and activism is painted through the lens and context of her family history set within the period. This book describes my own discovery of her, related by themes and in largely chronological order.

My granny's name was Nina Bahache de Bobrovsky, but I knew of her simply as Babu, short for 'babushka'. She was the granddaughter of Olga de Lebedeff. Babu's collection of antique photographs relating to the life of Olga have only recently been unpacked and examined. On the reverse side of a few pictures are her inscriptions, where Olga's name is featured under one of the following options:

- *Olga Borschoff-Kutaissov de Lebedeff*
- *Grand Maman Olga Sergeevna Lebedeff (Dlotovsky) née Borschoff*
- *Olga Borschoff-Kutaisoff*

One note in blue ink (Fig. 1) clarified that Olga had been married twice and gave a few other intriguing details. Another note cited a country house near Kazan in Russia and a villa near Lake Garda. A large portrait taken in Kazan was labelled 'Olga de Lebedeff, the famous Orientalist.'

It transpired that Olga de Lebedeff was well-known as an expert on Middle Eastern studies, and she was one of the first women active in that field. Two scholarly articles in English confirmed this.[2] Other sources, which were less accessible to me being written in Russian and Turkish, concurred and spoke of her as a distinguished Orientalist.[3]

Otherwise, there appeared to be no single archive, no memorial, no death certificate, nor any obituary. Olga de Lebedeff, or Lebedeva,

INTRODUCTION

appeared to have been all but forgotten in Middle Eastern Studies following the Russian Revolution. Her birthplace and background remained quite unknown.

Learning about Olga has meant discovering the part of my maternal family which originated in Imperial Russia. Family histories are often hard to explore in depth at the best of times and this is all the truer during or after a time of war and revolution, which disrupts or puts an end to 'normal' life,

Thus, I also found that place names, maps, entire alphabets, customs, and languages changed and were replaced over time. For instance, excepting French and Italian, even the various languages that Olga wrote in have altered: Tatar used to be written in Arabic script, now it is in Cyrillic; the Ottoman Turkish language is now obsolete, Turkish is written in Roman script; the German old Gothic script is no longer readily readable except to specialists.

One Hundred Years Later

After the Russian Revolution, the nobility ceased to exist. People like Olga with aristocratic status, the nobility, the intelligentsia or officers from the Tsarist army were termed 'enemies of the people' or just referred to as: *бывшие* ('former'). If they left the motherland, they would be stateless, and if they stayed, they faced discrimination without basic civil rights.[4]

Besides this, my research showed that the lives and histories of women tended to be little recorded in writing, except for details such when they were born, whom they married and the names of their children; an example of their subordinate role in society at the time. Husbands were defined by their careers and many family trees give exclusive priority to the male line. My mother's family tended to refer to their paternal lineage, the Bobrovskys, whose fathers and grandfathers were generals and historians, and who held the hereditary title of Count.

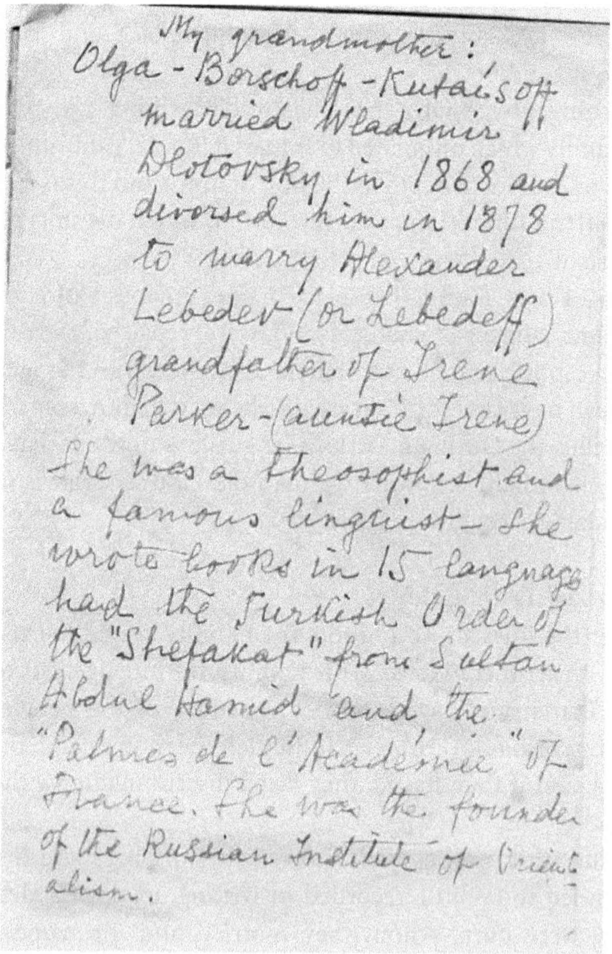

> My grandmother: Olga - Borschoff - Kutaïssoff married Wladimir Dlotovsky in 1868 and divorsed him in 1878 to marry Alexander Lebedev (or Lebedeff) grandfather of Irene Parker - (auntie Irene). She was a theosophist and a famous linguist — she wrote books in 15 languages, had the Turkish Order of the "Shefakat" from Sultan Abdul Hamid, and the "Palmes de l'Académie" of France. She was the founder of the Russian Institute of Orientalism.

Fig. 1
My granny's explanatory note in the family collection.

This book seeks to trace a different kind of 'maternal inheritance', through the story of Olga de Lebedeff, her daughters and other women in Olga's sphere, to reflect on the social influence that they too wielded.

Following the diaspora of Olga's descendants after the Revolution, and the break in relations between countries and peoples during the Soviet period, World War II, and the Cold War era, recovering their history is only possible some one hundred years later. This is thanks to

INTRODUCTION

the invention of the internet, email, and a window of opportunity when various archives have been made accessible.

Finding the Oriental scholar, Madame Gülnar

As mentioned previously, Olga de Lebedeff had a pen name of Gülnar, and friends in Istanbul (then Constantinople) called her Madame Gülnar.[5]

The aim of this book is to tell Olga's story, as well as to pay tribute to her contribution to Orientalism - or Orientology, as it is now known.

Her engagement with the Orientology of the period is significant, as she was one of the first women in this field at the turn of the twentieth century. In that period, even amongst Russian and European liberals, there were many who believed that women were physically and intellectually weaker than men and were incapable of serious academic study. Due to this, women's own opportunities for higher education were limited, except in the private sphere if finances allowed.[6]

***

In Book One, the narrative opens with the story of Olga's family background in St Petersburg set within the Russia of the 1850s, under her maiden-name of Barstchoff. Olga's childhood is sketched out in more depth by a newly translated cache of letters, which tell of her travels throughout Europe in 1860-1861. We follow her as a young woman, yearning to make a difference in society in the 1860s, and as she became disenchanted with a life of domesticity in the 1870s and 1880s.

Olga started life with the privileges enjoyed by the aristocracy, and this nineteenth century social network ensured that she was introduced to high society. But in her married life Olga had to learn to live with disappointment and loss. This led her to question the values of the society in which she lived, which in turn helped her to develop a new understanding of herself and what she could achieve in the public sphere.

In Book Two, translations of works by Olga de Lebedeff are presented for the first time in English. In addition to these, this volume includes a newly available biography of Olga, originally in Arabic and published in Cairo in 1907, translated by Professor Marilyn Booth.

For information about variations in dates, spellings of place names and on debates of the period, please see **Author's Notes**.

Olga's Family Tree

Great-Grandparents   **Grandparents**   **Parents**

- Ekaterina P. Tatischeva 1768-1855
- Alexandr M. Urusov 1767-1853
  - Natalya M. Urusova 1814-1882
- Prascovia P. Lopukhina 1784-1870
- Pavel I. Kutaisov 1780-1840
  - Hippolyte P. Kutaisov 1806-1851
    - Prascovia I. Kutaisova 1835-1900. 'Olga'
- Unknown
- Ivan Y. Bogdanov
  - Elizaveta I. Bogdanova 1804-1880
    - Serge M. Barstchoff 1826-1888
      - Olga S. Barstchoff 1852-1933
- Alexandra F. Dubyanskaya 1769-1798
- Sergei S. Barstchoff 1754-1837
  - Mikhail S. Barstchoff 1793-1862

INTRODUCTION

Principal Characters:

Olga de Lebedeff, born Olga Sergeevna Barstchoff, whose pen name was **Gülnar**
Mother: Prascovia Hippolitovna Barstchoff, born Countess Kutaisova (also 'Olga')
Father: Captain Serge Mikhailovich Barstchoff
Maternal Aunt: Countess Sophie Kutaisova
Paternal Aunt: Nadine Barstchoff
Godfather: Tsar Alexander II

First Marriage:	Second Marriage: Alexander Alexandrovich
Vladimir E. Dlotovsky ('Volodya'), Lawyer	Lebedeff, Mayor of Kazan
Children:	**Children:**
Nina Vladimirovna Dlotovsky	Alexander Alexandrovich Lebedeff ('Sacha')
Vera V. Dlotovsky	Olga A. Lebedeff ('Olla')
Vladimir V. Dlotovsky	Michel A. Lebedeff ('Micha')
Father-in-law: Erast K. Dlotovsky, General of the Infantry, President of the Supreme Military Court	

The Tatar Educationalists or Jadids	At Constantinople
Qayyum Nasyri, Teacher at Kazan	Sultan Abdülhamid II
Shigabudtin Marjani, Historian, Kazan	Nasri bey Bahache, Secretary to the Sultan
Ismail Gaspirali, Crimean Tatar Reformer	Ahmed Midhat, Ottoman publisher
	Fatma Aliye, writer
At Cairo	**Amongst the Orientalists**
Princess Nazli, President: *Alliance des Femmes*	Professor Josef Gottwald, Kazan
Qasim Amin, Jurist	Count Angelo de Gubernatis, Rome
Contessa della Sala	General Nikolai Schwedow, President of the Society of Oriental Studies, St Petersburg
Labiba Hashim, Founder of journal, *Fatat al Sharq* (Women of the East)	

Book One

Part I: On Becoming Olga de Lebedeff

1 Origins at St Petersburg

> You live as long as you are remembered.
> Russian Proverb

Centuries ago, the paternal Barstchoff ancestors of Olga de Lebedeff were boyars, courtiers who gave allegiance to the Princes of Muscovy.

Tsar Ivan the Terrible, who conquered the Tatar khanate of Kazan in 1552, was to later crush those boyars for their rebelliousness. In this way, a more subservient society was born.[7] The name of Barstchoff comes up again amongst the courtiers of the modernizing Tsar, Peter the Great, who built the city of St Petersburg as a 'window on Europe'.[8]

As for Olga's mother's side, ancestors were descended from amongst the most prominent names of nineteenth century Russian aristocracy: Koutaïssoff (Kutaisov) and Ouroussoff (Urusov). The first person to be called Koutaïssoff was Olga's great-great-grandfather, the infamous Count Ivan Koutaïssoff. He had been a true favourite of Tsar Paul I; his remarkable rise to power is told here separately in the Appendix. On the other hand, the Ouroussoff princes had ancient links to the confederation of the Nogai Horde nomads who had established themselves on the Steppes south of Kazan. Their heritage included the marriage of a sixteenth century princess of the Nogai Horde with a Muscovite prince.

By the nineteenth century, the paternal grandparents of Olga de Lebedeff retained strong connections in St Petersburg. The men of the family served in the government or army, and some of the women were handpicked as ladies-in-waiting at the Imperial Court.

Olga's paternal line in the nineteenth century

Great-grandfather, Sergei Semionovich Barstchoff (1754-1837) had fought in the Imperial Lifeguards Ismailovsky Regiment against the Swedes in 1790 and against Napoleon in 1812. He later served as Senator and Privy Councillor to Alexander I. His in-laws, who had a neighbouring estate near Lake Ladoga, were freemasons and descendants of the Confessor of the last two Empresses of Russia.[9] His sister, the accomplished Natalya Borschova, received a gold medal at the Smolny Institute from the Empress Catherine and became Dame of the Order of St Catherine in 1803, high honours indeed for a noble woman.

Fig. 2
Olga's Great Aunt Natalya Borschova, by Levitsky

Olga's grandfather was State Councillor and Chamberlain Mikhail Sergeevich Barstchoff (1793-1862). He inherited several properties including four apartments in central St Petersburg.[10] One of these was right by the Egyptian Bridge on the desirable Fontanka Embankment; the bridge's partially gilded sphinx statues and cast iron gates decorated with hieroglyphs were testament to an era gripped by Egyptomania. Another was a stone's throw away on Troitsky Avenue near the magnificent Trinity Cathedral [*Troitsky Sobor*] of the Ismailovsky regiment.

2

ORIGINS AT ST PETERSBURG

The family estate in Schlisselburg north of the capital was named *Porechiye*. This comprised a manor house and gardens, the surrounding arable land tilled by serfs, and whole villages. In his property portfolio there were also other estates in the Yaroslavl region at Zarechiye, founded by an uncle, and a manor at Bochatina near Ilinskoe-na-Shache.[11]

Grandfather Mikhail Sergeevich and his wife Elizaveta Ivanovna Bogdanova (1804-1880) retired to another quiet country residence at Turovo with gardens and arable lands, a shortish journey by carriage from St Petersburg near a fresh water lake.

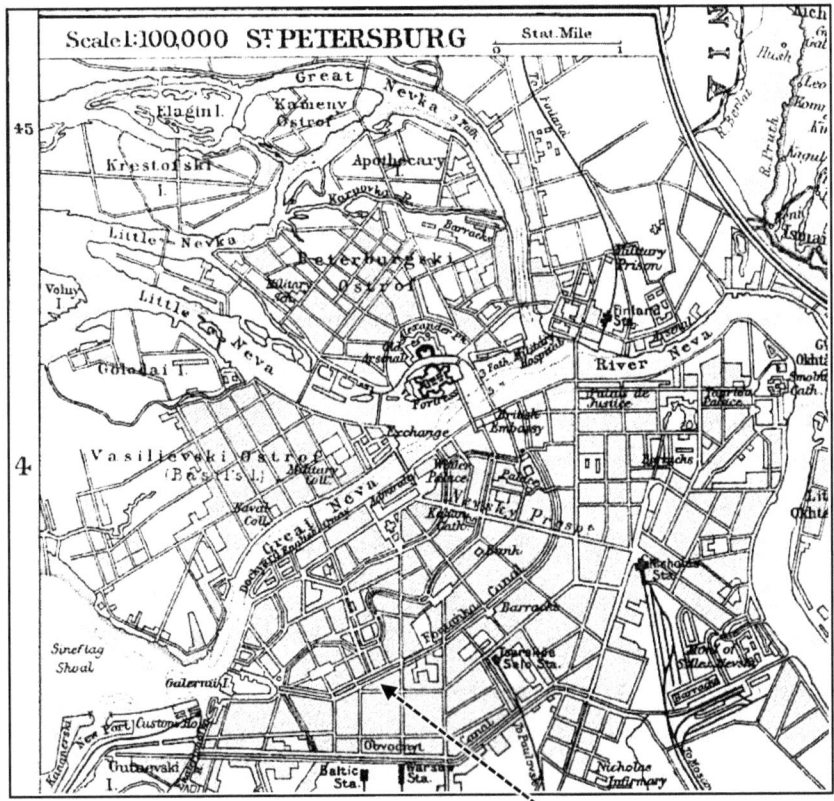

Fig. 3 Map of St Petersburg, 136 Fontanka Embankment[12]

Grandmother Elizaveta and the Grand Duchess Elena Pavlovna

The gentle-natured Elizaveta Barstchoff (née Bogdanova) spoke French to her children. The relationship was warm but outwardly restrained and formal; for instance, she used the French word 'vous' rather than the more intimate 'tu' in her letters to her son, Serge; but no doubt that was then the norm.

In her youth, Elizaveta had served as lady in waiting to the intellectual of the Romanov family, the Grand Duchess Elena Pavlovna. The Grand Duchess was the wife of Tsar Paul I's youngest son Michael Romanov, and so an aunt of Alexander II.

In 1854, when Florence Nightingale travelled to Turkey and began nursing invalids during the Crimean War, the Grand Duchess founded the 'Community of the Holy Cross Sisters of Mercy' in St Petersburg. Her nurses were trained to treat the wounded at military hospitals, such as at the besieged fortress of Sevastopol and at other battles.[13]

Grand Duchess Elena Pavlovna was an influential advisor to Tsar Alexander II, helping to convince him that it now really was time to emancipate the serfs. She also encouraged the tsar to found provincial secondary schools for young girls, otherwise they had to travel to St Petersburg or Moscow.

Fig. 4

A watercolour miniature dated 1827 of Grand Duchess Elena Pavlovna given to Elizaveta (Family Collection)

ORIGINS AT ST PETERSBURG

Years before, the grand duchess had given this miniature of herself to Elizaveta Barstchoff as a token of affection. Miniatures were often worn pinned onto the bodice. This denoted one of the highest forms of prestige a woman could attain in Russia at the time.

Serge and the Lancers Lifeguards Regiment

Known as 'Serge' in the French style, Olga's father Sergei Mikhailovich Barstchoff (1826-1888) was the eldest of six children: three boys and three girls.[14] The children were assigned and registered with the St Petersburg nobility.

Before the Crimean War, nobles were expected to serve as officers in the army. Traditionally, few in those days made a proper career of it, not least as service may have cost them a small fortune in equipment and display. Serge was with the Alexandria Hussars Cavalry (nicknamed 'the Immortals') in the regiment of the outstanding Field Marshal Count Paskevich—Erivansky on the Black Sea coast.

Fig. 5
Olga's father, Serge Barstchoff: the bushy 'mutton chop' whiskers were fashionable in the 1860s – 1870s, symbolising authority, and masculinity [15]
(Family Collection)

In December 1850, he was transferred to Odessa joining the Lifeguards of the Ulansky (Lancer) Regiment as Cornet. The regiment was famous for having fought in three battles against Napoleon and had fought bravely in defeat at the Battle of Austerlitz in 1805.[16] Additionally, the Tsesarevich, the heir to the throne Crown Prince Alexander Nikolayevich (1818-1881) was chief of this regiment.

Serge's social circle was formed in the company of other officers and their families, including nobles across the regiments in the region; twenty-eight per cent of recruits were married, but the majority were bachelors. Like other young officers, amongst them barons and counts, off duty Serge lived in style and enjoyed being one of the lads.[17] On Friday nights he would have his friends over for drinks and cards.[18]

Typically, in toasting the health of each person in the Russian manner, late nights were rowdy in a haze of cigar smoke and gambling. Alexander Pushkin opened his classic tale *The Shot* from the Tales of Belkin with this description: "Everyone is familiar with the life of an army officer. In the morning drill and riding practice; dinner at the regimental commander's or in a Jewish tavern; in the evening, punch, and cards."[19]

In such a manner, Serge once lost a fortune of 200,000 roubles playing cards, on a game with high stakes such as Faro. The huge and shameful debt was paid off eventually by his aged and ailing father. The story of the family's chagrin passed down the generations and confirmed his parents' impression that he was very unruly by nature.[20] Despite that particular loss, Serge was not alone in that misfortune; he kept one letter showing that he too had his share of winnings from a friend who became indebted to him at cards without any means of quick repayment.[21]

Olga's maternal line: the countess bride and her upbringing

The bride's mother came from the Ouroussoff family which nowadays is spelled *Urusov*. Princess Natalya Urusova (1814-1882) was the youngest of nine siblings. Her parents, Prince Alexander Urusov and Ekaterina Tatischeva, were said to be good and kind people whose daughters' education were a credit to them.[22] They spoke English amongst themselves. From age sixteen, Natalya was lady in waiting to the

ORIGINS AT ST PETERSBURG

Tsarina Alexandra Feodorovna for four years. Mixing in such circles it was evident that finding a suitable match for the beautiful princess would be easily arranged.

In 1834, Natalya married Count Hippolite Kutaisov (1806-1851), a commissioned cavalry officer in the Kieff Hussar's regiment, as it was then known. The following year, their first child Prascovia was born in Moscow. [23] Younger siblings followed every two years: Paul and Sophie. [24] My grandmother mentioned another son, Hippolyte Hippolitovich, but of him no other records remain.

Following the birth of their children, in the early 1840s the Kutaisovs moved to a provincial setting in the Tambov region, southeast of Moscow; there they moved in congenial circles of gentry and intelligentsia.[25] However, Hippolyte died in January 1851 and Natalya was to outlive him in Moscow by thirty-one years.

After the premature death of Count Hippolyte, swift arrangements were made for the marriage of their eldest daughter, Prascovia Hippolitovna.[26] Just three days after her sixteenth birthday, on 23 October 1851 Countess Prascovia Hippolitovna Kutaisova was married to Serge Barstchoff.

Fig. 6
Prascovia Hippolitovna Kutaisoff, 1835-1900 (Family Collection)

He was nine years her senior. The marriage was solemnified in Odessa, a popular seaside resort and port, as well as the fourth city of Russia. Serge was stationed there with the Lancer Lifeguards. One can well imagine that Serge invited all the officers from his regiment to attend the ceremony at the Orthodox Prokrovsky Church (the 'Pokroff') on Alexandrovsky Avenue.

Serge and his bride, Countess Prascovia Hippolitovna Kutaisova, also spoke in French to one another. Despite being christened Praskovia, she always liked to be known as Olga. The above portrait of her as a young woman depicts her as if at the theatre. This, and her hand on an open book symbolized her love of culture and the arts. Indeed, going to the theatre would prove to be an enduring favourite pastime.

Cornet to Cavalry Captain: The Crimean War

By July 1852, Serge was promoted to Colonel and in April 1853 he served as adjutant to the commander of the regiment's reserve cavalry. He was later transferred on the approval of the *Tsesarevich* as Cavalry Captain (called 'rotmeister') to the regiment's Lifeguards Horse-Pioneers Division, formed in connection with the outbreak of hostilities on the Russian Empire's Black Sea coast. The announcement of a promotion for Serge Barstchoff to lead the reserves' squadron was made by the Grand Duke Nicholas in May 1855. Though the squadron was supposed to remain in St Petersburg,[27] in July 1855 its regiment assisted troops in the Crimean War with cavalry and artillery.[28]

A very short summary follows of the Crimean War; a disastrous war for Russia caused by geopolitical tensions, which lasted nearly two and a half years. The Ottomans, with Britain and France as allies, declared war on Russia in October 1853. By January 1854 British and French naval fleets entered the Black Sea. On 22 April 1854 the Black Sea naval base at Odessa was neutralized by an Anglo-French squadron of warships. Russia ended up fighting against a coalition of the Ottoman Empire, Britain, France and Sardinia-Piedmont.

Six months into the siege at Sevastopol, Russia's main naval base in Crimea, there was a major blow to the morale of the Russians troops:

Tsar Nicholas I died on 21st February 1855. The rumour was this, that on seeing the flags of the British squadron through his telescope from his palace at Peterhof, the tsar took poison.[29] His son Tsesarevich Alexander Nikolayevich succeeded him on the throne.

Overall, the human cost of the Crimean War was enormous on both sides, but the Russians suffered greater casualties. The Russian defeat in February 1856 and the subsequent Treaty of Paris signed by Count Orlov and Prince Alexander Gorchakov, set out peace terms which were mortifying for the Russian side. The treaty 'crushed' the prestige of the Russian military and gave away Russian influence in central Europe.[30]

On the reform Emancipation of the Serfs

But this war would mark a turning point: Russia's surrender and losses in Crimea persuaded the new Tsar Alexander II that reform of the military, the law and emancipation of the serfs was vital to modernise the country.[31] The country was on its knees and there was a desire to avoid chaos. The tsar saw the need to restore Russia's prestige abroad and overcome Russia's isolation.

On 30th March 1856, when the Treaty of Paris was signed, the Tsar also announced to the Moscow nobility his intention to liberate the serfs. He told them it was better to grant emancipation from above, than wait for uprisings from below. Therefore, debates and deliberations began.

During this time, Serge Barstchoff was commissioned into a secret government committee of twenty noblemen in St Petersburg. Coming from a landowning family, Serge represented the Schlisselburg district. Formerly it was called Schlüsselburg meaning 'key fortress'; it was a region famous for the battle against the Swedes in 1702, before Peter the Great opened his 'window on Europe' with access to the Baltic.

The St. Petersburg Provincial Committee was under the chairmanship of chief of police, A.F. Orlov.[32] The task was to research the means of improving the serfs' living conditions, and plan terms for their emancipation. All the provincial committees had sent their proposals to the editorial commissions by the end of 1859. They were compared and systematized, and the first legislation for emancipation was drafted. In early 1861 these were revised by the Chief Committee and by the State Council.

Alexander signed the manifesto on the sixth anniversary of his ascension to the throne on 19 February 1861. This was to be the biggest of Alexander II's reforms, earning him the title of 'Tsar Liberator'.

Fig. 7 Signature of Alexander II[33]

The abolition of serfdom was a watershed moment in Russian history, a time when millions of peasants were introduced to civic life, and it was hoped by the reformers that revolt and revolution could thus be averted. Abolishing serfdom was believed to have ignited hatred from nobles who were hostile to the reforms, but the situation was complex as educated Russians felt shame about serfdom and there was an awareness that serfdom held back the country's economic development.[34]

Even after the Manifesto of Emancipation of the serfs, the relationship between landowner and former serfs was still tense. Although the serfs were freed, promises of land were slow in materializing and peasants lost free access to the forests and free grazing meadows. Government loans proved expensive for the freed serfs. The administration of problems, including disputes between peasants, was resolved through small local courts called '*volost*'. Here punishments were still meted out, including beatings by the foreman. Villagers formed their own rural societies to protect their interests, including from the arbitrariness of the foreman.

For many years thereafter, Serge was a permanent member of the Schlisselburg District for Peasant Affairs, and in 1876 oversaw this portfolio for cases and petitions.[35] He had already long retired from the army back in 1863.[36]

2 A Thousand Gracious Thoughts

> Petersburg, the most abstract and pre-meditated city on earth.
> Dostoevsky [37]

> Dans le courant des fêtes je me ferai un vrai plaisir de venir vous voir et de vous exprimer de vive voix l'assurance de mes sentiments les plus distingués.[38]

Within a year of their marriage, the young bride Prascovia Hippolitovna Barstchoff had returned to St Petersburg to have her baby.[39] Perhaps she even travelled on the new trainline which had recently opened between Moscow and St Petersburg; a huge project overseen by the then heir to the throne, Alexander Nikolayevich.

Prascovia's daughter, Olga Sergeevna Barstchoff, was born on 10/22 December 1852.[40]

Godfather - The Heir Apparent

Olga's christening took place thirteen days later in the neoclassical splendour of the Trinity Cathedral, with its famous collection of icons and four bright blue domes which soared over the city skyscape. This cathedral was right on the same street as one of the family's apartments on Troitsky Avenue, and in the same block as their other property on the Fontanka. Also bordering Ismailovsky Avenue, the cathedral served as mother church to the Ismailovsky regiment of the imperial guards, as each such regiment had its own cathedral.

Christening documents list Tsesarevich Alexander Nikolayevich, the future tsar, as one of Olga's godfathers.[41] She was in all likelihood one of many such goddaughters, as tsars typically gained godchildren from officers serving in their regiments; a tradition started by Peter the Great and followed by Peter's daughter Empress Elizabeth.[42] This was an effective way to garner support and demonstrate loyalty. Of Peter the Great, it was said that 'he was godfather to almost every one of the first-born children of all the officers and soldiers of his regiments of Guards…when the child was an officer's, the present was a ducat under the pillow.'[43]

Perhaps the honour was also conferred as the baby was granddaughter to a Count Koutaïssoff (Kutaisov), whose family had been closely linked for three generations with the monarchy.

Other godparents to baby Olga included close relatives: Grandmother Elizaveta Ivanovna Barstchoff, Prince Mikhail Alexandrovich Urusov, and Princess Alexandra Sergeevna Urusova, the wife of Prascovia's favourite uncle, Prince Paul Urusov. Family connections carried huge weight in such matters.

Prascovia Hippolitovna would link her maiden name to her married one in double-barrelled fashion: Madame Barstchoff-Koutaïssoff.[44] She sometimes embellished her headed notepaper with both crests.

Life in St Petersburg

Just over a year later, on 11 February 1854, a second child, Mikhail, was born and he was known as Michel (French style).[45]

In some correspondence from the young mother Prascovia to her husband Serge, we can discern that Prascovia was clever and confident, but 'quite reserved'. She liked to keep good relations with all her family including her in-laws: father-in-law was swayed into giving her an allowance to cover family expenses in Serge's absence. She sweet-talked her husband to forget his fierce pride and to humour his parents, with whom he clearly had disagreements.

The earliest letters to Serge, dated between February and May 1855 and all in French, provide us with an introduction to their family life.[46] While Serge was away with his regiment, the young family stayed in a hotel in Moscow, though costly, so as to visit their *grand-maman*. The antics of the two-year old Olga were remarked upon like this:

> Tell nanny, that Olga's furious behaviour is not a credit to her. Right now, she is being good, but she screams and is capricious all day long. I hope that *Michel* will not be so much trouble, as having one of that kind is enough.

At home in St Petersburg, frequent visitors were younger siblings, Sophie, and Paul Kutaisov. As the eldest, Prascovia Hippolitovna took them under her wing. Paul had just started at military college, and she followed his training with interest.

If father-in-law Mikhail Barstchoff arrived in town, he might invite Prascovia out to dinner at the Hotel des Princes in the Winter Garden, or to dine with friends, like the widow of Alexander Shishkin.

From the letters we learn the names of other acquaintances and friends : Durnovo ('Dournoff'), Larski, Saburov ('Sabouroff'), and Madame Sabanééff. These were not only fair weather friends it seems, as they took the trouble to pass by the house nearly every day on the occasion of her illness. A letter from 31 May 1855 details the experience of eight days of high fever, treated with a concoction and application of mustard plasters to bring down the fever (as mustard induces sweating) from the doctor Sadofsky.

We catch glimpses of other social and society events from other sources. In a letter from Petr Durnovo to his father, Petr mentions Madame Borshchova-Kutaisova (Mme B-K). On 18 January 1858, he writes: 'At Prince Gorchakov's [reception] I finally saw Mr Obrezkov, to whom I conveyed your greetings and who in turn bound me to convey to you, as well as Madame Borschova-Kutaisova, a thousand gracious thoughts'. Flowery and charming terms such as 'a thousand kind words', 'a thousand greetings' were much in vogue at the time ("*mille choses, mille tendresses, je vous embrasse mille fois,*" etc.).

Returning to Petr Pavlovich Durnovo: he lived in his father's mansion whilst his parents were away in France or Italy. Attached to the house was a large, heated glasshouse for growing vegetables out of season, and exotic plants with which to decorate the house. Petr Pavlovich was known to eat six course menus every evening, as dinner diaries kept by his kitchen staff reveal.

Rich and refined foods were eaten even in the autumn months, for instance, purée of asparagus soup, roast hazel grouse or quail with boiled artichokes and pineapple jelly, raspberry or blackcurrant soufflé with *crêpes* or 'meringue kisses with cream'.[47] There were, of course, more Russian sounding dishes too: *Pozharski* chicken cutlets (chicken patties in breadcrumbs), fillet of beef, sturgeon or trout Russian-style, stuffed turnips or buckwheat and fine *bliny* pancakes; also, Kaimak waffles, originally a Tatar dish. The cooks would prepare dishes in French style, English style or Italian, according to taste. The idea was that you could continue to eat the kinds of foods that you enjoyed abroad.

Fig. 8
Postcard of Senate Square, St Petersburg, with statue of Peter the Great looking out across the river Neva (Family Collection).

At the height of the summer's heat and until Serge returned from his latest assignment, Prascovia Hippolitovna took the children to the country. Her in-laws estate at Turovo had a lake, and here the children could cool off in the fresh waters.

When the Crimean war was over, the family might go on holiday to the south at Theodosia (Kaffa) to be by the seaside with its golden beach and mineral springs; or go back to Odessa where they had married.

But during the summer of 1857, Prascovia and her sister Sophie took the children north to Helsinki - then known as Helsingfors. Their departure by steamboat was announced in a local St Petersburg gazette. Thanks to an acquaintance, they managed to rent a house called La Villa Vilaina right by the sea, with a beautiful view. The Kingdom of Finland was then a Russian territory, but according to Prascovia, nowhere did anyone speak a word of Russian. She described Helsinki as follows: 'a charming town, it's just like a small version of St Petersburg - yet completely unpretentious.... we walk everywhere or go by boat.'[48] If needed, they could get a carriage for fifty kopeks an hour.

The prices in Helsinki were affordable, and Prascovia enjoyed the feeling, she exclaimed, of not worrying about spending money. She was all too aware that Serge tended to spend more than he was earning and not only on the important things of life, as the letters of the outstanding payments from suppliers attested; there had been the import of two hundred and ten bottles of Hungarian wine, and the urgent request for payment from the bronze foundry on Vasily-Ostroff.[49] It was, though, nothing out of the ordinary in those times. After all, amongst their friends and acquaintances – almost everyone lived beyond their means.

A tragic blow was to befall them. On 5 October 1857, following their return from Helsinki, little Michel died at age three and a half. The reason he died is unknown. He was buried in one of the expensive plots at the Novodevichy cemetery in St Petersburg.[50]

The Chancellor – Uncle Alexander Gorchakov

Of all Prascovia Hippolitovna's most influential connections, it was the Urusov aunts who provided her with the best introductions to high society. Princess Maria Urusova (1801-1853), previously lady in waiting to the Empress Elizaveta Alexeevna (wife of Alexander I), was a widow with six children.

In 1838 Aunt Maria remarried, and her second husband was a great catch: Prince Alexander Gorchakov (1798-1883). Gorchakov was a career diplomat. He would become Minister of Foreign Affairs and then Chancellor of the Russian Empire. In his time, was considered one of the world's most powerful politicians.

Fig. 9
Prince A.M. Gorchakov

Maria had two further children and died in 1853, but Prince Gorchakov was fond of his nieces and kept in contact. Prascovia and Sophie would be invited to certain social functions with his sister-in-law Princess Sophie Radziwill-Urusova (1804-1889). In her youth, Sophie had a reputation of being the queen of Moscow's beauties. Her tall height, bright expression and fair complexion mesmerized - as did her magnetic blue eyes and curly hair. She was a confidant of the Empress Elizabeth, having been her lady-in-waiting, though some said she had also been the Emperor's lover.

Fig. 10
Maria Gorchakov née Urusova and Sophie Radziwill née Urusova

A THOUSAND GRACIOUS THOUGHTS

The memoirs of Cassius Clay, US envoy to St Petersburg

Such events attended by Prascovia Hippolitovna ('Madame Barstchoff') are recalled some years later in the memoirs of Cassius Clay, the United States Minister to St Petersburg. Cassius Clay was an emancipationist, a friend of Abraham Lincoln. Speaking about international relations and the Russian Chancellor, he describes in 1865 how the 'Tsar Liberator' Alexander II and President Lincoln formed a close diplomatic understanding following the emancipation of the serfs. The emancipation in Russia pre-dated the abolition of slavery in North America.

Cassius Clay described the Chancellor Gorchakov as 'the leading man of Russia'. He says of him: 'In general ability and address he was not equalled in his time, though he had a great many rivals in the premierships of the nations – Bismarck, Palmerston, Disraeli, and others'.[51] Indeed, Gorchakov held the post of Chancellor for nineteen years and with his leadership is considered to have raised the prestige of Russia during his tenure (1863-1882).

The American Minister Clay was much sought after and in demand socially. He took great pains to study every rank in society and socialised with the first families of Russia; his main aim was to garner support in Russia for the Union in the American Civil War, and he was influential in the acquisition of Alaska, for according to him it was 'owing to the good relations I have been able to maintain with Russia that such a purchase was possible'.

In the meantime, however, against his wishes and due to the rigorous winter, his wife returned to America. Eventually she divorced him for his many infidelities. Returning to Russia without his wife Cassius Clay was lonely. Though he did not admit it outright, he is believed to have fathered a child out of wedlock in Russia, called Henry Launcey Clay (otherwise known as 'Leonid Petroff') whom he adopted.

'Liaisons are very common' [in St Petersburg society], and 'it is not thought discreditable to have a mistress'.[52] Whilst that may have been true for men, this was still not the case for women. Wishing to mention a few 'personal friendships of great value' to him in his diaries, Cassius

Clay mentions a few names 'to whom I owe especial remembrance' including the Imperial family. He recounts how 'with all of them I was quite intimate, and by them often entertained' including by Madame (Countess) Barschoff and her sister, nieces of both Prince Gorchakov and the Princess Radziwill. He wrote in his diary that Gorchakov's sister-in-law, Princess Radziwill turned somewhat colder '…when I began to like better the niece. But I mean no offence; they will forgive me in saying their beauty, as transmitted to the children of their blood, was still to me attractive'. [53]

The sister of Madame Barstchoff, Countess Sophie Kutaisov, remained unmarried and died of an unknown cause in November 1878. She was buried aged thirty-nine in a monastery called 'Spaso-Yabovlevsky' in Rostov-on-Don. Her grave was paid for and placed in a privileged position in the cemetery on the east side of the St Dmitri cathedral church, behind the altar.[54] No one knows why she ended her days in the convent; a clandestine liaison could have been the cause. Might she have been the French-speaking Countess mentioned as Clay's mistress in Richmond, Kentucky, on his return from Russia?[55]

Fig. 11
The Spaso-Yakovlevsky Monastery, Rostov-on-Don

3 Letters from the Grand Tour: Down the Rhine

> Man was born free, and everywhere he is in chains.
> Jean-Jacques Rousseau, 1762

A few years prior to these events, Madame Barstchoff, to whom the American diplomat referred, had set off on a long tour of Europe with her family in tow. Pleasure, education, and health cures were quite necessary, and the order of the day. After all, fairer southern climes were known to be the best medicine for all kinds of afflictions, constitutional and emotional. The tragic bereavement that the Barstchoff couple had suffered after the summer in Helsinki was proving so hard to get over. It was a disaster not written about, a trauma that could barely be mentioned. All Madame's energies would now be centred on educating the young Olga, totally *comme il faut*...that is to say, properly.

What follows is a rare story of a ladies' grand tour of Europe. Everything is described in a series of some sixty private letters dated 1860-1861. These were discovered in a Moscow archive, and they shed new light on Olga's early years. [56] All the letters are addressed to Serge Barstchoff. They reveal many intimacies of the husband and wife, and father and daughter relationships.

Lovely period details emerge of the all-women travelling party on their three-month travels. The journey culminates in a prolonged stay in Paris. Monogrammed stationary alternates with prints of the various cities through which they passed, giving a more tangible sense of their world. Suddenly, we are drawn into feminine preferences and prejudices. We hear about terrible toothache and the badly-behaved child. The purchase of diamond encrusted jewellery and visits to the opera contrast with heating bills, dreadful food and the stench of rubbish. Suspected intrigue, though nothing concrete, provokes marital jealousy. Sightings of Napoleon III and rumours about Garibaldi are reported on.

We meet Olga Barstchoff at seven years old. Eight of the letters are from the young 'obedient' daughter. We catch a glimpse of her strict upbringing and perceptive personality. Her mother quite often complains about her mischievous behaviour, but also expects a lot. Lessons come one after the other. It turns out that Olga was quite starved of the company of children her own age and missed her absent father's more light-hearted company.

On her travels she learned several languages: some Italian and then German at school. At home they spoke mostly in French, or sometimes Russian. Olga started speaking English with her governess. Having a Victorian governess was then highly fashionable in Russian high society.

To set the scene of these letters further, in the mid-nineteenth century European travel for Russians was a privilege mostly of the nobility. Business or studies abroad might force them to leave their estates back home for considerable periods.

Fig. 12
Monograms on the letters of O.B. (Prascovia Hippolitovna Barstchoff) in either blue, red, gold, black or green

For leisure, sunnier southern climes on the French and Italian *rivieras* were a true favourite. Many wives spent the winter there, with or without their spouses. On the way, health cures in the thermal hot springs of the Rhineland were a must. Russians loved the theatre and sights of the great European cities. They soaked in the more liberal political culture outside Russia. From Nice to Paris and Pau, the locals became used to the Russian associations, cafés, and Orthodox churches.

It was not unusual to live abroad through all the seasons of life, buying properties, bearing children, and retiring there.

For those with so-called 'westernizing' sympathies, European culture was always a reference point. European fashions in clothing, literature, food, manners were all popular; French and English culture were considered the most refined and civilized. Literature from Goethe to George Sand greatly influenced the Russians. Their country was, after all, experiencing a new era of outstanding poetry and prose writing. Though less famously, this also included the publication of women authors in literary journals.[57] Travels, like pilgrimages, inspired aesthetic and philosophical ideas and exchanges between authors of various nationalities. In contrast, the Slavophiles eschewed European customs in favour of those prevalent in Mother Russia and its expanding empire.

To dear Serge

As already noted, the letters from Prascovia Hippolitovna Barstchoff to husband Serge were written in French. Although she signed them as Olga, by choice her preferred name, to avoid confusion here she will always be Prascovia and her daughter will be called Olga or *Olishe*.[a] Prascovia's writing was elegant and even - so like her sister Sophie's, but neater.[58]

The extended trip through Europe was initially planned to be just a few months long, but they teased it out to be a new routine and way of life in Paris. Gaps in the correspondence reflect the times when the couple was reunited.

In June 1860 the whole family took a villa in the Rhineland, near the Prussian border at Bad Kreuznach. The town was famous for its warm saline springs for health cures and relaxation – as well as for its fine wines. Here in the summer season, there were festivals, concerts, and many public events to be enjoyed.

---

[a] Little Olga : 'Olishe' with the accent on the 'i'; though *Oliche* is the French spelling in the letters, in English it would be more easily pronounced as Olishe.

Fig. 13
Letterhead from Kreuznach

Prascovia's letters relate day-to-day concerns, describe the people, the scenery and food on their travels, and crucially, news about their daughter Olishe. The very first letter in this collection to Serge follows his departure from Kreuznach to Paris on business. There, he would be making enquiries for suitable hotel accommodation for his family when they arrived. His wife reveals a hankering for some comforting chocolate pralines from Paris:

> Thank you, my dear friend, for the toothpaste which I received this morning, and I am happy to hear that you are pleased with your trip especially the Paris part; I hope that this good impression continues and that you will not regret your absence from Kreuznach. We don't have any other news to give you, except that I am sorry to say we are having to wait a long time for the shoes.
>
> We are all doing well, and everyone sends you a thousand good wishes [*'mille compliments'*]. The weather is still cold and unsettled, which is very inconvenient, as we need to eat out at a restaurant, after nearly dying of hunger from the appalling food which we were getting at the house. That's why we decided to go to the restaurant, and yesterday we ate very well at dinner at Kauzenberg; we'll go there every day as the food is excellent and this is what we have closest to our place. It is true that it is frightfully noisy there, as the dining room is quite small and completely full; yesterday there were one hundred and twenty

people but we resigned ourselves to put up with the noise until you get back, in consideration of the dear maid; as, if we went there with you, without a doubt, you would never be able to put up with the shouts of the Germans and the racket of the service!

It is annoying that Reinholt seems upset, if he carries on like that, I don't think his presence is going to be of any use to you, on the contrary, it would be another embarrassment; especially in the civilized countries where you are, and where one is so well served. Adieu, dear Serge, I send you all my love and request you give my regards to Gary. Lots of love and thanks from Sophie, Nadine and Olishe, the Count sends his regards. All my love, Prascovia

P.S. If you can bring some chocolate pralines from Paris, we would love that, as here we can't find anything sweet at all.

Kreuznach 24 June 1860 (OS / 6 July NS) [59]

Before long, Serge returned to Kreuznach. After a month and a half, he departed again for Frankfurt and then back to Russia: to St Petersburg, Moscow, and then his parents' estate at Turovo. Regular correspondence from his wife and daughter followed.

The three sisters and Olishe started their journey southwards. Countess Sophie Koutaissoff and sister–in–law Nadine Barstchoff were both twenty-one, while Prascovia Barstchoff was twenty-five. The accompanying new English governess was called 'nanny' by Olishe, but her mother referred to her simply as '*l'Anglaise*' or '*la bonne*'. Nanny was clearly appreciated by her employer, who wrote: 'If she continues as she has up till now, I will always keep her.'

Basel – Geneva – St Jean-de Maurienne – Turin

Their three-month tour would be taken in style: first class rail travel and only the best hotels. First, south down the Rhine, and then across the Alps to Genoa by train. On leaving Kreuznach on 17/29 August (O.S.) they crossed into Switzerland. They stayed in Basel for one night at the magnificently situated and opulent Hotel des Trois Rois: "Here the

Rhine flows under the balcony and one thinks one is in Venice, as the building actually overhangs the water." On 18/ 30 August they made the ten-hour journey to Geneva. They had taken the fast train from Basel, including a change of carriage four times and a boat ride; first class for the family with free travel for Olishe and second class for their maid 'as fast trains do not do third class'.

> The journey from Basel to Geneva is wonderful, the whole way one has the most beautiful panoramas imaginable, the carriages are perfect (the best in the Alpes), with divans and tables, the Swiss are very polite and what gives me most pleasure is that my ears are not being split by hearing the German language.
>
> Olishe won over all the English people we met on the way and thanks to her they were also genuinely nice to us. On the steamboat this morning we met a friendly Englishman who played with the little one all the time and then during lunch he was extremely caring, which surprised us a lot for a man of his nationality, he reminded us of the charming Plehve.[60]

At Geneva they stayed four nights at the luxurious Hotel des Bergues on Lake Geneva. Two days later she wrote the following to her husband:

> My dear friend, I want to share with you how I am spending all my days, that is why I do not want to go to bed without having written you a few words, despite my long letter yesterday evening. We wanted to devote today to seeing all the remarkable things in town, but it rained all day and we have only seen the island of J.J. Rousseau on the way to the hotel which is not remarkable excepting the view of Mont Blanc which you can see from everywhere…Tomorrow if the weather is good, we will take a boat tour on Lake Geneva.

Instead, they spent much of the day in the watchmaker and jewellery shop *Ropel*. Here, all three ladies spent ruinous amounts of money. Mrs Barstchoff offset the costs by pawning jewels she did not wear from relatives like Prince Alexis Galitzine, and a brooch from her grandmother Praskovya Lopukhina. Her new watch was the size of a ten-kopek piece with her initials and a crown in diamonds underneath. She bought a magnificent new bracelet decorated with a large emerald and diamonds.

The following day the weather was also terrible. Bad toothache forced a visit to the dentist, to put lead on a tooth that had previously been poorly fixed. A visit to the theatre to see a play called *Family Drama* redressed the balance of a stay, which had not otherwise been of great interest.

On 22 August Mrs Barstchoff described how the panoramas on the onward journey were spectacular. The high Alpine scenery through the train window had quite taken their breath away:

> Looking out of the window I couldn't help thinking how happy you would have been, dear friend, to see what I am seeing. It is just the landscape that you love; imagine the wildest scenery, mountains which disappear into the clouds, waterfalls which deafen night and day, cliffs and in a word like a real tableau by Salvatore Rosa who painted beauties of nature with horrors…
>
> Olishe talks about you all the time and asks where you are right now.[61] I was tempted to stop off at Chambery to see the Emperor Napoleon who arrives there today at 4pm… I wanted to see him so much but decided it would be a waste of money because of the crowds and it would take an extra two days. The French people are charmingly polite, so far, we have only met friendly folk who make a point of pleasing us. I can just imagine how much you must be fed up, my dear friend, in our empty home, I will be happy to know that my letters give you gentle entertainment."

At one station, she fleetingly chanced upon an acquaintance, the Count Charles Lambert. A short stay at St Jean-de-Maurienne in the Savoy region confirmed Prascovia's preference for French cuisine. The only *auberge* provided food 'better than all the top hotels in Germany' and was quite clean.

Their onward journey was to the Kingdom of Sardinia-Piedmont. First impressions of Italy were poor, and the letters here reveal that the weary travellers were by now flagging, not least due to the scarcity of drinking water.

Fig. 14 Course of the Rhine: river and railway [62]

At the next inn where they stayed in Susa, supposedly the best in town, they were dismayed by the dire accommodation: the inadequate tallow candles barely lit the nauseatingly rank smelling room (certainly bug-ridden); the enormous spiders web and ten dead flies at breakfast next morning.

Pressing on with their itinerary, on arrival at Turin the travellers stayed at the outwardly grand Hotel Feder, recommended by everyone as the best. But this too they found to be disappointingly insanitary. Having not made a reservation in advance, they had been given the last available room on a mezzanine level. Prascovia described the meal which included frogs with lemongrass, as dreadful and inedible, leaving them hungry. She declared this less palatable than all the worst food they had eaten in Germany, which by comparison had been 'a feast of *Lucullus*.' Plus, the fruits were all unripe. A curious and unfamiliar confection here which made them chortle were potatoes covered in a sticky jam.

Sightseeing included the ancient convent and basilica of Superga, in the crypt of which the kings of Sardinia were buried. It was one and a half hours along a terrible road (reminiscent of those in St Petersburg). The view from the top of the high Alps, the Savoie, the plain of Marengo and Milan below was spectacular. But little else satisfied Mrs Barstchoff, whose disappointment about their visit in the city and its surrounds was heightened by the exaggerated boasting of Iotti, their Italian employee.

To top it all, they had been unable to find a good café, instead Mrs Barstchoff complained of the very squalid bars. The speciality truffles which Iotti had recommended looked repulsive, not only in appearance but in taste and smell. Butter, the dominant flavour in all the dishes, reeked of goat's milk. However, at last they had a passable dinner of risotto and roast chicken served with Asti wine at no extra cost and discovered 'a certain bread called *grissini*' which they liked.

Unwelcome news arrived about the behaviour of a cousin, Leon Galitzine and his wife. Mrs Barstchoff wrote how they had 'unpardonably' left their two- and three-year-old children Alexei and Alexander there in a foreign country, with a 'desperate' impecunious nanny. The rent at their lodgings had expired and they were about to be evicted from them.

After two days, Mrs Barstchoff and her party left for Genoa, not without, of course, having dropped off a note to the Russian consul at Turin.

A month on the Ligurian riviera at Genoa

After a journey of five hours, on 27 August (7th September N.S.) they arrived in Genoa. En route they had the complete surprise of meeting Charles Lambert again; it would not be the last time that his name would appear in the letters. She recounted that Lambert's doctor had ordered him directly to take a change of air to recover from an illness that had had him laid up in bed for several days.

Having inspected all the hotels, the sisters found a 'magnificent' five-room apartment, the best in the hotel. A former ducal *palazzo* of the Counts Gerbaix de Sonnaz, it was also named Hotel Feder. The apartment had two 'colossal' bedrooms with every conceivable comfort; the living room had a piano and was even decorated with gilt and bronze ornaments: all this for 140 francs per week including service charge. It had, they said, been occupied the previous year by the daughter of Alexander II, the Grand Duchess Marie (1853-1920). Three rooms for the ladies and two rooms for her staff, Reinholt and the English nanny. There were one hundred steps leading to the apartment; one advantage of this inconvenience would be the beautiful view of Genoa's harbour. They planned to stay for three weeks. She sent a letter to the consul, remarking that if any better recommendation or price could be found they would move if it were decent enough.

In case it seemed expensive, Prascovia Hippolitovna explained that the rate of 385 Francs per week included three meals a day. Breakfast, comprising tea, all kinds of biscuits, bread, and chocolate, was served in their rooms. On 8 September she wrote:

> I received both your letters of 27th and 30th August (O.S.) at the same time with the money, for which I thank you so much. I only fear that you have sent me too much, and that you are now completely broke. I beg you, my dear friend, not to worry that I am lacking money, you should know how economical and calculating I am, I never allow myself to spend too much, and life here is not expensive, to the extent that of the money I had before there's enough left to pay all my expenses in Genoa and I won't need the new money until my journey to Paris, where I shall probably stay one month.

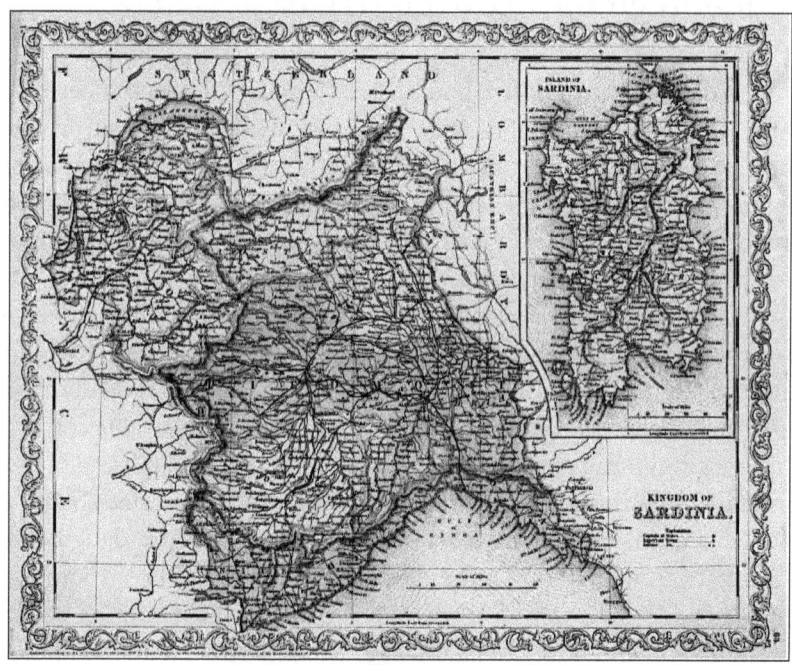

Fig. 15
Map of the Kingdom of Sardinia-Piedmont [63]

At one o'clock, they enjoyed a sit-down lunch with wine and fruits. A nine-course dinner was taken at five o'clock in the dining room. Later in the evening they would have some tea, or occasionally, soup. The staff also had three meals a day. So, considering all the above, Mrs Barstchoff explained that this was affordable.[64] The second week had only cost her two hundred francs.

In the meantime, Nadine had won the hearts of two nice gentlemen – an Englishman, and a Frenchman called the Baron of Thuret. But Nadine was only interested in marrying an Italian and finding a villa in Italy. She had even made some enquiries for a property for 80,000 Francs.

Just two days after their arrival in Genoa on 29th August, Mrs. Barstchoff received a visit from the Consul General, Mr Khvostoff. This was followed by an invitation to meet his wife and their daughter.

Fig. 16
Letterhead from their stay in Genoa, from Prascovia Hippolitovna[65]

The Consul's family had a house and garden and regularly invited the travellers over for tea or dinner. Of an evening, they would enjoy hearing Madame Khvostoff read aloud. Her choice of book had just been published the year before: *A Nest of Gentlefolk* by Ivan Turgenev, 'It's a very lovely story, and she reads very well'.

Genoa was delightful. They found the town to be a cache of antiquity and originality. All four were very happy. During the day the temperature was twenty-two degrees, and the evenings were wonderfully warm. The younger sisters and Olishe swam in the balmy and magnificent crystal clear azure sea, and they changed on the beach as there was no other option.

The food specialities here were more to their taste than the German food; a typical dinner would include local fish and mushrooms, and fruit and ice cream served with Asti wine and vin de table all for ten francs a head at the best café in town, the Café Concordia. There was a marble terrace planted with orange trees and a pretty fountain in the middle where musicians played every evening. Pricewise though, relative to the singing lessons with the best singing teacher in Genoa taken by Aunt Nadine, this meal was still expensive by local standards. Other shopping proved to be extraordinary value; Prascovia Hippolitovna was thrilled to buy some antique lace at such 'ridiculously low' prices that back home, 'one could get nothing at all' for such a sum of money.

Dear Papa

This first letter to her father Serge was, her mother avowed, composed and written 'entirely' by Olishe:

> Dear Papa, Congratulations on your name day. I am very bored without you and would like you to come back more quickly. I am learning English, and I have a piano teacher. Today I am going to the theatre. I bought myself two red Pulcinella puppets. Every day I go over to the Khvostov's to play in their garden. In two days, I am leaving for Paris, and I will buy a dress and an English hat with the money that you gave me. Bye, dear Papa, I kiss your hands, Sophie sends a hug and Nadine also - she is going to return to Petersburg.
>
> Your obedient daughter, Olga Barstchoff.
>
> Genoa 16/28 September 1860

Prascovia Hippolitovna wrote to her husband faithfully nearly every day, which she hoped he would not find tiresome, and urged him to write often. But it took nine days for his more irregular letters to reach her. Her letters were a comfort to him alone at home, he said. As well as describing what the family did in Genoa and commentaries about the Italians, Mrs Barstchoff also described her hopes and fears. Recently she had the surprising news from her mother that Cousin Olga Galitzine would be marrying a Belgian count (Raymond Graaf Cornet de Grez d'Elzius); the change of religion from Orthodox to Catholicism made it an unexpected match.[66]

Prascovia occasionally vented her frustration about Olishe, but her annoyance did not usually last long:

> I am maddened by the little one. She has taken to following us about everywhere. She never wants to stay with the nanny and wails when we go out. I think the bathing in the sea is too much for her, she is irritated and throws tantrums all day after swimming, though for the last two days she's hardly eaten anything and been a bit more manageable. I am going to get her a music teacher here…Nadine's singing teacher, who is the best in town charges two francs, so I am sure a piano teacher will be even better value.[67]

Next night, Olga had acute stomach pains and her mother was fearful of a fever. A doctor was called at four in the morning and after a calming potion the symptoms subsided: 'catching cold combined with digestive problems' caused the illness:

> The little one is very upset that I wrote to you about her bad behaviour and so she's become less capricious, she's already speaking some English quite well, for the short time she's had with the nanny.
>
> Being in Italy is remarkably interesting now, the success of Garibaldi and the enthusiasm he inspires are things you would not be able to imagine unless you had seen them with your own eyes. There is not an Italian who wouldn't sacrifice his life and his fortune, his name is on everyone's lips, even small children who can hardly speak can pronounce his name and call him *their father*.' I have only just been told this minute that Lamoriciete has been encircled on all sides by Garibaldi's troops, and so he is going to have to surrender – he's at Ancona.[68]

Prascovia explained to her husband that whilst the aristocracy supported the Austrian Empire, the business and townsfolk supported the revolutionary Italian general Giuseppe Garibaldi who had just seized

Naples. The people in the streets were jubilant and excited, music was played, and lights illuminated the town in celebration.

A routine of sorts developed: Olga had piano lessons each day, then there were excursions around Genoa or further afield such as to the villa of Count Pallavicini with its marble statues, alleys of lemon and laurel, lake, and stalactite grotto. In the evenings going to the opera was a favourite, and for 'only' an extra ten francs they could get one of the best boxes. They saw comic opera *bouffe* such as *Don Bucephalo*. Or they rode in a horse drawn *calèche,* an open carriage with retractable hood.

Apart from these pleasures and pastimes, the contrast between the riches of the town and the poverty including the muck on the streets appalled them. In the evenings the stench of rubbish was so strong that, so as not to 'suffocate' they carried bottles of smelling salts with them. The once beautiful and grandiose marble palaces along the narrow streets were in a state of disrepair, as the finances of the families that owned them were in tatters.

Meanwhile, Serge sent return letters from Moscow, Helsingfors (Helsinki), Warsaw or from home in St Petersburg. He kept his wife up to date with various relatives back home: brother Pavel Ippolitovich Koutaissoff, *Maman* Natalia Koutaissoff in Moscow, Uncle Prince Paul Ouroussoff, and great-grandmother *Grand-Mère* Prascovia Koutaissoff-Lopukhin.

A bill from Warsaw, for two hundred and ten bottles of Hungarian wine, attests to Serge's taste in fine 'juice of the grape'.[69] At the end of the week, he would invite his friends over to drink, smoke and play cards prompting his wife to write: 'Let's not renovate the house until I return to avoid the furnishings being spoiled.' As it was, the furnishings were antiquated and there were sad memories from the time that their son Micha had died three years before.

Evidently, the separation of the spouses was beginning to play on Serge's mind. Mrs Barstchoff had received several anxious and accusatory letters from her husband concerning the company of a certain old acquaintance the Count Charles Lambert whom they had met quite by chance at a railway station on leaving Geneva. Sweeping aside her husband's 'unjust, hurtful and cruel' concerns about her conduct, Mrs Barstchoff replied that all three ladies were on equally friendly terms with the Count, and that she was actually quite reserved.[70]

LETTERS FROM THE GRAND TOUR: DOWN THE RHINE

Having stayed in Genoa for a month, the lady travellers set off for the seven-hour journey to Milan on 1 October (New Style). They stayed there for a few days before setting off for Paris via the St Gotthard Pass.

Fig. 17
Olga's letter to her father Sept 1860[71]

4 Your Obedient Daughter: Paris

> I shall probably stay one month…
> Prascovia Hippolitovna Barstchoff-Koutaisoff [72]

The travelling party finally arrived in Paris on 8 October 1860 (NS). The next day, upset by the arrival of an injurious sounding letter from Serge, Prascovia Hippolitovna was quick to respond point by point:

> Regarding the matter of being cold, I don't know what you mean by the word, but I think I have never been colder to you than you have been towards me for some time, and given that all the attention and caring are towards Sophie, you often seem to forget that she's not your wife…so for pity's sake calm your ridiculous jealousies, as right now more than ever they are becoming insane, we are completely alone, without a single man of our acquaintance with whom to go out and no one to go out with us to the theatre or sightseeing, nor whom we would like to visit. You can be happy and at ease!

Her sister Sophie was, she later noted, in the habit of spending her day writing Serge 'long epistles'.

Two days later Olishe wrote to her father, sharing with him the annoyance she had felt hiding under the ladies' wide skirts on the journey, and now on their arrival it was cold and rainy:

YOUR OBEDIENT DAUGHTER: PARIS

Dear Daddy, Congratulations on your birthday and I hope you have a lovely dinner. We are in Paris and I am really happy about it, because on the way I had to constantly keep hiding under the skirts. It rains every day, so I can never go for a walk, I wanted to go and see the Royal Palace, and I couldn't. Nadine has not received the money and cannot leave with Mrs Khvostoff; she scolds Sergei Ivanovich [Reinholdt] a lot, he meddles in everything and knows nothing.

We are so cold that I would just like to curl up in my fur coat in my room. Mum has bought herself a French-style black lace net and Sophie has bought one with a crown; Sophie will send you her portrait, I will send you mine too as well as one for Paul. We have a piano and today I am starting my lessons with a lady music teacher. Mum sends you a hug. Bye dear Papa, I kiss your hands, and please reply to this letter and the other one. Say hi to everyone, and to 'Artichoke'. Your obedient daughter, Olga.

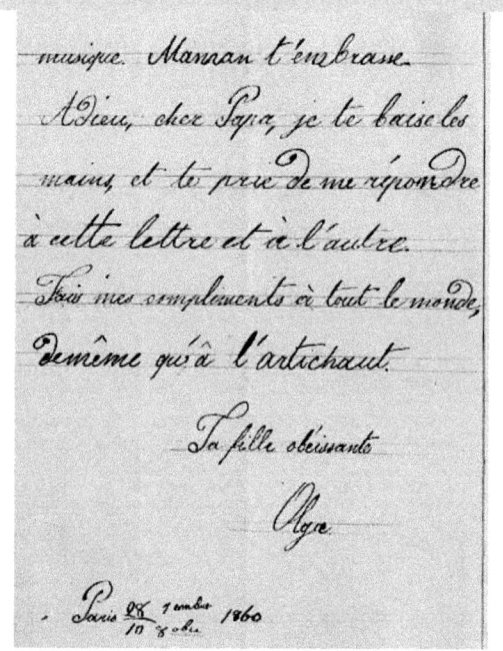

Fig. 18
Olga's letter, dated 28 Sept/ 10 October 1860[73]

The original plan had been to rent the hotel apartment in Paris for one month. Autumn and winter in St Petersburg were damp and cold, and pestilent illnesses including typhus, cholera and pneumonia abounded. A stay abroad in milder climes was most desirable.

The hotel apartment had been found by Serge. For their various ailments, the ladies were to enlist the services of a certain Dr Jobert de Lamballe. He was by reputation the best doctor in the city. But it was not long before the sisters complained that he was always too hurried.

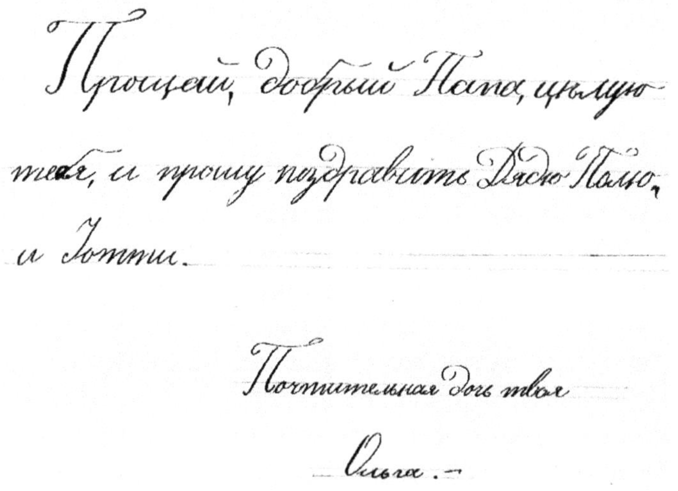

[Handwritten letter in Russian Cyrillic script]

Fig. 19
Letter 3 January 1861: "Goodbye, kind Papa, I kiss you and please wish Uncle Paul and Iotti a Happy New Year, Your Respectful Daughter, Olga" [74]

Aunt Sophie had a delicate constitution. Dr de Lamballe gave her injections of sulphur; a technique used by French doctors to reduce fever in cases of chest infections. Prascovia Hippolitovna was more robust, but she complained of 'inflammations', and a swelling she referred to as a 'tumour.' For treatment she used iodine and homeopathic remedies, or a common treatment at the time was bloodletting with leeches. Aunt Nadine, who had been worryingly thin and ailing and appeared to have something of an eating disorder, had improved after the summer cure at the baths of Kreuznach. The attentions of the best doctor in Paris were surely the true purpose of their trip.

Yet there were other advantages to staying longer in Paris, not least the concessions in meal payments and accommodation booked by the week or more. It was also all very convenient, as the young Olga was being educated at the hotel and learned English with the nanny. She took morning lessons in Russian and piano, and sometimes dance with a private tutor.

Four languages

After some weeks Praskovya Hippolitovna admitted that Olishe was bored with her own company in the mornings getting 'terribly naughty' [*horriblement polissonne*], and that she would be better off spending longer hours with children of her own age by attending more school hours.

In the early days of October, the new piano teacher recommended a school for young girls. This was because they had already been recommended a boarding school by Lambert's cousin, the Countess of Beives. However, after visiting the school, Olishe had been terribly upset at the thought of weekly boarding and had cried. So, on the piano teacher's suggestion they found another school for young ladies close by, at the *Pension de Jeunes Demoiselles* at 99 Rue Neuve des Petits Champs.

Lined with several impressive mansions, this street was named for the large gardens that used to be there. Olga was allowed to attend just in the afternoons from noon till five each day. She started on $17^{/29}$ October. For fifty francs per month, lesson subjects included reading, writing in French, arithmetic, German, and needlework. The school was run by two exemplary ladies. They promised to supervise her carefully and to give private lessons. Female teachers in networks of establishments like this one were fostering the latest educational skills and social values alongside the core subjects. This formative experience at the school in Paris proved to be very memorable and recalled by Olga many years later.

The school issued a report per subject and on behaviour each month: Olishe was in the first class, division three. Her school report on 12 January 1861 observed that 'Olga is sometimes not very inclined to work. She is a good child'. She scored very well in reading, writing ('when she wants to do it well'), grammar and German. February's report was also good. On 31 March 1861 Mademoiselle Demasier noted that she was 'très intelligente' and well-behaved.

YOUR OBEDIENT DAUGHTER: PARIS

Olga's piano playing was noticeably improving, as was the seven year old's English, taught by the excellent English nanny. 'Olishe will be able to write to you in four languages soon', boasted her mother to Serge 'to prove her *savoir faire.*' Interestingly, as the letters showed, Olga's French handwriting was much more advanced than her Russian; yet her mother stated that she was 'very capable' of doing it.

A few days later she commented: 'She has grown a lot and become very pretty, both her music teacher and at the pension are so fond of her, that they talk about her to everyone with the greatest admiration'. A portrait would be sent once they found a suitable outfit.

> Dear Daddy [Papasha], thank you for your letter and for your portrait; I will send you my portrait and my good school report, they are always really pleased with me. Yesterday I went with Mummy to the circus. I have a lady music teacher. Grandma wrote to us to tell us that Auntie Nadine is ill, and that she has white lips; please let her know we received all the money and that she should not worry but tell Iotti that he is the dirtiest and that I don't want to kiss him because he does not wash his beard. Bye dear Papasha, may you be healthy, Mother and Auntie send you kisses. Olga
>
> Paris, 19/31 October 1860

Fig. 20
Olga Barstchoff: 24 Nevsky Prospect, St Petersburg (Family Collection).

In a later letter she appreciates the kindness of the nanny, contrasted with the teasing of her school mates for wearing boots:

> Dear Papasha, Thank you for the letter. I haven't managed to get a portrait done because Mummy and Auntie are ill, but now that she is better, I will get one done tomorrow. I got the report from school, last month I had ten bad marks, because of my poor handwriting, and I will try next month not to have that. We have a doctor, Jobert de Lamballe, who talks like a bear, and always gets cross, and shouts at Auntie. Nanny sends her regards, I told her to be stricter with me, because I don't always listen, and she is too kind. At school all the girls laugh at me and call me 'Puss in Boots.'
> – Mother and Auntie send you a kiss. Bye dear Papa, I send a thousand kisses. Olga
>
> Paris, 1st December 1860

It was not long before Olga was kept 'too busy with lessons' to write to her father more than twice a month; he was told that she 'would write on her first free day'. She frequently asked her mother after him - where was he, and what was he doing, and when he would be visiting? Her mother would end her letters: "Sophie and I send you an embrace and Olishe sends her love [kisses your hands - *'te baisse les mains'*].

The large living room of their first-floor hotel apartment looked onto the fashionable Rue de la Paix. The two bedrooms faced the inner courtyard. Prascovia Hippolitovna shared one room with Olishe, and Sophie had the smaller room. They were most content with all this. Their location was just a short walk from the Tuileries Gardens and en route they would pass many of shops with their stripey canvas sunshades, boutiques with their irresistible-looking merchandise, fashion houses and elegant hotels.

At her hotel, Mrs Barstchoff felt very well provided for by the owner, Bussié. She considered that they had been given the nicest apartment in the hotel 'at a very reasonable rate'.[75] Their English nanny had to clean the apartment and look after their clothes. Nanny's room was on a higher floor, as was that of Reinholt, the *factotum*. He ran necessary errands and shopped for their basic needs. Although four or five other Russian families were also staying at the hotel, apart from Madame Alexandroff who was spending the winter in Paris, Mrs Barstchoff claimed that they kept themselves much to themselves.

Fig. 21
Olga's school report 12 January 1861 (TB = Très Bien)[76]

Fig. 22
Rue de la Paix 1860s, stereoscopy photo, Getty Images [77]

Wary of dining with one of her wealthier relatives who might be in the French capital, such as Aunt Princess Sophie Radziwill, Prascovia wrote that such an evening would require a whole new expensive set of clothes. But at the same time, she believed that on returning to St Petersburg Aunt Sophie would treat her favourably, providing all kinds of much needed contacts, commenting that 'the princess is an authority in society'.[78] Cousin Leon Radziwill who had recently been made a 'Gentilhomme de la Chambre' (a Chamberlain to the Tsar), was also expected to visit soon.[79]

Despite Prascovia's self-professed 'solitude' and her claims that they hardly socialised, she was excited about this chance to live in Paris with all its glamour and interest. The greatest pleasure was a regular visit to the theatre ('we are doing what you did here, it's our only outing otherwise we just stay at home'). When the circus visited town, Olishe was told that if she studied hard, she would get to see it.

Count Charles Lambert

An exception to any seclusion on their part was the reappearance of Count Charles Lambert. Their acquaintance from Genoa had a brother and several other relatives in the city and had recently arrived. He was staying on the same street at Hotel Mirabeau at 8 Rue de la Paix, a stone's throw from the Place Vendôme. Despite being busy with his own family and his own affairs, he would often make a brief visit in the morning, and if the weather were fine, he might accompany the ladies on an outing in the city.

It is clear from Prascovia's letters that Serge, her husband of nine years, continued to be bothered by this. Was she hiding her true intentions? These suggestions were heartily denied; his wife forgave him his jealousies, for this was not a new theme in their relationship. Pointedly, she stated that it was useful for the ladies to have some male company to respectably escort them out on occasion. She brushed off his concerns in sometimes cutting exchanges, at one point exclaiming that he was writing in an unnaturally tragic manner, saying *'tu as un air tragique qui n'est pas naturel'*.

YOUR OBEDIENT DAUGHTER: PARIS

Letters between Paris and St Petersburg usually took eight days; telegrams were reserved for important messages, such as announcing the arrival of more funds. Good news arrived from Serge at the beginning of November. He had been appointed an honorary member of the Economic Society. [80]

In between his consignments, Serge considered renovations to their home. The idea of stucco for the living room did not meet with Prascovia's approval. Neither did the proposed grey paint colour which would be too dark and hard to lighten up, but the stone fireplace he proposed for the study did pass. In turn, her inspiration came from what she had observed in Paris: the crystal doorknobs and glass plates on the doors - pretty and clean looking, which cost a trifle (*une bagatelle*).

Prascovia Hippolitovna sent records of all their expenses to the Italian accountant, Iotti. She assured her husband that although there were naturally many expenses plus medical bills (including her five trips to Evans, the dentist, which cost nearly one hundred francs, and earned him the epithet of 'brigand of the first kind'), their lifestyle in Paris was otherwise as *frugal* as possible. She gave a list of their money saving methods.

For example, Reinholt bought the essentials for the apartment including candles, tea, and sugar. The ladies washed their own small garments to avoid paying extra for the hot water in the hotel. They heated their rooms with wood they had brought in. A basket of wood cost two francs, that is, enough for one fireplace. 'When the money arrives, I'll go out to buy the wood myself', but she soon discovered that coal was cheaper than wood as well as heated the rooms better and for longer, and Reinholt obtained better prices than she could.

Paris, she now concluded, was quite the best place to be and even changing apartments was not worth the trouble. Especially with the onset of winter and the expenses that travelling would incur. There was now a more conciliatory tone. If Serge wanted her to have alternative plans, she added that she would of course cede to his preferences with pleasure but added the following: 'Everyone is amazed that I can manage to live in Paris, in the best street, feeding five people, plus heating and service for less than 300 francs per week.'

One of the things Mrs Barstchoff appreciated most about living in the city was the variety of people and observing the opportunities which were available to all of society. On 1 November she wrote:

> Paris truly belongs to everyone, the old the young, the rich and poor, one can live in any way and still find something fun to do affordably. For example, on Sundays I give the little one half a Franc. She goes down to the Champs Élysées where she can watch one or two children's shows or take a ride in a small carriage with two horses. She can climb in the playground and then buy some biscuits! Now she cannot wait for Sundays to come around.

On 15th November 1860, Olishe wrote to her father: 'On Thursdays I don't go to school, as I have dancing lessons.... On Sundays I go to the theatre on the Champs Élysées.' The family also attended the mass for Russians at church on Sundays, in the company of a large Russian congregation.

The following letter suggests that Olga was hoping to return to Russia to see her father. In the event, it would be at least a couple of months before she sees him again.

> Dearest Daddy [Milii Papasha], Congratulations on the holidays and I hope you are well. We went to St Germain; I liked the woods very much, and they told me that there are many deer and rabbits. We had a particularly good lunch there; they gave us some good chocolate. I go walking everyday with Nanny to the Tuileries, and sometimes with Auntie, along the boulevards or to the Royal Palace. Mum bought me a shawl, a sky-blue patterned dress and pale blue umbrella. I think that we shall soon return to Petersburg, and I hope that it will be wintrier than now. Good-bye dear Papa, I kiss you many times and look forward to your letter. Mum and Auntie send you a kiss. Your obedient daughter, Olga (*undated*)

Despite keeping the fireplace lit all day, during a cold spell the hotel apartment proved to be very draughty. Any warmth just escaped up the chimney. Indoors this temperature was quite unbearable; 'warm at eleven degrees' and the bedrooms were scarcely at nine and caused each of them to have a cold all the time. The cold increased the inflammatory pains that Prascovia wrote about: 'I used homeopathy and as usual it worked. So now after three days indoors, I feel quite fine'. In considering this, Mrs Barstchoff had hoped to go south to Cannes or Nice on 1st December, accompanied by Charles Lambert.

But plans changed because before mid-November, Prascovia had succumbed to a fever. Little Olishe too had come down with a whooping cough (*coqueluche*) that kept her mother awake at night. The now regular administrations and confusing advice of 'the devil called Jobert de Lamballe' and his medical colleagues in whose clutches she felt oppressed, increased her bills. The option to relocate to Nice was forfeited.

French doctors, she declared, were rude and brusque, so unlike more humane Russian ones. In any case, Nice would be awfully expensive, invaded as it was already by Russian compatriots. Another potential destination had been Pisa, but Pisa had a reputation from the Italians themselves as being 'dead' ['Pisa Morta'] – a place with scarcely any entertainment, or doctors, and only suitable for those recovering from tuberculosis. Her aunt Anna Koutaïssoff, married to the Crown Prince of Georgia, had left Pisa and was spending the winter in Florence instead.

Their so-called 'cloistered' life in recovery was soon remedied, starting with a trip to a Vaudeville theatre, a new form of polite entertainment with short separate acts.

Sighting of Napoleon III

Then on 6th December, they attended the premiere of a ballet called *Le Papillon* performed at the Paris Opera Ballet at the Salle Le Peletier. The emperor Napoleon III himself was there. The audience had applauded at length as he entered, 'and what was funny was that as he stood to salute everyone, the public – neither man nor woman – rose to their feet'. As they were sitting opposite Mrs Barstchoff had an excellent view of him: 'His person had such an expression of finesse and spirit that I liked him very much.'

The Christmas season in Paris meant that the streets were full of people and shopping booths: 'You can't imagine all the beautiful things of every kind on offer, you can spend the whole day looking without getting bored or tired!'

All the theatres were offering amusing comic reviews of the year's remarkable political and news events, one of which they attended on 23 December, a day after Olga's birthday. They also took a ride to the Bois de Boulogne to walk and watch the French and their favourite form of winter exercise': ice-skating.

After Christmas, rain, snow and mud, prevented their walks for a while. To mark the new year, the hotel manager sent Prascovia and Sophie two bouquets of flowers. After this short holiday break, Olishe was back at the *pension*. Her January report read: 'Olga is a good child. She is sometimes very little inclined to work.' School followed an early daily music lesson, and after school Mrs Barstchoff would make Olishe go over her lessons for the next day. Three times a week at five o'clock a dance tutor arrived, and the grown-ups had to be partners. They would eat at six in the evening. If there was no theatre, they would go for a walk around seven thirty along the boulevards till nine. At ten, they would take tea and Prascovia Hippolitovna would read aloud to Sophie. At midnight they went to bed: 'As you can see, my dear friend, our existence is as regular as clockwork'.

Summer – happy as a lark

The correspondence breaks for a month after March 1861, which suggests that Serge had in the meantime arrived in Paris from his posting in Kharkov. He had been unwell with an abscess which caused Prascovia much anxiety.

Olga had finished her classes in early-May, the piano had been taken out of the Paris apartment, and she was now on holiday. Olga had grown a lot. Though her mother worried that she been looking pale and thin, she had started to dress herself elegantly.[81]

The next set of letters is dated from May to August 1861. The ladies of the family were planning to take a cure at Europe's famous spa towns, Bad Ems in the Rhineland. They had in fact been plagued by health concerns : a swollen foot (Sophie) and a sore throat (Olishe) and more alarmingly, Prascovia was coughing up blood.

At Ems, Prascovia was prescribed to take twenty five hot mineral baths for her chest condition, with breaks in between. Sophie too had bathed in the thermal springs but found their effect to be tiring. The doctor had told her and her constant companion, Olga, to replace the hot springs with bathing in the River Lahn.

They were soon joined by Uncle Paul, and one or two acquaintances such as Plehve. Serge too was due to join them at some stage. Prascovia loved the peace and beauty of the scenery and wished that Serge could be there to enjoy it. If only she were an artist to paint the lush green mountains, the pretty pavilions, the charming river bank and the light graceful boats of different sizes which glided past them. The weather went from unbearable heat of twenty eight degrees in the shade to downpours.

Prascovia wrote that Olga would write to him in sad and solemn tones resembling Serge's, but it was a pose. In reality, she was lively and 'as happy as a lark', singing, leaping and chattering all day long. As everywhere, she had a large number of friends attracting attention by her kindness and mischievousness. There was one friend in particular, the little Tshilischeff, whom everyone took for her sister, though Olga was fair haired, and her friend a brunette.

In Spa it rained for two weeks incessantly, and Olishe complained to her father that whilst in Ems she had had a good time, at Spa it wasn't very nice because she hardly knew anyone. Though she had enjoyed seeing her grandmother, Elizaveta Barstchoff. Moreover, she had bruised herself jumping over some ditches, something she had been told not to do. Thus, she had been unable to write as she had hurt her hand. She blamed herself for her 'usual disobedience' (suggesting that the letter was in part authored by her mother).[82]

> Mummy told me not to jump across the ditches, but I didn't listen... I played *30 et 40* and lost 5 francs, which till now I can't forget. If I am sensible, which I am not always, Mum will take me to hear a concert.

They considered going to the Isle of Wight, but it seemed too expensive, due to the island's royal patronage, and anyway it was - by reputation Prascovia said - famously dull. More convenient to stay at Spa in Belgium, a scenic thermal water resort. The climate was usually good, the air fresh, pretty walks, a social scene with balls, concerts, and other pleasures.

Fig. 23
The Meeting Rooms at Bad Ems

The dancing lessons had eventually paid off: at a children's ball in August 1861, which had been requested by Olishe, the eight-year-old impressed with her graceful dancing. Her mother proudly commented that she was the 'Queen of the Ball' and partnered by a young Galitzine.[83] Passers-by started to remark on Olga's looks: 'Why do they say I am pretty, when you constantly say I am ugly?' she asks.

The sisters and Olishe eventually returned to Paris. Whilst Sophie still nursed a sprained foot, Mrs Barstchoff wrote of her perfect state of health, now no need for a doctor. Unlike at Ems where there were hardly any Russians, in Paris it was the opposite: 'one scan scarcely take a step without seeing a mass of compatriots.' She met the Princess Dadicene with Madame Moerder and the 'charming Evangelino'. Others were

Novosilzoff, Krylov, and a great number of other people. Included amongst this crowd were her dearest relatives, uncle Paul Urusov and brother Paul Kutaisov. The latter had graduated just the year before with first class honours from the Nikolaevsky Academy and recently returned from an expedition in the Caucasus.

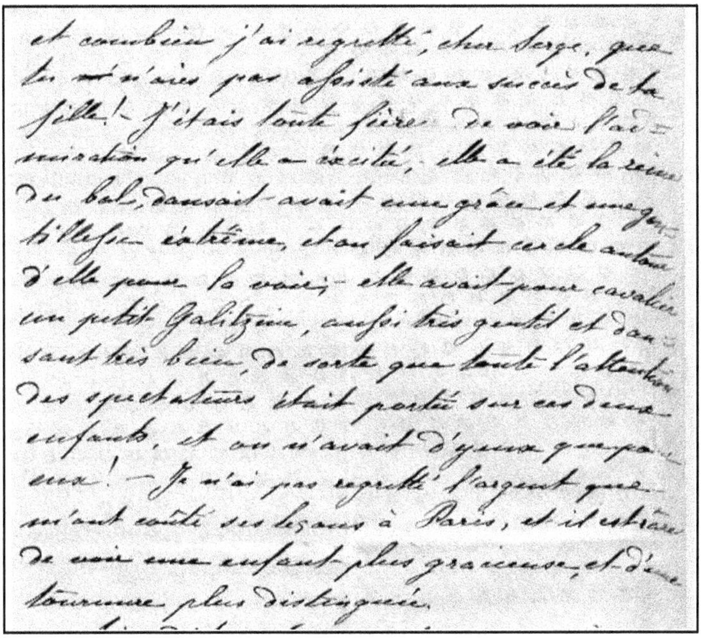

et combien j'ai regretté, cher Serge, que tu n'aies pas assisté aux succès de ta fille! — J'étais toute fière de voir l'admiration qu'elle a excitée, elle a été la reine du bal, dansait avait une grâce et une gentillesse extrême, et on faisait cercle autour d'elle pour la voir; — elle avait pour cavalier un petit Galitzine, aussi très gentil et dansant très bien, de sorte que toute l'attention des spectateurs était portée sur ces deux enfants, et on n'avait d'yeux que pour eux! — Je n'ai pas regretté l'argent que m'ont coûté ses leçons à Paris, et il est rare de voir une enfant plus gracieuse, et d'une tournure plus distinguée.

Fig. 24
Prascovia's letter letter, dark blue ink on pink paper

In Paris, in spite of the intense heat, they bought theatre tickets to see the military play *The Capture of Peking* and visited the Hippodrome and the chateau and gardens at St Cloud. With their impending departure in four days, they busied themselves with non-stop activities and so the time flew by.

The family's next plan was to travel to Livorno (Italy), where mother-in-law Elizaveta Barstchoff would also be staying, and then to head back home from there. Uncle Paul Urusov would provide the necessary money for the onward journey. Serge Barstchoff promised to meet them there and must have done so, as soon the correspondence again ends.

There was talk in the letters of Serge obtaining a placement in Warsaw through the new military governor of the city of Warsaw…none other than the Count Charles Lambert. Mrs Barstchoff encouraged Serge to think of taking up this post with the following words underlined in the letters for emphasis:

> I shall be the first in advising you to ask him for a placement, but in his current situation of simple <u>military governor of the city of Warsaw</u>, I don't think he will yet be in a particularly outstanding position; <u>reasonably,</u> it would be better to wait for his promotion, which doubtless won't take long. I am sure that you can count on getting an advantageous position if it depends on Count Charles to give one. I had a few words with him about this in Paris, as I told you, and he replied that a suitable position is certain to be available. With a promise such as that, coming from a man such as him, one can be perfectly relaxed and just wait until <u>his position becomes more consolidated.</u>

She knew that the job in Warsaw would supply better financial prospects to them as a family. She thought the weather better than St Petersburg but warned that 'you are mistaken if you think it better value there, as in Petersburg we can live as we like'. In fact, from other sources, it is possible to see that Serge Barstchoff did indeed gain a post in Warsaw. In 1861 he represented the Russian Government as an official of 'special assignments' under the governor general to the Kingdom of Poland.[84]

His resourceful wife had very cleverly set him up with a job, one that would more than help make their ends meet. However, not long after this at the age of thirty-six, upon his father's death in 1862 Serge inherited arable lands and various properties from his father's estates.[85] As eldest son he would have the pick of the best of them; he already had had the benefit of what the spouses privately called 'the emancipation of the paternal home.'

In the meantime, the final letter in this series on 22 August 1861 (O.S.) from Prascovia to Serge described their young daughter Olishe as awfully wilful and capricious. A letter from Serge had been timely, because in Prascovia's words:

YOUR OBEDIENT DAUGHTER: PARIS

There is no way to deal with her. We will have to place her in an educational establishment where she will be treated more severely than at home!

There is no evidence that Olga was put in an establishment, but her mother's complaints reflected the discipline she tried to put in place: respect and obedience were expected, submission to authority was essential. Olga's letters in Russian duly ended: 'Your respectful daughter'.

***

Years later and a photograph from Sicily

Our next news of Olga is an inscription in my grandmother's handwriting. On the back of the following photograph (below) we find that Olga has visited Sicily. The fashion details of her clothing and the softly waved short fringe indicate that the photo may date from the late 1860s. The close hip length fitted bodice emphasised a small waist drawn in with a belt and buckle. The blouse was fastened down the front with tiny buttons and the sleeves were narrow. Her light coloured skirt was a darker colour to the blouse. She is wearing pearl earrings and a string of pearls bracelet. The pastoral scenery utilises foliage in the foreground to create an outdoor looking setting, popular from 1860s studios.

On the reverse side of the photograph, we read: Villa von Stempel, Taormina [Sicily]. There is also an inscription in Ottoman Turkish which reads "unutmayınız beni" (transl. 'do not forget me'). This appears to have been written in her own hand and would be the earliest clue to confirm that by then Olishe had been learning the Arabic script for some time.

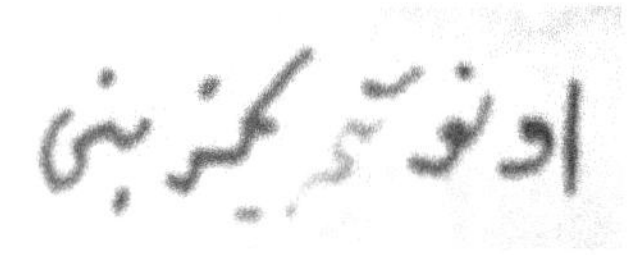

Fig. 25
Ottoman Inscription saying: 'Do not forget me.'

Fig. 26
Olga during a visit to Sicily

5 THE NEW FAMILY: DLOTOVSKY

> Therefore, I flung myself head foremost into that German ocean required to purify and regenerate me, and when at last I emerged from its waves I found myself a Westernizer, and so I have always remained.
>
> Ivan Turgenev

By coincidence during the same period that Mrs Prascovia Barstchoff had taken the young Olishe travelling, a twenty-two-year-old Collegiate Secretary called Volodya Dlotovsky had been abroad on leave. For three and a half months he passed through similar locations on his own grand tour. It was by no means his first such trip. A year before after graduation he had undertaken his first three month tour of Europe.

I found the details of each city he passed through on his travels stamped in two broadsheet-style passports. He left St Petersburg on 22 May 1860. His journey took him from Berlin in mid-June to Turin by the end of September 1860. In Marseille, Volodya received authorisation via the Russian Embassy in Paris from the Minister of Foreign Affairs, to remain abroad for a further six months until the beginning of May 1861.

The passports, amongst other original family papers, have survived the First World War, the Russian Civil War and two journeys across the Atlantic Ocean from Argentina (where they were kept by my grandmother). They include two professional service records, photographs, and other historical manuscripts. From each page of these documents, all in barely decipherable Russian script, comes a story.

The first had been the note by Nina Bahache (see Fig.1). There she described that the teenage Olga was married to Vladimir Dlotovsky, affectionately known as Volodya.

Fig. 27
Volodya (Vladimir Erastovich Dlotovsky) circa 1861

The couple were matched through the regimental connections of both their fathers in the Ulansky regiment and also no doubt through the family of the groom's mother Anna Zaborinskaya. Her relatives also had an estate in the same town of Schlisselburg, north of St Petersburg where Olga's grandfather had been an important landowner.

Fig. 28
Imperial Printing Emblem (above) and detail of Imperial eagles and heraldry (below) both on Volodya's passport (Family Collection)

The arranged marriage

Author and biographer Nikolai Ikonnikov cites this marriage as taking place in 1869. [86] It is unknown whether the marriage took place in Russia or abroad, but Vladimir's service record shows that that summer he took a leave of absence abroad for six weeks from mid-July to September. If it were a summer wedding, Olga would have been sixteen.

Fig. 29
Volodya (Family Collection)

That year Tolstoy had just finished his last volume of *War and Peace*; perhaps this was on their honeymoon reading list? In that book are two references to Olga's great uncle, the General Alexander Koutaissof (Kutaisov /Kutaysov). He had died a hero in the battle of Borodino on 7 September 1812 during the French invasion by Napoleon. It was a battle no Russian could forget. An extract follows:

> Mention was made in Kutuzov's report of the Russian losses, among which featured the names of Tuchkov, Bagration and Kutaysov. In the Petersburg world this sad side of the affair again involuntarily centred round a single incident: Kutaysov's death. Everybody knew him, the emperor liked him, and he was young and interesting. That day everyone met with the words: ...but what a loss Kutaysov is! How sorry I am![87]

As a young woman, Olga was of medium height, a brunette with dark eyes and of a lively disposition. The following portrait, taken by a commercial photographer in Kovno (or Kaunas), shows Olga in hand-sewn gown with bodice and wide crinoline skirt of a light colour decorated with contrasting draped darker lace and sweeping train. This was a fashion typical in Europe from the mid-1860s, which squeezed in the waist with corsets. Though producing beautiful silhouettes long-term usage of constricting undergarments could cause not only exhaustion but serious health problems. The tall hairstyle with plaits dates the photograph to the 1870s. Flowers in the hair were worn for a ball, or the photograph was taken on the special occasion of Olga's twenty-first birthday in 1873 – the pearl drop earrings and the strung rows of pearls a recent gift? The book on the chair symbolised her fondness for reading.

The artificial scene is typical of a photography studio of the time with plain background, drawn curtain and furniture as a prop and the patterned carpet in the foreground; a typical pose of the 1870s was to lean on the back of a chair. Whilst subjects did not smile for the camera in those days, the photographer and client intended to portray 'a pleasing expression' which denoted dignity or intelligent seriousness, and in the photograph her face is turned to the camera.[88]

Names from the ancient Primary Chronicle
Historical literary references relate to the couple's first names, Olga and Vladimir, which hold iconic status in the region. Originating from the old Norse, *Helga, or heilagr,* means blessed. The name *Volodimir,* means ruler of peace and is derived from Slavic roots. There were two venerated figures from the ancient *Primary Chronicle*: Olga queen regent of Kyiv (890-969) who spread Christianity, and her grandson Vladimir I of Kyiv (otherwise known as Vladimir the Great, 958-1015), who was also venerated as a saint. As ruler of *Kievan Rus,* he forcibly converted Kyiv and Novgorod to Christianity after a miraculous cure, marriage to a Byzantine princess and his adoption of the faith in 988. This marked the beginning of Christianity in Rus as well as the country's acceptance into the commonwealth of Christian nations, with the Christian culture of Constantinople as its Byzantine model. The rule of Vladimir I is looked back on as a golden age.[89]

Fig. 30
Olga Dlotovsky, née Barstchoff (Family Collection)

THE NEW FAMILY DLOTOVSKY

About Olga's betrothed, Volodya

Vladimir Erastovich Dlotovsky was fourteen years older than his bride.[90] He was an attractive man, in looks more like his mother than his blonde, blue-eyed father. His beard was clipped in the style of the time, and in all photographs, even on a picnic, Vladimir was immaculately turned out with suit and waistcoat. In later years, photographs detail a cigarette always in hand. His mother was kind and sweet natured, his father, a career military man, was a more distant, stern, and even fearsome figure, no doubt, a complete authoritarian.

Ivan Turgenev's *Fathers and Sons*, written in the period, describes the distant father-son relationship possible with extended absences due to unrelenting army service:

> 'The general returned to his division and his wife, and only at rare intervals sent his sons sheets of grey foolscap written and cross-written in the bold hand of the public scribe, and signed in a laborious flourish at the bottom ... Major-General'.

Paternal ancestors, the Dlotovskys came from the hereditary nobility of Polish nobles who lived southwest of Moscow between the ancient fortress city of Tula and Smolensk.[91] Their family records go back as far as Stanislav Dlotovsky from 1650.[92]

Fig. 31
Smolensk Council of the Nobility seal, family document dated 11 May 1848
(Family Collection)

When Volodya's parents had married in 1834, his father Erast Konstantinovich Dlotovsky (1806-1887) was stationed with the reserve regiment of the Second Ulansky Settled Division of Lancers south of Kiev [Kyiv]. He married Anna Ivanovna Zaborinskaya in the cathedral church of St Nicholas at Novomirgorod, now Ukraine. Erast Konstantinovich rose through the military ranks to the highest level, being General of the Infantry and President of the Supreme Military Court.[93] His career lasted sixty-two years under four tsars: from November 1823 under Tsar Alexander I, then Nicholas I, Alexander II[94] and finally Alexander III.[95] In that time he received twenty-five military honours.[96] His service included a time subduing the Polish uprising in 1863 for which he earned a reputation for being ruthless, undoubtedly fulfilling the Tsar's direct orders. His high salary of nine thousand roubles per year reflected his high level attainments.

Fig. 32
General Erast K. Dlotovsky and his wife Anna Dlotovsky (Family Collection)

The young Vladimir studied at the then-named Kharkov Imperial University and St Petersburg University, from where he graduated on 31 July 1859. He obtained his degree in Historical Philology standing for studies in Russian, French and the Classics; his dissertation was entitled *The Disintegration of Charlemagne's monarchy.*[97] The degree set Vladimir on course for life in the professions. His Diploma Certificate specifies that he was accepted as *Candidate* for the civil service 10th grade and had the right to be promoted to the rank of Officer.[98] Luckily for him, recent military reforms meant that university students were not called up for conscription.[99] Instead, after graduation, he set off on his first grand tour of Europe, having obtained a passport and leave for three months up till 1 October.

On his return, he joined the civil service as Collegiate Secretary, in the so-called land disputes office. After his second extended stay in Europe in May 1861, he worked at the Ministry of the Interior and an administrative committee chaired by his father: this reviewed district settlements and land disputes in the southern regions between the Ural Cossack armies and the Ural Kazakhs. This committee not only delineated borders on the left bank of the Ural River but acquired useful information on the geography of the region.[100]

Fig. 33
Vladimir's Passport (Family Collection)

Vladimir received a promotion on 17th April 1863 to senior Titular Counsellor ('*Sovetnik*'). Each promotion depended on having served two years at the lower level. He was awarded the Imperial awards of St Anna 3rd degree in April 1865,[101] and the Order of St Stanislaus 2nd degree two years later.[102] These awards were written out and signed by the presiding ceremonial '*Meisters*' and stamped with a waxed seal.

By February 1867, he was employed at the Ministry of Justice, in the legislative department.[103] This was a momentous time to be working as a lawyer. Trial by jury and a proper system of appeal courts were successfully introduced in Russia on the Western European model under Alexander II's recent reforms. The law of November 1864 eliminated the old feudal court system. It provided a new basis in Russia for *a swift, just, merciful court, equitable to all subjects*. Its aim claimed to be 'elevating the powers of the judiciary, to give it due independence and to establish among the people respect for the law'.[104]

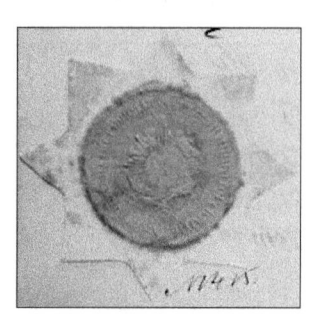

Fig. 34
Order of St Stanislaus 2nd degree with wax seal, 14 April 1865

The jury court was an independent court, with an oral and public legal process, and the equality of all people before the court. To start with, it enjoyed huge popularity. This reform removed an obstacle from Russia's path to industrial development, and in hindsight is considered the most democratic of all the institutions created by the Great Reforms (the courts were brought back into line with autocratic rule in the 1880s).[105]

The Ministry of Justice then appointed Vladimir at grade of Court Counsellor to be a district court prosecutor at St Petersburg. It was expected for lawyers to serve in several cities and regions of the empire, to increase their knowledge and experience. So as a Collegiate Counsellor he had his first posting as provincial prosecutor on 13 February 1870. He was to serve in the capital of the seven districts of the Kovno Province (a Russian Governate of Poland), right in the northwest of the Empire.

THE NEW FAMILY DLOTOVSKY

Fig. 35
Kovno (Kaunas)[106]

Family life in Kovno and public charity

Kovno - nowadays called Kaunas – with its picturesque red roofed houses and cobbled avenues and was home to Lithuanians, Letts, Poles, and ethnic Germans. There was a thriving community of Jews with a renowned centre of Jewish learning, and Russians were in the minority.[107] It was an area which had been affected by the Polish rebellion and its brutal suppression a few years before.

The young family moved here from St Petersburg whilst Olga was already five months pregnant with their first child. My great-grandmother Nina Dlotovsky was born on 21 June 1870, just nine months after their honeymoon.

Barely six months after this, Olga was expecting a second time. Vera was born on 1 October 1871, followed by baby Vladimir arrived a year and a half later, on 25 May 1873.[108] Thus, before her twentieth birthday, Olga already had three children. Nina and Vera were both very fashionable names: Nina, after a famous Greek saint from Cappadocia; while Vera means 'Faith.'

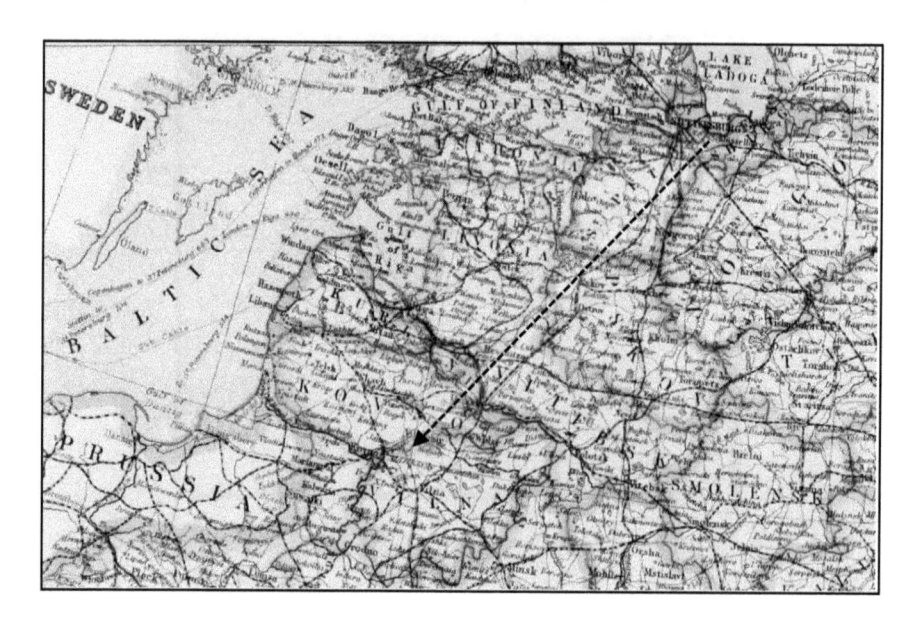

Fig. 36
Map of Western Russia showing St Petersburg to Kovno[109]

Fig. 37
Winter attire with a muff and fur coat to cover a long skirt (Family Collection).

All three babies were christened in turn at the Alexander Nevsky Orthodox Cathedral in Kovno. Prince Pavel Petrovich Lopukhin, 'His

THE NEW FAMILY DLOTOVSKY

Serene Highness,' was asked to be one of the godfathers; a great great-uncle and already eighty-three years old. He was also a childless widower with a vast fortune.

The following picture with the ladies dressed in long formal gowns and bonnets is, I believe, taken on Vera's christening on 20 October 1871. Even the toddler, Nina, is wearing a little cap, as must have been customary. Olga is wearing a decorated straw bonnet, favoured by younger women at the time, the thick dark ribbons hang untied. Based on Vera's christening documents, from left we may see: Olga Sergeevna Dlotovsky-Barstchoff, Nina, Kovno's Vice Governor A.S. Leonov, Prince Pavel Lopukhin (brother of 'grand-maman' Prascovia Lopukhina), Vladimir Dlotovsky, Grandma Prascovia Hippolitovna Barstchoff-Kutaisova. Baby Vera is not in view.

Fig. 38
A drink with godparents after the service (Family Collection)

If we take a close-up of this photo, the young mother of eighteen wearing a crucifix on a short chain looks straight ahead. She has barely touched her glass of wine, but her husband (viewed in the full photograph), looks across at her fondly.

Fig. 39
Close up of Olga with Nina

We learn more about Olga after her marriage from an interview she gave several years later. One gathers from this that she was frustrated to have to stop her studies to be married:

> She was unable to continue studying and reading, for she was married at the age of sixteen to the son of General Dlotovsky, at the time working as a public prosecutor in the Russian government. She focused on studying languages on her own. She studied Italian and drawing [or painting], and she played the piano in private charity association gatherings. Her fine playing softened people's hearts, and she charmed their minds with her eloquence and refined clarity of expression. She took unusual pleasure in serving invalids, aiding the troubled, and coming to the rescue of those in need. She read the Holy Book to female prisoners and consoled them for the calamities and afflictions they had suffered with her sweet words and delicate way of speaking.[110]

Olga was, in fact, recorded as being a Chair of trustees on the women's board of the Kovno prison committee, in the Vilnius archive Memorial Book of 1873.[111] The newly built high security prison was originally built for three hundred criminals, but was overcrowded with rebel leaders, peasant rebels and other political prisoners - of the kind probably put there by her imposing military father-in-law (he was also a member of the 'Prison Committee'). The three-storey high building with prison walls was certainly a feared place.

That Olga aided the troubled and played for private charity association gatherings reflects the distinctive ethos of the 'generation of the sixties' who prized compassion and a social conscience. They regarded service to society as a personal moral duty. People of this generation shared a passion for social change, serving the people, and as was noted a few years later by a writer on the history of women in Russian charity: 'since the sphere of activity for women in our country is much narrower than for men, all this pent-up energy was turned to public charity'.[112]

The reforms themselves were having a powerful effect on society: the abolition of serfdom especially, which had delivered more than twenty million people from bondage albeit imperfectly, had given hope that 'poverty ignorance and cultural backwardness could be banished by right-minded individuals.' The ethos of the 1860s left its imprint on many who became leaders of Russian philanthropy, those who were full of hopes for a bright future and wanted to work for progress.[113]

For Vladimir's service at the courts in Kovno, in 1871 he received a decoration for land arrangements made for former state serfs 1870-1872.[114]

Fig. 40
Vladimir's medal of distinction for state peasant emancipation (Family Collection).

Despite this distinction, it was also a time of turmoil: a great misfortune struck the young family, when baby Vladimir died.

By the end of May 1874, Court Counsellor Vladimir Dlotovsky was transferred to the Senate in St Petersburg for a few months. Here he was seconded to work in the department of the chief procurator. The 'Ober-Procurator' was an official in charge of the Holy Synod.[115]

Before his departure from Kovno he received a card (in French) from one of his team in Kovno dated 28 May 1874:

> If sometime, Mr Dlotoffski, you glance fleetingly at this letter you will always see friendly greetings from your very humble, devoted and grateful servant, who believe me, will never cease lamenting the day when he lost you as a benevolent boss. [116]

Vladimir used to take only ten days leave a year, but with this relocation for work, the family took a much-needed opportunity for a holiday abroad, with leave of absence of four months.[117]

Fig. 41
Nina Dlotovsky, my great-grandmother (Family Collection)

A new posting to Kazan

In mid-November 1874, Vladimir was appointed a member of the Kazan Court of Justice, one of the newly established courts of appeal. Vladimir was to stay in this post for six years. The Kazan court, which covered all criminal and civilian cases, was one of high status, the third after St Petersburg and Moscow. Kazan, or Kasan as it was previously referenced in some instances, has often been considered the third capital of Russia (see Fig.44). At that time, it was the most important of the provincial towns. Its position at the confluence of the Volga and the Kazanka rivers gave it great commercial advantages; its trade with the Ural Mountains, Astrakhan, Siberia, and countries such as China made it the emporium of Russian commerce with Asia.

It was certainly a promotion as geographically the Kazan Governorate was twice the size of that of Kovno; though its population was more rural and spread out, it was more numerous by some five hundred thousand people.[118] Even so the premises of the court were known to be very cramped for the procurators, notaries, advocates, and expert medics. Cases were often extraordinarily complex and court sessions often finished late in the evening or continued into the night; complicated trials lasted several days or even weeks which could make jury duty very onerous. On 1 January 1877 Vladimir was promoted to State Councillor, which meant that now he was now to be addressed as 'Your Honour'.

The birth of a fourth Dlotovsky child, another son, is recorded on 21 October 1876.[119] This baby boy was also named Vladimir after his father; it was common to rename a new baby after one earlier deceased. Yet, things were not going well between Olga and her husband. Disagreements and discord pre-empted an end of their marriage. Volodya took a month off work from 1 May to 1 June 1878, to try and resolve any differences, but to no avail.

In a matter of weeks, they were divorced. Olga is recorded as saying that she had 'been forced' to request a divorce.[120] She had applied to a different court which covered matters of church canon and spirituality, the Holy Synod.[121] Permission had been requested from the Sovereign, as traditionally divorces were granted by the Tsar – her godfather.

Divorce in those times was unusual, expensive and troublesome, and women had to prove causes other than adultery, such as desertion or cruelty to file for divorce. This young family was now bitterly split in two. For reasons not yet established, a year later the Kazan Diocesan Administration issued a document No. 2874 on 22 August 1879 specifying 'a prohibition for Mr. Dlotovsky to enter into a new marriage.'[122] With his knowledge of the law, it is inconceivable that Vladimir would not have disputed the terms for child custody.

It would not be long before Olga would again remarry. A meeting with a certain Alexander Lebedeff perhaps promised fewer constraints. There is no certainty about how they first met, excepting that Lebedeff who was from Kazan, had trained in law, and elite social circles were small. The date of the wedding recorded by relatives is 19 August 1878.[123]

Within the context of her new marriage to Alexander, Olga was now able to pursue her longstanding interest in Eastern languages. Whether the more conservative Vladimir might have allowed Olga to develop her interests in Turkish or Oriental studies is unknown. Turks were not Russia's allies and Turkish culture was not in vogue in 1878; Russia had, after all, only just finished another war with Turkey. Such an interest may have proved most unconventional for the wife of Vladimir Dlotovsky, the daughter-in-law of one of Russia's top generals.

Fig. 42
Original Art Nouveau postcard issued by the Red Cross: illustration by Ivan Bilibin in 1902 of folk legend called *Mikhailo Potyk and the Swan*. Words are about a swan (*Lebed*) who transforms into a beautiful woman to marry the hunter: *"Do not slay me but take me as your wife!"* A humorus keepsake referring to Olga and Alexander Lebedeff?[124]

THE NEW FAMILY DLOTOVSKY

The First Marriage of Olga S Barstchoff to Vladimir Dlotovsky
1869-1878

Parents	First Marriage	Their Children
Olga I Kutaissoff 1835-1900		
	Olga S Barstchoff 1852-1933	
		Nina Vl. Dlotovsky 1870-1947
Serge M Barstchoff 1826-1888		
		Vera Vl. Dlotovsky 1871 - ?
		Vladimir Vl. Dlotovsky 1873 - ?
Anna Ivanovna Zaborinskaya 1815-1903		Vladimir Vl. Dlotovsky 1876-1907
	Vladimir E Dlotovsky 1838-1907	
Erast Konstantinovich Dlotovsky 1806-1888		

6 THE MAYOR OF KAZAN

> Marriage is a big lottery – not everyone gets the winning ticket.
> Alexandra V. Bogdanovich

The new-found husband, long-time bachelor Alexander Alexandrovich Lebedeff, was nine years Olga's senior. Though not especially handsome, he was very wealthy, and enjoyed the good life. His family must have told him that it was time he settled down and produced a legitimate heir.

One memoirist of the period describes him as 'approachable, cordial and hospitable.'[125] A reputed trait of the upper echelons of society in Kazan was that guests were received at all hours. Reckless extravagance and 'a life of riotous pleasure nowhere surpassed' were the more imperfect customs of Kazan's aristocracy, as recorded by British author Edward Turnerelli some years earlier.[126]

To all appearances, Alexander enjoyed a successful political career. He happened to be a major landowner in the Kazan Province and neighbouring regions and became known for his works of charity. Being the age of industrialisation, it would not be long before previously inconceivable technologies such as telephones and electric lights would arrive, and Alexander would be amongst the first to get them.

He held the title of Chamberlain to the Tsar – traditionally a ceremonial post but one that at that time reflected the status of civil rank at court. He would occasionally visit St Petersburg to fulfil official duties as a delegate from Kazan's City Council and Olga as his wife went with him; their stays were often lengthy, not least as the journey each way from Kazan to St Petersburg was over one thousand five hundred kilometres [127] One of Alexander's tasks was to petition for the construction of the trans-Siberian railway to pass through Kazan from Nizhny Novgorod; he spoke of a Belgian company who would do the work, however, unfortunately this petition failed, and the line ended up taking a more southern route towards Siberia, bypassing Kazan altogether.[128]

Fig. 43
Portrait of Olga de Lebedeff wearing a tiara and white veil (Family Collection)

At the time of her second wedding, Olga was twenty-five years old. The white veil in the photograph (Fig. 43), suggests a wedding portrait. She looks much more self-assured in both her expression and style of dress with her decorative low neckline.

Olga appears to have taken the children from her first marriage with her, certainly the two girls. In several photographs taken in Kazan, they are stylishly dressed, ribbons tying their long fair hair. However, traditionally in cases of divorce, fathers had legal guardianship over small children, so it is possible he had custody over his youngest, Vladimir.

In an interview for a ladies' magazine some years later, Olga would describe her second marriage as a happy one. There, she described Alexander as being 'from one of the most venerable, notable, eminent, and wealthy families' of the area. [129]

The diaries of Alexandra Bogdanovich

However, the memoirs of a society lady called Alexandra Victorovna Bogdanovich, the wife of the General Yevgeny Bogdanovich, paint quite another picture to the happy one described. Memoirs need to be treated with some scepticism, yet this account discloses that in the first years of this new marriage Olga had some serious disappointments and difficulties.

I discovered this thanks to an academic from the St Petersburg Institute of History called Mikhail Druzhin. He first contacted me with questions about Olga and her family. He had found mentions of a certain Mr & Mrs Lebedeff in the memoirs that were intriguing. The historian explained that judging by the style and content of the memoirs, the General's wife Alexandra Victorovna was a mercurial, mistrustful woman whose prejudiced views about people's importance fluctuated according to her and her husband's need for them; the extensive diaries mention one thousand four hundred different individuals. People of both liberal and conservative views met at the Bogdanovichs' social and literary salon evenings, so there was a continuous exchange of information and rumours, enabling the General to become influential in public life and even in foreign policy. [130]

THE MAYOR OF KAZAN

Alexandra Bogdanovich took some interest in Mr and Mrs Lebedeff, to whom she referred only by their surname, and over several years recorded some short impressions. She first met them in January 1881 when Olga was six months pregnant. She described Olga as a 'lively lady' but did not take to her immediately. In May 1881 she writes that she is warming to Olga, the more she knows her - the better she likes her. The relationship improves to the extent that the Lebedeffs invite the Bogdanovichs to spend a holiday with them in August at Kaffa (Theodosia) on the Black Sea coast, but here the memoir breaks off.

Several years later in 1888 Alexandra's diary entry brings in a new theme. She starts to criticise Mr Lebedeff; that though he was rich and healthy, he was too frivolous, enjoying too much of a good time. She complains that like everyone else, he pesters her husband, Yevgeny Vasilievitch, for political favours. [131]

The descriptions about Olga herself appear indicting as well as intriguing, for at this time, in May 1888 Olga started to confide in Alexandra. The latter wondered how Olga could divulge so much about her personal life, when such things 'should remain private.' So, it transpired that all was not well with the Lebedeffs. In the circumstances, it was good that Olga could tell a friend what was going on in her marriage.

The memoir discloses that, by her own admission Mrs Lebedeff had spoken candidly of her second husband's infidelity - something that 'one would not normally discuss: though she found his figure unattractive, at other times Lebedeva found him adorable'. She had angrily admitted that Alexander had unfortunately fallen in love with a fifty-five-year-old Madame Golovinskaya, who demanded money in each letter. Olga herself is described as clever and sweet, but the memoirist finds her affected in some way.[132]

The diary contrasts Olga's virtuous demeanor with a stormy past [*un passé orageux*]. Doubtless, conflicting emotions towards her husband may have been hard to suppress. To what exactly this so-called 'stormy past' refers to, remains in large part, a mystery and pure conjecture.

About Alexander Alexandrovich Lebedeff

Alexander Lebedeff descended from the landed gentry of the Kazan Governorate of the sixth rank, and he was addressed as 'Your Excellency'. Anyone above the eighth rank had the status of hereditary nobility, and the sixth rank was generally reserved for ancient noble families (noble prior to 1785). The hierarchical caste system was made up of fourteen ranks tied to state service and landed privileges, with fourteen being the lowest and the first being the highest (such as chancellor, admiral, or metropolitan bishop).

Alexander's direct paternal ancestors were wealthy industrialist landowners. He had inherited lands, properties, and businesses from his father and grandfather.[133] His father is believed to have owned over a thousand serfs before they were liberated in the reform of 1861.[134] According to the Kazan National Archive, apart from extensive forests, Alexander Lebedeff and his forebears were proprietors of factories of various sorts including sawmills, potash, copper smelting, glass factories and distilleries in the Viatka, Spassky and Penzensky regions. Of the glass factories, Alexander inherited one at Konevo near Nizhny Novgorod (site of the famous summer fair),[135] which had been formerly owned by his grandmother's family of enterprising merchants, the Osokins. They were Old Believers, that is to say Orthodox Christian dissenters who rejected the liturgical reforms which Patriarch Nikon had made to the Byzantine rites in the mid-seventeenth century. Another glass factory was called Siuginsky, situated in the town of Mozhga in the Viatka Province.

With the products of the factories being marketed in Nizhny Novgorod and Astrakhan under the supervision of foremen, Alexander was termed a merchant of the First Guild, a major trader who was allowed to do business abroad; belonging to the First Guild entitled him to stand for city mayor, to carry a sword and to wear formal attire of the governorate. He was entitled to travel in a coach drawn by four horses, own river and sea vessels and country houses.

Both Nizhni Novgorod and Kazan provided commercial links between the centre of the country and the Urals, Siberia, and Transcaucasia, and with the neighbouring lands of Persia, India,

THE MAYOR OF KAZAN

Afghanistan, and China via the confluence of their waterways – the Volga, the Oka, and the Kama respectively. Though Alexander was born near Nizhny Novgorod,[136] he made his home in Kazan and he was a law graduate of Kazan Imperial University.

Alexander had followed his maternal grandfather, Governor Stepan Stepanovich Strekalov, into government service. By 1874, just barely in his thirties, he achieved the position of a Collegiate Advisor and had tasted the pleasures of the capital city, St Petersburg.[137] In 1882, he was appointed Collegiate Councillor in Kazan and the following year Mayor of the city for a three-year period 1883-1886. This was a role he would return to in 1887 and in 1899.[138] As well as these formal duties, over the years he fulfilled several honorary roles and trusteeships for schools and charities, such as at the School for Blind Children.[139]

Journalist Sania Safina mentions in her book *Lubiana, Land of the Foresters* (Lubyani, Rodina Lesovodov), that the name of the Lebedeffs would in time be made famous by Alexander's wife. At the time of their marriage, her aristocratic background added the prestige of her lineage to Alexander.

Apart from the initial allure of marrying someone charming and hospitable, Olga's new marriage maybe offered her the prospect of new opportunities; married women occupied ranks according to the grades of their husband.[140] Though Alexander was initially enchanted by Olga's energy and high culture, his lack of faithfulness (though common in those days), indicates that his focus on their marriage being a happy one was short lived. He tolerated her intellectual ambitions and scholarly studies, and dutifully provided her with a monthly stipend. This sometimes barely covered all her expenses including tutor fees and travel. Unless and until she had her own means via inheritance on her father's death in 1888, she had to operate within the bounds of this partnership. There were always going to be so many expectations to be conventional and obligations - *comme il faut*. Like in Europe, there was controversy and a-hundred-and-one limitations facing Russian gentry-class women's education and professional advancement.[141]

When Alexander served as the Mayor of Kazan and Marshal of the Nobility in the area, the couple were in contact with a wide range of people in society, across political, scientific, and other professional institutions. The social ties of wives - extended conduits of friendships and acquaintances - had the capacity to enhance their husbands' reputations and outreach. Olga was adept at putting people in contact with one another.[142] She was not afraid to use her influence when necessary, such as petitioning for aid during a famine.[143]

Connections with local land owning Tatars, wealthy Tatar merchants and scholarly Muslim prelates (ulama)[144] enhanced her ability to play this role, as quoted by one scholar:

> Thanks to her frequent dealings with Tatar labourers and local notables, she was already familiar with the Tatar dialect.[145]

Speaking the local language was vital, as noted by a nineteenth century Times newspaper correspondent, Scotsman Sir Donald Mackenzie Wallace who had toured the area a few years previously:[146] 'Educated Russians often speak one or two languages fluently, but the peasants know no language but their own, and it is with the peasantry that one comes into contact. And to converse freely with the peasant requires a considerable familiarity with the language – far more than is required for simply reading a book.'

In the early years of married life Olga had devoted herself to studying the arts of singing, drawing, and musical instruments as well as reading medical texts. The study of languages and the arts was well approved for young women by the government whereas interest in natural science was deemed too progressive and politically sensitive due to the rise in nihilism.[147] Olga's activities in those early years were described many years later in a biographical article (translated in full in Book Two):

> She was inclined by nature to help the wretched, and to serve invalids and those in need, she studied most of the available medical manuals, and learned the Tatar language in a short time, enabling her to become acquainted with the needs of people in trouble and those serving in her husband's properties. She did not stop with that; she mounted many musical soirées in aid of the poor. None of this deflected her from her determination to continue studying, reading, and writing.[148]

Excepting for its courses in midwifery for 'learned midwives', attendance at Kazan University was not yet officially open to women. Access to university education in general was a controversial issue before 1900 as some professors argued that women were incapable of serious academic study, and furthermore the government had barred women's entry to university from 1863 to 1897.

Press and scholarly articles cite that Olga gained access to the university's Society of Archaeology, Ethnography and History, which was open to the public; the university and society archives have no record of her name on either of their membership rolls. Yet, some sources claim that she graduated from the University of Kazan, so perhaps this is something that she herself had said. Afterall, with her husband's position of city mayor, it is probable that she was permitted to attend lectures even unofficially at the university.

However she managed it, Olga studied Oriental languages in a single-minded fashion, learning enough Arabic to read and write. At that time Tatar and Arabic used the same script. She studied elements of Persian, necessary for understanding Ottoman Turkish. Lessons were certainly taken with private tutors whether at home (or during a stay abroad). This is how over the next twenty-five years Olga de Lebedeff's language skills continually improved until she succeeded in becoming a renowned scholar and published translator of Tatar, Ottoman and Arabic texts, as well as an authority on the history of Kazan, and on Russia's Muslims.

The countryside estate at Lubiana, Viatka

Our scholar acquired the habit of spending several months at a time in the country; it was an ideal quiet place to work on her translations – a time consuming yet rewarding occupation, though punishing for eyesight and circulation. Some sources describe a family estate in the Spassky province south of Kazan, where perhaps Olga spent some of her childhood.[149] But the property documented in photographs is the one northeast of Kazan.

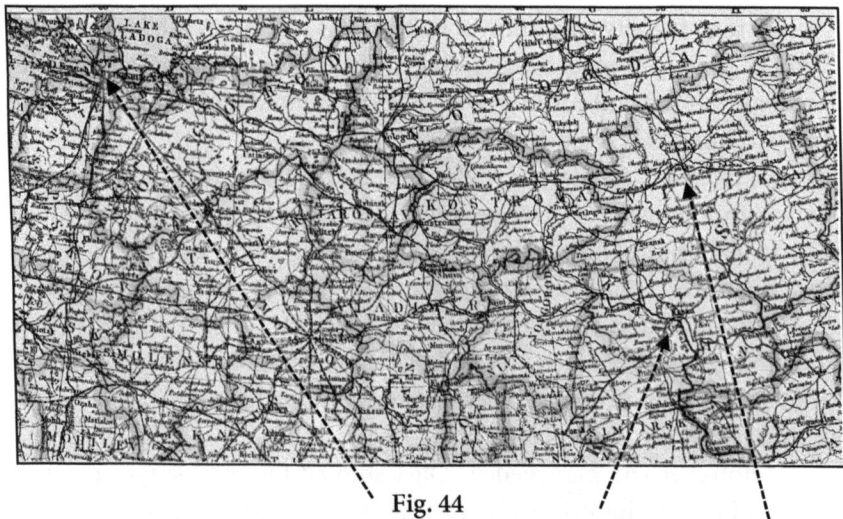

Fig. 44
Harmsworth Map of Russia St Petersburg, Kazan (Kasan) & Viatka

The extensive forest estates and lands owned by Alexander and Olga Lebedeff comprised an equivalent of over thirteen thousand hectares (measured in '*desiatiny*', where one *desiatina* is approximately 0.915 of a hectare) in the Mamadish district and over six thousand *desiatiny* in the district of Laishev by the Kama River.[150] One of the small villages in the Gurevka estate was called 'Lubiana' or 'Lubjan' of which I heard tell from my grandmother.

Her husband's grandfather, Evgraf Alexeevich, had originally founded the village; in 1872 Alexander Lebedeff was permitted to build a country house in Lubiana, by a summer stream of the same name, the 'Lubyanka', a small navigable tributary off the Viatka River.[151]

The manor and village of Lubiana were situated on the downstream left bank of the Viatka, which flows into the Kama River. The distance from Kazan was 168 km, then measured as 159 *versty*, in which one *versta* equals 1.06 of a kilometre). Once the ice had melted the cheapest and most convenient means of transport was by steamboat on a vessel with one of the following names: 'Grandpa,' 'Father,' 'Auntie,' 'Son,' 'Daughter' and 'Grandson.' The fresh waters were a paradise for anglers as the rivers abounded in carp, bream, perch, lingcod, and roach, although for just under half the year the rivers were frozen solid. In summer, though, they ferried thousands of kilogrammes of freight, then weighed in '*nyð*' - *pood* (where one *pood* equals just over sixteen kilos). The freight consisted of firewood, forestry materials and bread, up and down river.[152] This provided another business opportunity for the Lebedeffs, one which, with their steam-powered sawmill and timber from saplings to seventeen-metre-high trees, would make a legacy for the region. The undisturbed forest habitat was rich in biodiversity providing not only the high-quality timber for shipbuilding: oak, spruce, aspen, fir, lime, and black poplar but also the less prized elm, birch, maple, rowan willow and walnut which often were used for potash or firewood.

The remoteness of these forests allowed for a profusion of wildlife and easy roaming such as deer, bears, elks, wolves, foxes, lynx, ermine, and rabbits amongst others, which benefited hunters with their distinct types of traps and snares, providing a source for furs for which the region was famous.[153]

Researchers at the Tatarstan National Archive have described a typical estate of the period, which matches well the manor belonging to the Lebedeffs: 'The manor house was a kind of spiritual, social, and economic center of the estate. A classic family estate consisted of the manor house and various outbuildings; around the house with high porch and terrace garden was laid out. It had plenty of vegetation hiding barns, outbuildings for the housekeeper and workers, as well as stables, etc.'[154] Apart from the housekeeper, other servants included: coachmen, stable boys, washerwomen, cook, dishwashers, chambermaids and gardeners. They were treated, so it was said, according to the character of their master.

With its setting by the forest and with ample supply of all kinds of wood, it is unsurprising that this was the material used to build the new manor at Lubiana. It was constructed in the modernist or revivalist style of fashionable wooden architecture of the period. This echoed vernacular folk architecture with roofs of different pitches, turrets, hipped ends of lintels and cornices. The main house had three storeys (see Fig. 46). The interiors were floored with parquet, decorated with brass fittings, and heated with Dutch tiled stoves. From the smaller guest house with its two open terraces, one could walk along two rows of willow straight to the riverbank.

The gardens of the large manor house were planted with raspberry bushes and an orchard. The orchard was bordered by a solid painted fence and accessed through a wicker gate. Through the gate lay the clear waters of a huge pond ringed by pine trees. By the shore was a bathing area marked out by wooden boards. The estate owned a park of spruce and firs with an alley lined with lime trees, yellow acacia, white and purple lilacs, and meadowsweet.

Fig. 45
Postcards of the village and pond at Lubiana[155]

In the manor's two polygonal glass orangeries, exotic plants were cultivated, including palm and cypress trees in large pots which were brought outside during the summer.

THE MAYOR OF KAZAN

Stories which passed down the generations of villagers about the Lebedeffs' customs and 'comfortable' way of life made it sound quite idyllic:

> The family used to arrive in Lubiana during the summer months. They invited distinguished people and their close circle of friends to visit. Before entering the house, guests stopped to admire the sparkling fountain spray and the beautifully planted flowerbeds leading up to the front porch planted by the gardener Pyotr Kotsin. Sounds of music wafted through the house in the evenings, the elegant ladies enjoying their social time around the grand piano, with invited musicians, whilst their 'respected husbands gathered in groups to discuss politics and business.[156]

Fig. 46
Entrance to the large manor house at Lubiana (Family Collection)

There were stables and a coach house by the main house for carriage outings, and horse riding was also a pastime, side-saddle for the women. Other summer pursuits were picnics and boating, to which the ladies appeared in light coloured blouses contrasting their ankle length skirts of a darker hue and wide-brimmed hats.

The village had a post office equipped with a telegraph line. Horses were kept for the postal service. There were once weekly collections and deliveries along the so-called 'post road'.

Over the summer in 1894, Olga wrote to Leo Tolstoy from here. In those days you could address a letter to someone well known, simply with their name and the town where they lived and expect it to arrive safely: for example, 'To His Grace Count Leo Nikolayevich Tolstoy, Moscow, Russia'.[157] As a woman of letters, she herself also received correspondence in this way.

By 1897, this rural village of Lubiana had one hundred and thirty-two inhabitants of Russian and Tatar origin. A small school with fifty children was funded by Alexander Lebedeff; additionally, there was a fire engine, and a watermill for flour production.

The steam-powered sawmill by the river, also founded by Alexander, produced pine and elm planks and aspen and lime staves, and employed seventy-two workers. Though it was only operational for just over two months a year, the workers toiled in shifts to keep the sawmill working for twenty-three hours a day. The nearest doctor lived thirty-five kilometres away; provision of a vet and medical services to the local population was one of the main tasks of the district council or *zemstvo*.

Annual production earned the business over thirty-two thousand roubles (costs totalled about twenty-two thousand), however by 1909 these figures had practically doubled.[158] The goods were transported to the Caspian Sea down the Volga, Europe's longest river, well over a thousand kilometres to a representative in Astrakhan.

In winter and summer

The family was large, and typically for the time, the young children were taken care of day to day by tutors and governesses. As well as the offspring from previous relationships, Alexander and Olga had three surviving children of their own named Alexander, Olga, and Mikhail. None of them were born in Kazan, but it was said in Lubiana that a special tree was planted for each one. A first born of this marriage, a boy whom they had named Alexander, died in infancy.[159]

THE MAYOR OF KAZAN

Over at least two winters, Olga took her young family abroad to spend the season in Pau in south-west France. Evidence of this comes from newspaper cuttings. Escaping from the Russian winter even early in this marriage was a priority for Olga, and highlighted that travelling, and particularly overwintering, for them really was a preferred way of life.

Young Alexander ('Sacha') was born in Pau in February 1880 and baptised in the Russian Church there with both his parents present.[160] His sister Olga ('Olla') was born fifteen months later in April 1881 in St Petersburg,[161] a month after the shocking assassination of Tsar Alexander II.[162] By November 1882, Madame Lebedeff and family were back in Pau, lodging at the grand Hotel Beauséjour, situated in the centre of the city near all the main sights.[163]

Fig. 47
Hotel Beauséjour, Pau

Few details of the children are known except these from various archival sources. Sacha was schooled at the elite Alexandrovsky Lyceum in St Petersburg. Olla attended secondary school and learned five languages: Russian was her mother tongue, plus French (spoken in the family), as well as English, German, and Spanish.[164] The youngest, Mikhail (or 'Micha'), born in October 1886 in the capital, was baptized in the Court Equerries' Church of the Holy Image in central St. Petersburg. His godmother was Nina Dlotovsky, his half-sister.[165]

With a family of six young children of her own, some starting secondary boarding school in St Petersburg, life continued apace, replete with uncertainty and matrimonial disappointment. Despite the painful truth about her husband's infidelity, Olga for some time contended with the social obligations as wife of the Mayor of Kazan, together with the demands of parenthood.

In the meantime, she attended regular sessions at the Society of Archaeology, History (which used the Russian acronym of O.I.A.E.) at the University of Kazan, where the meetings were open to the public.[166] Here she met a mixture of scholars of various disciplines and amateur ethnographers. In Kazan, Olga took lessons in Tatar, Persian and Arabic from the well-respected Tatar scholar called Qayyum Nasyri.

Final revelations from the earlier mentioned memoirs of Alexandra Bogdanovich draw a further picture of betrayal and unhappiness; another conversation is recounted on 5th May 1888 about this 'out of the ordinary couple'.

Here, the charming and oft times 'secretive' Madame Lebedeff has revealed that each summer, her husband's three illegitimate sons have come to stay with her. Lebedeff does not pay his wife any attention. The skeptical and unsympathetic general's wife judges that whilst Madame Lebedeff appears to be virtuous, she is 'deeply flawed'; she typically cut a theatrical pose complaining of 'an imaginary migraine'. She had, apparently, been writing weekly to a monk called Father Antony, perhaps to assuage her conflicted feelings.[167]

Then, as though plucked straight from the pages of a novel, the memoir recounts the accusation that Mr Lebedeff lived frivolously with his mistress. He was in love, according to his wife, with a 'monster'. Then, apparently, after giving birth, Madame Lebedeff received her first husband back into her bedroom.

However, as for Volodya Dlotovsky, he had been posted to the southern city of Samara in 1880 in the law courts, so visits to Kazan must have been rare or infrequent. Marital tensions boiled over, and in January 1888 Alexander resigned his post of Mayor 'for personal reasons.'[168]

Despite the initial promise of the good life with Alexander - the magnanimous wealthy bachelor - family life had afforded Olga little lasting happiness. The indignity of her husband's affairs pushed her further towards self-reliance. But it was reported that for some time she maintained submission to his wishes even when absent;[169] one might speculate that she feared him, at least the power that he could exert over her. Legally, for instance, a husband authorized and approved passports for women and children when travelling, reinforcing the sense of subordination that wives then endured.

Although the second marriage had appeared to offer an escape, this albeit unverified account in the memoirs suggests that it was a decision that she may have regretted.[170]

In memoirs belonging to an Austrian Countess von Salburg, there is confirmation Olga would openly discuss her disinterest in Alexander.[171]

For years now, Olga de Lebedeff had set her own sights on new horizons though her studies. Despite all the privileges she enjoyed, it would require much courage and determination, not to say force of character, to bring any of her aims and vision into reality. She had now begun to see her work not only as serving art and truth, but also as a means of self-realization.

Second Marriage to Alexander Lebedeff
1878-1910

Parents   *Second Marriage*   *Their Children*

Olga I Kutaissoff
1835-1900

Olga S. Barstchoff
1852-1933

Serge M Barstchoff
1826-1888

Alexander A. Lebedeff (Sacha)
1880-1937

Olga A. Lebedeff (Olla)
1881-1962

Maria Strekalova
Dates unknown

Mikhail A. Lebedeff (Micha)
1886-1946

Alexander A. Lebedeff
1843-1910

Alexander Ev. Lebedeff
1798-1878

Part II: Introducing Madame Gülnar

7 Gülnar and the Jadids

> Generosity, knowledge, and justice arise from the mind.
> The greatest of these three is knowledge – for we receive
> learning and wisdom from thence as God's revelation.
> *Qabus Nameh*[172]

Finding space in her life to dedicate herself more to her studies, Olga de Lebedeff began to focus her attention on translations and her writing. This was a solace. In liberal public opinion being a translator or a writer was an increasingly respected occupation for a noblewoman. Above all else, beyond humdrum material obligations, she craved intellectual development.

Her interest in Tatar mores was partly attributed to her maternal ancestors. Olga had recounted this to a Lebanese writer in 1907: 'she had been born to a Russian father, with a Turkish grandfather from the city of Kutais.' Kutais was in the Caucasus, and her great-great-grandfather was Count Ivan Kutaisov, the notorious favourite of Tsar Paul I. His grandson Hippolyte Kutaisov 'married a princess… from a Muslim family in the Tatar region' called Natalya Urusov.

The Urusovs had in fact been Christianised for generations, but the story of the Tatar princess several centuries earlier must have aroused curiosity in Olga. The account went on: 'And so, the subject of the biography grew up with a natural fondness for the Turks and Islam.'[173] I had surmised this from looking at the family tree, knowing that the family names of Kutaisov and Urusov could not fail to be influential.

Furthermore, in *Notes on the new Ottoman literature* in 1912, Vladimir Gordlievsky, postulates that Olga's first knowledge of the 'Kazan-Turkish' language was learned in childhood.[174] Her conversational skills in Tatar were gained through chatting with local people and thus she acquired a Tatar accent.[175] Then, having arrived in Kazan with her young family at the age of twenty-two, Olga began to study eastern cultures in a city that had a strong tradition of Oriental scholarship. It was said that her 'interest in Turkish culture went far beyond that of ordinary academics...apparently she liked to wear Turkish costumes at home and to see her children wearing fezzes.'[176] She was even seen wearing a scarlet fez en route to Constantinople, for which reason she was called an 'orientalised European' by a rather aloof fellow Russian traveller.[177] Apparently, the wearing of red fezzes was considered quite 'de rigueur' for eastern travellers in Ottoman cities;[178] they were handwoven wool, water resistant, soft and elastic and some were artistically embroidered. Women in harems might wear smaller such caps made of red velvet and also richly embroidered. Apart from the clothing, Olga liked to sing Ottoman folksongs and translated some verses into Russian. It goes without saying that she was very partial to Turkish food and drink, one of her favourites being Turkish-style coffee.

Pen name of Gülnar

Adopting an Eastern sounding pseudonym, which contained two of the same consonants as her real name, gave Olga a way of establishing an identifiable Orientalized persona for herself. The name 'Olga' has no equivalent in Tatar or Turkish, but with the modern Cyrillic Tatar spellings of Gülnâr and Olga there is a certain similarity in 'ТӨЛНАР' and 'ОЛЬГА', a rhyming quality.[179] Additionally, given that Arabic is written from right to left and without vowels, this name might approximate her own quite well; it was a reverse play on the letters G and L in her own actual name, in keeping with her sense of herself as a translator, or hiding her identity. Others did this, notably Pushkin signed an early poem with letters minus the vowels in reverse: N.K Sh.P.[180]

Gülnâr' is a Tatar girl's name, [181] or more commonly 'Gülnara,' whilst similar Tatar names are Gülbahar and Gülnisa; the first part of the name 'Gül' means Rose in Turkish and 'nar' is pomegranate. Thus, the translation of Gülnâr is 'pomegranate flower.'

Apart from the similarity of the sound to her Russian name, Gülnar was a good choice for symbolic reasons. It showed respect for Tatar, Ottoman and Islamic culture. As a bright floral reference, it related to the cultural appreciation and motif of blooms in Ottoman society. Since ancient times, the flower and fruit of a pomegranate with its many grains represented fertility in Anatolia and the mother goddess. Pomegranates were depicted in golden threaded embroidery (for which Tatar women were famous), in Turkish handwoven rugs, and from Central Asia to China the fruit was painted on pottery or carved on wooden furniture. It had an additional figurative meaning in Arabic: beautiful. In parts of the Middle East, it carried the association of peace.

With or without her surname, the pen name is found in various renditions: 'Madame Gülnar' in French, 'Gospozha Gülnar' in Russian or 'Gülnar Khanum' and 'Gülnâr Hanım' in Tatar/ Turkish.

Olga signed all her letters to Turkish correspondents and some Orientalist colleagues in this way. It was also attributed to some of her published works, especially some early ones for the Turkish readership.[182] This is of interest, because as she herself noted: it was not yet permitted for Muslim women to write their works in their own name: *il n'était pas encore permis aux dames musulmanes de signer leurs ouvrages de leurs noms.*[183] Though many European women at the time also used pen names or *nom de plumes,* hers was not a gender ambiguous pen name or male alias however like George Sand or George Eliot; by using a Tatar or Ottoman sounding pseudonym, she must have also considered that writing from a woman's perspective was in itself an important statement.

For her as a woman writer, the pen name preserved anonymity and created a means of relating to Eastern culture. A romantic reinvention of her identity, it might even have afforded her a certain mystique, almost a disguise. Even more, without appearing to be a Russian outsider to Arabic and Ottoman culture, she was able to emphasise her ancestral link as an authentic way to appear less alien.

The first example we have of her using this name is in a brief note written in January 1887. The script is Turkic-Arabic script addressed to 'My dear Efendi Professor Gottwald' [she called the German professor Efendi, a sign of respect]. She wishes him a Happy New Year and for many more in the future. She signed her name *Gülnâr Lebedef*.[184]

Fig. 48
The signature of Gülnâr Lebedef [185]

Professor Gottwald

Professor Joseph Gottwald (1813-1897) was well known in Kazan as an orientalist. He had a wide circle of acquaintances amongst Tatar scholars and educationalists through whom he extended his contacts both in Central Asia and in other Eastern regions. One can deduce that he was a mentor figure to Olga and took an interest in her studies, not least because he and Gülnar shared the same teacher of Tatar.

Gottwald had taught Persian and Arabic at Kazan University from 1849-1855 until just after the department was moved to St Petersburg and he was a member of the Academy of Sciences. Head librarian in charge of ancient precious manuscripts and divers bibliographical riches, he oversaw the university's remarkable printing press, which possessed a rich collection of types from Arabic and Tatar to Mongol and Tibetan. He additionally acted as censor for twenty-seven years (till 1884). He himself owned an ample collection of rare books and manuscripts totalling in the region of two thousand five hundred (which has survived to this day).[186]

Besides this, Gottwald was the representative from Kazan University at four different International Congress of Orientalists over twelve years (1876-1889); he and his daughter would be travelling companions to Olga after her first congress at Stockholm in 1889.

Madame Gülnar's early 'sharqi' folk songs

Gottwald kept two Ottoman poems which Olga had written out in Arabic script and translated into Russian, signed as *Gülnâr Lebedef*. They were found at Kazan Federal University, Rare Books and Manuscript Department, in Professor Gottwald's archive from the 1880s.

The poetry used is a type of popular verse called '*sharqi*', which means 'song' in Turkish. The first poem is an anonymous folk song set to music by Latif-Aga (1815-1885) and is an early example of her writing in Arabic script.[187]

Copies of the English translations follow below.

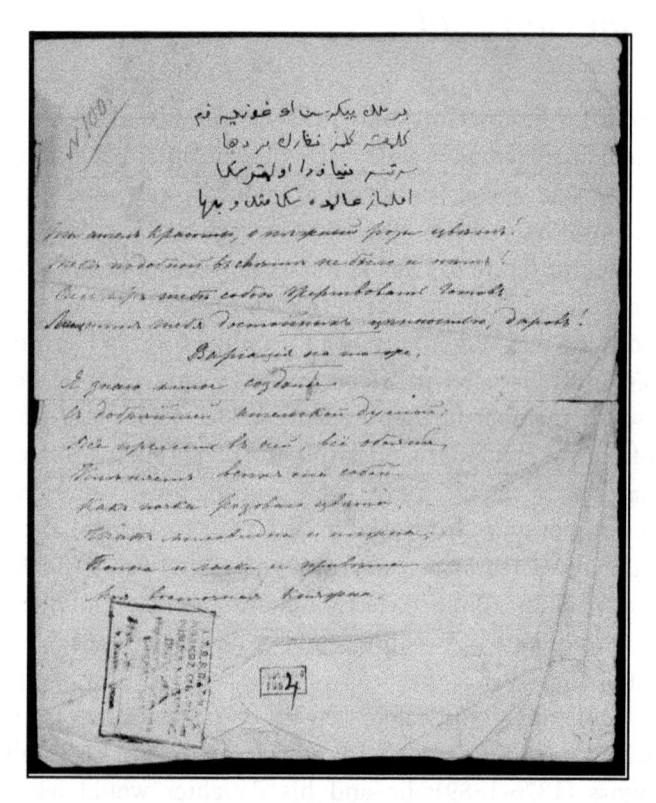

Fig. 49
Ottoman song (1) translated into Russian in Olga's handwriting.

GÜLNAR AND THE JADIDS

> You are an angel of loveliness, oh sweet rose bloom!
> Your likeness on earth has never been!
> For you we are all ready to surrender,
> But barely any gift would worthy render!

According to the account written by the prominent Ottoman journalist and fiction writer Ahmed Midhat whom Olga would come to know very well, Madame Gülnar learned and sang Ottoman songs, possibly these very ones; it was something which impressed him immensely.[188] As anyone who sings knows, singing in foreign languages reinforces language skills including fine tuning pronunciation. A joyful pastime, it also demonstrated Madame Gülnar's confidence as a singer to attempt them. Ahmed Midhat noted that Olga also sang in French, German, English, Greek and Russian.[189]

The second Ottoman poem, also anonymous, is thought by Russian scholar I. Zaytsev to be an Ashik (or Ashiq) of the kind sung and accompanied by a lute on the theme of worldly love.[190]

> Her face is as clear as moonlight.
> Her movements flowing and full of grace.
> As a cloud hides the bright morning star,
> So long eyelashes fall over her eyes,
> Curls are black as a crow's wing,
> Crowning proudly a snow-white brow.
> I never saw such beauty in all my life!
> Seeing her, I've lost my heart.
> I await your love, amazing vision,
> I'll wait for your love, helplessly and impatiently.

Through Olga's lessons in Eastern languages, she studied the cultures of Muslim-majority societies, including the Quran and Sharia Law [Muslim religious law] in written and spoken form in Arabic script. Her teacher in Kazan was Qayyum Nasyri, renowned for his beautiful calligraphy.

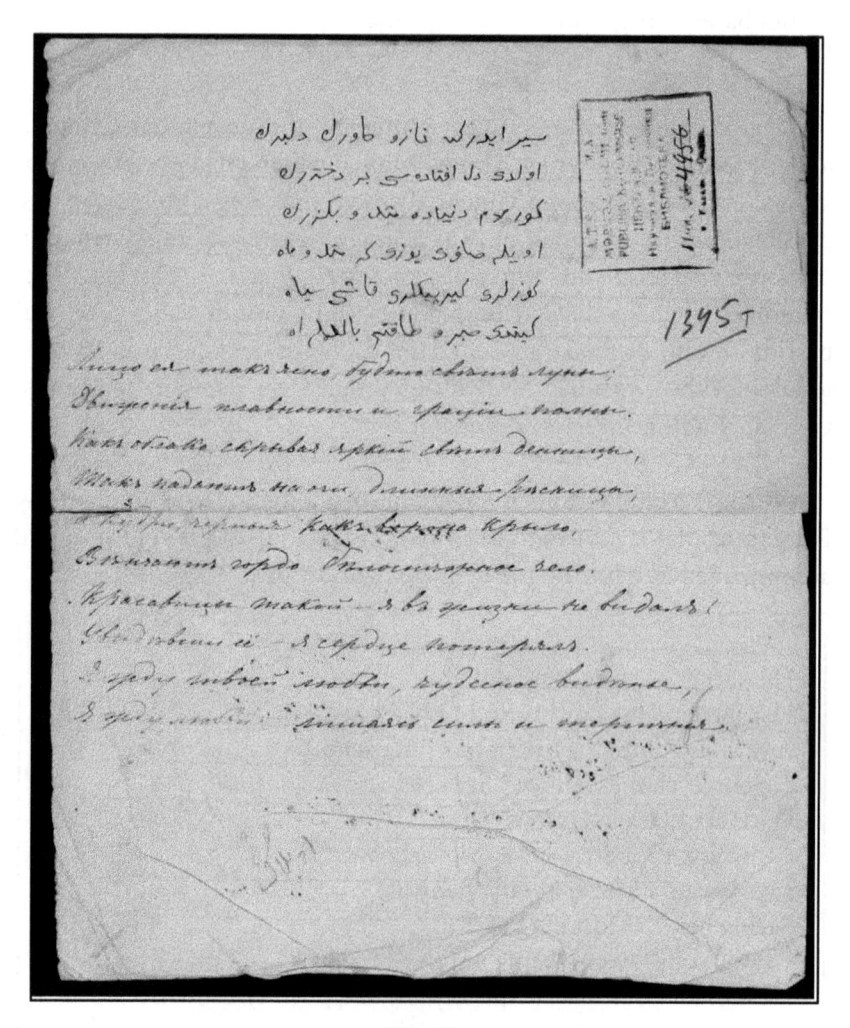

Fig. 50
Ottoman song (2) translated into Russian in Olga's handwriting.

GÜLNAR AND THE JADIDS

The Society of Archaeology, History and Ethnography (O.A.I.E.)

In Olga's day, Kazan was a gateway for 'Russia's Orient' not only as it was the most important commercial and cultural city of the Volga Tatars. It had been one of the earliest centres for Oriental Studies in Russia - since Tsar Alexander I had established the first professorship there in 1807, which created Kazan's first cohort of university-educated specialists. Leo Tolstoy took Turkish studies here in 1844 stimulating a life-long interest in Turkey.

According to Danielle Ross in her book *Tatar Empire*, the city had become the 'intellectual centre of Russia's colonial project'.[191] The university attracted orientalists of various specialisms and nationalities amongst whom were mostly Russians and Germans (the latter taught in Latin and German) but also a few Persians, Afghans, and Turks. Orientalist imperial concerns were focused on 'knowing, mapping, and ruling the diverse population of the empire's southern and eastern frontiers'.[192] Once trained, Kazan's orientalists were posted elsewhere in the empire to administer local provinces.[193]

The Oriental language department, the envy of Europe, was transferred to St Petersburg on 22 October 1854 and nineteen professors relocated there. Despite this, the Imperial University of Kazan continued to exert a significant influence on the town; however, due to the lack of a faculty for the study of non-Russians, research and pedagogy in regional Orientalist expertise was interrupted for many years, and a systematic study of related history and philology ceased.[194]

Following the Fourth Archaeological Congress in 1877 in Kazan, the Society of Archaeology, History and Ethnography was founded (it's Russian acronym was O.A.I.E.). This society became active in compiling information according to the subjects of its title, but predominantly in ethnography. In addition, the study and repairs to the relics of ancient Bulgar monuments to the south of Kazan were a priority. In Olga's own writing, she described how 'they are without doubt the most interesting monuments of Russian antiquity.' The buildings included two houses and a minaret. She explained how in 1881 Alexander II ordered the restauration of the ruins, including one named the Black Chamber, another which had the shape of a quadrangle believed to be a palace, and the White Chamber, which was almost certainly a bath or 'hammam'.[195]

Members of the new society were diverse. They comprised intellectuals including teachers and journalists, liberal social activists, and amateur ethnographers who mingled with university professors in the society as well as interested parties from the Kazan Theological Academy. Attendance was open to the public and the press.

Though Tatars totalled one third of the population, little of their culture was studied or spoken about until the late 1890s; it was perceived by Russians that being Muslim, Tatars lacked ethnic or national peculiarities. The study of Muslims was usually left to academic 'armchair' Orientalists, whose interests were usually confined to old Islamic literary texts, but who rarely ventured out to study relevant places and peoples. Another interested group were Orthodox missionaries whose work in the Kazan Governorate broadly set out to prove the superiority of Christianity over Islam.[196]

The Jadids

By the early to mid 1880s, the new society attracted several forward-thinking Tatars. Many played a significant role in compiling Orientalist knowledge.[197] They also studied the Russian language, unlike more conservative Tatars who did not in case it compromised their religion. When the authorities brought in reforms to institute Russian language training in non-Russian schools, rumours of enforced conversion to Christianity were spread. Many Muslims feared that learning Russian would make them apostates, [198] thus it was a contentious issue.

The progressives could see advantages in the advances in science, technology, and culture that they observed in Russian society and which they read about in periodicals from other areas of the empire. In particular, the Crimean Tatar language newspaper *Terjuman* (or *Tercüman*) meaning 'Interpreter' or 'Translator' founded by Ismail Gaspirali (1851-1914), debated these issues.

GÜLNAR AND THE JADIDS

In 1886, Gaspirali expressed his hope for the formation of an 'intelligentsia' among Russia's Muslims and introduced this as a new concept to his Muslim audience. A few years later he suggested that such an intelligentsia could take care of 'worldly matters', as religious affairs were already taken care of by Islamic scholars.[199]

Gaspirali himself highlighted the need for educational reform in a literary journey called *French Letters* serialised in *Terjuman* between 1887 and 1889.[200] Although the letters were fictional, they were inspired by Gaspirali's many travels across Europe from 1871. Through the fictional alter ego of Mollah Abbas, Gaspirali exposes weaknesses in the teaching in the madrasas of Bukhara in Turkestan. The imam that Abbas converses with lives in the utopian 'Abode of Felicity' in Andalusia and their conversation went as follows:

> We have heard that Bukharans are famous for their sciences and learning," noted the *imam*. "How are their *madreses* organised and what do they teach there?
>
> I recounted what they teach in the *medreses* of the Muslims. The old man shook his head and said:
>
> Perhaps, your countries and their people have no need for medical doctors, chemists, constructors, land surveyors; perhaps your rulers and Khans have no need for learned servitors, economists and the like, since from your story, I could see that apart from scholars of theology, you have no scholars in any other sphere of life…Does this mean that medical science, chemistry, geometry, the science of industry and wealth are not taught at all…It pains me to hear about the sorry state of your country and about its ignorance," noted the *imam* in a friendly voice, "and this is why I hope you will not be offended if my words will be hard on you.[201]

The progressives saw advantages in understanding political issues about which they read in Russian journals and newspapers. Moreover, these Muslim educationalists were coming to terms with the fact that if they did not reform education from within their own system, the Russian Empire would take over.

These reformists were called the 'Jadids' from *usul-e jadid* meaning 'new method'. The founder of this modernity movement was Gaspirali himself, who had instigated the teaching the Arabic alphabet in the phonetic method. But cultural reform had already been on the radar of Marjani and his former student Faydkhanov for some years and amongst the Volga-Ural ulama whose students began to travel widely, and who witnessed the colonization of Muslim lands by colonial powers. Marjani argued:

> It is necessary to learn Russian. It is obligatory and necessary that the people of [one nation] know the language of the press and the language in which the laws and regulations of the state are written. It is also necessary to preserve your own language. [202]

The group of intellectuals that met with Olga de Lebedeff in Kazan increasingly saw themselves as 'Russian Muslims', and not just as a separate people in their own independent society. But they also believed that it was vital to preserve their language and culture.

Historian Abrar Karimullin wrote two articles about the activities of Olga de Lebedeff in the Soviet era. In his article entitled *Gülnâr Hanum*, he mentions several Tatar scholars at the Society of Archaeology, History and Ethnography with whom she has connections. He singles out the eminent historian and akhund[b] Shihabetdin Marjani; the linguist and encyclopaedist Qayyum Nasyri; the pioneer playwright and ethnographer Gabdrajaman Ilyasi; and the teacher of Oriental languages at the university, academic Muhammedgali Makhmudov.[203] They were leading Tatar scholars of their time. Their reformist views were to have a profound effect on Madame (or, in Russian: *Gospozha*) Gülnar. Introductions to the first three of these exceptional scholars and intellectuals provide us with useful background information about how Olga's interest in local Tatar matters was influenced.

---

[b] Akhund: An Islamic cleric and theologian, a spiritual leader

Three Tatar Educationalists

Shigabutdin Marjani (1818-1889) [Shigabuddin bin Bagautdin al-Kazani al-Marjani] from the Machkara madrasa network was a Tatar theologian, an imam and historian. At the age of twenty-one, he had gone to study for ten years in the madrasas of Bukhara and Samarkand.[204] Due to his two-volume history of Kazan, he is considered the father of Tatar national identity. From 1876-1884 he taught at the Tatar Teachers School and was the first of just a few Muslim members of the university's Society of Archaeology, History and Ethnology. Here he lectured on ancient Muslim manuscripts.

Fig. 51
Depiction of Sh. Marjani as a young man

Marjani knew all the Orientalist scholars who had not moved to St Petersburg, such as Professor Gottwald, Vasily Radlov, Nikolai Katanov, a future president of the O.A.I.E. who would bring Tatar points of view to public attention, as well as Professor Kazem-bek and Husayn Faydkhanov, and many others. Marjani was fascinated by the objective scientific approaches to restructuring the past brought by archaeology, philology, and palaeography.

Qayyum Nasyri (1825-1902) still holds a special place in the affections of Kazan Tatars and is thought of as one of the most important representatives of Jadidism. He was a pioneer of education reform, writing many educational textbooks in Tatar; his pedagogical views were influenced by the forward thinking Konstantin Ushinsky and Lev Tolstoy. His house (on the same street as Marjani's) has been preserved as a museum, and there his calligraphies and manuscript collections are exhibited amongst other artefacts.

He is considered the father of the Tatar written language in the Arabic script and had wide knowledge of literature, folklore, and archaeology; his articles were even published in the Russian Geographical Society. One orientalist called V.V. Grigor'ev hailed him as 'the first Tatar in Russia who could view Islam with an objective eye'.[205]

Fig. 52
Qayyum Nasyri

Nasyri taught Olga de Lebedeff to read and write Tatar and gave her lessons in Persian and Arabic. Under his tutelage she translated into Russian *Qabus Nameh*, which he himself had translated in 1881 from Ottoman Turkish into Tatar. In addition, Nasyri was teacher to Josef Gottwald and another Orientalist called Maslovsky.[206] Nasyri was Olga's chief mentor in matters Oriental in her formative studies.[207]

Gabdrajaman Ilyasi was the same generation as Olga, born in 1856. He studied Tatar manuscripts and was one of the first Kazan Tatars to raise the question of creating a Volga Tatar periodical (inspired also by Gaspirali's Crimean Tatar periodical in 1883). Ilyasi is also referred to as an 'archeographer' which means a scholar of ancient writings, one who studies society, buildings, the natural world, and ethnography. In 1885 he joined the Society of Archaeology, History and Ethnography. It is notable that Ilyasi opposed the patriarchal way of family life and defended the rights and freedom of women.

In October 1887 the University of Kazan published his play, the first drama in the Tatar language: a twenty-minute tragedy called *Poor Girl [Bichara Kuz]* in two acts. The protagonist was a young girl called Magitab who refused her arranged marriage in favour of marrying a poor but well-educated young man.

The themes he presented were new in Kazan as he championed social equality, knowledge and morality over wealth and social status; amongst conservatives therefore the reaction to the play was mixed.[208] In the same year, he published in Kazan a book called *A Gift for Girls and Women*, a manual for raising children in the family.[209]

The acquaintance with Ilyasi is doubtless significant, given Olga's future campaigning for the emancipation of Muslim women in Russia and abroad.

***

As already noted, although other accounts mention that Olga de Lebedeff attended the Imperial University of Kazan and graduated in Turkish Philology,[210] actual confirmation of this from the university was not forthcoming. Correspondence from the University of Kazan Rare Books Department advised me that excepting the study of midwifery, women were not admitted to study at university until 1 August 1907.[211] In Russia as a whole, women were excluded from university between 1863 and 1897. As no archival record exists of Olga having attended or graduated from Kazan University, it may have been that due to those restrictions Olga audited courses as a private, non-matriculated student - languages could still be taken there for those with an interest. This is how despite the inconvenient official limitation and due to her influence and mayoral contacts, she nonetheless may have attended university lectures.

Following her first publication in 1886 and an attempt at publishing works in Turkey in 1888, she turned her sights on attending the International Congress of Orientalists. In the good company of the seventy-six-year-old Professor Joseph Gottwald, the delegate from Kazan university, Olga attended the 1889 congress in Stockholm.

This event was to open a new opportunity for her: just days after the congress she received a pressing invitation to visit Constantinople from a high up Ottoman publisher, the representative of the Sublime Porte, Ahmed Midhat Efendi.

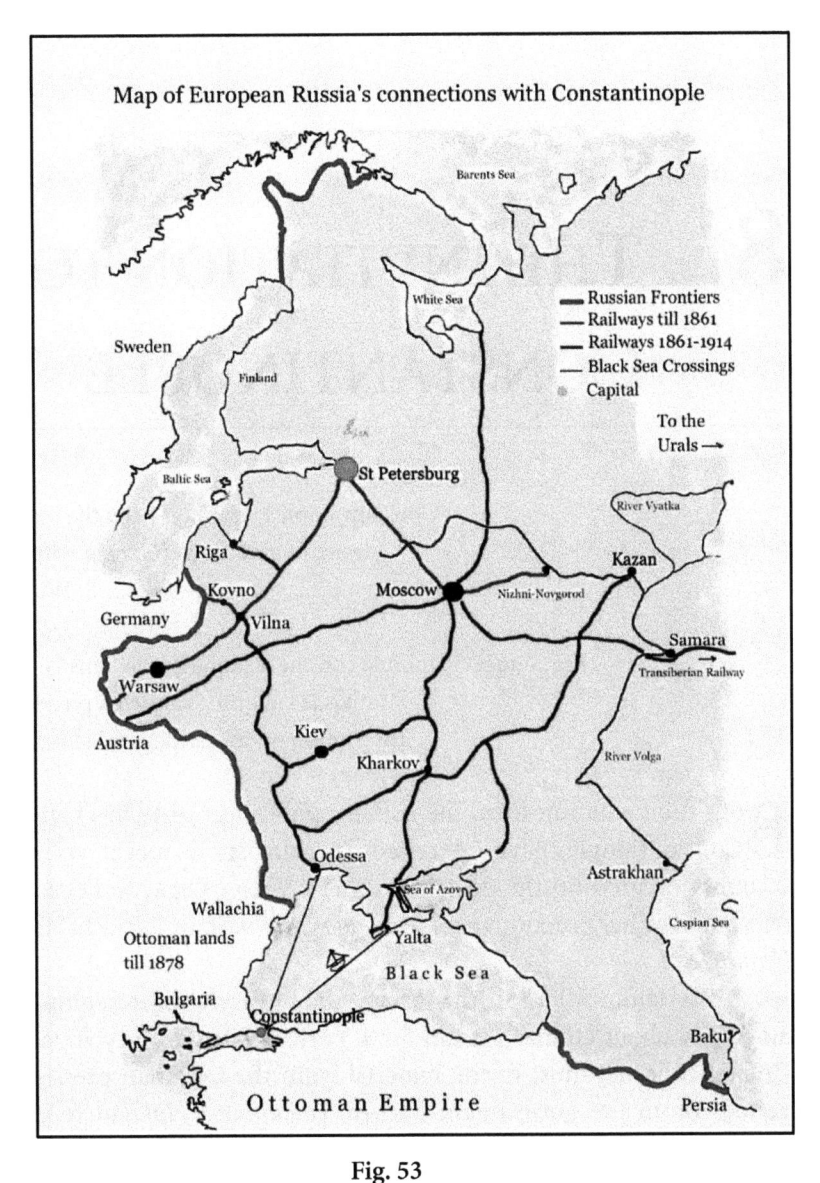

Fig. 53
Rail routes between Kazan, St Petersburg and Constantinople, and Black Sea crossings as taken by Olga de Lébédeff in October 1891 from Yalta and March 1894 to Odessa (quoted by B. Dukhovsky and J. Barber). Map by the author.

8 The Invitation to Constantinople

> Constantinople has always been the object of
> desire of ambitious rulers of nations.[212]
> S. Whitman

> J'ai conquis le monde comme le globe que je tiens en main,
> mais je l'ai quitté sans rien posséder.[213]
> Inscription on the Sultan's talisman globe

Both the invitation from the sultan's publisher, and Olga's visits to Constantinople, have interested Turcologists in recent years. Yet accounts of this mostly exist in Turkish, where Olga de Lebedeff is referred to by her pseudonym of *Madame Gülnar* or, in Turkish, "*Gülnâr Hanım*".[214]

The famous Turkish historian, Ömer Faruk Akün, compiled a biography about Gülnar Hanım for a Turkish Islamic Encyclopedia.[215] He had collected most of the material from the Ottoman press of the period. From the government backed *Tercüman-ı Hakikat* to avant-garde journals like *Servet-i Fünûn* and one of the best-selling newspapers *Ikdam*, articles were penned by the likes of Ahmed Midhat, Ahmed Cevdet Oran, and Mustafa Reshid.[216] Akün concluded that in both Turkish and a few Russian accounts of Madame Gülnar, information was often repetitive, inadequate, erroneous or contradictory and that no comprehensive research had ever been carried out.

Madame Gülnâr has also since intrigued scholars of literature, translation studies and women writers in Ottoman society. Ismail Karaca of Istanbul University expressed a widely held sentiment when he wrote:

> Madam Gülnâr won recognition because of her friendship to Turks, respect for Islam, knowledge and culture; also, her effect on Turkish readers and intellectuals continued for many years. [217]

The Russian sources describe Olga de Lebedeff's very first visit to Constantinople as taking place in either 1881 or 1888, but the latter date is the more likely. [218] Her fifth surviving child was born in St Petersburg in April 1881, so travel would have been impractical. Yet after April 1888, perhaps she had additional finance to enable such a trip to the Ottoman Empire, following her father's death?

To all intents and purposes, Olga had travelled with the hope of obtaining permission from the Turkish authorities to have her translations published. The translations were of works by Pushkin coinciding with the fiftieth anniversary of the poet's death. But to her great disappointment, the Turkish government suspected that she was a secret Russian agent and forbade their publication. A suspicion underlay the severe censorship in the Ottoman state hierarchy, that Russians and westerners alike would intrude into and subvert their affairs. So, despite tireless efforts on her part, she left Constantinople with a heavy heart.

Confirmation of that first date of Olga's first journey to Turkey as 1888 is to be found in an edition of the newspaper *Novoe Vremya [New Time]* dated 1893. [219] It is also hard to see that Madame Gülnar's translations into Ottoman Turkish would have been completed by 1881, before even the publication of her award-winning translation of *Qabus Nameh* in 1886.

Introducing the publisher Ahmed Midhat Efendi

The earliest Turkish account of Madame Gülnar was published in 1889 in the travel writing of Ahmed Midhat (1844-1912). [220] Ahmed Midhat Efendi was a journalist and prolific author whose novels and short stories would number about one hundred and fifty. His popularity in Turkey was comparable to that of Mark Twain or Charles Dickens.[221] He is now regarded as a leading and pioneer novelist of the late nineteenth century. Even his account of his meeting with Olga de Lebedeff, Turcologists say, reads like a novel.

After this in July 1891, a biography was published in *Servet-ı Fünûn* (transl. Wealth of Knowledge).[222] This periodical kept its readers informed about European and Ottoman literary and cultural movements as well as articles on contemporary writers. Without these early published accounts, the captivating story of Olga de Lebedeff and her meeting with Ahmed Midhat might never have been known in Turkey.

At the time they first met in 1889, Ahmed Midhat was the Ottoman delegate of the Sublime Porte at the International Congress of Orientalists in Stockholm and Christiania - the envoy of the Sultan. As an already experienced publisher, he had founded the daily newspaper *Tercüman-ı Hakikat* ('The Interpreter of Truth') with the support of the Ottoman palace in 1878, and he was now its editor. With this position he was a publicist for the Sultan, spreading propaganda and controlling his image. The subsidy for this newspaper came from the sultan's privy purse, which provided financial support and protection against mass competition.[223] Ahmed Midhat managed the Imperial Printing Office and had the know-how for getting around the censors, not least as he was the newspaper's part proprietor which gave him a certain independence.

Olga de Lebedeff must have known of Ahmed Midhat's influence with the Ottoman authorities: not only through her social contacts and Professor Gottwald, but also through her friendly contacts at the Ottoman Embassy. It is quite conceivable that she attended the congress knowing that Ahmed Midhat would be there, hoping to show him her translations. She arranged for an introduction through the Russian consul, the Arabist and Secretary General of the Congress, Carlo von Landberg. Olga Sergeevna herself was not listed as an official delegate or participant at the congress.

It was Ahmed Midhat's first visit to Europe. He had taught himself French and was well read in French literature; he could understand it better than he wrote it. He claimed that he had spent fifteen years researching Europe before travelling there.[224] Ahmed Midhat had even translated novels from French into Ottoman and had adapted versions of stories of European origin to suit the tastes of his Ottoman audience for their 'shared Ottoman morals'.[225] As he was concerned with protecting the moral values of the Ottomans, he is sometimes referred to as a 'moralist':

> For well I have learned that of the things that come from Europe, the rotten ones are far more numerous than the sound, and the bad number many more than the good.[226]

Ahmed Midhat was, however, simultaneously fascinated by the progress of Europeans in science, technology, and philosophy, but he did not approve of Ottomans who he thought were 'over-Westernised.'

Although by Olga's own account she sometimes wore Eastern style clothing at home, she knew how to impress in the latest of Parisian or London haute couture styles, such as from the fashion house of Charles Worth.[227] In the next photo, taken in Naples a few months before her first meeting with Ahmed Midhat, she is standing in profile with lorgnette in hand. Her tailored textured day dress comprised a high collared tightfitting bodice decorated with contrasting strings of pearls, a bustle, full skirt, and high sleeves with vertical puff at the shoulder. The short fringe was slightly frizzed, and a high chignon at the back showed off her dazzling diamond earrings.

At the Stockholm Congress in 1889

Despite this stylish portrait, her interest in fashion was reported to fall into second place to her intellectual pursuits. Ahmed Midhat recorded in his memoirs that all finery and diamonds at the reception where they met, she had not cared about such things or about how the other women were turned out; she had talked to him about intellectual matters.[228]

Having been introduced on Tuesday 3rd September 1889 on the second working day of the Congress, Olga de Lebedeff is reported to have astonished Midhat by introducing herself in fluent Turkish; "The name you should know me by is Gülnar." According to his later account of the meeting, he could not believe his ears.[229] She handed him her visiting card with the Arabic/Turkish name Gülnâr printed in gilt *ta'liq*-style script (Islamic calligraphy).[230] He was delighted to learn her name and replied: "Gülnar vakıa pek güzel bir isimdir", meaning 'Gülnar is indeed a beautiful name.' He spotted her real name preceded by 'Excellency' on an envelope, so she then divulged her identity as Countess Olga Sergeevna Lebedeva.[231]

Fig. 54
Olga de Lebedeff in Naples, March 1889 aged thirty-seven years old [232]

THE INVITATION TO CONSTANTINOPLE

He later wrote:

Her Ottoman was nearly correct. But she was speaking with an indeterminate foreign and charming accent such as that of the people of Daghistan or Bukhara.

Fig. 55
Embossed Header in gilt Arabic script: Gülnar [233]

When he asked how she had come to learn Ottoman Turkish, she replied that they lived in a large mansion in Kazan and had contacts with the large number of Tatars working on their land. She was helped by employees at the Ottoman Embassy in St Petersburg.[234] She showed him work that she had translated into Turkish, *Ilyas* which was a story by Leo Tolstoy about a Bashkir from Ufa.[235] This tale had previously been shown to an official at the Ottoman Embassy in St Petersburg,[236] very likely my ancestor Nasri Bey, and Olga had asked him to revise it prior to her attending the congress. Although she is said to have disliked some of the revisions, she had adopted others.

At the congress, she spoke to Midhat Efendi of her ambition to publish Russian classics in Istanbul and Ottoman literary works into Russian.[237] She already had thought of a plan and had prepared translations of other short stories into Ottoman. Ahmed Midhat too had some interest in publishing works for a European audience, which he said she had offered to facilitate.[238] He, for his part, was interested in learning more about Russian Tatars.

Johann Strauss explains the issues that Olga had with writing Ottoman: 'Thanks to her solid Orientalist training, she did not make mistakes in the spelling of Arabic or Persian words. But as far as words of Turkish origin were concerned, there were difficulties:

I do make mistakes in the spelling of Ottoman words since I pronounce them mostly in the Tatar way. In fact, the Tatars are not consistent in terms of spelling, everybody writes as he thinks best.'

Ottoman Turkish was utterly different from European languages, not only in its grammatical and morphological structures but also in terms of accepted literary style. If 'she lacked practice', any 'shortcomings in terms of spelling and expression, were of such a nature that even 'Ottoman males are not free of them.'[239]

Midhat Efendi was charmed and impressed by Madame Gülnar; he supported the idea that her work in Ottoman Turkish could be circulated amongst the reading population. It presented a unique opportunity: a literary partnership with this highly cultured Russian aristocratic woman who had lots of ideas of her own would be very interesting. Her identity was to be veiled under her pseudonym of Gülnar Hanım. As chief of the imperial printing works, Ahmed Midhat was in a perfect position to help Olga to achieve her goals.

During the congress, Midhat Bey had given a speech during the official opening, and chaired the Islamist section. Here, on the request of the Egyptian delegates, he translated from French to Arabic. Midhat had made a short, impassioned speech in French on women's rights in Islam for the benefit of the Europeans.[240] He was introducing a new book on this topic written for the congress by Egyptian delegate Hamza Fathallah (1849-1918).[241] It was published by order of the Prime Minister, showing the importance of the subject of Islam and femininity for local and imperial audiences.[242] Ahmed Midhat cut a striking figure with his flowing beard and red narrow fez: 'a giant ...with the width of two.' His spectacles gave his face a good-humoured expression.[243]

The journey across Europe to Paris

After the phase of the congress ended at Christiana (Oslo), Ahmed Midhat proposed forming a travelling party to accompany him on his way, or for part of his way, to Paris.[244]

So, on 12th September, he set off for Gothenburg on the evening train with Professor Gottwald and his daughter Nina Krelemberg, Doctor Boris Yanpolsky, a prominent St Petersburg physician, and Olga de Lebedeff. Most of the other congress delegates were also on board. Midhat's party travelled in the same train compartment. That night the

THE INVITATION TO CONSTANTINOPLE

travellers took turns telling stories until they fell asleep.[245] Madame Krelemberg was first, then Gülnar gave a summary of a short Russian novel and then another of a Russian opera. Ahmed Midhat told the story of Ali Pasha.

Fig. 56
Ahmed Midhat Efendi wearing gold embroidered dress uniform for state occasions: Salt Research, City, Society and Economy Archive [246]

The next morning, they visited the impressive waterfalls and factories at Trollhattan, and here Madame Gülnar agreed to play the restaurant piano for her fellow travellers.[247]

In his book *Tour of Europe*, Ahmed Midhat wrote of all his encounters at the congress and during his subsequent travels.[248] At least a fifth of this comprehensive travelogue is devoted to the time spent with Olga, as well as highlighting his many impressions of European customs.[249] After visiting Gothenburg on 13th September, the party set off for Helsingborg and the Oresund strait, visiting museums, castles, and ports en route. There then followed three nights in Copenhagen, where they went to the theatre to see Bizet's opera *Carmen*.[250]

The next stop was Berlin and without prior booking they all found suitable rooms for three days at the Hotel Friedrich. Ahmed Midhat consulted books on the history and geography of the German capital and took long walks alone in the early morning to familiarise himself with the city's sights, including art galleries, museums, churches, and libraries. He noted down each street name, every square and each sight he came across.[251] He and Madame Gülnar visited the Berlin Museum of Art together. Here, whilst Midhat appreciated the golden picture frames and the fine building, Madame Gülnar explained to him the paintings themselves and introduced him to the Dutch masters (Vermeer and Rembrandt for instance) and explained how the name Dutch School of Art came to be invented after the death of the painters involved.[252]

Ahmed Midhat seemed fascinated by the extraordinary difficulty of obtaining a theatre ticket in Berlin; one needed to pre-book at one of the twenty or so theatres. The travellers just managed to obtain tickets to the Opera House to see Verdi's *Rigoletto* thanks to the efforts of the hotel manager. Ahmed Midhat himself was not able to enjoy the performance, however, as he was quite exhausted and lost himself again in contemplation of the elaborate gilt ornamentation that surrounded him.[253] Afterwards they spoke of the ethics of the play. Another evening, they saw Wagner's *The Flying Dutchman*. Midhat wrote no less than one hundred pages on his three-day stay in Berlin alone. After this, whilst the professor and his daughter stayed behind in Berlin, Ahmed Midhat and Olga Sergeevna proceeded by train to Cologne for one night, before reaching their destination in Paris.[254]

THE INVITATION TO CONSTANTINOPLE

Throughout the course of the journey, the travellers exchanged views in French or Ottoman on culture, technology, science, fine art, and religion. Olga de Lebedeff and Midhat Efendi seemed to have been amazed at how their outlooks on life were strangely compatible. They talked much about the differences between the civilizations of East and West, commenting on how Westerners equate Christianity with civilization.[255] They covered such topics as women and family life, religion, morality, and literature. They did not agree on every subject however, particularly not on the issue of veiling, for Gülnar had objections to the hijab. Such discrepancies were dealt with diplomatically, however, and were not dwelt upon by either party.[256]

Their arrival in Paris coincided with that of fellow traveller Dr Yanpolsky. The extraordinary 'Exposition Universelle' or Great Exhibition was in full swing. Since the exhibition was to mark the centenary of the French revolution – Britain, Russia and Italy had only unofficial exhibitors. It was an occasion for France to mark progress in industry, the arts, and social ideas – and provided additional material for our travellers' discussion of the meaning of 'progress'. What fascinated Midhat most were the machines to be seen at the exhibition. He disliked what he perceived as moral corruption that came with material progress and especially the music halls of 'dissolute entertainment'. They visited the shops, from morning till night on one occasion, as well as parks, churches, schools, hospitals, museums, and palaces.[257] Her stamina for such outings was less than his and she often felt ill or needed more sleep and spent some days without leaving the hotel.[258] All this Ahmed Midhat records in his travelogue, where Gülnar Hanım features in the position of teacher.[259]

Ahmed Midhat had for many years been interested in foreign culture; in 1871 he had even published a compilation on Russian history. One of his goals was to make Europe better known to the Ottomans.[260] His conversations with Olga, however, were a revelation to him.

> I derived so much benefit hearing her explain to me the phases of progress traversed by Russian language and literature from the oldest times until today, that I turned into a person who had recognised and learnt the Russian nation anew.

During their long conversations, both realised that the problems faced by Russian and Ottoman society were very similar.[261]

He also asked Madame Gülnar about the situation of the Russians vis-à-vis the Turkic and Islamic peoples in Russia and about the latest developments in their civilization. He saw the backward state of the Tatars as being the fault of the Russian government and explained the need 'to warn and guide prominent Tatars.'[262]

Olga's account of the Tatars seems to tally with that of the elderly Gottwald: he painted 'a sad picture of intellectual stagnation' and believed that Europe had progressed 'in industry and science but not in wisdom'. Thus, Ahmed Midhat had a view of the old professor as 'a paragon of learned impartiality.'[263] This was the kind of frank exchange being made in their first days of travelling together. Comparisons were not only between the civilizations of East and West, and Christianity and Islam, but regarding matters concerning their own countries.

After seven days in Paris, some members of Olga's family arrived: her mother Prascovia Hippolitovna Barschoff-Kutaissov and her nine-year-old son, Sacha Lebedeff, who had a chest ailment. Following five more days or so of outings, this interesting interlude ended as the family received a letter of approval from Alexander Lebedeff that they should travel to Nice.[264]

This period coincided with the 'Russian influenza' epidemic that was sweeping across Europe; the sea air would do them all good. Judging by the list of foreigners in a local paper, *La Vie Mondaine a Nice,* they decided to stay in Nice for the winter: the newspaper entry on 19 December details that Olga Lebedeff and family were staying at 20 Rue de France, otherwise known as the Palais Marie-Christine, a short walk from the beach and the Promenade des Anglais.[265] Many of the Germans, Italians, Spanish and English listed in the town brought their families too, though the Lebedeffs were the only Russian family of the four other compatriots listed, who included the Princess Kourakine and Prince Paul Troubetskoy. Before they parted ways, Midhat Efendi extended a warm invitation to Olga to visit Constantinople, where they might continue to explore the themes that they had discussed on their trip and so she could perfect her Turkish. When they had dinner for the last time together, reminiscing about what they had experienced since the day they had met, they shed "a few very naïve and touching tears". Amongst things that they remembered and laughed about was the risk to which Madame Gülnar exposed her jewelry, which she preferred to leave in a box in the freight wagon...[266]

Fig. 57
Sacha: the marine theme of the masthead and ropes was a popular device at seaside photo studios in the 1880s (Family Collection).

In addition, Gülnar put forward a plan to translate literary works from Russian into Ottoman and vice versa. She sought his help for this.[267] Thus, with so many interesting perspectives to share, they resolved to translate a series of Russian classics into Turkish for Ottoman readers. Following the previous rejection of her proposal by the Ottoman government, we can only imagine what a relief and triumph it was to receive a formal invitation from Ahmed Midhat in 1889, since he was such an important and high-ranking publisher.

Ahmed Midhat left Paris for Geneva on 1 October and travelled with Dr Yanpolsky to Vienna.[268] Madame Gülnar remained a subject of their discussion until they parted. The Ottoman publisher had formed an opinion that both Russians were 'perfect' people.[269]

On returning to Constantinople, true to his promise of a continued association and starting on 25 December 1889,[270] Midhat published excerpts from his travelogue *Avrupa'da Bir Cevelan* [Tour of Europe] in the newspaper *Tercüman-ı Hakikat*. Here he chronicled his impressions of the West through Muslim eyes, 'to make Europe known to the Ottomans.'[271]

Crucially, he here introduced Olga de Lebedeff (as Gülnar), and portrayed her in the best possible light. Even before her arrival on Turkish shores the following year, she was already a focus of attention amongst the Ottoman intelligentsia and so called 'enlightened circles' as a learned woman who 'loved the Turks and their culture'.[272]

Ahmed Midhat first published Olga's translation of Alexander Pushkin's *The Blizzard* (otherwise known in English as *The Snowstorm*).[273] Pushkin's story, written in 1831, embodied an ingenious romantic plot and was one of five *Tales of Belkin* in which the author uncovers how destiny may work itself out through a series of unimaginable coincidences.

Olga's arrival in Constantinople, 1890

Ten months later and after the first publication of his travelogue, Olga took up Midhat's invitation to visit Constantinople, the Ottoman capital. She brought her children with her, as well as several translations which she had prepared.[274] She arrived on 13 October 1890 after the hot season, and stayed for seven months till mid-May 1891, leaving before the heat of the summer set in. This was the first of many visits when she would arrive by steam ship from Odessa or Yalta and pass through the Galata Customs House. Her arrivals and departures were recorded in the paper *Tercüman-ı Hakikat*,[275] as well as in other local newspapers such as the daily paper *Stamboul* which recorded a year to the day later after her first visit that that "Mme Olga de Lebedeff (Gülnar Hanoum), the

THE INVITATION TO CONSTANTINOPLE

distinguished writer arrived the day before yesterday in Constantinople where she plans to spend the winter." [276]

Fig. 58
Postcard of the Yildiz Palace and the Hamidi mosque (Family Collection).

On her first arrival in Constantinople in October 1890, Olga and family rented an apartment for seven months. They stayed at Hotel Belle-Vue on the at 27 Boulevard des Petits Champs in the centre of the fashionable Pera neighbourhood (Beyoğlu). [277] This area was where Europeans usually lived, and it was known as 'Little Europe.'

The Grande Rue de Pera, along which the French and Russian embassies amongst others were located, was a block away. The spacious halls of the Russian Embassy were richly furnished and boasted extensive gardens for hosting large receptions. Apart from the myriad shops, cafes, restaurants, and taverns, on the Grande Rue de Pera it was fashionable to have your portrait taken at the firm of the Sultan's official photographer 'Sebah & Joaillier' in a magnificent building next to the Russian Embassy. From Pera you could travel by tram, or underground train (only the second in the world) to Galata, or alternatively take a European-style hackney cab or carriage pulled by two horses.

Evidence of Olga's first stay at the Hotel Belle-Vue, so named due to the splendid views from every window of the Golden Horn and the Bosphorus, is recorded in the daily newspaper *Stamboul*. The paper's hotel list mentions 'Mme Olga de Lebedeff et famille' in over eighty entries between 16 October 1890 to 12 May 1891.[278] The two eldest boys, Vladimir and Alexander, were likely then at boarding school in St Petersburg, but otherwise she took Nina and Vera (twenty and nineteen), Olga (ten) and Micha (four).

From the hotel lists, we can see that apart from Olga's family, there were another three families using the hotel as their winter residence. The family of the retired Commander de Henk, a member of the German Conservative Party and other regular names on the hotel list were Sir Alfred and Lady Sandison (then Oriental Secretary at the British Embassy, and his wife). Sir Alfred had excellent Turkish as he had been born there and served for some time in the British Embassy in Constantinople. Also listed were 'General Blunt Pasha' and his wife.[279] Referred to here as the General, Sir John Elijah Blunt was British Consul in Salonika. He had married Fanny, the Sandison's daughter, and was known as a strong 'philo-Turk'.[280]

During her first three months in the Ottoman capital, Olga worked hard on her knowledge of Arabic and Persian. Midhat did whatever he could to promote her continued language studies and provided opportunities for getting her translations published. He found her a tutor in Persian: Habib Efendi. Her Arabic tutor was a thirty-year-old journalist called Ahmet Cevdet, one of the editors of Midhat's newspaper *Tercüman-ı Hakikat*. The translations into Ottoman and their corrections were labour-intensive work, often taking up to 'ten hours of study per day'.[281]

In large part thanks to Midhat's introductions, Olga de Lebedeff soon had a busy social life in Pera. After only three weeks, Olga was invited to visit the family of the leading civil servant and historian Cevdet Pasha and his daughter Fatma Aliye, who was a writer too and had children of a similar age:[282] 'Cevdet Pasha's daughter ... invited the wives of foreign ambassadors to her receptions at Yıldız Palace and Madame Gülnar was frequently counted among the guests'.[283] Olga in turn invited Cevdet Pasha along with his daughter to have breakfast at her apartment, something for which the pasha had to request permission from the Sultan Abdülhamid II himself.[284]

Other guests, both male and female Ottoman writers and intellectuals[285] like Mustafa Reshid and novelist Fatima Aliye and the poetess Nigâr Hanım, were invited to her apartment.[286] Nigâr Hanım also held famous salons on Tuesday evenings (separately for men and women).[287] Both these Ottoman women writers, with whom she struck up a lasting friendship and correspondence, were also able translators; cultured and elegant as they were, Olga regarded them as distinguished representatives of educated and enlightened Turkish womanhood.[288] In 1889 Fatma Aliye had been the second Ottoman woman to make her debut as a published author with a translation of a French novel (with her husband's permission) using the pen name of *Bir Hanım* - 'A Lady.' Olga would translate one of Fatma Aliye's books from Ottoman into French, *Women in Islam*, or *Nisvan-i Islam: Les femmes Musulmanes*, which discusses the status of women in marriage and social life in the Ottoman Islamic world and in the law.[289]

So it was that with introductions to society such as these, and through her own contacts from the Turkish Embassy in St Petersburg, Olga was permitted to visit the otherwise private world of the harems - to meet Ottoman women in their own homes and to learn about family life. Customarily, in powerful and wealthy families, women lived in secluded fashion, but they socialized and maintained a culture of their own in their own quarters, at the bathhouse and in celebrations. Some women acquired great influence in the family and administered their properties. 'Battles are won in the harem of the palace, not in the battlefield' is a quote from a current Turkish historical series, which sheds light onto the profound influence women always have wielded in society, often behind the scenes.[290]

Fig. 59
Order of the Shefakat

OLGA DE LEBEDEFF – A LIFE ACROSS EMPIRES

During Madame Gülnar's first winter in Constantinople, the Sultan Abdülhamid II awarded her the *'Order of the Shefakat'* (*Nişan-ı şefkat*) Second Class. This was an imperial Ottoman decoration of charity issued exclusively for women from 1878, and the meaning of the word Shefakat may be translated as tenderness or compassion. It was occasionally conferred on foreign wives or daughters of distinguished dignitaries or diplomats, in the categories of first, second or third class; the grand cordon first class of the order was reserved for royalty.

The medallion brooch which hung from a white ribbon bordered with green and red on each edge was an exquisite work of art which glittered with silver, gold, diamond, ruby and enamel. This was conferred on Olga 'in recognition for her contribution to Oriental Studies' and a reversal in fortune for someone who just a year or two before might have been dismissed as a spy. Olga would wear the brooch on special occasions with considerable pride.

Public occasions, such as the *Selamlik*, were a notable outlet for social life amongst foreigners: of the eighty guests assembled at the palace on 22 May 1891, which followed the Ceremony of Selamlik at the Yildiz Hamidiye mosque, the paper *Stamboul* names only four persons by name, one of whom is Madame de Lebedeff: the others were diplomats from Belgium, France, and Russia. 'His Imperial Majesty' the Sultan inspected the troops after his devotions at the mosque and then returned to the palace. A few of those present received Imperial salutations transmitted by His Excellency Mehmed Emin bey, Chamberlain of the sultan, if their name were familiar to the sultan. [291]

It was customary for Russians to announce their arrival and departure with the consul or ambassador. But Olga's attendance at these events, and her award from the sultan, would certainly have come to the attention of the Russian legation just round the corner from Olga's hotel. The longtime Ambassador Alexander Ivanovich Nelidov may have been most interested. His own wife Olga Khilkof-Nelidova was fond of literature and author of a novel under a male pseudonym – and had been tutored by Ivan Turgenev.

THE INVITATION TO CONSTANTINOPLE

Fig. 60
Olga wearing the Order of the Shefakat, approx 1891 (Family Collection).

Ordinary friendly and cordial relations were to be expected on both sides, but too much affiliation to the Russian embassy could lead to suspicions from the Ottomans about her motives, for Russia was often seen as 'the enemy at the gate.'[292] From Olga's family visits, we have no evidence to suggest that her activities played into any schemes of the Russian ambassador, no espionage nor Byzantine plots. But as a prominent Russian visitor to the city, her activities were doubtless followed with a mixture of admiration and at times, opprobrium. This filtered back to the Russian authorities too. The question must have been asked: what was she up to?

Fig. 61
Olga's children: Vera with Michel (Family Collection)

9 First Translations from Princes to Pushkin

> I am not a writer. I am a simple translator minding her own business, but I am definitely not what the Italians call 'traduttore - traditore' [translator-traitor]
>
> Olga's Letter to Tolstoy, 1 August 1894

At the time of Olga de Lebedeff's visits to the multi-lingual Ottoman Empire of the 1890s, translation was seen as a highly valued activity. It was in fact an essential tool and an area of huge growth, which carried with it an element of prestige.[293] Not only was it 'an artistic enterprise…. but in some senses a political act in the broadest sense, bringing voices from one part of the world to another'.[294]

Her work in this field earned Olga respect from 'forward-thinking' Russian men of letters like P.D. Dragonov. He praised her commitment in awakening interest in things Russian amongst Turks and establishing, as he put it, 'a closer connection between the two governments'. Later, others called her 'an ambassador of Russian literature in Turkey'.[295]

Olga's self-proclaimed motivation was 'to publish in Eastern languages books which would be suitable for and useful to the peoples of the East' as well as to introduce Eastern texts to Russian audiences.[296]

First publication – *The Qabus Nameh* – or *Book of Cavus*

During her years in Kazan in the 1880s, Olga had made a first-time translation into Russian of a Persian classic, the *Qabus Nameh*. She had translated it from Tatar. The censors passed her work on 18 December 1886, but it had taken a whole year for the book to be authorised – though she had finished it in 1885.[297] The text had recently been translated into Tatar in 1881 by Olga's teacher of Tatar, Qayyum Nasyri, so that 'it could be available to Russian Muslims.' Incidentally, the first time the text was published in English would be sixty-five years later by Reuben Levy.

The original text was an eleventh century *Book of Cavus* by the Amir of Dailam, the famous *padishah* and grandson of Qabus: Kai-Kabus Ibn Iskandar ruled from A.D. 1050 to 1087, and his book the *Qabus Nameh* was written for his favourite son. The Amir was ruler of the 'Land of the Sun', called Khorasan, or Khurasan, a historical realm south east of the Caspian Sea. In 1881, Russian armies crushed the Turkmen tribes of the area which they renamed Transcaspia, and established a new city called Ashkhabad six hundred miles from the Caspian.

Likened to the educational genre of Mirror for Princes for its political content, or of 'speculum literature' which tries to encompass encyclopaedic knowledge, it has also been defined as a textbook of ethics, or self-help guidebook for rulers: 'Most people imagine that buying slaves is like any other trading,' the author says, but in fact the skill is 'a difficult art…and a branch of philosophy'.[298]

In the Russian edition, forty-two chapters had all kinds of sage advice on how to live a good [Muslim] life with advice from father to son on the 'knowledge of God', 'the use of Prayer', the seasons, astrology, doctors, medicine, war, and love and so on.

This translation from the Persian and Tatar would have been of interest not only because the book had never been translated into Russian before, but as it was re-translated from Tatar, a language that had very little written tradition of its own.

FIRST TRANSLATION FROM PRINCES TO PUSHKIN

In her role as translator and bearing in mind her readers, Olga de Lebedeff tended to interpret. This is explained in more detail by I. Edijanov as follows:

> '[she] frequently elaborates on the content of the teachings, since she was familiar with the culture of Islam and the application of the translation sought not only to translate the text, but also to enrich it, make it more interesting, understandable and accessible to the Russian-speaking reader.'[299]

This tallied with a usual practice at the time of adapting a translation to make the contents more readable [or contextual].

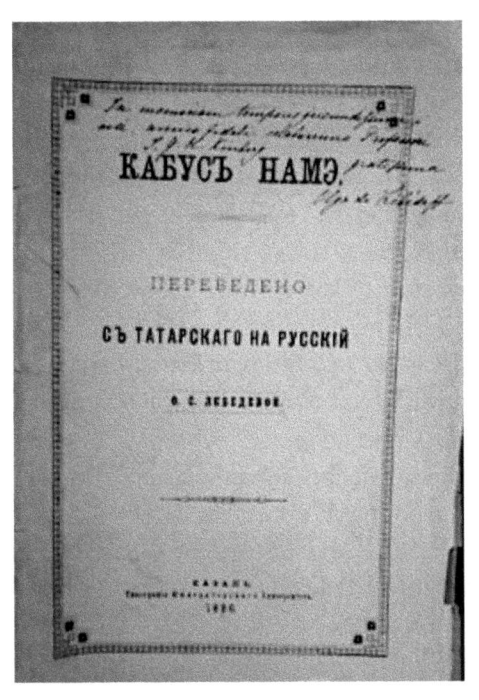

Fig. 62
Original copy with dedication in Latin to Professor JGH Kinberg

The translation won an award conferred by Charles Shefer, Professor of Persian and Director of the Paris School of Oriental Languages.[300] It is remarkable that the high merit of her translation was recognised abroad. This work was one she was rightly proud of and established her firmly in the Orientalist field of study.[301] For the Russian audience, her published name here was O.S. Lebedeva and not *Gülnar*. Could the increased censorship of Tsar Alexander III's reign have been a factor in that decision?

Having achieved this milestone, Olga began to set her sights on studying the richer heritage of the Ottoman literary language. This initiative was stimulated, it seems, by a meeting with diplomats at the Ottoman Embassy in St Petersburg. Another source notes that she took Turkish lessons with an Armenian from Istanbul.[302]

Refuting the French Orientalist, Ernest Renan

During her first documented stay in Constantinople, there were two joint translations by Ahmed Cevdet and Olga de Lebedeff which attracted favourable attention. These works represented important topics for the Ottomans: primarily, a welcome defence of Islam.[303]

The first was called *The Relations of Islam with Science and the Adherents of other Faiths* (1887) written in Russian by the Mufti of St Petersburg, A. Bayazitof.[304] It dealt with achievements of the Arabs in the field of science and Islamic education and morals.

The second was *The Refutation of Ernest Renan: Islam and Science*. Here, the Russian Mufti was objecting to the controversial thesis by the famous French Orientalist about the incompatibility of the provisions of Islam with rational knowledge. Renan's earlier work had originally been delivered at the Sorbonne in 1883. He depicted Muslims as having a hatred of science, nature and history.[305] A year later the Mufti in St Petersburg had put forward a counter argument about the fundamental compatibility of Islam and progress.[306]

The translations were done at the request of Ahmed Midhat,[307] who had been sent the Mufti's works.[308] He then arranged for the publication of this new translation of this polemic in his newspaper in 1890 or 1891.

The results of the translating partnership with Cevdet emphasized to Ottoman readers that Madame Gülnar cared about their culture despite being from another one. This work was one of substance relating to perceptions of Islam in the West. It would certainly have provoked ongoing interest in any of her subsequent translations.

As a foreign woman, a published translator, and a mother of six children, Olga Sergeevna as translator generated curiosity and allure. It was a novelty to have a highborn Russian lady both speaking to Ottoman society about Russian traditions and customs in their own language, and someone who even appeared to defend Islam.

Introducing new types of writing styles straight from Russian was interesting, not least as Russian literature was popular amongst French readers, and Olga's translations included works by several of the most famous authors.

She was the first direct translator from Russian masterpieces by leading figures in Russian literature (as opposed to a translation taken from a French version). Her translations into Ottoman were from poets and prose writers : Lev Tolstoy, Mikhail Lermontov, Vasily Zhukovsky and his protégé Alexander Pushkin. As powerful intellectuals, they had innovated Russian literary styles of the time.

Most of her translations were first serialized in instalments in Midhat's newspaper before being republished in collections of articles or books.[309] Usually there was an introduction or foreword by Ahmed Midhat to explain the text, which he or Ahmed Cevdet had edited 'so that Ottoman readers would find the text faultless.' Editions of these Russian stories enjoyed an unusually large circulation; it was said by some reports to have been up to 40,000 copies.[310] Olga's translation of Tolstoy's novella *Family Happiness* was retranslated into Arabic and published in a Beirut newspaper in 1892-3. This novella was written in the form of a moral fable or parable: that happiness is to be found in the true joys of home life. The underlying message encouraged the young to marry and build real family happiness based on trust and faithfulness.[311] The theme of domestic happiness was one that Ahmed Midhat also used in his novels.

In the context of Constantinople's publishing houses, it was largely thanks to the interest taken by Ahmed Midhat himself that so many of Olga's works ended up in print. One can also see the direction he guided her in with regards to which material to translate. Though the subject matter of his own novels frequently had a sentimental bent and portrayed the passionate sufferings and sensibilities of the heart versus the cold light of reason, he had wide-ranging interests including a deep interest in matters of religion and philosophy. As a writer he tried to 'remove any contradictions between Islam and [the concept of] progress and awaken in Turkish readership a love of knowledge.'[312]

It is a remarkable fact that her name was clearly published as the translator of these translations (whereas even today most presses do not put translator's names on book covers).[313]

The Poet Pushkin: His Life, Art, Works

Olga's work *'The Poet Pushkin'* has been translated here for the first time into English, by Şehnaz and Aykut Gürçağlar in Book Two.[c] It was originally serialized in 1890 in Ahmed Midhat's newspaper and the following year as a small book,[314] smaller than a postcard size. In March 1893, it was published separately in the contemporary style illustrated journal, *Servet-ı Fünûn*.

To acquaint Turkish readers with 'Russia's Shakespeare', as Madame Gülnar she penned a literary critique of Russia's master poet and most influential writer, Alexander Pushkin. Russia had recently marked the fiftieth anniversary since Pushkin's death, so this introduction to Pushkin was timely. As she put it in conclusion: 'Although Pushkin was considered an important writer during his lifetime, his significance increased among Russians even after his death.'

As well as a biography in which Olga de Lebedeff describes his formative influences, *'The Poet Pushkin'* details a synopsis and commentaries on the merits of Pushkin's most important works in prose and poetry. As a translator Olga is keen to convey Pushkin's personality as an author, as well as writing outlines of his texts. Several stories exemplify good and bad morality; others depict historical events in a fictional setting. The fact that Russian prose is 'rich in ideas and devotes itself to the exploration of moral dilemmas'[315] is one that would have appealed to Ahmed Midhat, the moralist. This verse from the poem *Exegi monumentum* translated by Catriona Kelly transmits Pushkin's sentiments about the power of the written word:

---

[c] The Ottoman Turkish title of 'The Poet Pushkin' is called *Şair Puşkin*.

FIRST TRANSLATION FROM PRINCES TO PUSHKIN

And for long I shall remain loved by the people
For awakening noble feelings with my lyre,
Because in my cruel age I have celebrated freedom,
And called for pity to the fallen. [316]

Olga's monograph on Pushkin includes descriptions of eight of his works: *Ruslan and Ludmila, Eugene Onegin; The Battle of Poltava; The Covetous Knight; Mozart and Salieri; The Captain's Daughter; The Bronze Horseman, and Boris Godunov*. Many of these stories - some in verse some in prose - depict historical figures and Russian tsars.

Mentioning that composers such as Glinka and Tchaikovsky (and Mussorgsky) had set Pushkin's text to music in the favoured dramatic genre of the time - opera – was another means to communicate the significance of Pushkin's work as inspirational within Russian culture.[317]

It is significant that Alexander Pushkin, who is often described as the father of the Russian literary language, was introduced to an Ottoman audience in this way, published and promoted with a foreword by Ahmed Midhat. It was quite an achievement to have found this way of interpreting her culture for the Ottomans. The word 'interpret' is particularly useful as the Ottomans and Muslims themselves used it to describe translation of the Quran: it could not really be 'translated' but it could be 'interpreted'. Ahmed Midhat's newspaper was *The Interpreter of Truth*.[318] In the foreword to her work, Ahmed Midhat stated:

> I would like to convey my gratitude to Gülnâr Hanım on behalf of Ottoman readers, as I feel obliged once more to express our feelings of appreciation to this honourable lady for her assistance in enabling us to benefit directly from this work. We are proud of the love she has shown for our language, science, and intellectual tradition."

He also refers to a previous description of edits made to the text.

> This time I am publishing an essay by Gülnâr Hanım by the title "Poet Pushkin". The work in question has been subject to some revisions; the degree of these revisions has already been taken up in the preface to *The Blizzard*, therefore making their repetition

redundant. However, there is a need to write a few words about the subject matter of the work....

From a translation point of view, translators of this text found that the language adhered to no consistent style, there were long sentences and a few inconsistencies; sometimes the Ottoman compounds were too flowery or repetitive. However, this early work of Olga's demonstrates the difficulties in translating from Russian to the hybrid Ottoman literary language where the style required a dexterous handling of prose style and considerable experience for appropriate use of Arabic and Persian elements.[319]

Conveying Russian culture in a quite different language was not an easy endeavour. Ahmed Midhat defended her, observing that Gülnar Hanım/ Mme de Lebedeff only lacked practice:

As far as the corrections in the works of our Gülnâr Hanım are concerned, we can see, thanks to our close observation, that in comparison with the corrections necessary for products of certain Ottoman pens these are very few.[320]

Midhat also said in his introduction:

This work is not only a biography [...] this work goes far beyond this definition. This essay focuses on the fruits of Pushkin's labour and is therefore an appreciation regarding Pushkin.

The latter was seen as a novelty. Modern literary criticism was just emerging in the Ottoman context, and Ahmed Midhat himself was a something of pioneer in this field.[321]

On the literary circle: The Souls of Arzamas

Pushkin was involved with a critical literary circle called *Arzamas* founded by the poet Vasily Zhukovsky in St Petersburg. Writing in her essay *The Poet Pushkin*, Olga wrote:

FIRST TRANSLATION FROM PRINCES TO PUSHKIN

This circle helped a great deal in opening the hearts and minds of the Russian nation. One of the leading writers in the Arzamas circle was Count Uvarov. The people who set up and constituted this circle studied the works of various writers with great interest and objectivity and searched and scrutinized ancient and foreign literature with a view to finding devices that would constitute a contemporary new Russian language. They established the essentials of Russian literature. At the time Zhukovsky, Batyushkov and even the historian Karamzin wrote a few works with the influence of the Arzamas circle [...]. During this period Pushkin published his first famous poem entitled *Ruslan and Ludmila*.

Members of the circle adopted Pushkin, even before he had finished school in May 1817. Though they loved literature, language and history, members were also boisterous to the point of buffoonery in reaction to literary pedants, but by mid 1817, the society whose adversaries had disappeared, finally fizzled out.

Olga described how they 'treated each other in a friendly and sincere manner and called themselves the "souls of Arzamas". In terms of Olga's sources, the above description tallies with the *Literary Memoirs* of Count Sergei S. Uvarov, the Minister of Education under Nicholas I. The memoirs describe how members of the society 'occupied themselves with a strict examination of literary works, with applying to their native language and literature all the sources of ancient and foreign literature, with seeking principles that would serve as a foundation for a firm independent theory of language etc.'[322]

Olga de Lebedeff added that Pushkin carefully researched the Russian language appropriate for the historical period of each story. He took Shakespeare's tragedies as a model for his *Boris Godunov*, which relates the life story of Russia's Tsar at the turn of the seventeenth century and is a commentary on kingship and legitimacy.

Olga de Lebedeff communicated the idea that literary circles like Arzamas had searched for devices for a new contemporary language (a literary reform) ... could this have had implications for Turks in the future?

Pushkin's works may also have been interesting to the Ottomans, not only because of his own exotic background having an African ancestor, but common themes might be relatable: the fairy-tale poem of *Ruslan and Liudmilla* referred to early Russian history between the Rus' and the Khazars, a Turkic-speaking tribe of the Caucasus; in Pushkin's time, this too was considered Russia's 'Orient'. Similarly, the choice of Tolstoy's *Ilyas* had a wise Bashkir Turk protagonist.

Another translation was of Pushkin's long narrative poem dated 1821-1822: a poetic legend called *The Fountain of Bakhchisaray*[323] together with a historical sketch of the Crimea.[324] This romantic tale of unrequited love of Khan Girei for a Polish princess in the former capital of the Crimean Tatars did not pass muster with the Ottoman censors perhaps because of its overtly Oriental theme including references to the khan and harem, the fakir, the Quran and Mecca. According to Professor Olcay, Olga may have had this published in Kazan instead; another source notes that this had remained unpublished.[325]

To elicit sympathy through fiction

Apart from the three translations already mentioned above, there were eleven other translations of Russian fiction published in the Ottoman Empire by Madame Gülnar. She wrote accompanying biographies in Turkish for three of the authors as a prefaces to their works. There were seven short stories, three poems and a novella, half of them were by L.N. Tolstoy. *Family Happiness* and *Ilyas* were first serialized in *Tercüman-ı Hakikat* and later published as separate books.

- *Family Happiness* by L.N. Tolstoy 1892, 1893, Novella
- *Two Old Men*: Folk Tales of Count Tolstoy 1892, Short Story
- *The Death of Ivan Ilych* L.N. Tolstoy 1892, Short Story
- *What Men Live By?* L.N. Tolstoy 1892, Short Story
- *Ilyas* L. N. Tolstoy (omitting translator) 1892, 1893, Short Story
- *Master & Man* by L.N. Tolstoy 1895,[326] Short Story
- *The Blizzard* by A.S. Pushkin in 1890 & 1891, Short Story
- *Queen of Spades* by A.S. Pushkin 1892,[327] Short Story
- *Demon (An Eastern Legend)* with Biography of Lermontof, M.Y. Lermontov, 1890 & 1891, Poem

FIRST TRANSLATION FROM PRINCES TO PUSHKIN

- *Angel* by M.Y. Lermontov 1892 and 1897-1898,[328] Poem
- *The Sail* M.Y. Lermontov 1897-1898, Poem

Other publications in *Servet-ı Fünûn* included a discourse by V.A. Zhukovsky: *Who really is a good and happy person?* (March 1892).[329] And an article (1893) called *The City of Kazan* [*Kazan Şehri*].

In 1893-1894 she presented the Ottoman readership with an overview of Russian authors entitled *Russian Literature* [*Rus Edebiyatı*, 1311] published by the Asaduryan printing house.[330] In it she introduced twenty writers and poets, beginning with the era of Peter the Great's reforms (using the Ottoman word *Tanzimat*, 'reforms', associated with nineteenth-century state reforms to the judicial and bureaucratic system).

'The first half of this 132-page book is about authors from pre-Pushkin times', writes Professor Hülya Arslan, '...even today we suffer from a lack of sources in Turkish that cover this period'.[331] Of course, also included are Pushkin, Lermontov, Gogol, Turgenev, and Tolstoy. Another intention was to make this material accessible to Russian Tatars who could read it in Ottoman Turkish.[332]

Olga described positive contributions by foreign specialists and skilled workers who arrived in Russia to help open and develop the country, highlighting that foreign influence could be positive. In his essay, Johann Strauss identified Olga's efforts in *Russian Literature*, to show 'different steps undertaken to open the country [Russia] to the West...a sort of panorama of Russian society as it embarks on a course of modernization'.[333]

However, the effort involved in composing these seventeen written pieces in Ottoman had been very time-consuming and exhausting. In a letter some years later to Nigar Hanım, Olga complained that she was always tired and felt as though she has been 'beaten by a whip'.[334] Following a diagnosis of 'neurasthenia', a condition characterized by fatigue, headaches, and emotional stress, the doctors forbad her to work for a time.

Despite her publications in Constantinople and a few mentions in the Russian press, not all her translations were printed at home in Russia. There remain works attributed to Olga de Lebedeff which have not survived, such as translations of an educational book by Leon Melos and *Old Man Eustace* from the Greek,[335] and an article on *The Tribe of the Chuvashes in Russia*.[336]

Following her translation of The Poet Pushkin into Ottoman Turkish, however, in 1896 the editor of a Kazan newspaper *Volzhskii Herald* wrote to Alexander Lebedeff with a copy of an article mentioning his wife.[337] The article by N.F. Yushkov was entitled: '*O.S. Lebedeva and her translations of Pushkin into Turkish*' which highlighted that the theme of Pushkin and the East was of interest to the Tatars. Yushkov put forward Olga's intention in terms of conciliation and entente, as follows:

> To elicit sympathy for Russia in Turkey and to establish an inward rapprochement between the two neighbouring states.

10 A Wedding and the World of Harems

> I married – continued Burmin – I married four years ago,
> and I don't know who my wife is, where she is
> or whether I will even see her again!'
> A. Pushkin from Метель, The Blizzard

In mid-October 1891 Olga had returned to Constantinople and checked in to the Grand Hotel de Londres.[338] This arrival of 'Madame Lebedeff' is remembered in the memoirs of Princess Barbara Dukhovsky, who by coincidence made the journey from Yalta on the same boat 'Oleg', with her husband and cousin Zoe, and stayed in the same hotel.

The Princess' memoirs describe how 'Madame Lebedeff' managed to obtain permission for the lady visitors to be invited to dinner in the harem of one of the Sultan's aide-de-camps, whose father-in-law was a former Vizier. She was informed that he 'like all modern Turks belonging to the upper classes, only had one wife'. The guests were offered cakes and preserves flavoured with attar of roses. Coffee *a la turca* was served in tiny cups supported by silver filigree holders brought on a silver tray by a black slave girl. 'I felt as if I were at the opera, and the curtain had just gone up on a brilliant act of Aida', wrote the princess. They were then invited to a twelve course meal served in tortoise shell inlaid bowls and with coral tipped ivory spoons and serenaded by a band of young girl musicians. Despite this excitement, the memoirs showcase derogatory comments that the princess felt towards Ottoman culture as well as towards her fellow compatriot.

Olga had procured cards of admission for them to attend the Selamlik, a grand state occasion. Here a terrace was reserved for the diplomatic corps, their wives and daughters and other notables on one of the wings of the palace.[339] Foreigners saw it as something of a pageant of pomp and ceremony. Despite this favour, Princess Dukhovsky noted that Madame Lebedeff came dressed in a grand outfit wearing her glittering medal from the sultan which had the unwanted effect of making her look pompous and patronising to the young Russian. However, the Turkish tradition respected by diplomats and other guests was to attend such events wearing one's best attire including decorations.

For her part, Olga had seen the newly opened Grand Hotel de Londres back in May. From now on, she would return here every winter till April 1894, according to the local paper, *Stamboul*. Established in 1891, the hotel was located at 53 Boulevard des Petits Champs, opposite the public garden and the Municipal Theatre (in hotel listings it is also referred to as the Hotel Belle-Vue). Board and lodging cost 15-20 francs (or 95 piastres) per day. This hotel was modern enough to boast a hydraulic lift, 'the same system as that used at the Eiffel Tower'.[340] Other advantages were its first-class European cuisine, telephone services, the comfort of new furnishings including the English-style toilets, all catering for European standards of comfort. The new hotel exuded elegance and was a fine place to celebrate her December birthday, Christmas and even the New Year.

The visits by Olga de Lebedeff to the Ottoman capital are now well-documented by Turcologists. Madame Gülnar is described in an essay by Johann Strauss, as occupying 'a unique place in the history of Ottoman letters.'[341] Strauss ends his essay noting that it was to a certain Ahmet Cevdet, her Arabic tutor, that Olga Sergeevna had promised a wedding: 'before returning to Russia, Olga Lebedeva had arranged a marriage for Ahmed Cevdet with a pretty girl from amongst her closest relatives.' The latter was a testimony from the publisher Ahmed Midhat's son.[342]

Both Olga's eldest daughters were now young women of a marriageable age - no longer teenagers. According to conventions of the time, they would need parental guidance in choosing a suitable match:

someone older and wiser, with solid financial means; someone who would provide them with the standard of living to which they had become accustomed. The likely candidate would need to be highly cultured and be of standing in society.

It is quite true that Olga arranged a marriage with an Ottoman subject for her eldest daughter, Nina Dlotovskaya. For her blue-eyed sister Vera, it might have been tempting to arrange a double wedding… there is, however, no record that Ahmed Cevdet became a son in law, so it is hard to verify any betrothal to him. We know that, in another ten years, Vera would be married to divorced Spanish pianist and conductor of the Italian opera at St Petersburg, Alonso de Cor de Lass.

Nina was quite a beauty, according to family lore. Apart from her physical attributes and excellent manners, she was always immaculately dressed (*très comme il faut*). Speaking several languages, French was her language of choice, and spoken at home. As was probably the norm in those days, Nina was known in later years to adjust her age for official papers using her feminine charms. Despite the dreamy, faraway look in the picture (below), she expected to get her own way.

Nina's education had included studies in history, philosophy, and literature. In many private homes, the influence of Voltaire, Rousseau, and Montesquieu was still to be found in the family library.

Two of her exercise books have been passed down to us. They detail studies in antiquity, covering the Egyptians, Chaldeans, Persians and Indians, the literature of the Hebrews and the Ancient Greeks. The second book focuses on French history and literature of the seventeenth and eighteenth centuries, including descriptions of La Bruyère, Fénelon and Moussillon, and the effects of the English writers Bacon and Locke on Voltaire, Rousseau, Buffon. Then follow sections on Corneille, Racine, and Moliere as well as descriptions of the writings of Fontanelle, Diderot, and d'Alembert. The separate subject of eighteenth-century Italian theatre is detailed on another page, evidence of another study. The quality of the handwriting and the detail of the subject matter speak of a rigorous and perfectionist learning. My guess is that these are lessons, dictated or copied out, since they are written with almost no corrections.

Fig. 63
Nina Dlotovskaya c. 1892 and Vera Dlotovskaya c. 1901 (Family Collection)

Nina's marriage to an Ottoman subject was arranged by her mother. She was betrothed with a large diamond ring to an experienced and sophisticated diplomat called Nasri Bey Bahache, a Secretary [Minister] of the Sultan.

Secretaire de S.M.I. Le Sultan Abd-Ul-Hamid Khan II

Nasri Bey, as he was generally known, spoke impeccable French.[343] From 1875 to 1892 he was posted at the Turkish legation in St Petersburg as first secretary and was one of the longest serving Ottomans there.[344] Nasri Bey had green eyes and was born in Aleppo.[345] His family were Latin Catholics.[346]

The wedding in Constantinople took place on Wednesday, 15th June 1892 at the Catholic Basilica of St Antony of Padua. The event was recorded in the daily newspaper *Stamboul*.[347] Though there were said to have been no formal invitations, the nave was full of friends. Russian-style hospitality would include an invitation by announcement for all

A WEDDING AND THE WORLD OF HAREMS

who wanted to come. The famous opera tenor Clement Marini sang Gounod's *Ave Maria*, his rich voice filling the Basilica accompanied on the organ by Professor Joseph Cagni. The ceremony included a nuptial blessing in French, reminding the couple that faithfulness towards God brings marital harmony. In the best of traditions, the happy couple went on honeymoon the following day. Their honeymoon was of long duration – from start to finish - forty-one days. Their return to Constantinople on 25th July was also recorded in the *Stamboul* newspaper.[348]

Nasri was much older than his new bride. But the union resulted in Olga's first granddaughter being born in Constantinople in March 1893, my grandmother, Nina. As Victor is the Christianized version of the name Nasri, the baby's Russian-style name was Nina Victorovna Bahache.

The baby Nina, whom they called Ninette, was baptised a Catholic in Constantinople. However, after about four years, mother and daughter returned to St Petersburg. There, the four-year-old was re-baptised in the Orthodox Church on 22 May 1897.[349]

The arranged marriage between Olga's eldest daughter and an Ottoman citizen emphasised the friendship Olga felt towards the Ottomans.[350] Supposedly, having a son-in-law in the diplomatic service might have offered some form of diplomatic immunity. Most of all, this tie cemented the gratitude she felt towards Nasri Bey, when he had helped her with her first translations into Ottoman Turkish all those years back in St Petersburg, before her visit to the congress at Stockholm.

During the next three years Olga and her remaining children returned regularly to the Grand Hotel de Londres. A memoir entitled *Mediterranean mosaics; or, The cruise of the yacht Sapphire, 1893-1894* by the American traveller Julia Langdon Barber describes her meeting Olga de Lebedeff on 23rd March 1894 which was towards the end of her time in the Ottoman capital.[351] Together they visited a harem. Barber references the American diplomat Mr Terrell when she describes her meeting with Olga:

> Madame Olga de Lébédeff, nee de Barstchoff, who has on her visiting cards, in addition, her name in Arabic, like this,

is a Russian lady. Her husband is, or was, Grand Chamberlain to the Czar, and she is an authoress of considerable fame. Mr Terrell interceded in our behalf, and she kindly consented to conduct three of us ladies to a harem. Madame Lébédeff says, that the Turks, even the pashas, seldom have more than one wife, and the word "harem" does not necessarily mean wives, but the entire household.'

Julia Langdon Barber then describes how, 'Madame de Lébédeff, who speaks Arabic, in addition to eleven other languages' managed to get them an audience in a harem during Ramadan at the home of one of the Pashas who had been Minister in St Petersburg [probably Marshal Chakir or Jakir Pacha who was posted there for twelve years as Turkish Ambassador]. By her account, the pashas would keep an open house at night for friends who might drop by, they also maintained the commendable custom of setting places downstairs for any poor hungry visitors.

Access to harems may have been limited for foreigners in general, but in correspondence with the novelist Leo Tolstoy dated 1 August 1894, Olga explains that having had access to harem apartments she could have confidence in writing about women's lives:

> I can say that women living in cities, and in particular the daughters of merchants and of high-ranking state officials, receive a good education. They have a European mentality, and they learn Arabic and Persian. The more upper class among them have foreign governesses. Among these women are some very well-educated writers and poets, perfectly capable of conducting philosophical discussions. Women are the tsarinas of their homes. Elderly ladies are treated with great respect. The law recognises their right to manage their own assets. However, social customs (religious values) require that they should cover their faces when they go out and that they should not talk to men they are not acquainted with.[352]

Both Ahmed Midhat and Fatma Aliye supported the idea that foreigners should be invited into harems to meet Turkish women and to see for themselves what kind of misperceptions and preconceived notions they may have entertained about them. This is reflected in a book by Fatma Aliye, called *Women in Islam*, designed to dispel erroneous views of Islamic women:[353]

> In order to know the Turkish character, it is necessary to understand the language and traditions of the country, and to be familiar with the people, both in their natural and family character.

To Ahmed Midhat's mansion on the Bosphorus

It was not only visits to certain harems that is of note. Olga was also invited to stay at Ahmed Midhat's house as an honoured guest at Beykoz.[354] Beykoz on the Anatolian side of the Bosphorus was, as Ahmed Midhat liked to say, the most beautiful place of Istanbul, and his home the most beautiful in Beykoz.[355]

The Asiatic shore had abundant vegetation and forests, and Beykoz was known for its extensive vineyards, fishing, and excellent water. Its three storey waterfront buildings had a unique character and at the landing stages one was met by locals who appeared more Asiatic, all of which made nineteenth century travellers realise that crossing the Bosphorus to the Asiatic side was 'really and truly journeying out of Europe and into Asia'.[356] Travellers could take some ten stops from the Istanbul by steamer and walk up the Giant's Mountain for a beautiful view of the Bosphorus and the Black Sea. Property was the preserve mostly of wealthy Ottomans, and the sultans had built their palaces here for hunting parties.

Though still registered at the Grand Hotel de Londres, Professor Olcay describes Olga's visits to Beykoz:

> During her first visit, Olga Sergeevna did not stay long at the hotel. Midhat invited her to live in his villa on the Asian side of the Bosphorus.

Here she was immersed in the social happenings at Ahmed Midhat's home. His hospitality reflected traditional ethics of his religion, as according to the saying attributed to the Prophet 'there is no good in the one who is not hospitable'.[357]

Fig. 64
Nasri Bey Bahache pictured second from right, Moscow (Family Collection). Here the Ottoman officials are wearing gold embroidered dress uniform.

A WEDDING AND THE WORLD OF HAREMS

Turkish men and women did not meet openly in public, but this custom was often evaded in private.[358] The invitation was certainly a testament to the strong connection and trust between them. We gather that over the years Midhat hosted women guests such as Madame Gülnar and the poetess Nigar Hanım,[359] whom he also held in high regard, as well as other foreigners of note such as the New York Herald journalist Sidney Whitman. Ahmed Midhat was famed for hosting literary gatherings of the most important poets and writers of the period on a Friday evening.[360] His son-in-law, was a good friend of his, the well-known poet Muallim Naci (1850-1893)[361] to whom he had married his daughter aged fifteen. Yet, though his family was large, women were not to be seen when foreign male guests visited.[362]

Ahmed Midhat built a tall wooden mansion around 1887 on the Beykoz waterfront. The spacious building catered for his large family in apartments of varying sizes, which over the years was extended and reached the number nine. There were three storeys with high ceilings and an attic upper storey, which in later years he converted into a neighbourhood school. High windows were elegantly decorated with classical style pediments.[363] Ahmed Midhat had a well-stocked library here and reception rooms for large social gatherings and theatrical performances.

He had sixteen children, six of whom were Christians that he had adopted. They lived under relatively 'plain but patriarchal' conditions.[364] Ahmed Midhat had two wives. The first was called Sofia Servet Hanim with whom he fathered his first child, aged sixteen.[365] Apparently, due to Ahmed Midhat's fondness for art and culture, each member of the family played a musical instrument, and music would often be heard wafting from the quayside windows.

Ahmed Midhat had taken a second wife in 1884, a seventeen year old Greek prostitute called Vasiliki, thereby rehabilitating her into society.[366] She converted to Islam and took the Turkish name Hafize or Anjelik Melek.[367] Ahmed Midhat wrote a novel *Still Seventeen Years Old*,[368] based on meeting his second wife where the issue of prostitution was discussed.

He was critical of the concept of 'civilization' and the decaying moral values of society which allows prostitution to flourish; he had been horrified by the behaviour of prostitutes in Europe.[369] Even though prostitution existed in the Empire, and though he saw prostitutes as victims of ill fortune and of social morality, Midhat tried to idealize Muslim Ottoman society and its ethical values. He believed that Europeans, by contrast, had brought immorality with them and were in fact to blame for the introduction of prostitution into the Empire.

Fig. 65
View from the European side of the Bosphorus [370]

In his comparisons of Islam and Christianity he invariably idealised Islam. As Olga would also have told him, prostitution and moral decline were also a problem in Muslim communities in the neighbouring Russian Empire; some blamed this on Christian domination and declared it alien in a decadent age.[371] Reports of immoral behaviour, from drunken brawls to sex outside marriage created strife in communities, and united Muslim reformers and traditionalist critics alike.

As for the newlyweds, Nina and Nasri Bey, their union in the city lasted some four years. Nasri Bey was awarded the Order of the Medjidie

A WEDDING AND THE WORLD OF HAREMS

[*Mecidiye Nişanı*] in September 1898, and a new position as deputy governor general of the *vilayet* of Adana in southern Anatolia.[372]

Fig. 66
'Les deux Ninas': the two Ninas, Olga's daughter and granddaughter (Family Collection).

The prospect of this posting much displeased his wife Nina Bahache, who had felt impelled to return to St Petersburg with Ninette.[373] The worrying increase in anti-Greek Orthodox sentiments towards the Armenians in Turkey may also have been a factor in her decision to leave their home in Constantinople, even if she and her daughter ran no appreciable risk of harm.

That most beautiful 'Queen of Cities' with its myriad mosques, minarets and spellbinding panoramas would still wait for their return.

Fig. 67
Nasri Bey's old friend, Ahmed Hafiz, representative of Bedouins to Ottoman government (Family Collection).

11 On Skilful Women Writers

> The mark of a country's degree of civilization is that women should be respected, but this is impossible unless their education is of the same level as that of men...We recognise however that any movement for the attainment of the object in view must come from Muslims themselves.
>
> *The Constantinople Messenger (1880)* [374]

Within Islamic communities in Constantinople and Cairo, women's problems and social issues were gradually beginning to be discussed in print, but these would be read by only a small proportion of the population. Invariably, women writers would need a mentor, as Fatma Aliye had Ahmed Midhat, and also approval from their husbands to publish their writing.

The vehicle for new ideas to circulate was often through association magazines and journals by subscription, or the literary evening salons of the active intellectual communities. The written word composed by women enabled an exploration of both local and foreign values. It increased their presence in the public sphere. By 1889, with increasing literacy thanks to State Primary and Middle schools and an increasing body of educated women, Constantinople had nine women's magazines, usually in the form of supplements for women, to cater for the widening readership. [375] The Egyptian women's press was also as active.

In Constantinople, Olga met Ottoman women writers from notable families such as the poet Nigar Binti Osman and Fatma Aliye, both who had recently started their writing careers. As many women writers, they also translated the works of Western writers. Traces of their correspondence with Olga, which lasted several years, are preserved in Turkish archives.[376]

Fig. 68
The Ottoman poet Nigar Hanım or Nigar Binti Osman (1862-1918). [377]

Fatma Aliye and Gülnar as a role model

Fatma Aliye is now widely acknowledged as being the first woman to discuss women's problems in the Ottoman Empire and who raised awareness on social issues and gender roles. Though she lived a traditional secluded life and been educated at home, she became a published author in Istanbul, Beirut, and Cairo and voiced her opinion in the women's press. Growing up, she had lived in the upper echelons of Ottoman society in Damascus, Aleppo, Janina (Greece) and in Egypt, as her father was a prominent government official, Ahmed Cevdet Pasha. She thus had a broad outlook and was one of the most highly educated women of her day.

At the time that Olga arrived in Constantinople, Fatma Aliye had not yet published a work in her own name. In 1891, Fatma Aliye and Ahmed Midhat jointly published a novel, where her name was substituted by 'a woman'. Ahmed Midhat in his role as Aliye Hanım's literary mentor, often set Madame Gülnar as an example and role model for Aliye, both as a writer and as a social activist. Midhat was interested in enhancing the status of women in Turkish life. Olga appeared to represent a role model figure for the concept of modern women.[378]

In 1892, Fatma Aliye published a book *The Muslim Woman and Family Life in Turkey: Women in Islam* which addressed the status of women in marriage and social life in the Ottoman Islamic world. This included 'arranged marriage, polygamy, infidelity, not being able to return to the family home, or concubinage'. [379] Described as a 'philosophical discussion', it was written in response to popular contemporary works by Westerners.[380]

Both Ahmed Midhat and Fatma Aliye were amongst those prominent intellectuals who criticized European representations of women in Islam. Fatma Aliye emphasised that Islam gives immense importance to women, and that patriarchal society could be challenged through Islam. In this way she hoped to affect cultural change. She thought that male dominated society enslaved women and that scholars and intellectuals ignored this. She maintained that there were also prejudice and misconceptions about the approach of Islam towards women. She supported education in the form of literacy and women's solidarity.

Fig. 69
Fatma Aliye (1862-1936) always appeared in Western clothing.

Representation at Chicago's World Fair in 1893

In August 1893, Fatma Aliye received a request from the cataloguer of the Women's Library to send her publications to the World Fair at Chicago. The Exposition was a trade show celebrating Columbus' arrival in the new world which lasted for six months from May to October. The Sultan Abdülhamid II had established a commission to refute the empire's reputation of the 'Sick Man of Europe'.[381] The sultan determined to put on a fabulous show of the Ottomans' progress in education, science and the beauty of its traditional culture.

Three of Fatma Aliye's books in Turkish were recorded to have been sent.[382] At the Women's Building Library Exhibit there were 7,000 books all written by women from all over the world. This included her book *Nisvan-i-Islam* about women in Islam. She was the only Turkish woman author recorded at the exhibition.[383]

The person who represented Ottoman women at the Exposition was a Spanish musician, Esmeralda Cervantes. In 1887 she had been appointed as harp tutor to the Sultan's harem. Esmeralda accepted an invitation to give an address *On the Education and Literature of the women of Turkey*.

In her speech, she chided the organisers for not appointing a representative of their society in Turkey, as in other countries. In other words, they had invited her as a European to give a talk rather than an Ottoman lady. It appeared that contact of the Board of Lady Managers with the non-Western societies had been very indirect; although in fact the chair of this board had written to Zaynab Fawwaz, a woman writer in Cairo during the preceding summer saying, '...tell me what in your Islamic faith prevents you from attending the exhibition.'[384]

Despite this, Esmeralda Cervantes declared that the nations of the West had misconstrued the level of education of 'Oriental women'. She noted that, although educational reforms had indeed become an important issue on the official agenda in the Ottoman Empire since 1856, there was a scarcity of precise information on 'public instruction' there which could be included in her address.

She made sure to emphasise that the list of famous women produced by Muslim society was very lengthy. She listed the names of some of the outstanding women writers living in Istanbul in the early 1890s, citing several contemporary women writers in Turkey 'who have obtained learning and become famous'.

Esmeralda Cervantes listed certain Turkish women writers including magazine editors and contributors, who were mostly from elite Ottoman families but who were active thinkers, as follows:

> Aliye Hanım, Maqbul Hanım (a writer on philosophical topics published every day in Tercüman-ı Hakikat); Layla Hanım (daughter of the late Isma'il Pasha), a poet published in Turkish newspapers; Mahrul-nisa Hanım (still very young). Articles in newspapers: Zayfar Hanım (wife of Hilmi Efendi), Qamar Hanım (book on Islamic beliefs); Amina Saniya Hanım (a mathematician with famous books including one for schools). I could go on mentioning women like this…

Though she was neither Turkish nor Muslim, Gülnar Hanım appears to have been included, referred to as a philosophical writer. The concept of a 'philosophical' writer could either refer to a writer of ideas, or as someone who engages with Islamic theology. In the Arabic translation of this speech, Esmeralda refers to Gülnar in this way: 'she is too famous to need definition'.[385]

The invitation to Fatma Aliye to send her books postdates Esmeralda's speech at the exhibition. This means that before the speech, Fatma Aliye was quite unknown and her book was untranslated from the Turkish.[386] An Ottoman female novelist representing Turkish women in print went some way to contradict the image of the recumbent and exotic looking Oriental woman stereotype (the 'odalisque'). It showed that Turkish women had a thinking mind and intellectual life.

The concept of a 'New Woman'

A few years later, Fatma Aliye's book *Women in Islam* was translated by Olga de Lebedeff into French, coming into print in 1896 in Paris.[387] It was the sole work by a female Ottoman writer that Olga translated, but the book was very significant, showing her willingness to help correct misconceptions about Ottoman women. Olga's literary activities may in turn have inspired other Ottoman and Egyptian women to publish their own works, and in their own name.

There were examples of Turkish women who had been able to get their works or translations into print, but not usually in their own name, for instance the first commercial women's magazine called *Terakki* was produced in 1869.[388] Before this, an article dated February 1858 records that a printing press has been delivered to Constantinople from Paris and placed in the harem of Ribardi-Efendi for the benefit of Turkish women.[389] The Efendi's wife was said to wish to publish in Turkish translation a collection of the best Western stories, starting with a Thackeray novel. This seems to predate by several years the beginning of secular publishing by Turkish women.

So, as we have seen, it was large part thanks to Ahmed Midhat Efendi's mentoring and patronage that Olga's publications in the Ottoman capital turned out to be some of the earliest by a foreign woman. Their unique collaboration flourished for a time, even though Ottoman censorship was severe, because Ahmed Midhat knew how to get past the censors. Not only had he helped Olga de Lebedeff to improve her Ottoman Turkish and meet some of the best known of the educated elite in Constantinople, but together they had produced and published a new collection of Russian works in Ottoman Turkish.

For a moralistic writer like Ahmed Midhat who was in the 'vanguard' of those who supported some form of women's emancipation, his appreciation of Olga de Lebedeff had been central to a new, more modern way of viewing women, though still a patriarchal one.[390] Ahmed Midhat stopped short of promoting women's right to work.

The wider social ideal of 'the new woman' at this time amongst other things defined women as independent, mentally acute and able to work or study on a par with men, challenging political orthodoxies of the day.[391] Women could be skilful writers, capable of writing as well as any man and profound intellectual thinkers, adding 'the honour of accomplishment to virtuous behaviour'.[392]

The embodiment he saw in Gülnar of a 'new woman' was an early evocation of the high-achiever image. This image is something Professor Carter Vaughn Findley has described as 'entering mainstream nationalist discourse decades later to justify the movement of women into public life under the Turkish republic'.[393]

Privately, for his part, Ahmed Midhat had expressed a hope that in Olga he had found an advocate for Ottomans and Islam, someone to counter negative views of Orientalists in Europe. This was mentioned in a letter to Fatma Aliye.[394]

Friendship and misunderstanding

Correspondence between Fatma Aliye and Ahmed Midhat frequently refer to their relationship with Olga de Lebedeff both in good times and bad. In a letter to Fatma Aliye, Midhat writes that his son-in-law has arrived and that 'our friend Gülnar is still with us'. He found in her a Turkophile, companion and intellectual counterpart.[395] Respecting cultural differences, he would call her Madame Gülnar, corresponding to her non-Ottoman-Islamic identity; on occasion he had even just called her *Gülnar* or referred to her as his 'companion'.[396]

He said that they spent the day with recitations in French and Turkish, with all the family gathering in the evening after dinner. Midhat's family would tell fairy tales from Turkey, and Gülnar would tell stories from Europe.[397] Such storytelling was a common bond and both cultures abounded in tales. Olga's Ottoman listeners knew very little of Russian culture, and she told these kinds of traditional fairy stories and those of Pushkin to entertain her friends. Visits to Midhat's villa might well be ten to fifteen days, according to letters Midhat sent to Fatma Aliye. Olga had on occasion been ill there. All the same, despite best intentions, there were bound to be consequences to this kind of familiarity and hospitality.

After some time, the visits to Beykoz 'sparked a wave of gossip' about Madame Gülnar and her Ottoman publisher, emanating from his literary opponents. Certain circles felt resentment that 'a Russian' would be given such a platform and so close an insider's view of Ottoman mores. One such critic was the Turkish journalist Ahmed Rasim.[398]

Professor Olcay defends the nature of their friendship in the following terms:

Reading Midhat's letters and the memories of his guests, we can unreservedly say that all the rumors were far-fetched. First, Midhat had just got married and was very happy. It was his second wife – at that time this was perceived as completely normal. And the whole large family of Midhat adored Olga Sergeevna. Sometimes her children travelled with her to Istanbul, and they also stayed with Midhat. In the evenings, everyone gathered in the living room: Midhat, his two wives, many children, guests of the house whilst Olga told Russian fairy tales, introduced Russian traditional culture - some of these stories are preserved in Midhat's diary.[399]

Yet, unanswered questions surrounding Madame Gülnar's purpose in Constantinople had also aroused uneasy suspicions in some quarters at the palace.

It had long been said that Olga de Lebedeff had come to Constantinople to perfect her Turkish and find out about family life amongst the Ottomans. She was perpetuating the habit of many years to overwinter outside of Russia with her children, perhaps for health reasons. There was also the romantic longing that her mother had spoken of in those letters of her early childhood, that Constantinople was the home of an Ottoman ancestor.

But on 10 July 1892, Fatma Aliye wrote to Midhat that she had been summoned to the Ottoman secretariat of the Sultan (the minister's office) by his chief companion to report to him what she knew about Madame Gülnar. Clearly, Olga was under the watch of the advisors to the Sultan, some of whom were opposed to foreign influences. Fatma Aliye was obliged to act as an informant on their private conversations. Neither was she inclined to contradict the palace's suppositions.

Suspicions also fell on Ahmed Midhat himself. Due to his numerous publications of her writings, his close friendship with the Russian writer, as well as his praise of her female virtues and intellectual aspirations, gossip claimed that Ahmed Midhat was a Russian spy.[400] He not only denied this or any affair between them, but also that Gülnar could ever be involved in political intrigues. Truly, based on her sincere affection for Ottoman and Tatar mores, she was an unlikely spy.

Yet, on 2 January 1893, Midhat wrote to Olga to tell her that their friendship was over.[401] He closed the doors of his house to his erstwhile

Russian guest. On her third winter visit till May 1893, Midhat not only did not receive her at his villa, but generally refused to meet and communicate with her; he did not answer any of her letters. Whatever the cause of their misunderstanding, which was surely a heated debate and not just the result of opinion or pressure, this represented a severe personal blow to Olga. She had lost a friend and could no longer count on him as mentor.

The approximate timing of this break in amicable relations coincides with the birth of Olga's granddaughter in Constantinople on 10 March 1893. Is it possible that a second marriage pledge of one of her close relatives, perhaps Vera, to Ahmed Cevdet had fallen through?

Through correspondence between Midhat and Fatma Aliye, we learn more about some of the other reasons Olga spent so long in the Ottoman capital. On 8th January 1894, Midhat wrote that Olga de Lebedeff had come to Istanbul for personal reasons. He remarked on her marital difficulties,[402] and that she could not have a good relationship with her husband.[403]

There was another rumour. Fatma Aliye wrote that Olga had come to Constantinople to avenge a person who had betrayed her; that she had come to the city to avenge a person who killed her relative.[404] It is not known whether this was a reference to blame attached to the death of either of two children in infancy. A separate source claimed that Olga arranged the marriage of her eldest daughter against her first husband's will.[405] There was clearly some unresolved complexity in this situation.

The rift with Midhat returned to some kind of appearance of cordiality six months later but stayed at the level of politeness rather than warm friendship.[406]

We can observe that any works by Olga that featured in Ahmed Midhat's paper *Tercüman-ı Hakikat* were almost all published in the years 1890-1892. Prior to this Ahmed Midhat had been planning to publish the collected works of Madame Gülnar.[407] In the end no collected works were published.

Despite this serious setback, Olga appears to have been resourceful with her local contacts. A different publishing house, *Servet-i Fünûn*, published three of her works in the spring of 1893. On 22 March 1893 her monograph about Pushkin called *Şair Puşkin* in book form was republished;[408] on 6 April 1893, her article entitled *The City of Kazan* came out; and on 11 May 1893, her translation of a poem Demon with her preface about the writer, Lermontov.

For Ahmed Midhat, there is a strong possibility that it was Olga's own foreignness was in the end an obstacle to him which could not be overcome, not least for political reasons. For him, she would always have to be an outsider.

His distancing from Olga de Lebedeff produced another shift: he increasingly promoted Fatma Aliye as the embodiment of a Muslim woman writer, transferring the concept of a 'serious' female from Gulnar to Fatma Aliye. Aliye had become his apprentice and devoted student in literary matters, particularly as they shared views on the theme of education for women. He had long called her 'my virtuous daughter' or 'my dear girl' - "fazıl kızım" and even published a biography of her in 1893. In fact, Ahmed Midhat was so fond of Fatma Aliye that he even named his granddaughter jointly after her and Nigar Hanım.

Disagreements between Olga and Ahmed Midhat are documented in his letters to Fatma Aliye, where Ahmed Midhat recounted how Gülnar had taken offence at some of his advice and called him a tyrant.[409] With his tall stature, broad shoulders and imposing presence, let alone his dark flashing eyes, he could surely come over as intimidating when displeased. Constraints were certainly evident in those friendships, and there was no doubt about surveillance and suspicions from the palace. People of note were anyway watched and reported on by informants paid by the palace.

Olga's departure from Constantinople

This is borne out in correspondence on 1 August 1894 to Leo Tolstoy. Olga discusses the matter of state control, and here one detects a trace of bitterness and resignation:

> There is incredible censorship...Everyone is observed. Those occupying high-ranking positions must be extremely careful when choosing whom to befriend.... They are afraid of talking in the streets. Such people are required to notify the Sultan whenever they have guests in their homes. [410]

ON SKILFUL WOMEN WRITERS

After five winter seasons in Constantinople, Olga de Lebedeff left the city perhaps for the last time. She departed not without nostalgia nor some disillusion. She had made many fond friendships and had enjoyed success with her publications, but these appeared to have run their course. Midhat himself would soon take on a new governmental role as Vice-President of the Sanitary Administration of the Ottoman Empire.[411]

Yet, following her departure from Constantinople, news about her did not disappear. Olga was still remembered by admirers including the writer, Mustafa Reshid.[412]

Referring to a meeting with her in St Petersburg, a warm tribute to Gülnar Hanum was published on 10 July 1895 in the Ottoman journal *Ikdam [Progress]*. Entitled 'Gülnar Hanım: Madame Lebedeva' the article read:

> Our readers probably remember the name of this wonderful translator of samples of Russian literature into the Turkish language, not previously made by any other Orientalist. On a recent trip to St. Petersburg, we had the pleasure of meeting this amazing woman.
>
> Listening to her opinions, accurate in the sense of criticism and good in deep humanity and love to the East, it seemed to us that we are seeing and listening to a woman of the future, a woman armed with extensive knowledge, sophisticated, with an all-encompassing love to spread peace throughout the world, brotherhood between nations ...
>
> Imagine a woman who speaks four European languages fluently, speaks Turkish, Arabic and understands Persian. Imagine a woman who not only reads the interpretation of the Classical Arabic of the Quran but also as an interpreter attributes esoteric or mystic meanings to the text. [413]

Olga returned to her homes in Russia, to St Petersburg and Lubiana. But now in the wintertime she would head to the Crimea, [414] or to her mother's new villa in the foothills of the Dolomites.

Her attentions would soon centre on the foundation of a national society of Orientalists in Russia, and outside of Russia, the International

Congress of Orientalists. Additionally, her preoccupation with the concept of the unity of religions drove her to seek out the opinions of the leading writers and academics of the time.

Through such activities, Olga's circle of contacts would widen, and it would not be long before she was drawn to another hub of the Islamic world, Cairo. Her personal association with that city and the Arabic language would eventually be as enduring, if not more so, than with the Ottomans in Constantinople.

All the while, she remained driven by the thought that education was a force for good, that reform had potential to open minds positively. This conviction was a confluence of all Olga herself had learned from the reforming movements in Russia of the 1860s - 1870s, and her interactions with Muslim educationalists in Kazan.

12 Islamic Revival of Volga Tatars

> *Abusus non tollit usum* et la religion Musulmane, bien interprétée est certainement une des religions les plus raisonnables et les plus compatibles avec la civilisation moderne.
>
> Olga de Lébédeff, *Abrégé de l'histoire de Kazan*

Whether in Constantinople or St Petersburg, Olga had meanwhile maintained connections with the Tatar educationalists at the Society of Archaeology, History and Ethnography (O.A.I.E.) in Kazan. She held the Tatar people in special affection, and considered their interests quite overlooked in Russian society and by the authorities. She undertook her own research into the history of the city, publishing first an article in Constantinople, and later a book on the subject in Rome. However, Olga's support for the new wave of progressive thinkers in Kazan was unconventional. At times, it caused quite a stir with the authorities.

Kazan, in the then-named Kazan Governorate and now the capital of Tatarstan, was a one-time political centre on the Silk Route linking China with the Mediterranean. Vital trade routes connected neighbouring Turkic Muslim peoples both within and outside of Russia's empire. The ancient historical connection between the Tatars and Central Asia may further be seen reflected in their languages.

Turkic in origin, Volga-Tatar is thought by some to be from a branch of the Altaic family. Including Ottoman Turkish and Uzbek, these three Turkic languages are related as three different branches of Common Turkic: north-eastern, south-western, south-eastern, respectively. Their common roots would render many words and phrases understandable. Take, for instance, the translation for our English word 'welcome'. In Tatar (transliterated from Cyrillic script) this is pronounced *Hoosh Kildenez*, in modern Turkish, *Hoş Geldeniz* (*Hoş* is pronounced *Hosh*). The pronunciation differs slightly but the words are recognizably similar.[415]

By latitude east of Mecca and Medina, and whilst situated on the European side of the Urals, Kazan is still a fair way to Asia itself either eastwards or southwards. To Bukhara and Samarkand, on the eastern side of the Caspian, it is a vast distance of two and a half to three thousand kilometres. Though distant, being culturally and physically connected to the swathe of territory inhabited by the Volga-Ural Tatars, these Central Asian lands represented an Abode of Islam - major centres of Islamic worship and study - that Muslims identified with.

About five hundred miles from Moscow, Kazan was long considered Russia's most northerly frontier between Muslim and Orthodox Christian cultures.[416] Russians, who had settled in the area, made up the majority in the Volga region. Other peoples and rural pagan cultures, like the Chuvash, Cheremises, Votiaks and Mordvins, lived in and around Kazan too. Religion united and divided. So, the city was also an outpost of Western culture, and an interface with non-Russianness, with peoples considered Eastern.

The term Tatar referred in historical writings to the feared Mongol invaders or Rus' and the rulers of the Golden Horde. Tatars were originally nomads, connected ethnically to the Nogai, Bashkirs, Metcheriaks and Kyrgyz Kazaks.[417] However, Kazan Tatars themselves preferred to think of themselves as Muslim and part of a larger Islamic community and identified as that, rather than as 'Tatar' within their own communities;: they used the term Kazan Tatars when in dialogue with the imperial state.[418] In Russia, relations with officials were formalized, and religious leaders who oversaw their communities needed to demonstrate loyalty to the Russian state, to the Tsar. This is how Islam became an anchor of stability for state authorities.

Dating back to the reign of Catherine II, the Tsars themselves offered patronage and protection to Muslims to garner their goodwill and support. Kazan Tatars had benefitted from Catherine's policy of toleration and co-operation.[419] Tatar colonies which formed after the conquest of Kazan by Ivan the Terrible were spread right across the East to China. Kazani merchants profited from this powerful trading empire in which Tatar became the language of commerce, and local administration within the larger Russian Empire. This had the effect of spreading their Islamic culture where they went. Prior to Catherine II, both encouragement and coercion to convert to Orthodoxy was the norm; missionary zeal was revived under Nicholas I, when the nationalistic ideology of 'Orthodoxy, Autocracy and Nationality' was instituted.[420]

Amongst the general Russian public, many viewed Tatars as a minority culture. They were depicted paternalistically at the time in books for popular reading where the term Tatar was often shorthand for all Muslims: Tatars were regarded with suspicion as 'dangerous ... untrustworthy and without honour.'[421] In common speech, sayings such as 'An uninvited guest is worse than a Tatar' added to a feeling that Tatars were not valued in society.

Pilgrimages and transnational networks

After the Russian empire's colonial conquests of Central Asian cities between 1863-1873, where only Bukhara had remained a protectorate, the advent of the railway brought new opportunities in transcontinental commerce in eastern provinces and with Asia. This generated yet more new wealth for Muslim communities, whose merchants had already long traded in paper, soap, wool, tea, and opium.

Going on pilgrimage and studying in renowned centres of Islamic learning strengthened ties with major transnational networks of scholars. But in ten more years, reports would spread via the new vernacular press that the prestigious reputation of scholarship in Bukhara and Samarkand was not what it used to be, and that students were receiving a limited range of knowledge. Kazan students were discriminated against, and thus the Kazan Tatars perceived the corruption of the Bukharan Islamic scholars, the *ulama*. The latter were seen to operate an educational system based on profits and connections.

The Tatars came to believe that their own scholarly studies were a truer expression of religious piety and rigorous training.[422]

Apart from this, by the 1880s Muslim heartlands were also seen by some Kazan scholars as becoming vassal states to Russia's imperial ambitions. This reinforced the sense that the Islamic world was under siege; the conquest of Bukhara appeared to threaten the survival of Islam itself. All the while, the Russian administration became increasingly alarmed at what they saw as Muslim puritanism and fanaticism, combined with the fact that Kazan Tatars shared a faith with recently conquered people in Central Asia. In fact, there in Central Asia, the 'struggle for souls' had no part in the imperial project.[423]

But to the Russian state, developments in the Ottoman empire appeared threatening not least as Sultan Abdülhamid II (1876-1908) claimed the title of caliph, leader of the worldwide community of Muslims: a non-Russian national consciousness had to be prevented. The first empire-wide census in 1897 counted fourteen million Muslims, though it was conceded that this figure had undercounted women as they had denied access to their homes and some claimed the figure was really double.[424] The official figure by the twentieth century would represent fifteen percent of the total population in the Russian empire, some twenty million Muslims - a larger number than under the Ottoman Sultan.[425] Additionally, resistance to Russian authority in the Caucasus became linked to Islam in the minds of officials and Islam was deemed an alien faith, a threat to be contained.[426] This was not unrelated to the fact that over a million Muslims were believed to have emigrated to the Ottoman empire from Russia in a 'great escape' between the years 1855-1866.[427]

The mistrust and suspicion of government and officials regarding activities by Tatar activists and advocates of Ottoman culture was something about which Olga was acutely aware, especially after her stays in Constantinople. Robert Crews writes that under Nicholas II 'the police targeted interaction between Muslims in various parts of the empire and communication with co-religionists…as strands of a Pan-Islamic conspiracy orchestrated from the Ottoman capital'.[428]

Even Professor Gottwald had formerly been accused, albeit in private by one the city's foremost orientalist missionaries Sablukov, of being pro-Muslim, due to helping Tatars overly with the editing and publishing of their religious books, seen as 'propaganda'.[429]

Missionaries

Missionaries at the anti-Islam division of the Kazan Theological Academy (serious scholars who wrote polemics against Islam), and those at the Kazan Teachers' Seminary and the Kazan School for Baptized Tatars, were looking for an Orthodox revival of their own. They were persuaded by the charismatic and influential Nikolai Ilminsky, a lay missionary-orientalist, that 'every encouragement to Islam becomes a detriment to Orthodoxy.'[430]

Ilminsky, additionally, aimed to stem Muslim Tatar influence over 'less confirmed' or nominal Muslims such as the Kazakhs through teaching in their own language but in Cyrillic script; he wrote about the danger of 'Tatarization' of other non-Russian Muslims so separating them by their language.[431] These views were backed by the Holy Synod's *ober-prokuror*, Konstantin Pobedonostsev. Thanks to his support, from 1880 missionary divisions in Kazan did experience a revival. Aspiring to convert Muslims to Christianity, the efforts by the Russian Orthodox Church were perceived to be in state interests, and so were, effectively, official state policy.[432]

Separately in 1870, the Ministry of Education had also founded a school system in the Kazan region called the Russian-Tatar schools. This accepted Islam as the religion of its subjects and used the Russian language to Russify them. Efforts towards this cultural assimilation was called 'civil Russification'.[433] Tatars still feared that these schools showed the government's disrespect for them and their traditions. Gottwald, and Olga no doubt too (based on her *Abbreviated History of Kazan*), perceived some of the missionaries' efforts and methods as an expression of contempt for Muslims.

However, all around in the towns of nearby Mamadishsky and neighbouring Chistopolsky to the east of Kazan, where Alexander Lebedeff was the Marshal of the Nobility and near his country estate, an Islamic revival was underway. A network of influential madrasas and scholarly families in the Viatka province were particularly influential, one of many neighbouring networks. Prosperous Tatar merchant families like the Apanaevs, who were merchants of the First Guild just like Lebedeff, acted as patrons of mosques and madrasas.

Influential madrasas

Something of a cultural and religious renaissance had already been in process for many years in the Volga Ural community, though for the educated few, living in poorer rural villages, things were still perceived to be backward. Yet by the mid-1880s literacy rates amongst Muslims exceeded those in Russian Christian communities.[434] As well as Kazan, the capital of the province, both the above mentioned districts had thriving rural madrasas where Kazani Muslims sent their children, boys and girls, to be schooled (though the new madrasas enforced stricter separation of boys from girls in the 1890s).[435]

In Chistopol, 140 miles southeast from Kazan, the madrasa housed between six to eight hundred students, most of whom were from outside the town.[436] From age seven upwards the schooling was free, thanks to the generous donations of rich Tatar patrons.[437] At the madrasa they studied literature, religion and jurisprudence. They learned to read Sufi poems, and Arabic-language texts to answer questions of their faith, and to analyze juridical and theological problems. They wrote in Tatar copying down the lessons and opinions of their teachers. Some debated in logic and philosophy.[438] Children studied for eight or nine years, leaving at age fifteen if required to help their parents' business, otherwise they could stay on at the madrasa to earn the honorable title of 'mollah'. Then they learned grammar, syntax, theology, Sharia, philosophy, cosmography, explanation of the 'hadiths' [tradition recording the words of Mohammad] and the Quran; furthermore, arithmetic and Sharia law in respect of inheritance.[439]

Muslim Tatars, whose numbers were approximately a third of the population of the Kazan province, formed networks connected to each madrasa, where Islamic scholar *ulama* wielded enormous influence. Interpersonal relationships forged through the madrasas generated the

ISLAMIC REVIVAL OF VOLGA TATARS

structure and authority amongst Muslims in the region. The influence of these madrasas extended over the whole Volga-Ural region, south and across the steppes and beyond to Bukhara in Central Asia.

One local network was especially significant: the Machkaran network in the village of Machkara (pronounced Maskara in Russian), to where many Islamic scholars had ties and which thus held real influence in the politics of Muslim communities across the region.[440] One scholar, the historian and imam (akhund) Shihabedtin Marjani (al-Marjani), had his roots there.[441]

Marjani, as we have already seen, was well-known to Olga through the Society of Archaeology, History and Ethnography at Kazan's Imperial University.[442] Along with one of his most outstanding pupils Faydkhanov,[443] Marjani realised that if Muslims did not adapt themselves and their educational systems to the current situation, then the Russians who had taken over in Central Asia, would impose their methods and educational standards upon them. He advocated critical textual interpretation, which had been practiced in early Islam and advocated by an earlier Kazan Tatar called al-Kursavi (1775-1813), a principle called '*ijtihad*'. Both Faydkhanov and Qayyum Nasyri also came to advocate this method of interpretation in the early 1870s.[444]

Later they were influenced by the founder of a new educational method. Ismail Gaspirali (Gasprinsky), a Crimean Tatar, pioneered a new method of phonetics called *usul-i jadid* and campaigned for new secular subjects to be taught, like maths, history, and science. Foremost in this long-term approach, which included the founding of the first Tatar-Turki newspaper, was the intention to modernize Muslim communities without losing their cultural identity.[445]

Qayyum Nasyri, Olga's teacher, had even taught this new literacy method in one of the new Tatar-Russian Teacher schools inspected by a German orientalist, Wilhelm Radloff; here Marjani had also taught Islamic theology for a while. These Tatar individuals represented reform and wanted to restructure Muslim education in Russia, but at the time they lacked a collective identity. They were later known as 'Jadids.'

One of Radloff's aims, as a more liberal educator, was to replace what were dubbed 'fanatical' teachings with a more moderate variant; however, the primary purpose of the school was to introduce the fruits of Russian culture and to bring closer ties with Russian-speaking society.

Without having a grounding in their own culture first, Marjani, thought this to be unacceptable. [446]

Gilman Karimov

An account of Marjani's regard for Olga is recorded by the historian Abrar Karimullin. Here, Olga is considered wise, energetic, erudite, and sincerely fond of Tatar people. Marjani recommended people such as his former pupil, the akhund and imam Gilman Karimov, to visit Olga to talk about delicate matters to do with more secular education for his madrassa, saying "She lives not far from Kazan".[447] A letter by Mr Karimov's daughter describes the encounter:

> Olga Sergeevna was well-known in the area, so it did not take much searching to find her. Upon arrival at her house, the butler looked with surprise at the newcomer. In front of him stood a Tatar with a camisole and tubeteika skull cap with wide, white homespun trousers and so on. He handed the butler a paper with his name on in Tatar. After a few moments, a richly dressed and beautiful woman met him with these words: "Welcome, dear Effendi, 'Hoosh-kildenez'!" There was no appointment in the diary, yet they spent more than six hours talking.[448]

Karimov explained how the teaching in local Tatar madrasa schools such as his in Minnibaevo[449] was inadequate and frustrating, with an absence of any sort of curriculum and he shared his thoughts on all this. Olga Sergeevna approved of his plans, and he returned to his village heartened by her advice. Following this encounter, they often exchanged letters, and Karimov continued to seek Olga's counsel. She gladly replied to his letters, one of which follows:

> Most Respected Teacher Gilman! I fully understand your intention and aims. I absolutely agree that your son is not getting the necessary education in the village. About your wish to move to the city and about organising a book publishing business, I expressed my thoughts during our meeting. Moving to the city would be the best resolution for that question. But this, as you

yourself know, is a difficult thing to do and incurs many expenses. After moving to Kazan, it will be a short distance. If you intend to leave the village altogether, you would do better to settle your choice on Orenburg, right on the junction between Europe and Asia, where you will find starting a business much easier. There you will find it easier to take European-style education to the population. Start by publishing books, and after that it will be possible to get authorization to print newspapers and journals.

Gilman Karimov took Olga's advice. Her suggestion not to move to Kazan but to Orenburg was also given on the basis that Kazan was not only a centre for Tatar culture, but for missionaries and their Theological Academy, which carried out a policy of Christianization of the 'native' peoples.[450] Karimov had also been guided by Ismail Gaspirali the owner of the Crimean Tatar newspaper *Terjuman* and founder of *Jadidism*. It was Gaspirali who had first alerted Tatars of the need to reform their educational methods.

Now Gilman Karimov saw his predicament as an opportunity to save Muslim societies from perceived backwardness, knowing 'that Muslims outside their scholarly networks were poor and ignorant.'[451] He relocated his large family to Orenburg; it was a difficult and risky choice.

However, Gilman Karimov was able to obtain permission and successfully open a private printing press in tandem with a wealthy local Tatar family to form 'Husaynov, Karimov and Co'. He and his son had struck up financial backing from the Husaynov brothers (who had also encouraged the family to move to Orenburg).[452] Together they published twenty-seven books, including Gilman's autobiography. In 1902, Gilman Karimov died when struck by lightning. But the business was continued by his son Fatikh Karimov (also known as *Karimi*). He had trained in printing in Istanbul and knew – perhaps not by coincidence - Ahmed Midhat.

13 Censorship and Discontent

> Civility costs nothing and buys everything.
> Lady Mary Wortley Montagu, 1756

The press had long been a wild card in political life in the Russian Empire. There was no legislature for passing laws, so the print war was a part of factional bureaucratic politics and tended to be seen as an organ of political persuasion.[453] Thus, Russian government blocked Tatar language newspapers being printed in Kazan and St Petersburg for many years, although educated Muslims in the Volga-Ural region could very well read Ottoman or Arabic newspapers, as well as Russian ones if they knew the language.

The first Tatar to have published a paper in the vernacular Tatar-Turki and Russian had been Ismail Gaspirali, down south in the Crimea in April 1883. The distribution of Gaspirali's newspaper *Terjuman,* or *Perevodchik* in Russian meaning 'translator', had become widespread amongst the empire's Muslim communities and influenced the most prestigious of Russia's Muslims; for years it would hold dominance of the Kazan Muslim periodical market.

It had taken Gaspirali three years to obtain approval from the Ministry of Internal Affairs, but he had argued that *Terjuman* would be an interpreter –a bridge to building a *Russo-Muslim* accord' and got his permission.[454] The permission stipulated that it must be written in both languages - Russian and Tatar (in Arabic script).[455] Gaspirali was something of an assimilationist and in 1881 he had published a manifesto entitled *Islam in Russia*.

CENSORSHIP AND DISCONTENT

In the Volga region, there had been a long history of unsuccessful attempts to get a vernacular paper printed for Kazan's Muslims, even before Husayn Faydkhanov petitioned for one in 1857.[456] Intellectuals believed that a newspaper and mass literacy could provide a means for popular enlightenment. It was this perspective which inspired Gilman Karimov to start up a private press of his own in Orenburg.

Olga's own attempt to use her influence with government followed efforts by her contemporary in Kazan, the writer Ilyasi. Upon her return from abroad, in October 1893 she arranged a meeting with the head of the central government printing department, whom she found to be well disposed to the ideas she then presented. Her aim was to publish a weekly Russian-Tatar newspaper in St Petersburg called *Chishme* (or 'Spring' in Tatar), whose educational objective would be to introduce Russian history and literature to the Tatar population. However, the reply from Evgenii Mikhailovich Feoktistov on 30 November 1893 declared that the Minister of the Interior [Ivan N. Durnovo / CH] did not deem it opportune to publish a Russian-Tatar newspaper.[457]

No doubt he was concerned with harmful political consequences. For instance, the authorities had been warned by the missionary Nikolai Ilminsky that the Tatar publisher Gaspirali wanted to unite the millions of Russians under Russian rule with science and civilization, and even to 'sow a Turkish germ among all the Muslims of Russia, the Ottoman language'; seen as Muslim propaganda, it was suggested by some that Gaspirali's newspaper should be restricted.[458] Ilminsky was suspicious of any activity which promoted an 'emerging national-political self-consciousness and unity of Tatars and Muslims throughout Russia'.[459]

This attempt by Olga with the authorities is described by senior researcher at the Tatar Academy of Sciences, Azat Akhunov:

> Her enlightened view was that there were two practical ways to educate the Tatars - the opening of secular Tatar schools and production of new Tatar-Russian newspaper. Arriving in St. Petersburg, Olga Sergeevna started to petition the government for these plans. Moreover, this activity caused her to fall under police surveillance, and under suspicion of conversion to Islam, which threatened all sorts of spiritual penalties from the church Synod, including being viewed as a heretic.[460]

Interview with a St Petersburg journalist

It was not an unusual problem for Orientalists (from any nation) to be considered spies, where their interests and loyalties could be called in to question by the authorities. This suggestion was put forward by Tatar historian Karimullin. He claimed that Olga's activities and influence with the Ottomans was played down by the St Petersburg newspaper censors that November.

When a newspaper, the *Novorossiskii Telegraph*, reprinted an interview with her on her return to Odessa from Turkey, the editor was called up by the state police to the department of political investigations. The interview with the sensational title for the time called '*A Russian Woman amongst the Turks*' read as follows:

> Apart from the desire to get rid of false impressions in Turkey about our country, Mrs. Lebedeff has still another aim for her fairly long stay in Constantinople.
>
> O.L.: I am learning there, I study the Quran, the Sharia, Turkish, Arabic and Persian.
>
> These are the very words Mrs. Lebedeff spoke to the reporter from the St Petersburg newspaper [the Sankt Peterburgskii Vedomosti].
>
> O.L.: You might ask why I need to do this, she continued, and my reply is this: to spread civilization amongst Russian Tatars, who are a totally forgotten, ignored people, whom I was able to closely observe at the time that I lived with my husband in Kazan, where he was Mayor. The Tatars are good, clever, and nice people, who now find themselves in a false, unnatural position. My goal is to educate them to the extent that they can merge with Russians.
>
> *How would you do this?*
>
> O.L.: By founding new Tatar schools, and with the help of half Russian half Tatar newspapers which would gradually introduce

civilized ideas and views. Our schools and universities are beyond the reach of the Tatars.[461]

Both Karimullin and Akhunov describe Olga's disappointment on hearing the result of her visit to the government press department:

The failure at having her ideas published in the newspaper was a heavy blow to Olga Sergeevna and destroyed all her plans. She left the capital dismayed, and returned to Kazan province, retreating to her estate in the Spassky district.

Here, she once again immersed herself in her translations and continued to explore the history and culture of the East, and often met scientists, Orientalists and Tatar educators at Kazan Imperial University.

Even the military mufti of St Petersburg, Gayatulla Bayazitov, who had first applied to publish a newspaper in Russian and Tatar in the 1880s, did not succeed in this until 1905.[462]

That year of revolutionary crisis which forced important concessions from the Tsarist government, marked the collapse of literary censorship in the Russian Empire and produced the first Tatar newspaper in Kazan in 1905. The person who succeeded in this effort was Said-Girei Alkin (1867-1919), a famous Tatar in the city, and a member of the first state parliament. He published and edited a newspaper called *Kazan Mukhbire* (The Kazan Reporter).

Pre-1905 censorship of Muslim teaching & Tatar discontent

Prior to this, Olga's own experience of having failed to get approval for a Tatar press for Kazanis, gave her the cause to vent her own frustration about the controversies over censorship and Muslim discontent in her *Abbreviated History of Kazan*. This was written for and presented to the International Congress of Orientalists in 1899. The publication written in French brought the topics so close to her heart to an international audience.

> If one has not forced them to embrace Christianity, on the other hand one has not done anything either to civilize them or increase their moral wellbeing. For several years foreign Muslim teachers have been prevented from coming. Thanks to the personal malice of an intransigent censor who is ignorant of Arabic and who has just a superficial knowledge of Turkish, Tatars have been accused of receiving Turkish books hostile to government policy ('a la politique russe'), something which is quite false, since such books do not exist.
>
> He has even gone to demand that all verses concerning the 'Jihad' or religious wars be expunged from all religious books printed in Russia these last years, such as Fikh, Tefsir etc. as if one would like to truncate the Gospel! This therefore comes back to depriving Muslims of the freedom of conscience which they have always enjoyed until now. This has resulted such a discontent that thousands of Crimean Tatar families have exiled themselves in Turkey, fearing that they are witnessing the beginning of a time of intolerance. [463]

Olga was scathing about the revised process by which the muftis were being elected. The first mufti had been appointed by the Empress Catherine II in 1788, but Alexander I had ruled in 1817 that the mufti should be elected by the Muslim community with approval from the emperor; most had been chosen from the Kazan Tatars. She wrote about the deteriorating relations between government and Muslims, and how the government was appointing muftis instead:

> One has also been shown to be just as intolerant by abolishing their right, till now uncontested, to elect their own muftis. From now on the Russian government oversees nominating the muftis, educated in Russian secondary schools who know their religion only imperfectly, and are completely ignorant of Arabic. It is with these examples of such petty-minded intransigence that the people are irritated, and the government loses prestige acquired after several centuries of tolerance. [464]

Fig. 70

A mosque in Kazan and some Tatar shops, original photograph (Family Collection)

On Tatar Schooling and Government Attitudes

The educationalist Tatar reformers, those Jadid teachers who wanted Muslims to modernize without losing their own Muslim identities,[465] and the intellectual friends she met through the Society of Archaeology, History, and Ethnography, made Olga aware of the pressing needs of the Tatars and how unequal their situation was in society. In the eyes of the Soviet-era Tatar historian, Abrar Karimullin, she was a staunch supporter of this "vanguard of progressive thinkers."[466]

Over the years Olga had been influenced by how others outside of Russia would perceive the situation too, including prominent Ottomans such as Ahmed Midhat. Jadids, increasingly, subscribed to the idea that the cultivation of knowledge brought power and progress, something that could be observed in Europe and Russia's economic and military superiority, and the colonized peoples were declining because of their lack of knowledge.

We can read about Olga's views on this in Part Three of her *Abbreviated History of Kazan*. Parts of this section, entitled 'Some Considerations on Tatar Civilization,' are translated below. With European Orientalists in mind, Olga tells of the religious dilemmas faced by Tatar families with respect to education in Kazan and remarks on the government's lack of interest in educating the Tatars. She openly states her views on the morality of these matters and alludes to the controversy between two opposing factions. In questioning the policies of the Russian government towards 'non-Russians' and other members of ethnic minorities, she holds the government responsible; Olga observes that as imperialist conquerors, Russians have long left the Tatars as 'orphans' in whom no one has invested. She wrote:

> The teaching programme does not meet the demanding standards of current European civilization, which they are beginning to want to have. It is true that they are permitted to enter Russian secondary schools and universities, as well as all the other kinds of teaching establishments; but this does not suit them, because there one cannot learn either Arabic or Muslim sciences which are obligatory for every good Muslim; at the same time, they have so much to study that they don't have enough time for this.
>
> The few Tatars who have studied at secondary school know nothing about their religion, and overall are neither Christian nor Muslim. So, it is not fanaticism that prevents the Tatars from sending their children to secondary school, but the risks they run of seeing them forget their religion, that is to say that they have to choose the lesser of two evils: to keep their religion and stay ignorant of European civilisation or acquire this civilisation at the

cost of losing their religious ideas, forgetting their duties and even their nationality, without even acquiring more elevated moral principles.

All the wealthy Arabs and Turks who have been educated in Europe have lost their religion and their Muslim individuality; they have become Europeans through their ideas and their tastes; they did not take care to avoid acquiring the unpleasant habits of Europe. To avoid such drawbacks, the Tatars have requested the government to provide Muslim universities, where all the European sciences would be taught in Russian, the Muslim sciences in Arabic, several European languages.... Russia should establish a certain number of schools based on the French schools in Algeria and Tunisia...unfortunately our ministers are not of this opinion and find it more advantageous for the Russian government to leave the Muslims in their initial ignorance. In the more than three hundred years since Russia conquered [these lands] has she done the slightest step to bring them out of the shadows of their ignorance? No one is interested in them, or cares to approach them, to offer them affection.

We can also find whole villages where the Tatars do not understand a word of Russian and consider Russian people with the distrust that practising Muslims always have of the infidel. They have formed a government within a government and live completely separately from the Russians. It is not sufficient to conquer a people; one should manage the conquest, educate the people, and attempt to assimilate them whilst treating them with kindness and fairness. Where is the merit in one who by adopting an orphan sends him or her to the kitchen so that they do not die of hunger? Is it not a moral obligation to cultivate his heart and intelligence and on no account to prevent the option of him becoming a useful member of society? Who knows if one would not find amongst the Tatars people of talent who would serve our common country as well as their Russian brothers?[467]

In her support of just Tatar causes, like other Jadid thinkers, Olga warned against ignorance amongst the Tatars in her *Abrégé de l'Histoire de Kazan* referring to the certain aspects of their civilisation:

> The Islam which they [the Tatars] accepted without understanding, instead of enlightening them - due to the false interpretation which they had invented - only brought different customs created through their barbaric and fanatical ignorance. That is how even the finest ideas create tyranny in the narrow-minded: but *abusus non tollit usum* (transl. 'misuse does not preclude proper use') the Muslim religion when well interpreted is certainly one of the most reasonable religions and most compatible with modern civilisation.[468]

It is useful to note that the exhortation to Muslim society to 'wake from a sleep of ignorance' holding them back from making progress was a favourite Jadid metaphor which underlay all other considerations. Jadids argued that Islam required knowledge, and it was knowledge that allowed one to be a good Muslim.[469]

The labelling of the ignorance as 'fanatical' might be regarded as a politically loaded concept. Here, in Olga's writing, I take it as narrow-mindedness based on the Jadid critique of ignorance. European and Russian imperialists often used the term 'fanatical' to label indigenous political resistance to continued European control of their countries and thus viewed fanaticism as a justification for further imperial encroachments; the word was used indiscriminately by non-Muslims denoting their conscious, or unconscious, bias towards Muslim religious piety. Whereas detractors like Professor Ilminsky believed that Muslim societies were doomed to stagnate in rigid fundamentalism, in this extract we can see how Olga de Lebedeff is still defending the principles of Islam as being compatible with progress, whilst stressing the importance of education, broad-minded thinking and ideals of enlightenment.

Ilminsky wished to prevent Tatar integration into society. Olga, along with Radloff and other heads of the Russian-Tatar schools, believed that as citizens Muslims were owed the opportunity to assimilate properly and believed in the possibilities of change.

Olga used the terms '*sblizhenie*' (rapprochement) and '*sliianie*' (merging, sometimes translated as administrative integration) and '*tsivililizatsia*' (civilization) to describe cultural integration that could be hoped for. The approach of secular education provided by the state was a legacy of the Catherinian view of tolerance with respect to religious minorities. In the late nineteenth century, in the Kazan region, these views clashed with both Orthodox messianism and Russian cultural imperialism, key terms being Christianisation and Russification.[470] The missionaries' attitudes were prevalent both in the state and Russian society at large.

With respect to education, the missionaries' efforts were actually focussed on preventing Muslim integration into Russian society and on preserving the separateness of non-Russians. Both the missionaries and the Russian-Tatar school system intended to turn their students into loyal subjects.

As a scholar of Islamic studies and culture, Olga rejected biases towards Tatars as intolerance. She advocated that Islam was compatible with reason and progress. Russian attitudes towards Islam were otherwise ambivalent. However, amongst certain Russian Orientalists, like Nikolai Ostroumov - close to the colonial administration of Tashkent and a former student of Ilminsky - the view was that Islam was not compatible with progress.

The kind of written criticism she levied towards the Russian government for their failures post-conquest to educate, assimilate and treat the Tatars as equals was not repeated publicly (in print) in subsequent years; at least no surviving document to this effect has been identified. It is noteworthy that her Russian version of the *Abbreviated History of Kazan* (1899) was prepared for publication but did not pass the Tsarist censors.[471]

In future years, Olga was to channel her energies into teaching tolerance through secular cultural exchange through the foundation of a new Society of Oriental Studies in St Petersburg. In this venture, she was assisted by one of the great figures of Russian politics of the time, Sergius Witte, the then Minister of Finance.

Education for women and girls

The Society of Oriental Studies, which she founded in 1900 in St Petersburg, opened branches across the empire. Through this society, Olga was able to give voice to an aspect close to her heart: how in general, ordinary Muslim women had little opportunity in educational terms – both at home in Russia and abroad.[472] In 1900, she would refer with enthusiasm to the kind of charitable efforts in education for Muslim women in French Algeria and changes in the law there in a booklet she published in Russia and in France (this will be explored more fully in a later chapter).[473]

Aiming to bring the subject of education for girls to the fore in cities such as Tashkent, in 1901 she wrote to the editor of the *Turkestanskie Vedomesti* newspaper.[474] The letter explained that a new branch of her society in the city could help to establish schooling for girls in Russian and their native language bringing them the knowledge of European civilization. She advocated that the process of setting up the society would be quite straightforward.

Her view was aligned with other European women activists, that European civilisation had made great strides in humanitarian values and rights ahead of the East, and that through the advance of friendly relations between peoples the goal of permanent peace would be achievable. In her salon evenings devoted to questions concerning Russia's Muslims she doubtless described these sorts of views.

She proposed that with the right intention it was possible to achieve lasting friendly relations between peoples of different religions and nationalities, circumventing religious and political obstacles. With hindsight, scholars have noted that European imperialists including Russians accepted the civilizing mission of Europe in the world. Edward Said observed that imperialism was an educational movement.[475]

In the above mentioned letter, Olga de Lebedeff advocated the tuition of both Russian and the native language to girls to give them the best chance to learn about the world. She gave the example of successes in Algeria and Tunisia in the establishment of new schools and the education of young girls. Perhaps her belief was not that one language was superior to the other (i.e., Russian superior to a native language), but rather that the knowledge of both would lead to educational advantage in a changing and modernising world. Was this approach imperialistic or primarily practical?

CENSORSHIP AND DISCONTENT
Stories of famous women from Bulgar, Sarai and Kazan

A little later, work on women's rights and education began to be evidenced in Russia from other writers. Of note, it was Karimov's printing house in Orenburg which produced a book in 1903 by the Mufti theologian and educator Fakhretdin.

Rizaetdin Fakhretdin (1858-1936) was one of the first Tatar scholars to teach about women's rights in the Volga-Ural region, and he was aware that this would not be easy, since many stereotypes in traditional Tatar society would need to be overcome.

With similar themes to those in Olga's own work on women's emancipation, this book was called *Famous Women* (*'Мәшhур хатыннар'* in Tatar, transliterated as "*Mushur khatynnar*").

Writer Ilmira Gafiyatullina describes the content of this Tatar account of *Famous Women* as follows:

> In particular, this work *Mushur khatynnar* can be conditionally divided into several thematic blocks: The rulers of ancient states; Mothers, daughters, wives of kings of various dynasties: Ghassanids, Sassanids, Umayyads, Ayyubids, etc.; The closest circle of the Prophet Muhammad, his associates (səhəbulər); Mothers and Wives of the Prophets; Messengers of hadiths (məhəddisələr); Holy women in Islam (əyliyalur); Muslim women lawyers (fəkihəlur); Illustrious rulers of the East; Women Patrons of the Volga-Ural Region; Writers and Poetesses in the Islamic World; Preachers (vəgyizələr) and orators (khatybulər); Teachers of gymnasiums for girls (madurrisulur); Doctors (tabibulur); Women-calligraphers (yazu hənərendə mahirəlur).

> The collection also includes the biographies of Muslim women from Bulgar, Saray, Kazan; female heroes (bahadirlər); pilgrims (хаҗ idychelər), mothers of many children, etc. It is noteworthy that the book pays special attention to the biographies of women from the inner circle of the Prophet Muhammad (peace and blessings of God be upon him). And this is no coincidence, because, as you know, women of the early period of Islam

occupied a prominent social position, enjoyed great prestige among men. Their stories have inspired millions of women throughout the Islamic world. Based on their examples, the author of *Mushur Khatynnar* tried to encourage Tatar society to reform to provide women with rights and full education. [476]

More than seven hundred women are mentioned in the above text, from Islamic Spain through to the Middle East, Central Asia, Siberia, and the Far East. Fakhretdin outlined the activities of the wives of the prophet and their companions, rulers of ancient states, and those mothers and daughters who down the centuries left an indelible mark on the Muslim community.

Following the 1905 revolution, another activist succeeded in expanding education to women and girls: in 1906 in Bakhchisaray (Crimea), Gaspirali was allowed to start publishing a women's magazine called *Galyame Niswan* (Women's World) in Crimean Tatar. It was a supplement to his newspaper *Terjuman*, and in 1907 his wife became the editor. He had been campaigning unsuccessfully since 1887 for permission to publish a periodical for women. The topics in the new publication included the rights of women in Russia, the position of women in various countries, activities of famous women, tips for housekeeping and raising children, carpet weaving and embroidery; it published prose and poetry and corresponded with subscribers who were from as far away as Turkestan, Egypt, India and Japan. [477]

A new Tatar poem for Madame Gülnar

Fond appreciation for Olga's progressive ideas is still being recorded in print by modern day Tatars. The Tatar Encyclopedia published in 2005 in Kazan has an entry for Gülnar Hanum, describing her as a social activist and publicist, one who spoke out about the government policies of increasing Christianisation towards the Muslim people, the question of schooling, and who described the fight for emancipation and rights for Muslim women in different eras and Muslim countries.

CENSORSHIP AND DISCONTENT

In 2011, the Tatar poet Gazinur Murat wrote a poem dedicated to Olga's memory, which mentions several of the personalities mentioned in previous chapters including progressive reformers and scholars, and also the poet Fatikh Karim (son of Gilman Karimov).

The poem is translated into English for this volume below, entitled *Madame Gülnar («Гөлнар ханым»)*. The poet recalls Gülnar's support to Kazan's 'orphans', the incomprehension of the establishment, and the respect she engendered amongst Tatar intellectuals of Kazan.

It demonstrates the fact that Madame Gülnar is not forgotten today and has relevance to Tatarstan's reckoning of its own past. In referencing orphans, the poet may be speaking for survivors of Tatar oppression in the nineteenth and twentieth centuries. The term *Hoosh Kildenez!* means 'Welcome.'

Madame Gülnar (2011) by Gazinur Murat (b. 1959-) [478]

Let the last century's wild path be damned!
Quickly let its name be extinguished.
Why would our people matter
To the wife of Kazan's mayor?
Sarcastic folk snigger, has she lost her mind?
How does a refined Russian,
A woman, need Marjani?
Respectfully, she calls him Teacher.
Always speaks well in Tatar,
Studying with Qayyum Nasyri
In Persian, Tatar, and Turkish.
As the gates of forty gardens open up to her,
She greets the father of Karimov
With 'Welcome': *Hoosh Kildenez!*

She can talk with anyone,
Whether Arab or German.
But They do not understand her language,
Her own country is unfathomable!
Those nasty folks suspect her:
What does she want and why -
What would a woman, like Our Lady,
Want with the Tatars?
See, she seeks solace
For Kazani orphans!
Mindful and honouring
In troubled times.
See, she seeks a bright future
For us citizens without a home!
So holy men respect
And bless Olga Sergeevna.
At least one kind woman here
Understands our orphans' lot:
For she always greets us with the welcome: *Hoosh Kildenez!*

14 An Account of the Conquest of Kazan, 1899

> Our land is vast and abundant, but it is not well ordered.
> Russian saying

> To the orientalists at the congress of 1899: This essay is dedicated to you despite coming from my inexperienced pen. If it makes too poor an impression in comparison with works brought of more considerable erudition, I hope that they will forgive me for suggesting that I too, even though in a more modest fashion, would like to contribute to the advancement of 'Science' which draws us all here together. I trust that in this I may succeed![479]
> Olga de Lebedeff

At a time when little attention was being paid to the Tatars in Russian ethnography or Oriental Studies,[480] Olga de Lebedeff was actively engaged in this field. For Russians, Kazan was a window to the East and Islamic cultures. Olga produced her first article on this theme in 1893 called *The City of Kazan*, published in Turkish in Constantinople.[481] The intended audience was Ottoman, as Muslim Ottomans were interested in finding out more about Muslims in Russia.

Her monograph of ninety pages called *Abrégé de l'histoire de Kazan* [The Abbreviated History of Kazan] was published in Rome six years later. This was printed for a European and wider audience at the

XII International Congress of Orientalists (1899). It was one of the earliest descriptions of the history of the city and the Tatar people in a Western European language.

In 1854 the artist Edward Tracy Turnerelli had published a two-volume work on the history of the city in English. Kazan was, he said, a *terra incognita*. His account covered the city's founding up until a terrible fire of 1842. His lively anecdotes and favourable sketches of life in Kazan were written to arouse in his 'gentle readers' an interest in a place which he feels has been unfairly dealt with by foreign writers.

Olga's book was concerned primarily with the founding of the city by a series of Tatar Khans up until the dramatic final conquest by the Russians in 1552. Firstly, she introduced the history of the Volga –Kama region, then followed by these three sections:

Part I: On the frontiers of the Golden Horde and customs of the Khatun

Part II: On the History of the Khans, their infighting and demise

Part III: Several Considerations on the Tatar Civilization

In the third part, she reflected on the effects of the continued subjugation of the Tatar people by the Russians across the centuries and assessed the impact that coercive methods have had on Tatar education and freedoms. The edition made for the congress was finalized in Rome by the congress hosts, but several crucial pieces of information did not make the print run: omissions were photographs of Kazan plus amendments, references, and a dedication (see epigraph above).[482]

References and Sources

In some papers belonging to her daughter Nina Bahache, I found four photographs stuck onto pieces of cardboard with inscriptions underneath by Olga. The photos are slightly damaged and faded with the passage of time, but they are original copies of the ones Olga sent to

AN ACCOUNT OF THE CONQUEST OF KAZAN, 1899

Rome (Fig. 70, 71, 72 & 74). The other omissions mentioned above are included here too.

The range of references and sources found in letters to the Count de Gubernatis for this work is impressive:

- Ibn Battuta (1304-1368)
- Prince Andrei Kurbsky (1528-1583)
- Professor Sergei M. Shpilevsky (1833-1907) Legal historian
- Professor Nikolai Zagorskine (1851-1912) Historian of Russian law at Kazan
- Father Zariansky
- Mollah Chinab-ud-dine
- Frachu

An outline translation of Abrégé de l'Histoire de Kazan

Translated from the French, the following passages are an outline of Olga's text. Her book starts by specifying the connection between the khanates across the region. This was reflected in the provenance of utensils and armaments from Crimea which in turn arrived from Egypt and Constantinople:

> The Khans of the Crimea always entertained good relations with the Egyptian Sultans, who sent them rich gifts and precious objects of all kinds. They also sent them slaves, rare animals, horses, camels, monkeys, and parrots.[483]
>
> The khanates were interconnected along on the Silk Road long before they were discovered by Western explorers from Europe, and their stories remain little known in the West.
>
> Tatars had founded this city at the end of the fourteenth century, though as the stone weapons and ruined human habitations show [from an archaeological point of view], the land had been

inhabited from time immemorial, the names of whose ancient nomadic warrior peoples were described as the 'Tchoud, Tcheremisse, Meria, Mouroma, Vess, Mordva and Perm'.

On the right bank of the river Kazanka was the place which became known as the 'Old Town' of Kazan, the foundation of which is closely tied to the conquest of Eastern Europe by the Tatars, after the sacking of the 'great city' of the Bulgar Khans (a civilization much superior to their own) in the autumn of 1236 after several years of fighting.

The conquered Finnish tribes of the Votiaques and the Tcheremisses converted to Islam and became Tatars. The first fortified encampment called 'Yourt de Saïne' was set up by the Batu Saïne Khan ('the good, the generous') who sent his emissaries to search for a suitable place from which to observe the feats of the princes of Ryazan, Vladimir, and Moscow. The encampment enabled them to repulse Russian attacks, defended as they were by thick forests and marshes. It also was a convenient stopping off place for the Golden Horde and for other envoys and a place to survey the other tribes who lived around the right bank of the Volga, bordered by high places.

The place was situated in a kind of ravine surrounded by hills which is where the name 'Kazgan' – later Kazan – came from. Kazgan means 'cauldron' in Tatar. For over ten years there was complete calm in the region, which was only interrupted when Grand Duke Vasily Dmitrievitch [Basil I whose rule lasted 1389-1425 and who was enthroned without the sanction of the Golden Horde /CH] decided to show his anger at the Horde by invading Nizhni-Novgorod. This was followed by the pillaging of nearby towns of Rostov, Dmitrov, Serpukhov and Nizhi-Novgorod by Edigey, an Emir of the Khan Tokhtamysh, and ended with his siege of Moscow at Kolomensk. Subsequent squabbling between the Emirs and Khans of the Golden Horde ended by shaking the foundations of the kingdom, from which the frontier countries of Crimea and Kazan would soon detach. [484]

In **Part 1** of the book Olga continued to describe the second foundation of Kazan:

According to different historians this took place in either 1422 or 1437 by a khan of the Golden Horde called Oulou-Mohammed[d] (Oulou means the Great) who is considered the true founder of Kazan. Having fought back against the Grand-duke Vasily, he retired to Kazan and declared all the surrounding lands along the Volga riverbanks conquered, independent of the Horde, and named it the Kingdom of Kazan. He drew many inhabitants from the territories of the Horde, promising them a return to the sumptuousness of the times of Sultan Uzbek-Khan. This sultan possessed an immense empire, exterminated the enemies of Allah, and fought for the Faith; Sarai on the river Volga was his capital and here he had built a madrasa for the sciences, as he loved science and men of letters. According to the *Récit d'Ibn-Batuta* the Turkmen womenfolk played a key role in the affairs of the government since the times of Sultan Berke about whom it is written: 'the opinion of the Khatun (ladies) in this matter coincides with that of the Emirs.'[485]

Part 1 (ii) depicted the early connections between Kazan and the Golden Horde and the alliances with the princes of the Horde to the south in Astrakhan, Azov, and Crimea.

Other authors claim that the Old City of Kazan was founded by the eldest son of the last Khan of Bulgar, Altyn Bek several years after the kingdom of Bulgar was destroyed by Tamerlane ('Timour-Leuk') in 1397. Oulou-Mohammed founded a stronghold close to the old site, which had been ruined by the Muscovite army in 1399; but his new citadel was a kilometre and a half up on a hill, an improved strategic position. He made a new Horde by drawing a mass of Tatars from the Golden Horde at Astrakhan, Azov, and the Crimea. The legends concerning the era of the independent existence of Kazan begin and finish with the

---

[d] Also written as Ulugh Muhammad

myth of the winged serpent or dragon [the dragon was later emblazoned on the city's coat of arms], noting that the inhabitants of the Volga-Kama region were no strangers to the cult of serpents; the Arab Ibn-Fadlan visited Bulgar in the tenth century and claimed that the country abounded in snakes that no one killed. (Additionally, in the language of Muslim peoples, the serpent represents victory of Islam over the paganism of idolatrous natives of conquered lands). The Russian Chronicles lose trace of events for five years until 1445 when which Oulou Mohammed takes prisoner the Grand Duke of Muscovy, Vasily Vasilievitch [*Basil II*] at Suzdal. This triumph was short-lived. Hearing of conspiracies against him by his son, he released his prisoner and hastened back to Kazan. Here his two sons, Mahmoutek and Jacob, murdered him. Following this regicide there was a series of Muslim sovereigns who fought against the Grand Duchy of Muscovy for the next 107 years.[486]

In **Part II**, Olga de Lebedeff explains the rise of Kazan as an important political and commercial centre and the establishment of a famous fair (prior to the one at Nizhni Novgorod).

The last of the khans descending from Oulou-Mohammed dynasty, who were antagonistic to the Grand Duchy of Muscovy, died around 1518. However, the next Khan of Kazan, the grandson Ahmed of the Horde, was elected by the Russian Grand Duke Vasily Ivanovich [*Grand Prince Basil III Ivanovich of Moscow and All Rus, ruler 1505-1533*].

However, he was pushed off the throne by Sahib-Girei, the Crimean Khan's brother in 1521, who was hostile to the court at Moscow, but proved to be a cruel ruler. He consulted with the Ottoman ruler Suleiman the Great [*now referred to as Suleiman the Magnificent or the Lawgiver*], who proposed that Kazan be declared part of Turkey.

This infuriated the Muscovites who assembled a force of a hundred and fifty thousand men and in the battle that ensued one night in 1524 it was said that 60,000 Tatars lost their lives.

Fig. 71

Tatar Tower of Suyunbike (or Suyumnbeka) also known as the Mausoleum of Shah Ali Khan was the only surviving Tatar edifice. [487]

A new khan was invested on 29 June 1531, one who swore allegiance to the Grand Duke of Muscovy and after this time Russia enjoyed friendlier and more influential relations with Kazan. For a brief period, Djan-Ali Khan reigned peacefully. He married a Nogai princess, great granddaughter of Edigey, called Suymnbeka.

But a former pretender to the throne, the penultimate Khan Sefa-Girei, murdered Djan-Ali Khan in 1535. He was given the hand of the Queen Suyumnbeka; even so the khan became unpopular with his people. In 1545, under Ivan IV two Russian armies converged on the environs of the city burning and pillaging everything, without attacking the city itself.

Fig. 72

Portrait of Söyembikä, or Suyunbike regent of Kazan in 1549

In this city, to where Olga de Lebedeff had moved, and which was a bridge to Islamic cultures for her, it is significant that she wrote this history in 1899. She describes how the early vestiges of Tatar culture and history had been eradicated at the overthrow of the town by the Russians several centuries earlier in 1552; whilst the mosques from that early period and the Khan's palace were made of stone, the remainder of the buildings were made of wood and there was little trace of contemporary Tatar culture.

The stone *kremlin* built by Ivan IV in 1555 was almost entirely destroyed by the 'imposter Pugachev' in 1774.[488]

AN ACCOUNT OF THE CONQUEST OF KAZAN, 1899

Fig. 73
Kazan Kremlin. Original photos from Olga's collection

In an account about the demise of the Tatar civilization she emphasised the point: [489]

> Even at the heyday of the Muslim khans of Kazan, any civilisation there was the preserve of the elected few.[490] There were no local Tatar products beyond embroidery or ordinary objects for everyday use and no real art had remained. Though the khans, their wives, and people of the court (who were all foreigners) were undoubtedly educated people, their culture came from outside as the erudite Arabs, Persians and Turks who spent long stays in Crimea and might have travelled north …. as far as Kazan, but there is no certainty on this.
>
> Though by the end of the nineteenth century when there were approximately thirty thousand Tatars living in the city [*corrected*

by her later to 45,000[491]], Kazan was still a window to the East and important as a historic Tatar and vibrant Islamic cultural hub. 'Volga Tatars' were Hanafi Muslims, one of four religious Sunni Islamic schools of law predominant amongst the Ottomans and historic khanates or sultanates of Central Asia. The city had eleven 'médressé' (madrasas or colleges) run by Tatars themselves plus, five government primary schools and one 'Teachers' School' also founded by the government. [492]

The following is a summary of Part II, sections XIX and XX, which covers the final siege and battle for the city by Ivan the Terrible and his troops.

The reign of fourteen Muslim khans finally ended with over a month's siege of the city in September 1552 by the Russian forces of Ivan IV (Ivan the Terrible). The Tsar's proposal for *Kazanis* to submit themselves to him was rejected: "we do not fear you, and we will either all die, or we will save our city." [493]

Although the city was well defended against the Russian attack, a couple of fugitives told the Russians about the defensive battle plan and of a secret tunnel. The Russians troops blew up the underground tunnel with gunpowder, thus producing an enormous breach of the city wall, raining stones and earth over the inhabitants of the city. Now the city's clean water supply was cut off. The bloody battles that ensued finally ended on 2 October 1552. Ivan the Terrible made his triumphal entrance on 4 October preceded by his confessor bearing a Cross. The tsar chose a spot for a new cathedral to be built called the 'Annunciation of the Holy Virgin' and a small wooden church was put up and consecrated in a single day to mark the capture of Kazan. Tsar Ivan IV left after six days leaving behind a governor, dignitaries, and subalterns,

AN ACCOUNT OF THE CONQUEST OF KAZAN, 1899

three thousand infantry soldiers and a detachment of Cossacks. So ended the reign of the Muslim Khans of Kazan.

Fig. 74
Memorial Monument to the capture of Kazan 1552 (Family Collection)

The land registry of Kazan throws light on the fact that a military regime controlled the city during the second half of the sixteenth century. The mosques, the Khans palace and city towers were turned into munitions depots; it had the atmosphere of a town constantly under siege.

Tatars were forbidden to live within the city walls or to enter the city fortress. Ivan IV ordered a new stone kremlin to be built. (The word kremlin is Muslim in origin 'kharemlik' which would become the description of all fortresses or imperial palaces surrounded by walls in ancient Russia). [494]

However, taking the city of Kazan was not synonymous with subjugating the whole Kingdom of Kazan.[495] For six more years up till 1558 the aristocrats who had managed to save themselves did not cease in attempting to revolt in the surrounding areas: the Finnish tribes gave staunch support to the rebels, which did not cease even when one thousand five hundred and six thousand nobles, princes and mirzas from Kazan were killed. Their revolts continued till 1584. Till the end they had relied on help from Turkey, Crimea, Astrakhan, and the Nogai Horde. The Tsar felt obliged to exterminate all the rebels and almost all the Tatar people. However small insurrections continued into the seventeenth and eighteenth centuries, however, each time they were stifled.

Reflections on the text

In just seven years the city would fall dramatically for the last time to the Russian forces of Ivan the Terrible. In celebration, Ivan IV built St Basil's cathedral in Moscow's Red Square.

The conquest of Kazan and afterwards Astrakhan in 1559 by this Tsar crowned the first 'Tsar of all Russia', marked the beginning of Russia's expansion towards the east; it was an expansion beyond the lands occupied by Orthodox, ethnic Russians. The foundations for Russia's future empire were laid. This gave Russia control of the whole length of the Volga, down to its delta on the Caspian. It opened the way for an unimpeded advance across the Urals and into Siberia.

After Moscow's liberation from the Tatars, and the fall of Byzantium to the Turks the previous century in 1453, Russian monarchs now began to self-identify as the sole defenders of Orthodoxy. Just the Tatar domain in the Crimea was still under Ottoman suzerainty.[496]

AN ACCOUNT OF THE CONQUEST OF KAZAN, 1899

A Russian prophecy was born from the conquest of Kazan that four hundred years later, that 'in 1854 Constantinople would fall into the hands of the Russian Tsars.'[497]

Fig. 75
Original photograph of the military church, the old city wall, and the town hall (Family Collection).

From Olga's account, the Ottoman ruler Suleiman the Great [r.1520-66] proposed that Kazan should become part of Turkey, at a time when the Ottoman Empire was at its peak. The Ottomans had after all conquered eastern Hungary including Budapest and gone all the way to the gates of Vienna (inspiring, it is said, the croissant -with its crescent shape - and inadvertently introducing coffee to the city).[498]

If the Ottomans had controlled Kazan this would have changed the geopolitics in the region and in the minds of the conquered forever.[499] Amongst Sultan Suleiman's titles was 'Lord of Lords of the world, East and West'. The Ottoman expansion westwards during the sixteenth century had already 'started a craze for Turkish styles and artefacts – Europe's first experience of 'Orientalism''.

Alliances were being forged between Protestants in Northern Europe and the Ottomans against the Catholics; the Sultan was seen as 'Luther's best ally'.[500] As ostracised by Catholic Europe, Queen Elizabeth I had made a strategic trade alliance with Murad III, the then Ottoman Sultan. Still by the nineteenth century an alliance of trade and geopolitics would still hold good against the Ottoman's Orthodox neighbour to the north.

This account of the subjugation of the Volga Tatar peoples by the Russian armies explained much about the ongoing search for identity of the Kazan Tatars and why research into their own history and the Muslim religion itself became so important during the latter half of the nineteenth century.

As a curious aside, influence from the Tatar language remains to this day in several adopted loan words and sounds into Russian, especially those related to finance or war: for example, the words for money – *'dyengi,'* shop - *'magazin,'* bazaar - *'bazar,'* kiosk, deposit - *'zalog,'* and even the word for a Russian noble, a boyar - *'boyarin.'*[501]

Two more points of interest: the first, the style of men's clothing predominant till Peter the Great was the kaftan, a long suit or jacket; the second, prostration before those in authority (including in church). It is disputable whether the preference for strong leadership resulted from submission to the Tatar yoke.[502]

On the 'civilising' of Asia

Since Ivan the Terrible's conquest of Kazan, Russians ruled over Muslims for five hundred years. Observing how Russia gained its status as empire and its drive eastwards provides us with an interesting perspective on how Imperial Russia came to view its own Orient by the nineteenth century: a pan-Russian consciousness of being a unified nation in opposition to external enemies.[503]

The 'tsardom' lasted for one hundred and sixty years under different monarchs. But by the end of the sixteenth century, the Russians

AN ACCOUNT OF THE CONQUEST OF KAZAN, 1899

led by Cossack Ermak had crossed the Urals and captured the Tatar city of Sibir also called *Qashliq* or the Khanate of Turan. Sixty years later they had crossed Asia and reached the Pacific. It was only after the defeat of the Swedes in the Great Northern War of 1721, that Peter the Great adopted a new title for himself of *Imperator* or 'Emperor of all Russia' to reflect a homeland within European civilization and 'a vast, but foreign, extra-European colonial periphery', so transforming Russia's political identity and geopolitical self-image.[504] Expeditions continued across Siberia, despite all the obstacles and climatic hardships; Peter sent a Dane in the Russian Navy, Vitus Bering on an extensive expedition, which ultimately resulted in the discovery of the Bering Straits.

A century later, explorers, noble officers and scientists from the Russian Geographical Society, were expanding the empire's reaches ever further. They were inspired by European explorers like Captain Cook, David Livingstone, and Alexander von Humboldt, and especially the latter's Central Asian expedition of 1829. Members of this society helped shape the sense of imperial destiny and of their own nation through the fields of science and continental geography: 'imperial exploration with a national purpose'.[505]

One such champion of Russian colonization [who knew Olga de Lebedeff,[506] perhaps not least both their ancestors were in the Ismailovsky Lifeguards Regiment] was the Vice-President of the Russian Geographical Society: Pyotr Semyonov (1827-1914). Nicholas II later bestowed him with the name Tian-Shansky after the mountain range in Central Asia he had explored. Semyonov wrote that 'Russia moves forward, as Providence itself has ordained, in the general interests of humanity: the civilising of Asia'.[507]

The expeditions served to promote Russian expansion and colonization, with the aim of bringing European civilization to the Far East; achievements they envisaged as comparable to the colonies of Spain, France, and England. In 1886 Semyonov referred to Prezhevalskii, a famous explorer of China and Tibet as 'a pioneer gathering the scientific material that is necessary for the definitive conquest of these [Asian] lands for culture and civilisation.'[508]

However, in the mid-nineteenth century Pan-Slavist scientists such as Nikolai Ia. Danilevskii strove to distance Russia from Europe. They downplayed Europe's presumed superiority in all things, affirming the gradual flowing of Russian-Slavic colonists into empty territories across a single dominating contiguous, 'unipartite' landform, a "natural geographical region". [509] Danilevskii's ideas included that 'great civilizations had been created not only by Europeans but also by Asians, using China and Egypt as the main examples'.[510]

There had been a lack of serious study about the Tatars or their language at the University of Kazan or within the O.I.A.E. society. Olga and some of the older Orientalists like Professor Gottwald considered that the intellectual development of the Tatars had not progressed since the time of the Russian conquest.

In 1893, Gaspirali presented the common complaint amongst Muslim intellectuals:

> It is completely true that our Muslim people are one of the most backward, the level of their knowledge and the productivity of their labour and industry stagnate behind necessary and desirable levels.[511]

The question of neglect and lack of development is addressed by Olga in **Part III** of her history of Kazan:

> In subjugating the Tatars, the Russians left them freedom of conscience, and did not oppress them in any way; but on the other hand, they did not concern themselves with civilizing or educating them, with the result that there is not any difference between the intellectual development of a Tatar from the year 1552 to a Tatar in the nineteenth century.
>
> Therefore, since the Russian conquest of Kazan, this ancient civilization has not developed. This is almost the opposite of what we could support. From where in fact could the Tartars draw the essential culture for the life of their people?
>
> From the Russians? The Russians kept them apart and were pleased with this, perhaps to better maintain their domination by letting them live in ignorance; and besides, at the beginning of this domination, the Russians themselves were scarcely more enlightened: the same ignorance, the same fanaticism, the same

persecutions exercised by some in the name of Mohammed, by others in the name of the Orthodox religion and all saints.

From the Orientals? Since 1552, these had sent only their merchants to Kazan. Moreover, the few descendants of the Tartar aristocracy who had escaped the massacres, who survived the conquest and who could have exercised a civilizing influence on the mass of the people, converted to Christianity and immediately mingled with the Muscovite aristocracy." [512]

Although Olga de Lebedeff and Professor Gottwald blamed the neglect and lack of advancement of the Tatars on the policies of the Russian government, it is worth noting Olga's opinion of education amongst Russian peasants in general. In a letter to Count de Gubernatis from 1899, she gives details of the state of affair in the countryside:

> The officers of the Red Cross are looking after matters in the needy villages; it is very necessary, but it also makes peasants so lazy that they don't want to work; they say that the Tsar will not let them die of hunger.
>
> Our peasants are very demoralised and need a completely different education system than the one that exists in Russia. It is not for nothing that the ancient Rus begged the Varangians to rule over them saying: *Our land is vast and abundant, but it is not well ordered.* This situation continues in many senses. We only have external order maintained by the police, but the majority is uneducated. [513]

The Abbreviated History of Kazan describes some of the ongoing tensions between the Russian authorities and the Kazan Tatars. As already mentioned, Olga had prepared a Russian version of the text, but it did not get published: the centuries old mutual mistrust still remained through differences between their religions, written and spoken languages and cultural identities.

PART III: AWAKENING

15 Letters to Tolstoy & on the Unity of Religion

> All your views, of every kind, are of utmost importance to me.
> Olga de Lebedeff, Letter to Tolstoy, 1894

Leo Tolstoy, who generally refused to be addressed as Count, wrote to *'The Russian Gazette'* and *'New Times'* on 16th September 1891. Here he made a statement, much to his wife's annoyance, which allowed anyone who wanted to publish or translate his works 'which have been written by me since 1881' to do so free of charge in Russia and abroad, either in Russian or in translation. This was a public renunciation of his copyright.[514]

Dear Sir, Count Lev Nikolayevich!

Having already translated and published five of his works in the Ottoman capital, it was only afterwards in the summer of 1894 that Olga introduced herself to Tolstoy. Writing from her countryside estate at Lubiana on 23 June 1894, she informed him about the translations and said that she was happy to answer any questions he might have on the Turkish civilization and way of life.[515]

Her mission to educate the Ottomans about Russia and European culture and vice versa (a goal shared with Ahmed Midhat), is played out in this correspondence.[516]

> Working on Oriental languages, I have studied in special depth the Turkish language and its literature. With this aim in mind, I spent some time in Constantinople and got to know many intellectuals. This gave me the chance to see for certain that they could avidly enjoy your wonderful works in French translation and could appreciate your genius through them. Their popular writer, a moralist and novelist, Ahmed Midhat has translated *The Fruits of Education* into Turkish and published it in his newspaper 'The Interpreter of Truth' (*Terjuman-i Hakikat*). Wishing to acquaint them further with the thoughts of my great fellow countryman, the pride of each patriotic heart, I dared to take it upon myself, without your permission, to translate several of your short stories such as *Family Happiness, Ilyas, Two Old Men* and *What Men Live By*. Unfortunately, due to extremely rigid and absurd censorship, the choice of works was very difficult, and one just had to be limited to these.[517] All the translations enjoyed much success and were in great demand. *Family Happiness* was retranslated into Arabic and published in a newspaper in Beirut.

Those stories contained all themes that were approved by Ahmed Midhat. In the second letter to Tolstoy, dated 1 August 1894, she responded to Tolstoy's friendly reply saying:

> Please do not think, dear Count, that it will be difficult to answer your questions. On the contrary, it will be an immense pleasure for me, and if I don't know something, then I will endeavour to learn everything that you want to know.[518]

She described how Turks lived and the constraints of state control imposed upon Ottoman society, even high-ranking officials:

> In Turkey there are many newspapers, but they are all devoid of content. Half of the newspapers are full of panegyrics to the Sultan. And the other half consists of articles from foreign

newspapers and novels translated from French. There is incredible censorship....[519]

Another female writer of the time was more categorical. Mary Mills Patrick, an American living in Constantinople for several years, wrote later that during the years 1876-1908, the very idea of progress had been prohibited.[520] This was a sentiment Olga had previously countered, but the outcome of her experience in the city had evidently led to some disappointment.

There were subsequently three other letters to the famous novelist, now kept at the Tolstoy Museum. Of this written record, Dr. Hülya Arslan from Okan University in Istanbul writes:

> What most excited me in these letters, the originals of which I saw at the Lev Tolstoy Museum in Moscow, was the approach of Olga Lebedeva. As Olga Lebedeva saw it, a language she learnt was not just a medium of scholarliness to be restricted within the lines and pages of books or to be used for mutual comprehension by people belonging to different societies whenever they met each other for whatever reason. Neither her family's nobility and great wealth, nor the fact that that she was the spouse of someone who had risen to the rank of governor constrained her. As someone who was deeply attached to the language and culture that she had learnt, she tried to instill the values of her own society, which she represented, in Turkish society; but at the same time, she also tried to make unknown aspects of the Ottomans and Turks understood or at least known in Russia. [521]

Fears about hostility towards Christians

Olga also shared her anxiety about the kindling of hatred in Turkey towards Christians (following the first Hamidian massacre of Armenians at Sasun that year). [522] This was now a theme that was closer to home, as Olga's daughter was a Christian, married to an Ottoman Christian.

Tolstoy had studied some Turkish at Kazan University and had a long-standing interest in the Turks and their culture. He was also a pacifist having been influenced by letters from British and American Quakers[523] (though he did not agree with women being 'liberated by Christianity').[524]

Fondness for the Turkish people can be seen in Olga's second letter to Tolstoy (1 August 1894):

> I want to tell you that I love Turks and Muslims very much…. They have many characteristics in common with us. Peasants live in poverty in this fertile land. The reason for this is the way the landowners confiscate the crops. The people are extremely docile, good-natured, and deeply devout. They are kind not just towards Christians, but also towards all living creatures. They believe in fate to such a degree that they accept everything they consider to be God's will.

Parallel text on the unity of religion (1894)

For some time, Olga had been reflecting on the similarities in Islam and Christianity. Her thoughts revolved around publishing a book to bring about rapprochement between Russia and Turkey, as well as for Christians and Muslims in Russia.[525] Her letter dated 1 August 1894 began in this way:

> Dear Count, for the last three years I have had an idea that I have been mulling over. I want to write about the shared characteristics of Christianity and Islam. Also, since there are many Muslims living on Russian lands, I think that this would be beneficial for both communities. I intend to extract lines from the Quran and Gospel that resemble one another, to comment on them, and compile a book. I shall be very happy if you would like to read the preface that I have written, dear Count. However, if on the other hand you think that I am an unrealistic dreamer, please tell me so openly. All your views, of every kind, are of utmost importance to me.

On 18 August 1894 she sent him the draft she was writing. Though draft itself has not survived, we know from his reply that in a 'Prologue' she had outlined the common moral ideals of Christianity and Islam; she proposed how the texts of both holy books could be shown to demonstrate a converging of religious values. His reply was this:

> This is a very important issue, as you have said you have devoted your life to it. For this reason, I will tell you directly what I think.

He found the aim attractive. He agreed that it was a fine, good idea in principle, but stressed that the prologue she had already written needed to be reworked many times:

> [it should be re-written] at least twenty- or thirty-times making use of everything that has been written on the subject to date ('the articles by Max Müller on the question of the unity of religion are excellent') to ensure it met with the kind of reception that you intend. Please forgive me for my blunt honesty and receive the assurance of my complete respect.

Tolstoy himself was prone to 'write and revise everything innumerable times.'[526] Having had the difficulties in undertaking such a venture pointed out, Olga thanked Tolstoy and promised to rework the prologue. Till now, it was believed that this project did not see the light of day. In historian Shifman's view, the political conditions were not yet right for such a publication either in Russia or in Turkey; Russian officials then saw the massacres as a manifestation of the fact that the Ottoman Empire was 'in an advanced state of decay.'[527]

However, despite no surviving manuscript, there are two pointers that Olga did write on this topic. The first evidence is that in September 1894 she sent the Geneva Congress some leaflets she had authored in Arabic and Turkish for distribution;[528] she later refers to the information being in Turkish, French, Russian, English, German and Arabic. Seeing it as a campaign [*propagande*] she called for 'the need to reject all petty feelings of nationalistic or religious enmity; and to extend the hand of friendship to the peoples of the East. To go forward with them towards a truth proved by reason and lit up by science....in order to build lasting relationships beyond politics or religion'.[529]

Both a biography in an Arabic journal Fatat al Sharq (1907) and a short biographical account written by Isabella Grinevskaya (1864-1944) quote that Olga wrote an article on the *Unity of the Religions*.[530]

This interest in Theology and the religious textual comparisons reveals that instead of polemical studies of the Russian missionary theologians at Kazan for instance, Olga was interested in inviting dialogue and a more inclusive concept: one that stressed the common spiritual element which if embraced would lead to societies of different religions that could live peacefully together. [531] She, like other contemporary intellectual thinkers, recognised how exploring the intertwining legacy of both Islam and Christianity could serve as a base for greater understanding.

The next year she finished another translation of Tolstoy's works, a short story: *Master and Man*.

Babis and Baha'i

The exchange with Tolstoy then took a new, but related turn. Olga introduced him to the ideas of the Persian preacher called Ali Muḥammad (1812-1849) from Shiraz. Between 1840-1844, he was known as the Bab, a mystical name meaning *The Gate of Knowledge* or *The Door of Truth*. He was hailed by some as a messiah figure. The Bab did not reject Islam but preached that one should not live merely by the letter of the law, but by its spirit through contemplation. After repression of the movement, the followers of the Bab, the 'Babis', made a formal break with Islam in 1848.[532] The Bab was one of the forerunners of the Baha'i. After years of persecution in Persia, many Baha'i families made a new life in the Russian Empire in Ashkhabad, Transcaspia.[533]

In a follow-up letter on 18 August 1894, Olga told Tolstoy: "I have even found a Muslim sect very close to Christianity, by means of which it might be possible to affect the unification of Muslims with Orthodoxy. This is the sect of Babids or Babis. You have heard of it?" He wrote back to her on 22 August, but there is no copy of this letter.

Two weeks later, on 3rd September 1894, Olga de Lebedeff summarized the Babis' theology, listed their sacred books, and described their current situation in the Ottoman Empire. Although Tolstoy still welcomed her attempt to find common ground between Islam and Christianity, on 4th September 1894 he warned that a mechanical juxtaposition of similar passages from the Quran and the gospels would do little to further the unity of religions: he contended it would be better to gather the passages expressing the following:

> [the] fundamental vital experiential-moral religious truths, which are...identical in all religions, and second [to show] that Christianity and Islam have the same sources and they differ only in their deviations from these sources, and that it will only require Christians from their perspective and Muslims from theirs to abandon these deviations and both religions will then inevitably coincide.[534]

Fig. 76
Letter to Tolstoy at Tula [535]

On 12th September 1894, Olga sent a pamphlet translated from Persian about the Bab, and notes about the Babists by the Russian Orientalist and military man Alexander Tumansky, who had had friendly relations with the Baha'i at Ashkhabad.

Tolstoy's diary entry of 16th September 1894 records his feelings that day, that though all was going well, he was feeling sad. He read his day's correspondence including Olga's letter and article about the Babists, without finding anything of major significance.[536] On the evening of 21 September he wrote back to her again and another letter to his assistant Chertkov. Dated 22 September the letter said that he said he had found the information about the Babists interesting, and asked to borrow some books she had in English if 'you could spare them…I will make sure to return them'. He added:

> "I was glad to know that you took my advice so kindly about corrections to your prologue and with which intentions to follow it".[537]

The Baha'i advocated equality between men and women; they saw women as playing a predominant role in the establishment of world peace, and gender equality as a precursor to peace. One can see how the latter intentions of the Baha'is would tally well with Olga's own views on these subjects; she must have seen them as enlightened ideas, albeit very far from what was acceptable to many of her friends in Constantinople, who would see the Baha'i religion as heretical. Tolstoy, for his part was not particularly interested in women's emancipation per se. Their correspondence on the matter ends.

However, it was not the end of Tolstoy's interest in the subject, according to his response to the five-act play *The Bab* by Isabella Grinevskaya, which was later recounted by Tolstoy's secretary, Valentin Bulgakov:

> Count Tolstoy read this drama Bab with great interest and sent a letter to Mrs Grinevsky praising her work and telling her he was in sympathy with these teachings of the Baha'i Movement. His letter to her was published in the press of Russia. Next Count Tolstoy read a booklet by Mr. Arakewian that described further the history of the early followers of the Bab and gave a short account of the teachings. He studied it with eager interest … Count Tolstoy's heart and soul were in all universal movements like the Baha'i Movement that aim at the unity of all humanity.[538]

A year later Tolstoy would become much more interested in the fate of the persecuted Caucasian sectarians in the south of Russia called the Dukhobors. In a letter to the Editor of 'The Times' (10 September 1895) he explained his thoughts on persecution and how to deal with it:

There is only one way to help the persecuted, and more particularly the persecutors who know not what they do – publicity – the presentation of the case before the court of public opinion which, having expressed its disapproval of the persecutors, will restrain the former from their cruel acts, often only perpetrated out of darkness and ignorance, and keep up the spirits of the latter and give them comfort in their sufferings. [539]

However, in view of Olga's correspondence with Tolstoy, it may be significant that in 1909 - 1910 he published a pamphlet entitled *Muhammad's Sayings Not Present in the Quran*, [540] based on a selection of hadiths.

Despite Tolstoy's earlier recommendation to Olga, there is no record of direct correspondence with the Professor of Sanskrit and comparative religion Max Müller. [541] However, substantial correspondence has been found with another professor of Sanskrit, who was based at Rome University: a person who was interested in her ideas, and who in time, would become her new mentor.

16 The Draw of Cairo

> I have been twice to the Vice-Queen Mother, who is still young and beautiful.
>
> Olga de Lebedeff

The world of eastern religious thought, ancient and modern, was a fascinating subject for Olga and her fellow Orientalists. Her wide range of friends and acquaintances in the field of Oriental Studies included specialists in comparative religion. Amongst her correspondents were Russians, Ottomans and Europeans.

The largest surviving collection of her letters found outside of Russia is kept at the Biblioteca Nazionale Central in Florence: twenty-seven letters in the archive of Count Angelo de Gubernatis (1840-1913), a prominent Italian Orientalist.[542] Written over a ten year period, dating from 1898 to 1908, they cover several important life events: Olga's first visit to Egypt, her mother's death, the founding of the Society of Oriental Studies and notes for the publication of her book *Abrégé de l'histoire de Kazan*. Except for two in Italian, they are all written in French.

The Italian Count de Gubernatis

By the Count's own admission, he was '*a tireless worker, an indomitable fighter, an incorrigible idealist*'.[543] One of the greatest objectives of his intellectual life had been to make his country better appreciated abroad and vice versa. Many of these Orientalists had similar goals, not least as communicators between different countries and cultures. De Gubernatis also became a firm advocate and activist for the peace movement including writing plays in verse on the subject.

Count de Gubernatis was Professor of Sanskrit in Florence and then in Rome. A prolific writer, including essayist and playwright, he founded several journals and set up the Italian Asiatic Society. He established an Indian Museum in Florence. He was a regular attendee and at the International Congress of Orientalists including at St Petersburg (1876), Florence (1881) and Stockholm (1889). At Geneva (1894) on the penultimate evening, 'he made a brilliant speech in praise of the city of Geneva and the lady visitors'.[544] He was Secretary General of the Florence Congress and the President of the organising committee at the two-week Rome Congress in 1899.

Fig. 77
Golden embossed monogram with initials O.L. [545]

Alongside his intellectual studies on India and Asia he studied classical and contemporary European literature. He had a longstanding interest in Russia. Indeed, he was married to a Russian called Sophie de Gubernatis Besobrasoff. She was the sister of a Russian economist and senator,[546] and a cousin of the famous exiled anarchist revolutionary Michael Bakunin (1814-76), who also advocated full equality between women and men. The Count's 'excellent wife' as Olga called her, was a translator of Russian works into Italian: Turgenev (*Spring Waters* and *Virgin Soil*) and Lermontov (*The Demon*). Their daughter Cordelia, to whom Olga frequently referred to as 'charming', was on friendly terms with Olga's daughters, Vera and Olga.

As a man of letters, the Count encouraged women writers to take part in intellectual pursuits; his sister Terese Mannucci de Gubernatis was an educationalist and had been the director of schools for girls at primary and secondary level as well as a novelist, his other sister Caroline was also the head of school: l'Istituto Bellini in Novara.[547] In 1881 he had founded an educational journal for young girls called *Cordelia*.

The Count clearly appreciated and believed in the ability of women to be accomplished writers. Amongst his female correspondents with pen names was Dora D'Istria, author of *Women in the Orient*,[548] who lived in Florence; and the writer Marchioness Maria Majocchi Plattis (1864-1917) known by the pseudonym of 'Jolanda', who became the editor of the later more entertaining *Cordelia*.[549] He published his sister-in-law Lezi Bezobrazov under the pen name of Tatiana Svetloff in his magazine *Rivista Europea*.[550]

As organiser of the 1899 Rome Congress, the Count invited three women to present their work: Zelia Nutall, an American archaeologist expert on Mexican codices, Emmeline Plunkett (British) on the astronomy of the *Rigveda*, and Olga de Lebedeff on the history of Kazan and a talk on Muslim women at the time of the Caliphs.

De Gubernatis invited Olga to become a member of the Italian Asiatic Society and she was honoured to accept; offering to give a report to the Italian Asiatic Society on the history of the International Congress of Orientalists. She subscribed to the Count's monthly magazine called *Vita Italiana*.

From the length of her first letter in Italian from Cairo in March 1898, following her visit to meet him and his family in Rome, we can at once tell there is a warm friendship between Olga and the Count, and that he has become something of a mentor.

Other early letters concern her upcoming participation at the Rome Congress in September 1899, where he encouraged and guided her in his capacity as congress President for the organising committee. In them, Olga expressed her estimation and affection for the Count saying that he, together with the Choskvitvoffs, are her dearest friends in Rome.

When they met there, the Count gave Olga lessons in Sanskrit - 'language of the Devas'; for this reason, she calls herself his 'disciple' (in Sanskrit: *shishya*), signing her letters as 'your devoted', 'affectionate' or 'respectful disciple'. She also calls him 'dear venerated guru' or 'dear friend' and after her absence from Rome, resolves to take up the study of Sanskrit on her own. In his early days, De Gubernatis espoused radical political views, but these mellowed with age. His wide sphere of interests, ranging from literature and the peace movement to an appreciation of

Eastern religions would render him extremely interesting company.[551] Some of his views on religion were quoted in an article in the Proceedings of the Florence Congress of Orientalists:

> One thing is certain, no quarrels would happen in the world if egoism did not predominate, alike with individuals and nations, if Christian charity were not a dead letter, if religion, on which so much is spoken and written, for which people and governments profess to strive so hard, had only some true and deep efficacy on life. But religious dogmas are learned like Greek and Latin, in order that people may know something about them, not with the view of putting them into practice. The habit of meditating on the practical obligations that a knowledge of religious truth imposes is but slight. Few, I repeat, seek to confirm the actions of their lives to it. If only [they] did so, and got a rule of life for all, new studies in religion would be superfluous. I think more serious occupation of the mind with the subject is needed and should be placed at the foundation of our life. [552]

To make the subject better known, in 1902 he published a five act play in Italian verse, entitled *The Buddha*.[553]

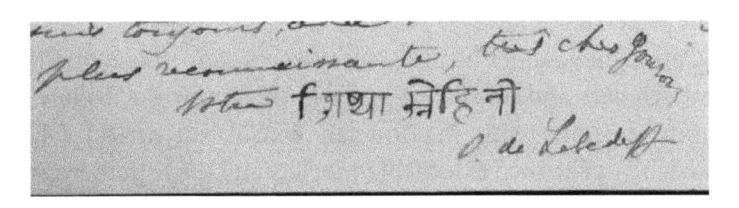

Fig. 78
Signed 'your affectionate disciple' in Sanskrit.[554]

First impressions of Cairo (1898)

It is through a letter to Angelo de Gubernatis that we learn of Olga's first visit to Cairo. [555]

In March 1898, she wrote to the Count towards the end of her stay from the Hotel Continental. As she planned to visit Beirut for two weeks on the way back to Italy, she hoped to visit the Count's brother, Henri, whom he had told her was the Italian Consul there. She wrote in Italian: 'Dear Count and distinguished *Maestro*' please have the kindness to let him know about me so that when he gets my letter it will not be a surprise ('*Vengo dunque a pregarlo di aver la bontà d'informarlo sulla mia persona affinché non sia sorpreso, quando riceverà la mia carta*').

She continued that she had first arrived by boat from Naples to Alexandria. Even in the cooler months, the climate proved difficult to get used to:

> As for me, I was very unlucky during the first part of my stay in Egypt. I arrived during an unseasonably cold spell; then came the '*hamssin*' when clouds of sand rose to the sky. Gradually it has got warmer, but this wind is very unsettling, and the noise in the hotels and streets - unbearable; there is no quiet. In this place all they think about is charging us foreigners extortionate prices...

The crowded, atmospheric streets with their latticed windows and minarets nosily bustled with myriad bargaining shopkeepers, tall camels, pedestrians, and veiled women some riding donkeys. As the weather changed to be 'like a furnace', the temperature reaching forty-three degrees Centigrade, even at night the outside temperature was too hot to open the window.

Cairo, then under British rule, was host to some of the most eminent scholars and intellectuals of the Muslim world. Following the usual introductions with the Russian consul, on arrival Olga was fortunate to be presented to local high society and made numerous useful international contacts. Her letter referred to meeting learned men of the country and a good Arabic teacher. She also recalled the sadness at the death of the illustrious French Orientalist Monsieur Shefer, who in his dying delirium was reciting verses in Persian.

> I came down with flu and was so ill that I had to forgo the pleasure of visiting the Upper Nile, and instead go to Helouan [Helwan: CH], a small village in the desert, known for its clean air. After being a recluse in that prison for more than three weeks, I returned to Cairo; and it's only now in the last days of my stay here that I have found a very good teacher of Arabic; I have made

THE DRAW OF CAIRO

many acquaintances in the 'harems' and with learned men of the country.

Following all the initial problems with illness and in adjusting to the climate and way of life there, plus the visits and lessons, Olga professed to not having had time to write anything for the congress yet; but she had translated, studied and 'tried to acquire some religious and moral influence: which I try to acquire in all Muslim countries - and which could work well for a book for the Congress'. This suggests that she already had in mind to contribute to the next congress, which would be organized by the Count de Gubernatis in Rome the following year.

One great outcome of her stay was that thanks to the Consul's wife and a new friend, the well-connected Contessa della Sala, she received many invitations to harems. This included visits to the *Vicereine*, who held receptions every Tuesday and were quite a feature in the social life of the city:

> The wife of our consul Madame Koyander is a good person, *'simpatica'* and very intelligent; the Contessa della Sala (a Russian married to an Italian) is an excellent person. These two ladies treat me as if I were their relative, and they take me to meet all the important people of the country.
>
> I have been twice to the Vice-Queen Mother, who is still young and beautiful. I attended a very interesting wedding; the party cost one hundred thousand francs. There were (dreadful) dances, music and singing, and a splendid buffet. The bride was dressed in white satin covered in gold, with a long veil of a fine golden fabric, a diadem very heavy with diamonds and threads of gold that hung on both sides of her head to her shoulders. Entering the hall, she was preceded by richly dressed women, who sang a melancholic tune, clapping with their hands on drums shaped like large bottles. The bride came towards them, supported by two friends, and two others held her train. They led her to a small platform at the end of the room with two armchairs around which were beautiful plants that formed a kind of tent overhead.'

Fig. 79

Period Postcard of Cairo (Family Collection)

After this first visit, Olga would return many times to Cairo, a place she felt increasingly drawn to - the Nile even reminded her of the River Volga back home.

THE DRAW OF CAIRO

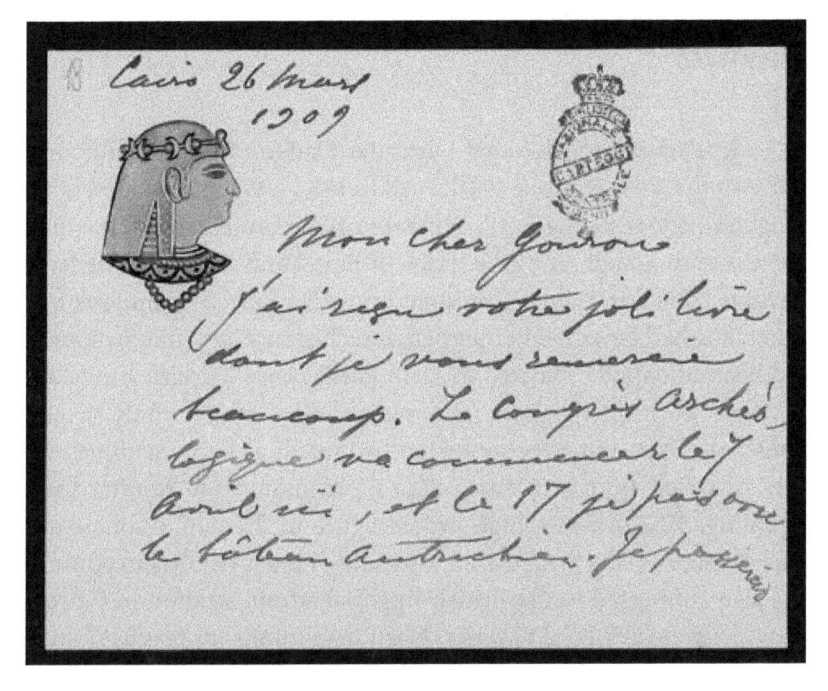

Fig. 80
Postcard to the Count [556]

Arriving in November when many hotels were still closed, she stayed until spring at the grand four storey Hotel d'Angleterre, a family hotel located centrally in the Ismaili quarter. She always took Arabic lessons with a sheikh at the al-Azhar University. She continued to meet many local and international scholars, religious leaders and certain women writers.

Society in Cairo was described by one traveller at the time as a perfect kaleidoscope of new faces and strange encounters. But friendships from here would be enduring. One such friend was Countess della Sala who had access to the high society harems. Countess della Sala had lived in Cairo since before the British Occupation.[557] Renowned for her quick wit, she was intimate with the Cromers, Princess Nazli and with the leaders of the foreign colonies and provided Olga with all the best introductions.

Famous women: Princess Nazli and Zaynab Fawwaz

It is most probable that Olga met Princess Nazli in 1898 on her first visit to Cairo. Princess Nazli Fazil (c.1852—1913) was eldest of three daughters of Mustapha Fazil, Minister of Foreign Affairs of the Sultan; she was granddaughter of the Pasha of Egypt and a niece of the famous Khedive Isma'il in Cairo.[558] Brought up with a European outlook by her father, she had bewailed her perpetual seclusion as a young woman. She had been unhappily married to Halil Pasha, once Turkish Ambassador in Paris and thirty years her senior. The couple only lived in Constantinople, and after taking her two maids as his concubines, Nazli later divorced him with the Sultan's permission for ruining himself gambling.[559] Nazli was a high-profile figure in the public sphere at the time of Olga's visits to Cairo, an associate of the jurist Qasim Amin. She was also connected to the British Imperial administration in Cairo and so associated with Lord Cromer. Nazli held salons, or teas as they were known, with the intellectual elites of the day. She received male visitors every afternoon, opening her palace to the diplomatic corps and their wives, receiving them with her face unveiled.[560] Thus, her salons became known as the 'Nazli circle', and hers was something of a political salon.[561]

Nazli was involved in 'women's rights' but not in a way that everyone approved. She was joint president of the *Alliance des Femmes* [Women's Alliance], an association which aimed to foster peace through education. The aims of this society were to provide mutual assistance and understanding between Eastern and Western countries, by encouraging friendship in the interests of 'permanent peace'. These aims are quoted in Olga's work *On the Emancipation of Muslim Women*, translated here in Book Two.

Another writer living in the city who attained renown was Zaynab Fawwaz (1860-1914), a Lebanese Shi'i Muslim. Her book donated to the Chicago exhibition Women's section some years before had arrived in time for the start of the exhibition; it was sent as a gift and a presence for Arabic women at the Exposition. Her Arabic biographical dictionary on famous Muslim women was called *Scattered Pearls on the Generations of the Mistresses of Seclusion* and, as the title suggests, comprised life histories of women in their generations. Writing biographies of so-called exemplary women in Islamic circles was a well-formed literary tradition, and the genre was encapsulated in the term 'Famous Women'. Accounts of exemplary women revealed to readers what they could aspire to and what they might also be able to achieve (a 'new model of selfhood').[562]

Fawwaz was one of the first women 'to participate in an emerging discourse on gender's centrality in Egypt's struggle to wrest independence from colonial subjection'.[563] Of Fatma Aliye, she praised her for her exemplarity, writing:

> One source of pride for the secluded women of Islam, unequalled by Eastern and Western women alike. She lives in Istanbul. May God increase her likes, and with her may God extend the sciences and learning to our female sex.[564]

A history of heroines: Young Woman of the East

Several years later, an Arabic biography of Olga came out in Cairo in a new woman's journal called *Fatat al-Sharq* [*Young Woman of the East*] under the title 'Famous Women'. The journal, founded in 1906 by Labiba Hashim (1880-1947), a Syrian Christian resident of Egypt, provided a collective history of heroines and their life narratives. It covered historical and literary articles and stories by women, emphasizing unity among Muslims and Christians, Syrians and Egyptians.[565]

A whole section was dedicated to inspiring women throughout the Middle East and advocated women's liberation and their right to education and political participation. Celebrated was the idea of women's awakening, important to the success of a wider cultural and nation-based challenge to the dominance of the West.

The journal announced in 1906 that it would publish items about women famed for their refinement and knowledge. The biography of Olga de Lebedeff was featured here on 15 April 1907. Being included in the journal as a subject was notable because despite having an Oriental sounding name of Gülnar, or *Jullanur* in Arabic, Olga was not from the

Middle East, but had come to Egypt. A translation of this was shared with me by Marilyn Booth and may be found here in Book Two.

The accounts of famous women published by the above authors in Cairo were not only a means of honouring the memory of exemplary women but provided encouragement to others to envision their own future.

17 THE CALL FOR WOMEN'S EMANCIPATION

> I have always been personally devoted to the cause of emancipation of Muslim women - within the limits indicated by their Prophet - who founded a religion which is perfectly compatible with all modern advances, on condition that it is correctly interpreted and bound with sincerity...
>
> O. de Lebedeff, Algiers 1905

Towards the turn of the century, the international women's emancipation movement was gathering momentum. Not all European women were behind it, due to divisions of class, status, colour or religion, and so unity was hard to achieve.

The call for Muslim women's emancipation in those days was controversial, even though it was not totally new. The Babists and the Baha'i already advocated equality between men and women. In Persia in the year 1848, one of the followers of the Bab, Fátimih Baraghání (*Tahirih*), became an inspiration for the cause of emancipation. In Cairo, the scholar Al-Tahtawi had sown the seeds of feminist thought and influenced the opening of the first primary schools for girls in 1873.

In the 1890s, amongst Olga's circle of friends and associates in Russia, Constantinople, and Cairo, there were Muslim voices who highlighted and challenged views on women's rights in education. Gaspirali and Ilyasi, Ahmed Midhat and Aliye Hanım, Princess Nazli and Qasim Amin exposed traditional views about the patriarchal social system and empathized about the inequalities experienced by women in the Islamic world.

We know that Olga was thoroughly devoted to the cause of women's rights, and she believed that women in Christian societies needed it just as much as women in Muslim societies. She understood the issues of the day, not only by being a guest at harems many times, having friendships with Ottoman women and being a translator of Fatma Aliye's famous book on Muslim women, but also by being familiar with inequalities in her own country and more widely in Europe.

A new opportunity presented itself to Olga in 1899. The organiser of the International Congress of Orientalists at Rome, Count De Gubernatis, invited her to give an address to the congress.

The theme they agreed on was entitled: *Muslim women at the time of the Caliphs* (see Book Two). The emancipation of Muslim women was becoming an important topic amongst men and women of letters in the Ottoman world, though ideas of reform were strongly resisted by clerics and traditionalists.

In composing her talk, she had used material from an article by the Bengali jurist Syed Ameer Ali which she had translated. Syed Ameer Ali was a prolific author, an intellectual educated in Kolkata (Calcutta) who specialised in Anglo-Muslim law and was a judge at the high court in Calcutta. In London he had attended female suffrage meetings with Millicent Fawcett.

Ameer Ali's work on the topic of the emancipation of Muslim women had come out earlier that year in the major British journal *Nineteenth Century*. It followed the tradition of extolling famous Muslim women.

Olga knew several of Ameer Ali's works including his article *Eneniça fil-Islam*. She had already translated his book *The Spirit of Islam* into Russian. Like Ameer Ali, Olga often went to print without revealing her sources.[566]

THE CALL FOR WOMEN'S EMANCIPATION
On the Emancipation of Muslim Women 1900

Several months after the Rome congress, she published an essay entitled *De L'Emancipation de la Femme Musulmane* [On the Emancipation of Muslim Women]. Here, Olga de Lebedeff discussed the 'important question' of how women in Islam could avoid being reduced to living subserviently, almost as slaves, and in difficult conditions; there were prejudices that needed to be fought. She urged Muslim lawmakers to embrace a more progressive view: to allow women an education for the benefit of society at large. The audience was not intended only to be the European Orientalists.

Though hers was not an isolated voice, it was pioneering at the time for a woman to have discussed this topic in the public sphere and published a work in French on it, thus making it more widely readable internationally. Many ordinary people in Islamic society together with intellectuals and men of the law, were concerned about the fact that women were treated as second-class citizens without certain rights.

Muslim reformers were presenting the rationale. They said that it is not Islam itself that prevents the development of women but pre-existing pagan customs. A number of jurists from diverse and far-flung countries endorsed the views, in other words it was a transnational discourse. In the year 1899, both Syed Ameer Ali in British India and Qasim Amin in Egypt, then a British protectorate, wrote publicly on this topic. It has been argued that these views repeated European discourses and assumptions; that those kinds of writers were 'colonised thinkers' in the service of 'nation' and 'progress' rather than feminism per se. [567]

But by basing the arguments used by these jurists, with their status as well-known experts on Islamic law in her own publication, as a non-Muslim herself (and not from Britain or France), Olga de Lebedeff, knew that quoting their authoritative opinions (using Islamic principles) was essential in writing about the status of women in Islam. Besides, in Egypt in the 1890s the growing emancipation discourse in newspaper columns included the aspiration for girls' education, promoted by well-known writers such as Zaynab Fawwaz.

From her time in Egypt the previous year, Olga had been introduced to many of the leading public figures which included influential women in their harems and some of these she quoted in her essay. She studied Arabic with a teacher from the renowned al-Azhar University. Her experience of the more liberal atmosphere of Cairo gave her additional confidence in writing on the theme of emancipation. The severe rules for women she had known in Constantinople were less evident in Egypt, the main restriction was the wearing of a very thin and transparent veil on going out.

The books by Qasim Amin, President of the Court of Appeal in Cairo were, however, a big inspiration. Amin's two Arabic publications addressed to Egyptians were entitled *Tahrir al-mar'a*, 1899 [*Emancipation of Women* or *The Liberation of Women*] and *al-Mar'a al jadida*, 1900 [*The New Woman*]. They had both had a controversial reception, causing something of a furore.

Amin was amongst the group of male Egyptian intellectuals who founded Cairo University in the first decade of the twentieth century. His education had been Egyptian, but he also had received a four-year scholarship to study law in Montpellier, France. Years later, Amin would be considered as one of the Arab world's 'first feminists', even though earlier writers had made many of the points he made. The *Oxford Dictionary of Islam* describes how 'he advocated greater rights for women and spawned great debate over women's issues throughout the Arab world' but he was later criticised as being overly 'pro-Western'.[568] Statements such as this added to that supposition: 'There is no doubt that man's decision to imprison his wife contradicts the freedom which is the woman's natural right.'

He spoke openly of the state of 'slavery' of Muslim women, how 'a woman could be a prisoner in her own house and worse off than a slave'. Amin was even more controversial because he disapproved of the veil and the associated gender-segregation system, at least in its more extreme forms. He and others, such as his close associate the Mufti, Muhammad 'Abduh, proposed a legal system that would give women more protection in cases of divorce.

Between 1899 to 1905, Olga brought this discourse to the Orientalist congress three times. There, typically, high-ranking government officials and diplomats from around the world were also in attendance. Initially, the rights she advocated related to education, and then for rights to enjoy the same standing in society as Muslim men. She

THE CALL FOR WOMEN'S EMANCIPATION

contended that all this was possible within the bounds of the Quran - as shown at the apogee of Islam and as declared by high-ranking and influential Muslims themselves. She also warned against the pitfalls of a superficial modern world with its superfluous temptations. In terms of 'emancipation' Olga was not arguing for Muslim women's suffrage. But she believed that holding women back from being educated would not bring about a thriving society.

In 1902 she quoted Amin's work on women's legal rights called *The New Woman* [*al-Mar'a al-jadida*, 1900] eleven times. [569] This outlined changes in the justice system that would make a significant difference to women's lives, such as in the context of divorce or mistreatment by a husband. A translation of this address to the congress called *Les Nouveaux Droits de la Femme Musulmane* [The New Rights of Muslim Women] may be found in Book Two. Reactions to the talk are discussed in Chapter Twenty.

How Muslim Tatar women lived in the Russia had been touched upon in her history of Kazan, published in 1899 and offered to the congress of Orientalists. [570] The last chapter described the marriage customs and way of life of middle-class Tatar women: traditionally they lived isolated lives, receiving their education at home, not leaving the family home or socialising, and not meeting their husband till their wedding day.[571]

Olga had obtained her impressions of women in Islamic societies both in Russia and in different parts of the Ottoman empire. In her own life she had benefitted from some independence and the privileges of the social elite that most women had not had. By travelling in Europe and in Russia and through her education, she experienced a life which contrasted with the more secluded lives of many of her 'Eastern sisters'. From her perspective of being a woman, she publicly highlighted the complex subject of Muslim women's emancipation, during those times – the age of Empires.

Fig. 81
A postcard in the family collection (possibly Algiers)

She explained in her essay *De l'Emancipation de la Femme Musulmane* the situation that women found themselves in at the turn of the twentieth century. Aiming at a Muslim audience as well as for Europeans, she outlined how in times gone by, women in Islam were not excluded from positions of high office and responsibility as could be seen from the biographies which were passed down in the tradition of exemplary and 'famous women'. Thus, the work incorporated a retrospective of Islamic women in history.

Olga was at pains to highlight the impetus of the emancipation movement evidenced in Beirut, Constantinople and Cairo through the appearance of serious articles and novels in Arabic and Turkish journals written by women authors. She gave examples of modern women authors as inspirational and exemplary models for contemporary women:

THE CALL FOR WOMEN'S EMANCIPATION

I may not fail to mention several contemporary educated Muslim women, who have themselves appeared in the field of education and philanthropy.

Amongst those mentioned were Zaynab Fawwaz, famous biographer of Muslim women, and prose writer Marian Halil [Maryam Khalil]. [572]
She made sure to send her old mentor, Ahmed Midhat, a copy of this work (see Fig. 84).

The Russian copy

The same year a Russian translation of this text was printed in St Petersburg at the press of Isidor Goldberg. The Russian and French versions vary slightly; the Russian one is smaller in size but longer. It included an explanation about the founding of her new Oriental studies society in St Petersburg and addressed key reasons why Muslim theologies had misrepresented the Quran.

Olga was able to increase her campaign in the Russian Empire through the foundation of the Society of Oriental Studies in St Petersburg. With her new public profile as Honorary President, she wrote letters to provincial governors and to the press in cities across Russia raising awareness of the matter of women's education, sending out copies of her booklet.[573] Here she explained that a new branch of her society in the city could establish schooling for girls in Russian and their native language, bringing them the knowledge of European civilization.

She pointed out fanaticism and ignorance (in Russian the latter word used means 'lack of education') not only on the part of many Muslims but also several Europeans who do not know Islam, whose prejudice in this regard, she argued, needed to be countered. She went further than in the French copy with some additional notes: not only did 'the prejudice need to be fought but also to be eradicated, because it goes against the authentic teaching of Mohammed, as set out in his Quran'. She wrote:

> The Quran recognizes a woman's rights as well as her duties.... Of the blessings conferred to man by God, the woman is not the least of these. God united man with women so that they would love one another and mutually support one another.
>
> Men must remember the solemn promise given by you to women, because the Quran speaks of the equality between men and women... There is no question regarding the existence of laws which prescribe a secluded life for Muslim women, the need to cover their faces or whose purpose is merely to serve the pleasure of husband and master. Muslim theologies have distorted the meaning of the Quran where all that is being asked of a woman is that she lives honestly and dresses modestly, in order that the gaze of strangers only see hands and face; in other words, what is now happening in the Muslim world is completely the opposite.

It is doubly interesting to have quoted from the Quran in Russian, given that at that point the Quran was mostly transmitted to Muslims in Arabic. Writing as a woman made the material more potent. Olga de Lebedeff goes on to state that at the time of the apogee of Islam there was never any obstacle for a woman to receive the same learning as a man nor to receive the same rights (p.6):

> We can cite a range of examples and facts proving this distinguished role which Muslim women used to have. Traversing the Crimea and Sarai, we know that the wives of Crimean and Sarai khans lived in full freedom. At the very court of the Uzbek khan, an Arab traveller Ibn Battuta gave this witness: 'The faces of Turkmen women were not covered. They were accorded much honour, and the khan's wives played a key role in government affairs. Even since the time of Sultan Bereket they wrote on paper: "the opinion of the Khatun in this matter coincides with that of the Emirs." Each Khatun (lady or wife of the khan) received a portion of the state's revenue.'

In Russia, by promoting the latest ideas of emancipation for Muslim women Olga became widely recognised as their first female advocate. This kind of activity still provoked strongly critical reactions in missionary circles.

Abrar Karimullin quotes that the writings of Olga on this topic were further published in Russian in Baku (1905), in Tatar in a publication called *Bayanel Hak*, Kazan (1906), and as a separate book in 1907.[574]

The international women's movement in 1900

Though ideals of women's emancipation had been just a talking matter in many regards in Europe, America and Russia, by the turn of the century in those places the feminist movement reached its peak. A public awareness was developing through print media that although the nineteenth century was a century of emancipation, women's rights were barely appreciated. In Russia, as elsewhere, the movement campaigned for educational opportunity, family law reform and other civil and economic rights, but there the factions were divided between socialist and liberal feminists. Some countries like Switzerland, France and Germany did offer tertiary education and university places to a few women, so many travelled long distances to obtain their education.

In Paris, the heart of the French colonial empire, the emancipation movement was represented in 1900 at the world fair, the *Exposition Universelle*. There, international women activists gathered, and Olga was with them.[575] The Second International Congress of Feminine Works and Institutions even succeeded in obtaining financial backing from the French government.[576] Some felt that this endorsement made it the first 'official' international women's congress, and the events were recorded in eight volumes.[577] Amongst the representatives of women to the Congress was May Wright Sewall, American peace activist and founder of the International Council of Women.

The fourth plenary was chaired by one of the great pioneers of French feminism, Sarah Monod (1836-1912), who as a Protestant philanthropist and peace activist, had great 'moral authority'. The session on 22 June included reports by the following: Mrs Hyacinthe Loyson on the *Alliance of Eastern and Western Women*;[578] the Turkish writer Miss Selma Riza on *The Legal Situation of Women in Turkey*; Olga de Lebedeff on *The Emancipation of Muslim Women*; and Jeanne Schmall on *The Salary of Married Women*.

These activists, a product of their times, believed that European or Western civilisation had made great strides in humanitarian values and rights ahead of the East, and that through the advance of friendly relations between peoples the goal of permanent peace would be achievable. The Paris based Alliance of Eastern and Western Women, led by Presidents Princess Nazli and Emilie Hyacinth Loyson, connected many groups of like-minded thinkers including the International Council of Women.

An advocate in E. Groult: 1899 & 1901

Following the speech in Rome on *Muslim Women at the time of the Caliphs*, two press articles eventually appeared written by Edmond Groult (1840-1907), a French lawyer. These articles give us some useful insights on the contents of Olga's presentation and the endorsement she received in certain French intellectual circles. The first came out in Tunisia, in *La Dépêche Tunisienne* on 18th December, where we read: [579]

> On 11th October at the Congress of Orientalists in Rome, there was a paper on 'the emancipation of Muslim women'. The author was a Russian 'grande dame', highly respected for her knowledge, Her Excellency Madame de Lebedeff. With finesse and tact being a speciality of a female author, Madame de Lebedeff introduces us to the Muslims in the golden age of Islam, quite different from the current situation.
>
> The examples cited by Madame de Lebedeff in and of themselves prove the mistaken prejudice which tends to believe that Islam has excluded women from social life and prevents them from receiving the same education as men and prevents them from being able to do things in the world. Some women fulfilled the highest public roles. There were some that were queens who personally commanded their armies; others who were gifted in the science of law and who oversaw courts of justice: and others

THE CALL FOR WOMEN'S EMANCIPATION

who were distinguished philosophers or who were brilliant in literature and poetry.

Amongst these high profile women were representatives from Granada and Persia, individuals who reigned over different Muslim peoples such as: Sitel-Molk, the sister of Hakim in Cairo and Razia Begum in Delhi. The article continued:

> After the crusades, the Tartar invasions swept away civilization in the East and prepared for the subjugation of women. Madame de Lebedeff whose speech was analysed very thoroughly by Monsieur Edmond Groult, director of regional museums at Lisieux, showed us a testimony of the intellectual awakening of women in the East. Right now, there are newspapers being founded written by women in Constantinople and in Egypt. Additionally, special schools for the education of young Muslim girls are being set up in Egypt.
>
> In finishing, Mrs Lebedeff made an urgent call for the creation and propagation of societies of Orientalists which will teach us to know the intellectual needs and moral standards of these peoples. In that way we will be able to create lasting relationships outside of all religious or political issues between these two worlds, who still know each other too little. We cannot but applaud these ideas of Mrs Lebedeff and hope that the indigenous Tunisian race, still considered as one of the finest amongst the Arabs, will quickly join this movement of feminine liberation.

As a lawyer and a man of letters, Edmond Groult himself had for some years made a study of the situation of women especially in the regions colonized by France, Algeria, and Tunisia. A previous article he had written was called *Improvement of the Condition of Muslim Women for the Congress of Carthage*. [580] He claimed that this report was reproduced in several journals in Algeria and Tunisia and a substantial number of Muslims approved of it.

He made a second reference to Olga's 1899 congress speech on 23 November 1901 in the Paris daily newspaper, the first one produced by women called *La Fronde* (meaning 'The Catapult' or 'Spirit of Revolt'). The article was entitled *The Forum: On the Improvement of the condition of Muslim women in Algeria and Tunisia* and the editors noted that the subject of women in all countries and especially in French colonies was of constant concern to their readers, showing that there was great public interest in this topic. [581]

Groult's vision included a hope that such improvements for women would add to the glory of France by increasing its power in the Orient. Thus, these views may outline the superiority of European attitudes to women (and West over East), pointing to what might be classified in hindsight as an imperialist approach to the colonies. But at the time, he and other 'friends of civilization and progress' saw their support for work in the colonies as humanitarian.

In the article, Groult began by saying that on arrival in Algeria or Tunisia 'one is struck by the elegance and nobility of the representatives of the Arab people, even the poorest'. He noted that while the men are dressed fiercely draped like ancient Romans in togas, the women are covered in unsightly garments, their faces masked with a thick veil, with only a hole through which to see. 'One feels pity, he wrote, 'seeing them walking alone, or in two and threes.' He commented that 'it is in vain that one searches the Quran for a text which obliges women to dress like this, and that the Berber and other tribal women refuse this kind of slavery'.

> When they leave their home, no man is allowed to speak with them, neither are they allowed to speak, not even if they have something interesting to say, such as that a child is ill. They pass like shadows and are in fact more shadow-like than women. They have an incomplete personality, a rudimentary soul. Instruments of pleasure in rich homes, beasts of burden in the slums or tents, they are considered inferior beings, somewhere between man and beast. In the seraglio, the inner most circles, their existence is sad and faded. Mostly deprived of intellectual culture, they have a vegetative existence, which could have some charm if in the benevolence of a kind master, but for certain, this would not suit our French women. Very often there is terrible hatred and dreadful jealousies amongst the rivals who are forced to live under the same roof or to share the same tent.

THE CALL FOR WOMEN'S EMANCIPATION

Women prepare their husband's food, but they do not eat together and do not have the right to show themselves when he has guests. For them there are never evening parties, balls, or outings to the theatre or a concert. They do not even have the consolation of religious ceremonies. Only the old women might sometimes go to the mosque where their presence is tolerated. They group together in a dark corner and the believers pass next to them without more acknowledgement than they would give to a bundle of clothing.

It is not unusual for Muslim husbands, thinking they have cause to complain about their wives, to hit them with the end of a club till they die, or till the women, to avoid that cruel end, take poison - more unconscious than criminally. It has become like the night in the frustrated awareness of Muslim women, it is time that one tried to bring in the light.

He now continued:

This subject was again taken up in 1899 at the 12th Congress of Orientalists in Rome. It was raised by 'une grande dame russe', Her Excellency Madame Olga de Lebedeff, who showed with remarkable erudition, that from the first period of Islam Muslim women enjoyed great liberty and that they occupied the highest stations in society at that time. She cited the name of several amongst them who were educated in literature, the sciences, and arts. It was since the time of the crusades that Muslim women suffered setbacks. Their husbands were brutalised by the need to defend themselves and were to lose their appreciation of women's poetry and culture. The same event instigated the start of emancipation for European women, who had taken control of administering their domains during the long absence of their husbands, many of whom never returned.

During her very learned and remarkably interesting report to the Congress in Rome, Her Excellency Madame Olga de Lebedeff showed us the first signs of emancipation of contemporary Muslim women.

She showed us several journals, books and brochures published in Turkey and in Egypt, which aim to develop their intellectual culture and to make disappear their outmoded traditions under the covers of which they are submissive, contrary to the Quranic texts when interpreted soundly. In Cairo she quotes Princess Nazli, the Honorary President for the 'Alliance of Women both Oriental or Occidental for progress of friendly relations amongst all nations and the establishment of permanent peace.' In France the President of this useful society is Madame Hyacinthe Loyson.

Of Emilie Hyacinthe Loyson and her husband Charles Loyson (or Père Hyacinthe, an excommunicated priest and orator theologian) we know that having undertaken a study of comparative religions, they advocated radical unorthodox religious views.[582]

On the Emancipation of Muslim Women (in French) was finished in December 1899. It was privately printed in Lisieux in the hometown of Mr Groult and his wife Madame de Besneray. Bearing in mind the support given by Groult to this cause, this may point to them being sponsors for this publication.[583] In the Preface to the French version, Marie de Besneray, described Olga de Lebedeff as 'a talented historian':

> Speaking many languages, including Turkish, Arabic, and a student of Sanskrit, she has skillfully traced a thousand precise and charming pictures of these countries about which we know so little. She has opposed prejudices and mistakes, has refuted erroneous stories, and like Aliye Hanum - a great lady from the East – she has shown us the world of the Ottomans in a more accurate light[…]To enable women of all nationalities to care about ideas, to teach them moral truths, and the eternal rights of conscience, will always be the worthy task of a great mind.

In the text, Olga referred to the work of Groult and the founding of schools for young girls in Algeria and Tunisia to improve their living conditions as a mark of progress. She remarked on the intellectual awakening of women in Syria helped by Europeans and celebrated that in France the question of emancipation for Muslim women had already entered the realms of reality.

THE CALL FOR WOMEN'S EMANCIPATION

Ideologist of the Young Turks

In Cairo, the Ottoman free-thinker and ideologist of the Young Turks, Dr. Abdullah Cevdet (1869-1932) reprinted this work. His monthly *Idjtihad* journal was a social and literary journal of East and West.[584]

Dr. Cevdet's association with and support of Olga de Lebedeff is significant. He regarded the education of women to be essential for progress in Ottoman society. He was a modernist intellectual who would influence Kemal Ataturk with his secularizing reforms. Interestingly, he too was an advocate of Baha'ism.

Dr. Cevdet's journal published *De L'Emancipation de la Femme Musulmane* in April 1906 under the title '*De la Psychologie du Monde Musulmane*'.[585] He explained how his journal aimed to publish articles concerning the 'psycho-sociological' study of Muslims.

> Our very honourable friend, friend of the Turks and Muslims in general, Her Excellency Olga de Lebedeff, the illustrious Orientalist, about whom we will be speaking for a long time to come, has agreed to place her remarkable dissertation on the emancipation of Muslim women at the disposal of our magazine *Idjtihad*. We have pleasure in starting our series of articles with this charming and precious study which we share with our readers in full.

It is a testament to the interest aroused by the themes in this essay, that over nearly twenty years it was republished in full several times in translation, not only in Cairo, but in Baku and Salonika. The last edition in 1919 was in Istanbul.[586]

The following related works are translated into English for the first time here in **Book Two**:

1899: Speech: *Muslim Women at the Time of the Caliphs* (Rome)

1900: Essay: *On the Emancipation of Muslim Women* (Lisieux)

1902: Speech: On *the New Rights of Muslim Women* (Hamburg)

1905: Speech - International Congress of Orientalists (Algiers)

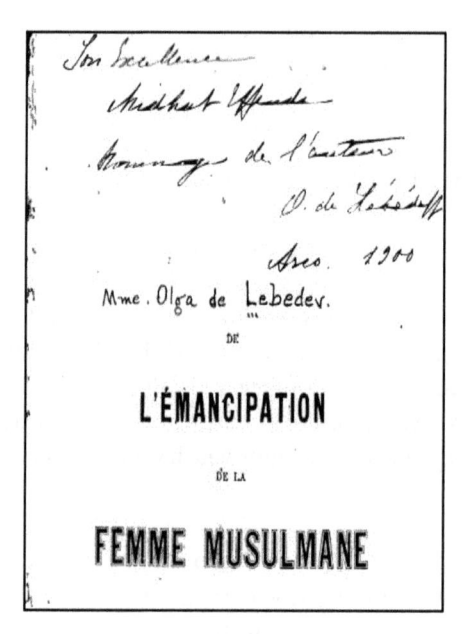

Fig. 82
An original copy with a dedication:

Son Excellence Midhat Effendi, Hommage de l'auteur, O. de Lebedeff, Arco. 1900 [587]

Part IV: Oriental Studies

18 AT THE INTERNATIONAL CONGRESS OF ORIENTALISTS 1889-1899

....to take stock, to compare notes, to see where we were, and to find out where we ought to be going; and second, they gave us an opportunity from time to time to tell the world where we were, what we had been doing for the world and what in return we expected the world to do for us. The principal idea ...was that of tracing the reciprocal action of the East and West on each other, in consequence of the modern revival of Oriental studies.[588]

Max Muller
1874

There is one danger, however, you must take care not to fall into, i.e. unconditional Turcophilism. I mean to say you must avoid all sentiment in dealing with politics.[589]

A. Vambery
1913

AT THE INTERNATIONAL CONGRESS OF ORIENTALISTS
1889 – 1899

At the International Congress of Orientalists, which occurred every one to four years, linguists and philologists presented papers alongside archaeologists and ethnographers. There were a few eccentrics amongst them, and some attracted fervent disciples. This new forum in Oriental Studies became a major and highly prestigious gathering.

Delegates to the congress arrived from societies such as the Geographical, Archaeological, Asiatic and Orientalist societies, or perhaps from an Academy of Science in their home country. The most distinguished were invited as honorary members. At the congress, translators and university lecturers rubbed shoulders alongside diplomats, royalty, nobility, and political personages, who gave the event semi-official status. It was an occasion for academics and representatives of relevant societies to advertise their institutions with written offerings and talks, so being seen to be actively engaged in the field.

Membership of the long-established learned societies, such as the London based Royal Asiatic Society, was exclusively male. [590] Most members had been to university or were recruited with experience on the ground in the East. The society's journal was the most important publisher of Oriental scholarship in Britain.[591] Specialists in their fields included figures in colonial administration, such as military consuls, who had turned out to be outstanding linguists or archaeologists; they contributed to the field through their writings and collections of manuscripts or artefacts. This bred a fascination for culture, adventure, the exploration of monuments and urban and rural history. Exotic beauty and sensuality also had its allure and was a feature of many a scholars' experience abroad.

Over a span of twenty-three years, Olga de Lebedeff attended the International Congress of Orientalists, from Stockholm to Athens. In this chapter we take a look at Olga's contribution at the congresses up to 1899. Apart from contributing papers to the congress, it was here that she gave addresses to the delegates on the rights of Muslim women, which were later published in the proceedings and as separate publications.

The congress environment provided Olga with many invaluable contacts, influences, and opportunities both through the lectures and the social events that formed part of the entertainment. Each congress offered a social programme of outings, so that the host country could show off its famous sights; such events could draw huge crowds, estimated on occasion to be several hundred thousand.[592] The largest contingent of attendees was invariably from the country hosting the congress. The public frequently had access, and ladies were allowed to attend, either as members, or as the wives and daughters of the participating gentlemen. Free rail travel was granted to participants. Usually, the congress lasted for one or two weeks.

Reports on the lectures and speeches were recorded in the 'Proceedings' of each congress; in one volume you might have several European languages, most frequently English, French, German, Italian, and the language of classical scholarship, Latin. They were not recorded wholly in any of the Asian or Middle Eastern languages but were occasionally interspersed with extensive quotations in Japanese or Arabic scripts.

At Stockholm, though leading scholars participated, the scientific nature of the event was said to be 'somewhat impaired by the almost excessive hospitality of the Scandinavian hosts.'[593] Undoubtedly, here many lasting friendships were made in the camaraderie of such social events.

Amongst the international participants who encouraged Olga's contributions over several years were Ahmed Midhat, Ignace Guidi, Count Angelo de Gubernatis and Ignace Goldhizer.

Stockholm VIII Congress: 3- 12 September 1889

Not yet registered as a delegate at her first congress, Olga's own interest had led her to attend the congress in Stockholm. Before this she had made a name for herself with her Tatar-Russian translation of the Persian classic *Qabus Nameh*, winning a prize from Charles Shefer (Paris). She had taken other translations to the congress with the hope of meeting the right person who might publish them, and indeed here she had met Ahmed Midhat, the Ottoman sultan's publicist and representative.

According to Ahmed Midhat, who now had an ideal opportunity to observe the orientalists: 'while Arabic was more widely known than Persian, most European orientalists could only pick their way through texts word by word'.[594]

Geneva X Congress: 1894

Although she did not attend the Geneva Congress in person, Olga's name is listed on the proceedings as the author of leaflets sent for distribution.[595] These leaflets were produced in several languages (Turkish, French, Russian, English, German, and Arabic). In them she wrote about 'the necessity to reject all petty feelings of nationalistic or religious enmity'.[596]

Between the congresses: 1895 -1897 & The Spirit of Islam

During this period, apart from her publications in Constantinople, it appears that Olga was busy with another project. From late November 1895, three North American newspapers reported that she was working on a translation of *The Spirit of Islam* from English into Russian 'in order to encourage the Russian Tatars to read Russian'.[597] The full title of the book was *The Spirit of Islam or The Life and Teachings of Mohammed* (1891) by Syed Ameer Ali, the Bengali jurist.[598] The author was considered an interpreter of modernism in Islam both to the West and to his fellow Muslims.

A record of Olga's intention to get this translation published in Russia is preserved in the archive of the Russian Academy of Sciences, in a letter addressed to the Dean of the Oriental Language Faculty of St Petersburg University, Baron Viktor Romanovich von Rozen (1849-1908).[599] The letter, in cursive Gothic German script, was a challenge to decipher. Here Olga explained about her hopes to get her translation published in Kazan as it was 'an instructive work for European Orientalists'.⁶⁰⁰

A translation follows here:

> Hotel de France, Kasan [sic] 2 October 1897
>
> Esteemed Baron! I recently completed the translation from English of The Spirit of Islam by Saïd Emir Ali, which I would like to publish in Russian. Dear Baron, the contents of this book must be freely known to you, and it enjoys a well-established reputation among European Orientalists as an instructive work. I now take the liberty of asking Your Excellency to allow me to publish this book on my own account, rather than troubling the Academy of Sciences to publish it. In the hope, esteemed Mr. Baron, that you will be kind enough to fulfil my request, I now ask you to kindly send the permission to Kasan [sic] as soon as possible, as I want to have the book printed here at lower costs. Please receive my greetings with special expression of my appreciation. Olga von Lebedeff [followed by a further postscript and her signature *Gülnar*, both in Arabic].

Throwing a light onto what kind of text this was by Syed Ameer Ali, below is an excerpt from the original book, printed in the *History of the XIX Century* by Lavisse and Rambo. Ameer Ali described a new spirit amongst forward thinking Muslims and liberal reformers under British rule in India.⁶⁰¹

> Modern-day stagnation in the Muslim community is mainly due to the view, ingrained in the minds of all Muslims, that the right to use one's personal critical judgement ceased with the first lawyers (the four canonists) ...that a Muslim, in order to be considered a faithful follower of the prophet, must completely subordinate their judgement to the opinion of people who lived in the IX century, and could not have any idea about life in the XIX century. ... Religion and state merged; the caliph was an imam, a secular sovereign as much as a spiritual leader. Over time, as despotism penetrated into the habits of the people, the canonical spirit took possession of the minds of all classes of society.' The same scholar concluded: 'The law (sharia) in some

AT THE INTERNATIONAL CONGRESS OF ORIENTALISTS
1889 – 1899

points is irreconcilable with the modern needs of Islam, whether in India or Turkey, and requires changes.

Though censorship in the Ottoman Empire hampered distribution of such ideas, they still found their way into newspapers and journals there and therefore would have been read by Russian Muslims too.

A testimony from Tatar historian Karimullin claimed that Olga hoped to introduce foreign literature into Russia, including translations of writings by Ahmed Midhat and Qasim Amin (the Egyptian jurist), but these were not permitted to be published in Russia.[602] Karimullin proposed that the situation highlighted political tensions at the time between the two empires, not least as the Russian government very much feared Pan-Islamic fundamentalism.

Olga had had plans for an anthology of ancient and modern Persian, Arabic and Ottoman literature. Compiled under the mentorship of Ahmed Midhat in 1891 and intended for the Congress of Orientalists in London, they had named it *Anthologie Orientale*;[603] it featured information about Islam and social life in Turkey.[604] By 1899 it had still not been published, so Olga offered it to the organisers of the Rome congress instead.

Rome XII Congress: 4 to 15 October 1899

Ten years after her first congress, Olga attended as a contributing participant. Since Stockholm, her engagement with Ottoman society and the literary contributions she had made in Constantinople had established her as an Orientalist of note. Apart from translating famous Russian works into Ottoman Turkish and as a translator of Fatma Aliye's famous work *Women in Islam* [*Nisvan-i-Islam*], she had made the two translations of the *Refutation of Renan* into Turkish commissioned by Ahmed Midhat.

The book she offered the congress was on the history of Kazan [**Abrégé de l'histoire de Kazan**], which included *Some Considerations on Tatar Civilisation*.

In a letter dated 14th August to Count Angelo de Gubernatis, President of the Organising Committee, she enclosed the photographs for her book on Kazan; but these did not make the final printing. [605] The photographs were found amongst family papers and are printed in this volume along with a detailed description of the work.[606]

Included in the mailing was a dedication, which revealed her determination, as well as nervousness, at the prospect of participating in the forbidding male-dominated world of orientalists. The dedication also missed the publication but is detailed below:

> To the orientalists at the congress of 1899: This essay is dedicated to you despite coming from my inexperienced pen. If it makes too poor an impression in comparison with works brought of more considerable erudition, I hope that they will forgive me for suggesting that I too, even though in a more modest fashion, would like to contribute to the advancement of 'Science' which draws us all here together. I trust that in this I may succeed! [607]

Olga and the Count corresponded with the about the subject of an address she could offer in person. The proposed themes had been discussed as either history, literature, or civilisation in the Muslim world. She had suggested reading a paper on the 'Civilisation of the Arabs at the time of the Caliphs at Baghdad' or presenting her *Anthologie Orientale*.

However, in the end they agreed on this: *Muslim women at the time of the Caliphs*, a theme she knew well. Yet culturally, this was a controversial topic, because both the ideas of emancipation of women and the emancipation of Muslim women were derided and disputed.

A week later, on 21 August 1899, Olga sent the Count the new discourse that she had prepared to read out at the congress. Whilst she spoke of being extremely excited about the double task of producing a work (not just a translation) she was also anxious about putting herself forward to speak in public for the first time with her talk on Muslim women. She hoped that she would not lack the courage to do it saying, 'je tremble d'avance'.[608] Additionally, she wrote:

> Please let me know frankly if you find it worthy of being read out; please correct anything that you think needs it. You don't need to

AT THE INTERNATIONAL CONGRESS OF ORIENTALISTS
1889 – 1899

tell me just simply do it bluntly, as I don't mind that, and I would rather a thousand times be silent than make a fool of myself.

The support of the Count in getting this speech agreed to, points to the forward-thinking views of De Gubernatis, as well as his encouragement of Olga personally.

Apart from being the first opportunity that Olga had had to present her views of women's emancipation for the attention of members of the congress, it must have been a particularly emotive moment of hopefulness for a better world on the eve of the new century. Her daughters, Olga and Vera attended in support of their mother.[609]

The article in praise of Olga's talk given on 11th October *Muslim women at the time of the Caliphs* given appeared on 18 Dec 1899 in the Tunis newspaper *La Dépêche Tunisienne*. It pointed to the tact and finesse of Mme de Lebedeff. She had, it seems, called for the creation of Societies of Orientalists:

> At the end of the talk, she gave an urgent call for the creation and propagation of Societies of Orientalists to understand the intellectual and moral needs of Eastern peoples. That way we can establish lasting relations outside of all questions of religion or politics. We cannot but applaud the ideas of Mme de Lebedeff and hope that the indigenous race of Tunisians, always considered one of the finest amongst the Arabs, will speedily enter this movement of women's liberation.

This talk resonated with like-minded people in Europe, as well as intellectuals from Cairo to the Caspian.[610]

The British newspapers had previously taken much interest in the goings on at the International Congress of Orientalists and this year was no exception. On 19 Oct 1899 *The Pall Mall Gazette* describes the closing of the highly successful Congress in Rome. It gives an extra perspective on Olga's participation at the congress with a mention of some entertainment that she laid on for delegates:

> At one point there were nearly 800 people in attendance, and the congress lasted two weeks instead of one. Excursions were to Tivoli and Hadrian's Villa and the Forum Romanum. There was an original

play written by Angelo de Gubernatis (President of the Reception Committee). The length of the stay enabled 'congressists' to entertain each other rather more freely than has sometimes been the case. Thus, Mme de Lebedeff, the learned author of a history of Kazan, the Romanian Consul and Mrs. Ginsburg, the wife of a well-known English delegate, have all given entertainments which have been numerously attended and much enjoyed."[611]

If Olga hosted her reception at a hotel like the Majestic, formerly called Hotel Suisse where she sometimes stayed in Rome, we can imagine that this would truly have been a grand event; presumably some of those from the Russian delegation such as Professor S. de Oldenburg, A. Pozdneev, V. Radloff, and Baron Victor von Rozen also attended.

Fig. 83
Olga's postcard from the aptly named Hotel Majestic sent to Angelo De Gubernatis[612]

19 Society of Oriental Studies: St Petersburg 1900

> Hier on m'a télégraphié de Petersburg que j'étais enfin autorisée à fonder la Société d'Orientalistes laquelle j'ai travaillée depuis presque cinq ans. Ce printemps même, elle sera ouverte.
> Olga de Lebedeff, 21 March 1900, Arco[613]

Two important events had changed the course of Olga's life at the start of the new century. The first was her mother's unexpected death on 8/20 February in Arco (South Tyrol). The second was the fulfilment of many years work: the creation of her Russian Society of Oriental Studies on 29th February 1900 (OS).

Confirmation of the society's founding charter arrived in Arco by telegraph a week later, on 9 March (OS) from St Petersburg. The ambition to found this new '*Société d'Orientalistes*' had been conceived 'after a long stay in the Orient'.[614] To her mentor and confidant, the Count de Gubernatis, she wrote that it had been nearly five years in the making. The Count, a seasoned expert in Oriental studies, was one of those who greatly supported the idea that such a society could bring greater understanding between cultures. The concept of its creation was very close to her heart. 'You know how passionately I love the East and everything to do with it' she had written to Baron von Rozen. He was the dean of the Faculty of Oriental Languages at St Petersburg University, an Arabist who also headed the Oriental department of the Russian

Archaeological Society. In 1897 she asked the Baron about how to establish a new society:[615]

> Seeing as too few people here are interested, even though we have so many Eastern peoples in our lands, I would like to create a circle of academics and enthusiasts to unite diverse elements and to awaken a lively interest. As you are considered the "Doyen" amongst our scholars, there is no one better than you to lead and advise. That is why I earnestly request that you do not decline to come to mine for the meeting with other well-known scholars and interested parties on Friday at 8pm.

This letter shows that the Society originated from her founding activities at her own home in St Petersburg in the company of other like-minded individuals. Doubtless there would be accompanying drinks and refreshments, a welcoming speech, and discussions, as at other salon evenings she hosted. But this gathering was something extra special, the first of many, drawing together a circle of Orientalists. She was well-known by many of them including the Turcologist V.V. Radlov, P. Semyonov Tian-Shansky, V.V. Barthold, N.I. Veselovsky, and Yu. I. Krachkovsky, [616] F. Knauer and N. Stréboulyaef, and many others including Asianist advisors to the government like E. Ukhtomsky.

Key questions facing Russia: A Unified Empire

Oriental Studies were perceived as one of the strongest disciplines in Russian academic circles and was also most widely recognised internationally.[617] This was due to the fact that Russians had developed perhaps the most extensive institutions for Oriental studies at Kazan and St Petersburg universities.[618] By the 1890s, it was the second largest area of research after Slavic Studies in the Imperial St Petersburg Academy of Sciences, the leading research institution in Russia.[619] In addition, the community of Russian Oriental scholars believed that their work was 'central to the key questions facing Russia at the time'.[620]

Olga's new Society of Oriental Studies would help popularize secular knowledge about the empire's Eastern cultures and make them more accessible. This must have struck a chord with officials keen to capitalize on the identity of the empire as multinational and thereby consolidating and authenticating Russia's place in Asia. In fact, in his memoirs the Finance Minister Sergei Witte himself describes the Russian Empire as 'having swallowed up non-Russian peoples' to become a 'conglomerate of nationalities'.[621] Responsible for the state built trans-Siberian railway and for various international commercial treaties, Sergei Witte was one of the government ministers most knowledgeable about the Far East. It was Witte who ratified the official papers for the Society. In his view the Siberian railroad would provide a commercial link between the Far East and Europe; he had even proposed greater migration from European to Asiatic Russia, which was agreed to be in the interests of the state.

Simultaneously government ministers had been 'at loggerheads' over Far Eastern policy (over the taking of Port Arthur in the Liaotung Peninsula in Manchuria for instance), therefore the aims of the Society appealed to those who saw trade and education as a means to improve relations. [622] Witte's vision of a unified empire, where toleration for Muslims included 'full equality of rights with other subjects, freedom in the conduct of their religious needs and non-intervention in their private lives,' made him a firm supporter of the tradition of enlightened rule established in Russia by Catherine II. Witte's approach was that railroads and not repression garnered loyalty from the empire's subjects.[623]

The founding of the Society of Oriental Studies was established by government decree (No. 45).[624] Royal patronage came from a senior member of the royal household who had held the post of President of the State Council for many years: His Imperial Highness Grand Duke Mikhail Nikolayevich, uncle of Tsar Nicholas II. His personal connection with Olga was that his brother Alexander II had been Olga's godfather. He had knowledge of the Caucasus having lived in Tbilisi as governor for twenty years; this experience and knowledge of administrative management would greatly help the direction of the Society. With his tactful and kind personality, contemporaries regarded the elderly Grand Duke as a peacemaker. His private and public life were known to be exemplary.

As well as the outstanding statesman Sergei Witte, amongst the Society's nominated honorary members were other major figures, representatives of the government including P.A. Stolypin and General Kuropatkin, the Minister of War. Though Olga de Lebedeff started as President, due to her increased absences abroad and particularly in Cairo, she took the title of Founder and Honorary President.[625] In July, General Lieutenant N.K. Schwedoff also took the title of President. In her letter to De Gubernatis, Olga described how Schwedoff worked 'very energetically and with know-how.'

As a matter of comparison, these early origins were not unlike those of the Royal Asiatic Society in London. This society started off as a meeting of literary friends in the home of Henry Thomas Colebrooke in January 1823. In those days few Oriental scholars could call themselves professional as such. But they had connections to the colonies and rare knowledge of the empire. The founders of this British society took action to obtain a Royal Charter, find rooms, establish a library and a journal. They had started off dealing with scientific, economic, and commercial subjects and over the years articles on language, literature, history, archaeology, and native culture followed.[626]

Aims of the Society of Oriental Studies

From its small beginnings, the organisation of the Russian Society of Oriental Studies developed gradually. At the end of May 1900 Olga wrote to Count de Gubernatis an update from St Petersburg:

> We still have a huge amount of preparatory work to do which will soon be finished and then in two weeks I will set up a General Assembly...., dear teacher and friend, though you have suggested giving some talks for us in August, reluctantly I must dissuade you of this as all the towns are empty then, but if you come in November, I can guarantee a full hall in Petersburg and Moscow.

In her letter to him on 17 November 1900 also from St Petersburg she clarifies how the project developed after its founding:

> Some of our members have gone to Persia to see if they can do some business there... the academic dimension has not yet been

touched. Without enough money, we are unable to establish an Institute of Modern Oriental Languages – but we have a small place of our own. I have imagined opening three courses teaching Persian, Japanese and Turkish...as we have plenty of teachers for these two languages; as for Turkish, I will start teaching it myself, until we have the means to pay a good teacher. One must start everything with something - and once this business is set in motion, I hope that the Minister of Finance will give us a subsidy. We also hope to receive some concessions on train travel. I feel sure that in time our society will be as well-funded as it is significant. [627]

The aims that Olga de Lebedeff proposed had been cultural and educational. They reflected her own interests:

- to educate with exhibitions, lectures, courses, libraries, expeditions, and published works
- to engage mutual goodwill between East and West
- to provide cultural and scientific studies and commercial exchanges
- to deliver society from religious or nationalist hatred
- to promote truth, displayed in the intellect, through education.

Schools would teach both Russian and Eastern languages set up under an 'Academy of Practical Oriental Courses'. [628] It would have two divisions, for commercial industry and for Eastern languages. Studies were to cover all 'the Orient', not just the Muslim-majority areas. Japanese was taught as one of the first languages. Formally the society espoused three goals:

1. academic and cultural, through the study of the 'Eastern' countries (archeology, history, local history)
2. educational, with a view to organising schools in countries of Asia, mainly with a commercial focus, teaching Russian language; and, in Russia, courses of Oriental Languages
3. commercial and industrial

In two essays about Olga de Lebedeff, the Soviet era historian Karimullin made the point that this Society was influenced by Tsarist politics. Yet, the society could hardly have existed without official endorsement. The letter quoted to her friend and mentor De Gubernatis as mentioned above shows that she hoped to receive subsidies from the Ministry of Finance.

Head offices in St Petersburg were established at 6 Candle Lane. It housed a library and museum of eastern manuscripts and objects.[629] A second branch was established in Tiflis (Tbilisi). This was the Empire's administrative centre of the Caucasus. Grand Duke Mikhail Nikolayevich had many contacts there as former governor. Tiflis was also the birthplace of Witte, where he had received his early schooling.

The branch was 'composed of all the most enlightened and most influential people in the country', Olga explained to Count de Gubernatis.[630] By 'enlightened' people, she meant the most intellectual. Eventually, separate branches were set up in other cities across Central Asia to Vladivostok (Ashkabad, Astrakhan, Baku, Blagoveshchensk, Bukhara, Vladivostok, Omsk, Amur, Khabarovsk, Tashkent, Tehran, Harbin, and Yerevan (then known as Erivan)).[631]

With the society and its members attached to public life, the knowledge imparted here would have the effect of enlarging civil society. The cultural and commercial interests of Japan, China, Afghanistan, and India were explored. Yet, in the end, the government's failure to establish peaceful relations with Japan resulted in the Russo-Japanese war of 1904.

The Society's logo and seal was circular in blue and white with the Russian lettering of the society around the edge: 'ОБЩЕСТВО ВОСТОКОВѢДѢНІЯ'.[632] In the centre was a drawing of the rising sun and its rays dawning on the horizon.

After the Grand Duke died in 1909, the Empress Alexandra Feodorovna became the royal patron, so only then was the society given the formal title of 'Imperial Society of Oriental Studies'.[633]

The Ministry of Trade and Industry co-signed the Charter of the Practical Oriental Academy on 28 October 1909. [634] The Ministry of Trade and Industry required reports on the Academy's educational and economic activities from the Society of Oriental Studies. Full courses lasted three years, with two semesters per academic year from September to May. Graduates received a diploma.

SOCIETY OF ORIENTAL STUDIES: ST PETERSBURG 1900

Fig. 84

Tsar Nicholas II & Tsarina Alexandra Feodorovna (Family Collection)

Studies included training in business and regional administration. Consular work included studies in history and international law. There were other educational programmes towards and during World War I:
- History of the Middle East [Near East] taught in 1914-1915.
- History of East Asia [Far East] taught in 1914-1915.

- Consular and Diplomatic Law in the East, a 3-year course starting in 1911-1912.
- Organization of the Armed Forces of the East, 3-year course starting in 1914-1915.[635]

Over the course of its eighteen-year history, a wide range of Eastern languages as well as English and French were taught: Persian, Chinese, Mongolian, Japanese, Armenian, Georgian, Ottoman Turkish, Serbian, Bulgarian, and Sartsky (a Central Asian language).

By 1912 there were one hundred and sixty-three people working for the society. Many eminent Russian Orientalists were members: for example, the Sanskrit professor Fëdor Knauer (1849-1917) from Kiev University; the Arabist Stréboulayef professor at the Institute of Oriental Languages and interpreter for the Russian Government; the army officer A.E. Snesarev (1865-1937) who studied both in India and at the British Museum; and for a time Vasilii Bartold (1869-1930), who would later be one of the fathers of Soviet Orientology. Barthold was a specialist in Islam and Turkic peoples and became famous as a historian of Central Asia, but he has also been described as a 'closet scholar... who insisted on the great political potential of seemingly irrelevant and 'abstract' studies of ancient manuscripts and dead languages of the 'East'".[636]

From 1900, her new prestigious position as founder and honorary chair gave Olga de Lebedeff more authority to speak about the rights and freedoms of Muslim women both at home and abroad.

Letters to newspaper editors promoted her Russian edition of *'On the Emancipation of Muslim Women,'* which ended with the words:

> We are already partly coming near to a better future, and that's why we must actively try to hasten the return of rights historically belonging to Muslim women, and to give them that life which is in accordance with their religion and today's civilization![637]

Described by the newspaper's editor as the 'famous activist, indefatigable and energetic O. de Lébédeff', Olga and General Nikolai Konstantinovich Schwedow proposed the founding of a branch of their society in Tashkent. How to set up a branch was described in Olga's letter dated 26 April 1901 to the editor of the *Turkestanskia Vedomosti*.

SOCIETY OF ORIENTAL STUDIES: ST PETERSBURG 1900

Between them, they advocated women's education in Central Asia, and the need to found secular schools for girls (and boys), following successful models in Algeria and Tunisia. This, they asserted, would lead to the intellectual emancipation of Muslim women, and bring benefits of European-style education. Schwedow requested the Governor-General of Turkestan to take the founding of their society's branch under his own patronage and protection.

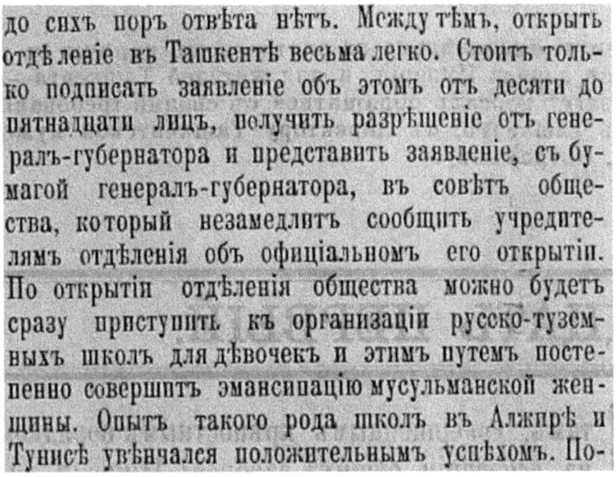

Fig. 85

Excerpt from Olga's letter to the editor in Tashkent, 1901

Books and dictionaries compiled by the Orientalist brothers Pozdneev and other teachers of Oriental languages were produced under the auspices of the society. Other publications of the Society were called 'News', 'Works' and 'Notes' and others specific to Persia, China, Japan, Georgia, and Central Asia. They included diverse works from Kalmyk grammars to the Turkestan-Siberia railway, and the essentials of Buddhism for Buryatian children.[638]

By 1913 topical questions of Pan Islamism and Pan-Turkism in Russia were discussed in the Society's journal, *Mir Islama* ('*The World of Islam*'). It was edited by Baron von Rozen's disciple Vasilii Barthold. In June 1914, the society was drawn into government talks to discuss 'The Muslim Question'.[639]

The independence of the society as a separate entity ended in 1918, with the demise of autocracy and the murder of the Society's royal patron, the Tsarina.[640]

Then, the Society was absorbed into the Institute of National Economy. This was a special educational institution for training specialists with knowledge of Oriental languages to work in various fields of activity on the eastern outskirts of Russia and in neighboring states. It was managed from then on entirely by the Ministry of Trade and Industry.

One hundred and ten years later, quoting this original society, a new Society of Orientalists was re-registered in Kazan at the Federal University: 'continuing to play a role as a bridge between Russia and the countries, peoples and culture of the East.' [641]

International recognition

For ten years, Olga de Lebedeff represented the society at the International Congress of Orientalists, attending in Hamburg, Algiers, Copenhagen, and Athens. In the years leading up to the revolution, she divided her time between St Petersburg, Kazan, Arco and Cairo. Olga maintained contact with the next generation of Orientalists such as Ignaty Krachkovsky, who in time would become one of the founders of the Arab School of Soviet Studies.[642]

On 15 June 1903, Olga received an honorary title of *Officier d'Academie* from the Ministry of Public Education and the University of Paris. The honour was given to her 'as an author of distinguished and valued writings on orientalism' and for being the founder and Honorary President of the Russian Society of Oriental Studies in St Petersburg.[643]

In addition, she received a gold medal from the Romanian Academy, and a Serbian award, the Cross and Star of St Sava ('the Enlightener'), in recognition of a trade agreement. The order of St Sava was one of the oldest orders dating from 1772. This had not ever been awarded to a woman.[644]

***

For an assessment on Olga's activities amongst Russian scholars, I turned to the expertise of Russian historian Victor Dzevanovsky-Petrashevsky who has a special interest in Orientologists from the imperial era and who has published biographical articles on several of them. In 2021, he was a speaker at an online conference 'The Beginnings of Turkology in eastern Europe and its importance for Turkic minorities' about Olga's involvement in Russian Oriental Studies.[645]

Academicians and women in the field

Dzevanovsky described the influence of Baron Viktor Rozen as more powerful in Orientalism at home and abroad, but behind the scenes with courtiers Olga had the most powerful levers. He went on to explain the following:
- Students of Rozen followed strict rules that he had established. They preferred not to participate in affairs outside the Faculty of Oriental Languages or the Geographical and Archaeological societies. But there were 'defectors' like Samoilovich, Shapshal, Khashchab, Martinovich, Pozdneev and others. They were accepted everywhere, but not, he said, taken so seriously by the academicians.
- In European Orientalism a woman scholar was a novelty; perhaps more likely to be accepted than in Russia. Prejudiced attitudes towards women did not put Olga off her mission. She proceeded to break through barriers, 'like an icebreaker': she had talent and courage but even the audacity to combine science and knowledge in the field. She found interesting people and attracted them to work for the society.
- All the while, she kept going with her translation work. She used her right as translator to translate conceptually rather than always in a literal style, moreover, she did it all with pleasure. Other academics worked to the dictates of society, but she had to fight for her status every day as a woman in the field. Above all, she succeeded by boundless willpower.
- After Rozen's death in 1908, women gradually began to appear in the Russian academic sphere. [This was also made possible, for example, by the fact that the Imperial University of Kazan began to admit women in 1907].

- Wives of Imperial Orientalists had often aided their husband's work, accompanying them on expeditions and preserving their legacy: Elena Oldenburg, Varvara Zhukovskaya, and the two sisters of Iranist Valentin Zhukovsky: Maria Bartold (1868—1928) for Middle Eastern studies, and Alexandra Marr (1864-1939) in Caucasus studies. The first woman to be employed by the Asiatic Museum was the Egyptologist Natalya Mikhailovna Diakonova [m. Alekseeva] (1890-1973) in 1918.[646] Arabist Vera Krachkovsky (1884-1974), became a lecturer on Central Asian history and art as a woman in her own right in the 1920s, an authority on Arabic paleography.[647]

Building bridges

In the light of these comments, the aspirations and active contribution to the public sphere of Olga de Lebedeff seem more remarkable, especially since the Tsarist government opposed the formation of private educational groups or organizations.[648]

With various innovative aims based on a reciprocal exchange, her main goal had been expressed in the founding charter:

> To spread accurate and true information about Russia amongst the peoples of the East, as well as to introduce Russian society to the material needs and spiritual life of Eastern cultures.[649]

The society provided an alternative route to study the 'Orient' in a range of practical ways outside of missionary Orthodox colleges or the purely literary approach of the universities. By engaging with the languages, culture, commerce and history of Russia's eastern lands and its neighbours, the society was well placed to 'build bridges' between diverse cultures. This was a move away from remote scholarly learning which typically resulted in, for instance, the speaking of Arabic in a way that was so pure and poorly pronounced that ordinary Arabs could not understand it.

The international community of Orientalists she had met at the congresses had inspired Olga in forming this society. Importantly, she advocated that Orientalists had a duty to educate others in the cultures they had themselves studied. An exchange with those cultures was even considered necessary for the common good.

Improved education and rights for minority peoples including women and girls were at the heart of Olga's mission. She served as a role model for women, who in later years took up the study of Arabic, Turkish or Persian and succeeded in studying at university. She showed that women were not intellectually inferior to men and capable of professional work, ideas which prior to 1900 were current amongst many Russian and European liberals, and academic professors.[650]

***

All the while, in Orientology and society at large, a whole raft of academic, religious and political discourses competed; in Russia, the search for national identity and imperial ambition vied for prominence.

By 1917, a School of Oriental Studies had opened in London. British Orientalists had sold the idea to the government that the school would be an imperial training centre. Funds were limited, however, and earning a living teaching Eastern languages was also limited; academics could not abide the concept of vocational training. This school was to become SOAS, the School of Oriental and African Studies.[651]

20 At the Congress: Hamburg to Athens (1902 -1912)

> Orientalism in the early twentieth century was to a considerable extent a collaborative European enterprise.[652]
>
> R. Irwin

> Let us awaken the East from its slumber! To this end let us propagate as much as possible the societies of Orientalists to teach us about the ethics and cultural needs of these [Eastern] peoples. We can also establish lasting relations outside of any religious or political concerns between the two worlds of East and West.[653]
>
> O. de Lebedeff

At three of the following events, Olga presented a total of three first-time Arabic translations and gave two addresses on the theme of rights for Muslim women.

Hamburg XIII Congress: 8 September 1902

The Hamburg Congress marked Olga's first attendance under the official auspices of the Society of Oriental Studies that he had founded in St

AT THE CONGRESS: HAMBURG TO ATHENS (1902-1912)

Petersburg two years before. Amongst the twenty-eight-person Russian delegation were Baron V. Rozen and General N. Schwedow (President of the Society of Oriental Studies).

At the congress, Section VI was dedicated to Islam. Here, Olga presented her *Récits de voyages d'un Arabe* (110 pages), comprising the description of ancient wonders of the world from Aleppo to Alexandria. This was a translation from an Arabic text, by a Christian Arab from Aleppo.

In addition to her written offering, she wrote a speech *Les Nouveaux Droits de la femme musulmane* [The New Rights of Muslim Women]. This was printed in full in the proceedings and translated for this volume.[654]

The Hungarian scholar Ignace Goldziher read out the address on her behalf. Goldziher, described by Bernard Lewis as 'one of the founders and masters of modern Islamic studies', was a fervent attendee of the Orientalist congresses. He believed that giving lectures at such events was just as important as publishing articles'.[655]

This speech explained the new rights for Muslim women. It was based on the latest views of Muslim lawmakers and scholars, in particular the second Arabic work by Qasim Amin called *The New Woman* [*al-Mar'a al-jadida*, 1900]. She rebuffed the conservatives and detractors of Qasim Amin; his first work on the subject in Arabic *Tahrir al-mar'a* in 1899 had caused controversy by condemning the Egyptian attitude to women, whilst advocating education and cessation of the veil:[656]

> The Egyptian prime minister sent [him] an open letter showing his sympathy for these latest ideas saying they should be widely spread to the public. The mufti of Egypt and Sudan Mohammed Abdou and more importantly the rector of the Muslim theological college El Azhar [al-Azhar University], show deep sympathy for his emancipated ideas.

The speech provoked quite a strong response amongst the male participants. The 'Proceedings' of the Congress were recorded in German, and the discussion on the talk is translated below:

> During this discussion in which several speakers took part, Mr. Ignace Goldziher emphasized the consideration that the matter in

question could not be answered in any definitive manner. The position of women in Islamic society varies from one cultural setting to another due to both ethnographic antecedents and historical influences. The uniform codification in *madhhab* law [legal schools of Islamic jurisprudence][657] could be contrasted with the fact that, throughout its lively development, the theological handling of this subject does not present a uniform picture. From the hadiths one could readily select instances of conflicting opinions about specific details pertaining to the question of women in Islam. For example, there are many textual instances of sharply disapproving sayings about divorce.[658]

A vivid description of the reception of this talk comes from across the Atlantic. *The Washington Evening Star* 18 Oct 1902 published a summary of the debate:

A paper read by Mme Olga Lébédew on the "legal rights of the Mussal woman in marriage" created some diversion in the congress, from the fact that the presentation made by Mme. Lebedew, which was based on investigations of her own in the Mohammedan provinces of Russia, was hotly contradicted by the Mohammedan men, who had left their wives at home. They declared that these women were the happiest and contented with their lot of any women in the world. The showing by Mme. Lébédew was that while the physical wants of the women were supplied, and while their legal status in most respects were not bad, they were kept in ignorance and not allowed the enlightenment of education.

The rebuttal to this paper by the Muslim men in attendance is reminiscent of the popular response in Britain expressed by the politician James Mills in the 1820s. James Mills' assumption that all women in Britain lived happy lives, never mistreated by their male relatives, was lampooned in his own lifetime. This was at a time when women of all social classes were viewed as third class citizens, less important than men or their own male children. Women were, as many women pointed out, 'little better than slaves'.[659]

AT THE CONGRESS: HAMBURG TO ATHENS (1902-1912)

Algiers XIV Congress: 6 - 19 April 1905

The delegates at Algiers, many of whom were already old acquaintances from previous congresses, gathered on 18th April in a private reception at the Hotel Excelsior. They entertained one another warmly in many different languages ('parlant toutes les langues connues'). On 20 April, in the daily newspaper *La Dépêche*, a special correspondent cited Madame de Lébédew amongst the foreign speakers at the congress, the only woman to be mentioned.

During the solemn opening ceremony, held in the Grand Hall of the Consular Palace on 19 April, Olga had given an address representing the 'newly established' Russian Society of Oriental Studies together with two other delegates, Knauer and Stréboulayef. A full translation of her speech is in this volume. She began her speech as follows:

> Our society has given me the mandate to wish the discerning members of this Congress every success on the path of the advancement of knowledge, and for the joint work undertaken to bring about the rapprochement of East and West.[660]

A large part was dedicated to highlight her hopes for the emancipation for Muslim women. This represented the third time that she had brought the topic to the congress. Now, though, the host country was an Arabic country, albeit a colony of France.

In Section III entitled Muslim Languages comprising Arabic, Persian and Turkish, she offered a translation. It was from Arabic to French, entitled *A History of the Conversion of the Georgians to Christianity* by Patriarch Macaire of Antioch.[661] A commentary on this by Professor Marilyn Booth features in this volume. Professor Ignace Guidi had recommended the translation of this manuscript from the Vatican library. In the Preface, Olga explains that the translation concerns the second voyage of the Patriarch of Antioch to Russia, invited by the Tsar Alexis, to judge the Patriarch Nikon.

There followed articles in the *Revue du monde Musulman*, Paris Nov. 1906 and the *Revue Africaine* amongst others.[662]

A copy of *Les Nouveaux Droits de la Femme Musulmane* and the Discourse given at Algiers was approved by the Russian censors and printed in St Petersburg on 17 May 1905. To follow up her efforts at the congress, a copy of this was sent to the Governor General of Algeria on 16 December 1905.[663]

Just a small amount of correspondence may be found that relates to this period. Olga lived in Cairo at least during the winters, sometimes staying in a hotel or at Emad El-Din Street 8.[664] She held salon evenings about Russia's Muslims. Her article on this subject is quoted in the bibliography of a magazine *Arafate* in 1906.[665]

Fig.86
Olga age 53 at home in Lubiana, Russia, in 1906 (Family Collection)

Copenhagen XV Congress 14 -20 August 1908

Olga appears to have attended this congress, but not contributed with any papers or talks. The *Proceedings* of this congress listed her as living in Cairo and a representative of the Russian Society of Oriental Studies together with A. Snesarev and Professors Fedor Knauer and Strebulyaev.[666] Her friend from Cairo, Contessa della Sala, was also invited to take part in the congress as an official delegate of the society.[667]

Correspondence from this period include letters from Cairo to the Count de Gubernatis which mention other Orientalists: her old mentor Professor Ignacio Guidi and his student, the historian Prince Leone Caetani.[668] One letter points to not having seen Prince Fuad (later King Fuad I) in March 1909. A month later, she left Cairo following the Archaeological Congress and headed back to Rome again, via Naples.

Between this congress and the next, Olga continued with her studies in Arabic in Cairo for several months each year.

Athens XVI Congress: 6-14 April 1912

Attending the event in her fifty-ninth year, Olga arrived early on 2 April from Cairo. It turned out that she spent much of the event in hospital with bronchitis. She wrote to a friend: 'Everyone has been very kind, but all the same it's very sad.'[669]

On 10 April 1912 her new translation was presented. The Sufi text comprised a partial translation of the Risalah of Al-Qushayrī' from Arabic to French: *Traité sur le Soufisme de l'imâm érudit Abou 'l-Kâsim Abd'Oul-kerim Ibn Hawazin el Kochâirî*.[670]

This was an early and important work, the original document dated from 1045 C.E. It was an epistle to the Sufi community from Abd al-Karim b. Hawazin al-Qushayrī. Her translation of Chapter Two explained the expressions used by this community underlying the theory of Sufism. The full text explained the beliefs of the Sufis, whilst lamenting the decline of contemporary Sufism in the eleventh century.

According to a recent publication, this was a difficult work to translate.[671] The meanings of the words themselves were intended to be hidden from outsiders, to protect the mysteries from being spread amongst those to whom they do not belong. This makes a knowledgeable appreciation of her work to be outside of the scope of this book.

However, it can be noted that in 1915 the German Arabist Richard Hartmann gave Olga's translation a harsh review. The criticism of his thesis was levied at her non-literal interpretation, saying her sometimes free translation misrepresented the text's original wording.

To the non-specialist, her interpretation made the complexities of the text relatable and readable, as well as accessible for the first time to European readers. [672]

Ahmed Midhat, the Ottoman publisher, had previously observed that for European Islamicists, Theology and mysticism were the subjects of greatest interest, but they often remained foreign to the spirit of those fields.[673]

Concepts in Sufism were familiar to Olga, based on her interaction with Tatars in the Kazan region. During her lifetime, mystic Sufi thought was very much alive and well under the Ottomans and across Central Asia, carried there and amongst the Kazan Tatars by Sufi missionaries. Olga's ongoing interest in the mystical aspect of religious thought and experience was clearly a motivator for her in choosing this text; on the basis that her knowledge of Sufi practices in Tatar communities would have been long-standing and that colleagues regularly slated each other's works, a new assessment of this translation would be useful.

In summing up, through her dedication to the congresses over all those years, we can say that Olga de Lebedeff aspired to bring East and West closer together in harmonious accord, as she urged others to do, by finding points in common and through solidarity one with the other. This resonated with the ideal set out at the first Congress by Max Müller in 1873:

> The principal idea …was that of tracing the reciprocal action of the East and West on each other, in consequence of the modern revival of Oriental studies.[674]

21 Old Wisdom - Theosophy in Cairo

Ex Oriente Lux

No man in becoming a Theosophist need cease to be a Christian, a Buddhist, a Hindu; he will but acquire a deeper insight into his own faith, a firmer hold on its spiritual truths, a broader understanding of its sacred teachings.[675]

Annie Besant

Whilst Orientalists delved into ancient texts and the meaning of lost civilizations, the first translations of Hindu and Buddhist texts provided inspiration and a source of spiritual renewal to several generations of Romantics who were inclined to reject rationalism and materialism.

Preoccupied by the mystical, the supernatural and the subconscious, the Romantic movement at the time emphasized personal feeling, individuality and dramatic expressiveness (such as in the music of Rossini, Verdi, Chopin or Debussy). There was disillusionment with the Church and some concern about the pace of European industrialized civilization. Instead of perceiving the East as 'other', they embraced the

Orient in a reconciling vision of wholeness.[676] However, a darker side of this so-called Oriental Renaissance was drawn into racist nationalism by French Orientalists such as Gobineau.

During the years that Olga dedicated her time to Oriental Studies and travelled between Kazan to Cairo, she became increasingly drawn to a new movement, one which by 1901 was gaining popularity both in Russia and abroad. It was founded by an exiled compatriot by the name of Helena Blavatsky, born Helena Gan (1831-1891). Theosophy, as it was termed, was a 'wisdom tradition' claiming to unite religion, science and philosophy into one great synthesis.[677]

This was a parallel, but opposite trend to the philosophy of Romantic Orientalism of the second half of the nineteenth century. Helena Blavatsky's doctrine, laid out in her book *The Secret Doctrine* (1888), was a mystic-religious philosophical system. Like Spiritualism, it was considered - and often sensationalised, as occult. Yet it attracted an enormous and respectable following, not least as occultism was a current intellectual craze; avant-guard artists and intellectuals alike became fascinated by the world of possibilities opened up by the esoteric.

Helena Blavatsky had founded the society with an American, Colonel Henry Olcott (1832-1907). Their Charter of the Theosophical Society was first formalised in 1875. The term Theosophy was derived from Greek meaning 'Divine Wisdom' (*theos:* 'god' and *sophia:* 'wisdom'). Annie Besant (1874-1933), another leader of the movement from London, explained how the concepts of Theosophy could be integrated into existing spiritual practice. A cornerstone of Theosophy was to encourage the study of comparative religion, philosophy, and science.

In the early twentieth century, Theosophy presented a forward-thinking approach, and its objectives were described as threefold:

1. To form a nucleus of the Universal Brotherhood of Humanity, without distinction of race, creed, sex, caste or colour.
2. To encourage the study of Comparative Religion, Philosophy and Science.
3. To investigate unexplained laws of Nature and the powers latent in man.

Intellectuals in Olga's circles had been frustrated by the apparent hypocrisy and contradictions in their societies and mainstream religion. The concepts in Theosophy offered a truth beyond all political and geographical boundaries. It was cosmopolitan and international. This was a time of great intellectual ferment and social unrest, when many were searching for eternal truths, a strong moral ethic and a sense of personal dignity.

In Russia, the Theosophy movement also attracted many serious and respected scholars, writers, artists, and scientists. They looked to the 'revaluation of all values' and the birth of a new culture at a time when the concept of and faith in science was almost seen as an equivalent of truth, progress and radicalism.

Other Russian Theosophists

Whilst there were Theosophical centres in most European capitals, unless they travelled abroad Russians were only gradually introduced to Theosophical writings in Russia via smuggled books in English or French. They began to see in Theosophy a spiritual union of East and West 'that would bring Russia out of its long sleep and send it forth to save decaying Western civilization from the deadening hand of positivism and scientific materialism.'[678] Before 1901 there were only a few individual Theosophists and a few private circles but after this there was more press coverage and once Russian censorship regulations were liberalised after the Revolution of 1905, a new journal appeared disseminating Theosophical articles.

In her book, *No Religion Higher than the Truth*, Maria Carlson explains that Theosophy offered a strong moral ethic in the face of a crisis in materialistic culture, crime, social alienation, and decadence:

> Theology's implicit social agenda, its answer to the question "How should we live" was also attractive to the Russian intelligentsia. Its program dealt with everything from toleration of race and religion to vegetarianism... One of Theosophy's greatest temptations...was its promise of the Great Synthesis: of

science, religion, and philosophy, of matter and spirit, and of East and West. [679]

Amongst some of the many famous Russian Theosophists were writers and philosophers such as Vladimir Soloviev, Andrei Belyi, Nikolai Berdiaev, and Nikolai & Helena Roerich; others such as the artist Wassily Kandinsky (1866-1944) were influenced by Theosophy. Several Orientalists disseminated information about Eastern thought, making it appear less 'exotic'.[680]

Two famous Russian women in this society were the philanthropist Anna Filosofova (1837-1912), one of the founders of the Russian women's movement and campaigner for women's education and employment, and Anna Kamenskaya (1867-1952).[681] The latter was President of the Russian Theosophical Society, and active in social work and the growing Russian Women's Movement.

Influence of Theosophy on Olga de Lebedeff

Inspiration from Theosophy may be shown in Olga's writing in the period 1899-1900, when she referenced harmony and light. It may be seen that the concepts on the unity of science and religion found in the Theosophical movement had some resonances with the beliefs of the Baha'i. There was appreciation of each other's lack of dogma and prejudice, if not a total match of one another's belief system.

At a geographical crossroads between Europe and the East and between the two hemispheres, Egypt was a crossroad of faiths, and it was here on 7 May 1908 that Olga founded a Theosophical Society Lodge.[682] Remarkably, this was four months before the official registering of the Russian Theosophical Society in St Petersburg. The Theosophist magazine dated 10 July 1908 describes this as the first lodge founded in Egypt, and Olga is referred to as countess: 'Son Excellence Madame La Comtesse Alga [Olga] de Lebedef'.[683]

She named the lodge *El Hikmet El Kadim*, literally meaning Old Wisdom or Ancient Philosophy (in modern Arabic, *al-hikma al-qadima*). [684] This was a translation into Arabic of the concept of Theosophy as coming from ancient traditions. The lodge owned a hall and library and provided public lectures in French.[685] It flourished for several years.[686] It is hard to imagine that, as its founder, Olga would not have been very active within the new lodge.

In 1911, she visited the Baha'i Abbas Effendi on his visit to Alexandria. Details of her visit to him were recorded on a tablet he wrote to one of his disciples (where he referred to Olga as Gulnar), as well as on a postcard she wrote to Isabella Grinevskaya. About Theosophy Abbas Effendi wrote:

> As for the Theosophical Society, shouldst thou attend their gatherings and speak of the oneness of humanity; of the contents of the Divine Tablets; of the spirituality born of heaven; and of equality, concord, love, and harmony among the children of men; and consort with them with the utmost attraction, this will doubtless be beneficial.

Meanwhile, Olga continued to be based in Cairo during the winter months until at least 1913.[687]

Olga's choice of translations

It can be no coincidence that all the Tatar and Arabic translations undertaken by Olga had a religious or philosophical theme, starting with the early text of *Qabus Nameh* (a Persian classic).

Two of the Arabic manuscripts were stored in the Vatican library. The first was by a Christian Arab from Aleppo: *Voyages of an Arab* (on travels in the Holy Lands). The other author of *A History of the Conversion of the Georgians to Christianity* was the Patriarch Macaire of Antioch.[688] As mentioned previously, Olga's translation of the eleventh century epistle by the Sufi Al-Qushari explored the mystical concepts and practices of the Sufi religion. All were translated into French and presented at the International Congress of Orientalists over ten years between 1902 and 1912. This was a contribution to scholarship and enabled the comparison of religious texts. Importantly, the works were first-time translations into a Western European language.[689]

Fig. 87
Olga de Lebedeff wearing the Order of the Shefakat, approx. 1891 taken in Kazan (Family Collection).

Part V: Life in and out of Russia

22 Arco, Austro-Hungarian Empire

> Know you the land where the lemon trees bloom?
> Goethe

> I dreamed in a dream I saw a city invincible to the attacks of the whole of the rest of the earth, I dreamed that was the new city of Friends.
> Walt Whitman, 1867

This chapter takes a retrospective look back to a pivotal time in Olga's life when she began to visit the town of Arco, a place which for over thirty years would be a home and later a refuge.

Since the summer of 1894, her family had holidayed near Lake Garda in what was then Austria-Hungary. Her widowed mother, Prascovia Barstchoff, had bought herself a handsome villa in the small, picturesque town of Arco in South Tyrol, for the price of 8,840 silver Austrian Florins.[690] Prascovia's maternal aunt Princess Radziwill (Sophie Alexandrovna Urusova) had recently left her at least a little money.[691]

Newly built in 'all'Ovo', the three-storey villa was situated a short walk from Arco's medieval square. The sixteen rooms even had electricity, the gardens of 800 square metres were planted with palm and cypress trees.[692] The mild climate suited Prascovia Hippolitovna better than in Russia, so this place became her permanent residence. She could never know how important this purchase would be for her descendants in later years.

Arco was fashionable with the Hapsburgs, European nobles, or people of means. They could arrive by train on the Brenner line connecting Innsbruck to Verona. Many foreign incomers bought properties or rented rooms for the winter whilst taking a pulmonary cure in the health resort, known in German as a 'Kurort'; others passed through on a six-week tour of the Tyrol.

The region was known for the fresh quality of the air between the mountains and Lake Garda. The Dolomites sheltered the town from northerly winds; though snow would thickly cover the mountains till spring, the sun in the valley was still warm. In summer, it was much cooler than Rome. In this lush Mediterranean microclimate where vineyards and olive groves flourished alongside pomegranates and lemons, both nature and scenery were felt by many who visited to be healing for body and soul.

Fig. 88
The town of Arco with its high rock and castle (Family Collection).

Over the old town towered a rocky outcrop with the ruins of a medieval castle, owned by the Counts of Arco. The buildings below were built in an arc around this rock, giving the town its name. The original inhabitants, the local Italian speakers, lived in the old town.

The new hotel opposite, Hotel Erzherzog Albrecht, bore the name of the Hapsburg Archduke Albert, Duke of Teschen. Arco was a favourite location for the Archduke, who visited the town regularly with his entourage, until his death there in 1895.

Fig. 89
Fair of Sant' Anna, c. 1900 Arco [693]

The memoirs of one right wing Austrian aristocrat, the outspoken Countess Editha von Salburg of Graz (Krieg-Hocfelden), describe the period and her neighbours through a critical lens. [694] She lived near to the Barstchoff-Lebedeffs between 1898 and the start of WWI. Countess Salburg looked down on the local Italians and was disparaging in her description of other nationalities.

> Arco now looked questioningly at us… a group of Russians, less numerous than the English; a couple of rich Jews, who lived there. There were only a few real Austrians. The local Italian families remained, it must be said, in gloomy isolation from the Middle Ages, with undoubtedly underlying hatred …Amongst the river of people and personalities, who, at that time, passed by me in these large rooms of an Italian palace, many nice enough, there

ARCO, AUSTRO-HUNGARIAN EMPIRE

were Austrians, Hungarians, Baltic, Russians, Poles, English, a few French (barely any), and Italians.

Though she holds back from mentioning anyone by name, Countess Salburg refers with irony to her foreign neighbour Olga as 'Her Great Excellency'. She wrote how the old Countess Prascovia lived there for most of the year looking after her villa, enjoying the company of an old Austrian, whom she regularly invited for lunch.

Fig. 90
Prascovia Hippolitovna Barstchoff, née Countess Kutaisova, c. 1879 standing in front of an ornate tableau holding a white rose (Family Collection, the photo is from Kazan).

The death of Prascovia

Following a sudden decline, Prascovia Barstchoff died in Arco on 8/20 February 1900. In her final years, she had put on a great deal of weight. Her sweet tooth (recalling her predilection for chocolate pralines) no doubt resulted in her contracting diabetes, noted as the cause of death on her death certificate.

Her daughter rushed back from Rome, deeply shocked. Writing to the Count de Gubernatis, Olga exclaimed:

> 'I haven't had the heart to write till now, it was a huge shock...completely unexpected'.[695]

The Orthodox priest from Merano presided over the funeral at the villa, attended by a few neighbours. The mourners, including Countess Salburg and General Nikolai Schwedow, observed that the old countess was buried in her finery in the open coffin.[696] The burial took place at the Protestant Cemetery in Arco, which you pass on the left as you arrive from Riva del Garda. No remnant of the grave remains. Russian newspaper *Novoe Vremya* published notices about her memorial services in two churches in St Petersburg in the days that followed and an obituary.[697]

In her memoirs, Countess Salburg noted that 'the General' was a regular visitor. She may not have known that Nikolai Konstantinovich Schwedow was about to become the President of the Society of Oriental Studies.

Villa Lubiana and its guests

With its new owner, the house was renamed *Villa Lubiana*, after the wooded estate in Russia. Every year from then on, Olga would return to work on her translations, and to escape colder climes.[698] For Olga, visits to Italy also served as a convenient stop-over en route to Cairo, crossing the Mediterranean from Naples to Alexandria.

ARCO, AUSTRO-HUNGARIAN EMPIRE

At Villa Lubiana, life was by no means solitary, as Olga de Lebedeff was gregarious and loved company. Apart from General Nikolai Schwedow, other invited guests were Mr. Groult and Madame de Besneray, friends from Lisieux.[699] Her children and grandchildren arrived in Arco for holidays with their governess. From Arco they visited Milan, Lake Como, and Venice; the spa town of Salsomaggiore near Parma was another favourite.

Fig. 91
Ninette with mother Nina / Micha in Arco 1895 (Family Collection).

The General had clearly had his own designs on property in Arco, as he had previously owned an adjoining vineyard. Municipal records confirm he sold a portion of these (176 m²) to Olga, in exchange for the use of two rooms.[700] Countess Salburg considered this a plan on Olga's part to tie the General down, though unsuccessfully. As they were heard chatting together in German, Countess Salburg made a dig at the linguistic slip ups the two Russians were prone to make.

Schwedow was said to enjoy the patronage of the Tsarina Alexandra Feodorovna, but his detractors and competitors considered him something of a 'wedding' general, in other words, rather unimpressive.[701] Yet, an Abyssinian mercy mission Schwedow had led in 1896 had been a success, and in St Petersburg he held the prestigious post of Russian Red Cross Vice President; with his connections at the palace, he was certainly able to pull some strings.

Fig. 92
General N.K. Schwedow

Was it through the Red Cross that Olga had first met General Schwedow? She received the Order of the Red Cross through her work for the Russian Red Cross, recorded in her biography *Famous Women* (see Book Two).

Evidence of her activities in this field comes from the Library of Congress concerning the grain harvest failure in 1898 around Kazan.[702] Peasants were said to be begging for food, cattle were eating from the straw roofs. Olga appealed for relief for their distress to the Red Cross in the United States. She contacted an American diplomat, the Hon. A.W. Terrell, former Minister in Constantinople, whom she had met staying at the same hotel in Constantinople some years before[703] and he in turn wrote to the Red Cross. Though the petition did not result in American Red Cross aid because their work in Cuba was unfinished and the coffers were stretched, it shows that Olga used her influence as best she could.

A million rubles and personal loss

It was well known to friends and acquaintances that Olga and her husband Alexander Lebedeff lived very separate lives. No photographs of him were passed down in the family collection. But despite their differences, the Lebedeffs did not divorce. To some extent, there were useful advantages to maintaining appearances, with him being Chamberlain to the Tsar and she a renowned Orientalist. Divorce would have been messy, expensive and invited scandal, so they put up with one another. They were both godparents to granddaughter Irina[704] born in 1904 to Olga Alexandrovna (married to the lawyer Vladimir Mikhailovich Gorloff).[705]

The fortune Alexander had amassed was over a million rubles.[706] In Kazan, his lasting legacy was a bridge named *Lebedevsky Bridge*; it was financed with 20,000 rubles from his own funds when the city council money ran out. [707] On 25 June 1910, the journal *l'Ideal-Journal* announced his death. Quoting a eulogy in a Kazan journal, he was referred to as 'a great altruist, universally acclaimed for his works of charity.' [708]

Both Olga's first husband and the second died within three years of each other. Olga's eldest son, Vladimir Dlotovsky, had an untimely death a few months after his father in 1907.

Fig. 93
Family and Friends: Vladimir (son, 1st right), Vladimir Dlotovsky (3rd right), Vera Dlotovsky-Cordelas (5th right) circa 1906 (Family Collection).

23 Russian biography, Revolution and Revelation

From some archived letters, it can be observed that around the time of WWI Olga had returned to Kazan. It was safer there than in Arco, as war had reached Austrian South Tyrol, where Italy sought to claim lands which it believed were rightfully Italian.

There remains scant correspondence from this period, which reveal just one or two snippets of information about Olga's health and her connections with other writers. For instance, a postcard to the Orientalist Krachkovsky, written in January 1915, requested a useful contact for someone else, and described how she had failing eyesight.[709] She now relied on others to help with reading.

This was confirmed in a letter that year to Isabella Grinevskaya. Olga wrote a few pleasantries: that her health had improved overall; the weather was hot; she would go to Lubiana from mid-May; the post was in a dire state.[710]

The friendship with Isabella had one further outcome: Isabella produced the only biographical account of Olga written in Russian. It was just two pages, intended for a dictionary of writers compiled by S.A. Vengerov, a literary historian and collector of biographies.

The two pages describe Olga's published works, family background, honours awarded and the eleven languages in which Olga had fluency: 'French, German, English, Italian, Turkish, Persian, Arabic,

Latin, plus a little Hebrew and Sanskrit';[711] omitted are Tatar, Greek, Spanish, and of course, Russian which totals fourteen.

In the letter from April 1915, Olga asked how to obtain a copy of the dictionary and thanked for her kindness in remembering her. No copy of this work has yet been identified, or indeed whether Olga was finally included in it.

At the Revolution

Following his father's death, Micha, the youngest Lebedeff, had inherited the family estate at Lubiana where he maintained the local school of twenty students.[712] As landowner, he served as Marshal of the Nobility up until the Revolution.[713] After this, everything was to change.

Sensing the turning tide of revolution in 1917, he sold the estate. He said his goodbyes, arranging for the priest to bless the villagers. From here he set off across Siberia to Vladivostok. He crossed the Pacific Ocean to Victoria in British Colombia on a British built steamer, the 'RMS Empress of Russia', which boasted the quickest journey time across the Pacific. The ship's record states that his intended destination was New York. Micha arrived with one thousand dollars, some twenty-three thousand dollars today. He then sailed from Victoria to Seattle on 17 September 1917 on the Princess Adelaide.[714] Significantly, under 'next of kin', the ship's record states that his mother Olga was still living in Kazan, a time when city was not yet taken by the Bolsheviks.

Micha settled in Manhattan for a year attached to the Russian Consulate General. He signed up for the US Army WWI in September 1918.[715] Though the war was soon over and so he did not see active service, he had returned to Europe. One year later in November 1919, he returned to New York for good. Micha got himself a job as a stock trader in Manhattan for Goodbody & Co. [716] He never married and lived in rented communal flats by Central Park, near the Russian Orthodox church.

Meanwhile, the Lubiana manor in near Kazan underwent a looting in what locals referred to as a 'pogrom'. This included the smashing of the windows and furniture, and the burning of books. A fire threatened the whole building. It was put out by a former employee. Valuables such as icons and cutlery vanished. The orangeries were dismantled and the exotic plants, deemed of little use, were eventually taken off to the botanical gardens in Kazan.[717] The village heard stories of Admiral Kolchak's forces as they passed through the region; the Red Army also trekked through the village in 1919.

It was truly the end of an era for the Lebedeff family, but also for the city of Kazan itself. The last detachments on the Volga line of defence, the Russian People's Army, held out against the Bolsheviks together with Allied troops of the Czech Legion. They were forced to retreat when Kazan was finally taken by the Bolsheviks on 6 August 1918; fear of the Red Army was so great that 30,000 inhabitants of the city left with the retreating forces. [718]

This must have been a chance window for Olga to leave before the city was taken; a way to evade the world war as well as the Russian civil war. There are no exact records of her departure. The most frequent escape routes were through Poland or Sweden, or south via the Bosphorus through Turkey and the Balkans.[719] Travelling in whichever direction was perilous, as till October 1918 Ottoman forces were still fighting in WWI.

Reflection: During the revolution itself in the Kazan region, one of the most pressing questions in public life revolved around the issue of emancipation for Muslim women in Russia. Demands for extending voting rights to women were thus promoted during the years of revolution. In the twenty-first century, Olga de Lebedeff is credited as having been an inspiration to the movement since her activities at the 1899 International Congress of Orientalists in Rome. [720]

Destination Arco

Arco was where Olga lived out most of her elderly years. Her three daughters, Nina, Vera, and Olga survived the revolution too. Nina and

Vera both stayed for some years in Italy; but it was Vera who lived with her mother. For some, this survival was thought of as 'the bitter bread of exile'. But returning to their villa of many years, though refugees and stateless, they were very fortunate to have a home of their own.

Fig. 94
A locket sized miniature of Olga de Lebedeff (actual size 2.4 x1.7 cm) with a note in my grandmother's writing (Family Collection).

They feared for Sacha Lebedeff, the only one of them who had stayed behind in Russia. Depressing stories from there abounded: of repression, arrests, and famine. Food parcels were sent, including flour, pasta, rice, corn oil and milk powder. Aid from the Red Cross reached even the small village of Lubiana. Micha sent food packages from New York. These were remembered by the former cook, who spoke in glowing terms about her former boss: 'proud of the care and attention he showed her'. [721]

In Arco, Olga and Vera were by no means the only stateless people of Russian origin. Elena Galitzine and Tatiana Ignatieff were a few doors down. Tatiana turned her home (formerly the house of Countess Salburg) into a guesthouse, where it was said that for a certain time only

Russian was spoken. Olga and Vera also had the company of Liubov [or Aimée] Dostoyevsky (1869-1926), daughter of the famous novelist. Aimée was a good friend of Vera's and stayed as their guest whilst recuperating at the sanatorium just months before she died in late 1926.[722]

After World War I, Arco became part of Trentino, Italy. Olga should have been owed war damages after clashes between Austro-Hungarians and the Italian forces damaged the building. But not being an Italian citizen, she did not qualify for war damage repayments.[723]

The Arco town archive had just one or two more important nuggets to show. The first, was that Olga lived at Villa Lubiana until October 1928.[724] Was it financial need or poor health that precipitated the house sale? [725] The second record cites that the council did offer to pay war damages two years after they had already left the town, with no onward address. The villa had been in the family's keeping for thirty-four years: a home during the age of empire, through WWI, the Russian Revolution and Civil War and up until well into the years of fascism. Alarmingly, the fascists had begun to dominate daily life and arrests were now normal; the slogan "Mussolini is always right" was pervasive.

Crucially, the population register in Arco indicated that Olga and Vera left for France on 24 December 1928, just after Olga's seventy-sixth birthday.[726] A few postcards written by Nina and Vera remain as further clues as to their whereabouts. They indicate that Vera lived on the French Riviera at Menton during the 1930's. The rail journey from Arco to Menton most likely took two days: from Verona with a change in Milan, then on to Genoa and along the Italian coastline to the French frontier. Menton lies just across the Italian French border. Where exactly Olga went to in Menton is still uncertain. The Russian community had established their own Russian Home for Convalescents. Perhaps this home was her destination?

The Pearl of France

Often known as the 'Pearl of France', between the wars Menton was quiet and more run down than in its earlier heyday.

RUSSIAN BIOGRAPHY, REVOLUTION AND REVELATION

There had been a sizeable Russian community for many years. Visitors also came from 'old Europe' – English, Austrians, Germans, Russians, Dutch, and Scandinavians - as well as Americans and Australians. The English and Russians established their own churches, and the English had their own society newspaper *The Menton & Monte Carlo News*. As a Count Moszynski who used to spend the winter in Marseille commented, 'The English have the habit of fleeing their country from the autumn like swallows only to return home in the spring'.[727]

Fig. 95
Postcard from Vera to Nina, Menton (Family Collection).

Those visitors had over-wintered here in hotels, pensions and villas and perhaps took cures in hydrotherapy and heliotherapy. The temperature rarely dropped below sixteen Celsius, and the air quality of this microclimate, not unlike Arco's, was beneficial to those with lung complaints. Yet in 1929, many hotels were going out of business.

Following the Russian Revolution and Civil War, on the eastern coast of the Cote d'Azur near the Italian border were more than 3,300 Russian émigrés. Amongst them were famous writers, musicians including Rachmaninov and Stravinsky, painters such as Chagall and the dancers of the itinerant ballet company *Ballet Russes*, and members of the White Army regiment of General Wrangel. Associations and committees had been set up to welcome the émigrés some of whom had exceedingly difficult financial circumstances. Many took any job going, from taxi driver to hotel pageboy.[728]

A revelation in Sacha's confiscated letters

The unhappy fate of Sacha Lebedeff has been uncovered in the *Memorial Book of the Nizhni Novgorod District*.[729] Sacha had stayed behind in Russia. Details of his mother's death are tied up with his own.

Prior to the revolution he had had an excellent education and served as Marshal of the Nobility in the district of Laishevsky. After the Revolution he was classed 'a former person', and like all members of the nobility, was stripped of any privileges.[730] Sacha fought with the White Guard and funded their cause against the Bolsheviks. His sentence in the memorial book states that in 1925 he was accused of spying in Moscow, for which he was sent to a concentration camp for three years. Afterwards, he earned his living as an accountant for a large restaurant chain.

Aged fifty-seven, he was arrested on 26 August 1937. He was sentenced by a three-person commission, and shot three weeks later without trial, a victim of Stalin's purges. His pseudonym is written in brackets: *Bedokurov* – meaning 'mischief-maker' or joker.

Before his death, the FSB archive (formerly KGB) in Moscow confiscated Sacha's personal correspondence. There, letters record that his mother, Olga de Lebedeff, died in Menton in 1933.[731]

Fig. 96
Some Postcards and Stamps of the era (Family Collection).

Epilogue

In 1947, my mother Veronica was given a photograph of the garden at Villa Lubiana in Arco by her grandma Nina Bahache. It was a touching memento of a well-loved place, given with a hope that one day she would perhaps go there. Over sixty years later, Veronica did attempt to find the villa, but it was in vain as she did not know the exact location. Upon further enquiry and a chance meeting, she was later sent the address, and it became clear that the name of the villa had changed.

Fig. 97
Garden at Villa Lubiana, Arco (Family Collection).

With this new information, in October 2017 (eighty-nine years after it was sold), I visited the previously named Villa Lubiana. The house had recently been painted a beautiful light pink colour, and the palm trees in the garden were now fully grown. As I walked up the front steps and into the hallway, I felt a warmth and sense of welcome as well as an

EPILOGUE

intriguing excitement and gratitude for this home and refuge - so much loved by my grandmother and her family in years long gone.

Fig. 98
Villa Lubiana, view from the back garden (Family Collection).

Of the years in between, a few postcards, archive materials and threads of memory fill in a few gaps. The records show how Olga's daughters and grandchildren were scattered across continents.

According to Vera Dlotovsky's last postcard in November 1937, Vera had moved to Beaulieu-sur-Mer in the south of France. She wrote that she was looking after an elderly Countess Faletary. Though her trail ends in this beautiful town, it would not be too much longer before the occupation of the Riviera by German troops. An undated postcard from her wishes the recipient spiritual joys and peace of mind as the only consolation to overcome human trials and tribulations:

> Je te souhaite des joies spirituelles et la paix de l'âme. C'est la seule consolation dans nos épreuves ! Des ailes, des ailes pour planer au-dessus des misères humaines.

To Vienna and Cannes

What happened to Olga de Lebedeff's youngest daughter, Olga Alexandrovna? She and her family had moved away from Russia during the First World War in 1916, where her lawyer husband Vladimir Gorlof (1871-1948) was first secretary in the Paris Embassy. Olga Alexandrovna lived there with her children until 1929. They moved to Warsaw where Vladimir was Head of Mission. He was concerned with the 'refugee question' and the White Russian movement. Before the Red Army occupied Warsaw, and because the Nazis still occupied Paris, in 1944 the Gorlofs moved to Vienna where their younger daughter (also called Olga) married an Austrian. Upon being widowed in 1948, Olga Gorlof moved to Graz with her Austrian 'Foreigners' passport to live near her daughter and then Salzburg from 1951-1956. Finally, she spent the last six years of her life in Cannes at a retirement home where she died in 1962, aged 81. On her application to France as a Russian but stateless refugee, the paperwork stated that 'for political reasons' she did not wish to return to Russia.[732]

To Nottingham

Aunt Irene was another of Olga de Lebedeff's granddaughters: In her fifties, Irene Gorlof became a British citizen. She married an Englishman from Nottingham called Wilfred Parker, a widower; they had no children of their own. In 1953, her naturalisation documents were put under an injunction not to be opened for one hundred years. There are too many of such files for the National Archives to look through, which is why they are closed until a request is received to open them. Here it showed that Irene Gorlof worked for the RAF in Vienna. She was an interpreter there for two years after the war; then she applied for asylum in Britain, and later naturalisation. She spoke excellent French, English, German, Polish and Russian. She never openly spoke of her trials in getting to the UK, so my parents were quite unaware of them.

To South America

Olga de Lebedeff's eldest daughter was my great-grandmother, Nina Dlotovsky-Bahache. After leaving Italy for the last time, she moved to Latin America. She had travelled with the last of her remaining funds - and a few borrowed ones from her daughter, Ninette. She tended to live life lavishly, as my mother said 'like an oligarch' – and travelled constantly as she had always done, until her funds ran out. She took her treasures and personal effects with her, most engraved with her initials [N.B.] underneath a crown: there were a silver-plated samovar, a silver mirror and brush vanity set, silver teaspoons, silver framed icons and the

EPILOGUE

oval-framed holy relics from Rome (fragments of bones of the saints). Her father's brown leather photograph album, and her ancestors historical papers, were safely transported too.

These documents are the ones I have translated to make sense of this history. There were also original photographs and postcards of the Russian royal family; the kind that would have been confiscated by the authorities in Russia in the Soviet era.

In 1929, Nina took Argentine nationality. She initially lived with daughter Ninette and family, the Bobrovskys in Asuncion, Paraguay. Never quite able to fully adapt to this new life and customs of the New World in extreme humid heat, the sorrows of the past few years took their toll on her now fragile mental health.

To London, Japan & South America

My grandparents had met and married in London in the last months of the First World War, when Russia and Britain were allies. Ninette Bahache worked as a translator for the allied war effort and lived with her mother at Smyrna Mansions in Smyrna Road, London. She fell in love with Major-General Sergei Bobrovsky (1875-1957). He was eighteen years older than her, divorced, and the head of a Russo-British engineering project called BECOS (The British Engineering Company of Siberia). They married in August 1918 and had their first child, also nicknamed Olga, in London.[733]

Joining the counter-revolution against the Bolsheviks, my grandfather commanded a ship, the Mogilev, which collected about four hundred White Russian officers from ports en route to Vladivostok. Their plan was to help with the civil war effort supporting Admiral Kolchak and his White Army on the Eastern front. However, the Mogilev was damaged in a storm and diverted to Japan, where it faced a long delay in repairs. In the meantime, Kolchak was executed and Vladivostok fell to the Bolsheviks. Most officers returned to Europe or stayed in Japan.

After two years in Japan and the tragic death of their firstborn, the Bobrovskys relocated to South America where Sergei was offered work for the Ministry of Engineering in Buenos Aires. A former military engineer, he was soon invited to work in Paraguay. There, he founded the Faculty of Engineering in Asuncion and was its first Dean. He was involved in the design and building of over four hundred projects of roads and bridges. The couple had three more children in South America: Sergio, Tatiana and Veronica. Due to glaucoma, Sergei gradually lost his sight. Then he would ask Veronica, to read aloud Tolstoy's *War and Peace* or recite poetry in Russian - having insisted that she learn the language with a tutor and at home, alongside Spanish and French.

I have a few impressions of my grandmother, referred to as 'Babu', from hearsay: a strong, but warm personality; someone of high expectations. On her desk lay a flurry of paperwork, that no one should touch. The words *'grande dame'* were applied to her, perhaps not least as she had many interests, read extensively and was an engaging conversationalist.

Also like her grandmother Olga, Ninette was an accomplished pianist, her book of Bach *Preludes* is annotated one prelude per day, and she had a fine singing voice. She continued the tradition of reading aloud Russian stories and poems like Pushkin's *Tsar Saltan* in a singsong and expressive voice. A snippet below of this lengthy poem was taught to me in Russian by my aunt Tatiana, with my English translation as follows:

Ветер по морю гуляет	Across the swelling sea
И кораблик подгоняет;	Speeds the small boat -
Он бежит себе в волнах	Skimming the waves
На раздутых парусах	Sails swollen:
[Мимо острова крутого,	[Past craggy isle,
Мимо города большого:	Past tall town's pier,
Пушки с пристани палят,	Then cannon fire
Кораблю пристать велят.]	Directs the boat to dock.]

Ninette de Bobrovsky had worked as a translator and my mother said that she knew some twenty languages. This included the main European ones, Turkish and some Japanese. In Asuncion, she worked for a time for the Paraguayan Foreign Service, and during the Chaco War as a Red Cross nurse. She was even offered a prestigious post as chief translator for an international organization in New York, but due to the ill health of her husband was unable to take up the offer.

EPILOGUE

Some final thoughts about Olga...

Reflecting on the missions and life's work of Olga de Lebedeff, one of her main interests appears to have been in providing a bridge between different cultures and finding a common understanding. She cherished the ideal of international harmony, outlined in her work *On the Emancipation of Muslim Women*. Here she urged her readers 'to reject all petty feelings of nationalistic or religious enmity and to extend the hand of friendship to the peoples of the East', and she stated that 'we can establish lasting relations outside of any religious or political concerns between the two worlds of East and West, by learning each other's ethics and cultural needs.'

Through her scholarly work at the congresses and her enduring activism for Kazan Tatars and for Muslim women, Olga was connected to a wide circle of intellectuals which included scholars, reformists, and government officials in the international sphere: Russians, Tatars, Turks and Ottomans, Egyptians, French, Italians, Germans, Austrians, Hungarians, Romanians, and Serbians.

In her activism and as founder of the Society of Oriental Studies, she grappled with the central issue of how neighbouring countries, as well as Muslims with non-Muslims, could live side-by-side in peace. One might say, from Russia she had looked through both the so-called 'window on Europe' from St Petersburg, and the 'window on the East' from Kazan.

As the Ottoman Ahmed Midhat realised on his tour of Europe with his new friend Gülnar, Olga de Lebedeff was brilliantly versed in the customs and languages of both Eastern and Western countries and loved to find the connections between them and promote the best of each.

Looking back at her life, it seems that in many ways she succeeded in her quests. On a personal level, I hope that now, in some way by recording her story, Olga's efforts may continue to inspire.

Book Two

Translations

The Poet Pushkin (1891) p. 300
Translation from Ottoman Turkish by Şehnaz & Aykut Gürçağlar

Muslim Women at the Time of the Caliphs (1899)* p. 327

The Emancipation of Muslim Women (1900)* p. 329

The New Rights of Muslim Women (1902)* p. 341

Speech at the Algiers Congress (1905)* p. 348
* Translations from French by: C. Hamilton & M. Atkinson

On the Conversion of the Georgians (1905) p. 350
An Appreciation of the Arabic text by Marilyn Booth

Famous Women (1907) p. 354
Translation from Arabic by Marilyn Booth

THE POET PUSHKIN (1891)

The Poet Pushkin has been translated into English for this volume by Şehnaz and Aykut Gürçağlar.

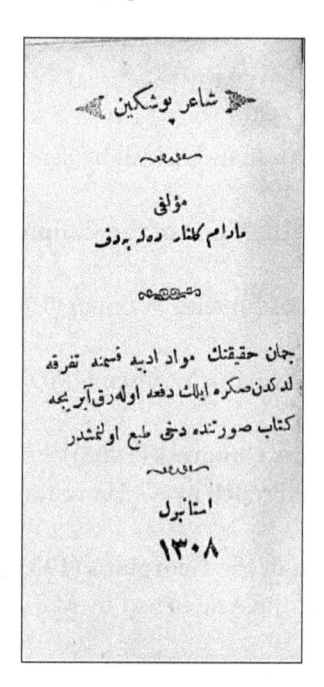

Note: Original Ottoman Turkish page numerals feature above the following English text.

THE POET PUSHKIN

1

A Translation of *Şair Puşkin* **by Madame Gülnâr de Lebedeff
With** *A Statement* **by Ahmed Midhat Efendi**

This work is being published in book form for the first time after being serialized in the literature section in *Tercüman-ı Hakikat*.

Istanbul
1891 (1308)

« براؤاده »

فضيلت‌پروران مستشرقيندن كنار خانم افندى — كه اسم صحيحلرى مادام اولغا ده‌له‌به‌دفر — السنه وعلوم وادبيات شرقيه‌يى تحصيل ايله مشتغل اولوب بومناسبتله وتجربة قلم يوللو يازدقلرى بعض آثارى عثمانليلق عالمنده نشر ايچون بوعبد عاجزه توديع بيورمش اولدقلرينى « اورو پاده برجولان » « مژده بيان ايلمش وآثار مذكوره‌دن » قار فورتنه‌سى »

2 ٢

A Statement by Ahmed Midhat

I had explained in my *Avrupa'da Bir Cevelan* (A Trip Through Europe) that Gülnâr Hanım Efendi (whose real name is Olga de Lebedeff), a lover of virtue and a follower of knowledge, studied and occupied herself with Oriental languages, sciences, and literatures, and that she gave some of the works she wrote to a humble servant like me to be published in the Ottoman world. I recently published one of these works under the title *The Blizzard*.

3 ٣

This time I am publishing an essay by Gülnâr Hanım by the title *Poet Pushkin*. The work in question has been subject to some revisions; the degree of these revisions has already been taken up in the preface to *The Blizzard*, therefore making their repetition redundant. However, there is a need to write a few words about the subject matter of the work. Pushkin is among the leading authors of the Russians and died about sixty years ago.

4 ٤

The reason I call him a leading Russian author is because he is not among those who have imitated their predecessors but a poet who has greatly contributed to the linguistic and intellectual innovation of his country.

As it has been proven in the case of many others, the true greatness and value of such men are acknowledged after their passing and the importance of their writing leaves national borders once they are fully appreciated within the borders of their own nation and assumes a general civilizational importance. Nowadays Pushkin is not only perceived as a Russian author but also judged as a great man as part of general human civilization, thus leading to the translation of his works into European languages such as German, French, and English.

THE POET PUSHKIN

5 ٥

This work, which bears the title of the great poet, is not only a biography. A biography is the specific life history of a man, while this work goes far beyond this definition. This essay focuses on the fruits of Pushkin's labour and is therefore a work of appreciation regarding Pushkin. The appreciation of a work shows two aspects: one of these is its linguistic capabilities, while the other is its intellectual capabilities. We are not able to appreciate the linguistic capabilities of the work, as we are not competent in the Russian language.

6 ٦

In any case, this aspect of the appreciation of a work is limited to the members of the nation that the author belongs to and cannot leave this area. Yet the second aspect is where advanced nations share common ground. Taking this point into consideration, Gülnâr Hanım has provided us with the synopses of Pushkin's major works. Through reading these, our readers will develop an idea about this literature as if they had read the works of this masterful poet and memorized his expressions themselves.

7 ٧

Thus, the reading of the summaries will not only introduce our readers to Pushkin but also enable them to benefit more as if they have read his most select works. As a final word, I would like to convey my gratitude to Gülnâr Hanım on behalf of Ottoman readers, as I feel obliged once more to express our feelings of appreciation to this honourable lady for her assistance in enabling us to benefit directly from this legacy. We are proud of the love she has shown for our language, science, and intellectual tradition.

شاعر بوشكين

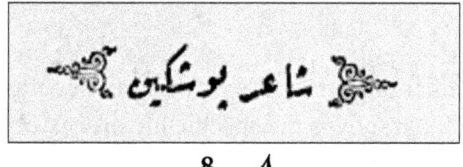

8 ٨

The Poet Pushkin

Alexander Pushkin was born in 1799. He was born to one of the most respected families of Moscow. His father was a descendent of an ancient lineage of Pushkins, that of the Boyar Grigory Pushkin, Ambassador to Poland during the Reign of Tsar Alexei. His mother was the youngest daughter of the famous black man Abram Hannibal. Her father had gained the favour of Peter the Great who even had him baptized.

9 ٩

Abram's son General Ivan had gained fame after the capture of Navarin. As an educated man for his time, Pushkin's father was an exemplary person with his good morals. Since he was a very hospitable man, his home was open to Muscovite nobility, as well as famous poets and authors. These poets and authors included Derzhavin, Karamzin, Dimitriev, Zhukovsky, Batyushkov, etc. Pushkin's father always discussed literature with them and did some writing on his own, a part of which was in French.

10 ١٠

Apparently, French governesses supervised young Pushkin's education. Growing up under the instruction of these governesses, Russia's future poet naturally did not develop any competence over Russian customs. The major shortcomings in his education were remedied and corrected by his nurse Arina. This nurse told young Alexander many Russian stories, songs and legends and taught him Russian literature [sic].[734] Like all talented and easily affected children, Pushkin loved to read very much. His father's library was composed of works by the most famous authors of the

THE POET PUSHKIN

18th century and the young boy read them with great enthusiasm and as he read more, he wanted to try his hand at writing.

11 ١١

When he was fifteen years old, he wrote a comedy in French and performed it only for his family.

In 1811 Pushkin was sent to the new school founded at Tsarskoye Selo. Although his education thus far was poor, his intelligence became quickly apparent. At that time students at the Lyceum lived in great affection just like big families. The libraries in the Lyceum were always open for the students and students had a keener interest in literary studies than other subjects.

12 ١٢

Several students at the Lyceum published a newspaper. Pushkin's poetry started to appear in publication starting from 1814. Naturally, Pushkin's writing at the time echoed the ideas by Russian and foreign writers that he was most influenced by. However, after 1817 his poetry started to display motifs of a national character. His verses were harmonious and sounded exquisite. His poetry during his years at the Lyceum displayed an extraordinary variety and included rubais, elegies and satirical poems.

13 ١٣

After completing the Lyceum in 1817, Pushkin obtained a position at the Foreign Ministry. However, he had already joined the ranks of famous poets; he did not pay much attention to his job and tended towards mundane pleasures and delights. Again, it was around this time that he became a member of a critical literary circle called Arzamas. This circle helped a great deal in opening the minds and hearts of the Russian nation. One of the leading writers in the Arzamas circle was Count Uvarov. The people who set up and constituted this circle studied the works of various writers with great interest and objectivity and searched and scrutinized ancient and foreign literature with a view to finding devices that would constitute a contemporary new Russian language.

14

They established the essentials of Russian literature as required. At the time Zhukovsky, Batyushkov, and even historian Karamzin wrote a few works with the influence of the Arzamas circle. Although this was an important and serious circle, its members were unceremonious in their interactions. They treated each other in a friendly and sincere manner and called themselves the "souls of Arzamas". During this period Pushkin published his first famous poem titled *Ruslan and Ludmila* whose contents are described below.

15

Ruslan and Ludmila

As Ludmila, the daughter of Prince Vladimir called the "beautiful sun", and the knight Ruslan are holding their wedding, darkness suddenly falls over the world and sounds of thunder and similar noises start to be heard. Within a few minutes all the invited guests fall into a slumber and become unconscious. After a while the darkness disappears, and the sleepers suddenly awaken. Yet when they see that the bride has disappeared, they realize that all was the doing of the famous wizard, long bearded dwarf Chernomor. Upon this, all the knights present there set out to look for the bride everywhere.

16

After many challenges and adventures Ruslan finds poor Ludmila in the beautiful and sumptuous palace that Chernomor created with his spell. Ruslan kills Chernomor with a magic sword he once found in a battlefield and rescues Ludmila. Before he dies,

Chernomor inflicts the girl with a sleeping sickness. He has thus avenged himself of the rescuers of Ludmila. Ruslan takes Ludmila away in this state and takes her to their home, puts a spell-breaking ring on her finger and manages to wake her up. Thanks to this wonderful result the mother and father of the girl are enveloped in a sea of happiness and the wedding is held amid much pomp and splendour.

17 ١٧

This poem was written in such beautiful Russian that readers became mesmerized by its artistry. However, because the poet invented expressions that had hitherto never been used, certain old-school writers criticized this new language. Yet scholars who had modern ideas and greater sagacity appreciated and admired Pushkin's inventive talent. They considered this work the foundation of a Russian language that was just emerging. Although the story told in this work is fictitious and completely imaginary, its expression and style are highly sophisticated. The poem forms a unity of grace, elegance, and harmony.

18 ١٨

Glinka, the famous composer of the first Russian operas, created an opera out of the poem and masterfully composed its music.In 1820, Pushkin was exiled to the Caucasus by the government who disliked the satirical pieces he wrote criticizing the corruption made visible by the new European style of civilization in Russia. The charms of the region, its wonderful air and water and the unforgettable vistas were an inspiration to Pushkin. That is why the Caucasus region had such a positive impact on the poems Pushkin wrote there.

19 ١٩

Pushkin not only wrote descriptions of natural landscapes, stories, and poetic legends. He also wrote a great deal about history and politics. He studied Lord Byron's works with great interest. The intelligence of this English poet provided the inspiration for his famous novel *Eugene Onegin*. (Around five-six years ago the famous composer Tchaikovsky adapted this novel into a wonderful opera). A summary of the novel follows.

Eugene Onegin

One of the most brilliant young men of Moscow society, Eugene Onegin, travels to his country estate in the summer.

20 ٢٠

One day his childhood friend Vladimir Lensky introduces him to a family who are his neighbours. This family is composed of a widow and her two daughters. Both girls are very pretty and the older one (Olga) is engaged to Lensky. The younger daughter (Tatyana) is only sixteen years old. Olga is always gay and merry, while Tatyana is her opposite, dreamy and pensive. Tatyana grows fond of Eugene and after waiting and enduring patiently for a few weeks, she decides to write Eugene a letter. In her letter she discloses her deepest feelings and tells Eugene that she believes that he is sent by God to make her happiness complete.

21 ٢١

She thus declares her love for the young man and requests Eugene to come to the garden to speak to her to reach a conclusion. Eugene arrives at the place she suggests. However, he tells the girl that the affection and love she has displayed is merely an ignorant and childish act. He confesses that he is created to court the whole world and that he is not a man that can dedicate his heart to one girl only. He therefore advises her to give up on this idea and find a man capable of making herself happy. Naturally enough, Tatyana was extremely saddened by his response. After some time, Tatyana's mother organizes a ball where Eugene is also invited.

THE POET PUSHKIN

22 ٢٢

When Lensky sees that Eugene and his fiancée Olga dance together for a long time and become friendly, his heart is struck by jealousy, and he challenges Eugene to a duel. When the opponents face each other in the battle ground, they remember that they were friends since childhood and avoid shooting their guns. Finally, when the witnesses goad them, they take to their weapons and Lensky dies from a bullet wound. The young man falls into grief and regrets having killed his best friend over such a trivial matter of jealousy. He leaves the place to travel abroad.

23 ٢٣

Lensky's fiancée cries only a little over their separation and finds a lover whom she marries. Poor Tatyana thinks about her departed love day and night and becomes increasingly frail. Hoping to end her suffering, her mother takes Tatyana to Moscow to entertain her and introduces her to high society. Eugene travels in Europe for a few years to deaden the pain he feels inside. The day he returns to his homeland, a fancy ball is organized in Moscow and of course he is among the invitees.

24 ٢٤

Among the guests, Eugene notices an exceptionally beautiful, graceful, and elegant lady arm in arm with a general but does not recognize her. This general is Prince Garemin, who is an old friend of Eugene, and after bidding him welcome, introduces his wife to Eugene. It is then that Eugene recognizes that this attractive woman is none other than Tatyana who once declared her love for him and feels an extraordinary passion in his heart. In fact, Tatyana's stance and demeanour had since undergone great change and Eugene watches this symbol of perfect beauty in great amazement and starts to look at this treasure of happiness with sorrowful eyes.

۲۳

سیاحت ایلدی . لنــکینك نشانلیسی شو مفارقتدن طولایی یالکز براز مدت اغلادقدن صکره کندیسنه ینه برسوکیلی بولمش وآنکلـه ازدواج ایتمش ایدی . بیچاره تابانا ایسه عاشقندن آیرلدیغی ایچون کیجه کوندوز دوشونمکده و کیندکچه صاراروب صولقده ایدی . والدهسی آرتق بو اضطرابانه نهایت و یریرم امیدی ایله زواللی قزجغزی مسقوا شهرینه کوتوروب اکلاندیرمك ایچـون کبار جمعیتلرینه تقدیم ایلدی .

یوکهئ برقاچ سنه لراورو پاده دونوب طولاشـه رق درونندهکی دردی ازاله ایلدی . بعده وطنه عـودت ایتـدی که او کون مسقواده غایت طنطنه لی بر بالو

THE POET PUSHKIN

25 ٢٥

Flames of love invade his heart. The next day when he goes to visit General's home, he finds Tatyana alone and goes down on his knees to confess his love. Alas! Tatyana has become a virtuous and loyal wife, strictly observing the rules of marriage. She speaks to Eugene and tells him that although she has not been able to banish him from her heart, she is now a part of somebody else's name and feelings; she proudly instructs him to never have any hopes and politely warns him to never set foot in her home.

26 ٢٦

In addition to the high morals it reflects, the simple and pleasing composition of the novel is worthy of attention. In several places in the novel Pushkin ridicules the ignorance of Russian women of the time. And in one instance, someone says:

"Am I to fear women readers? There are no women who read on Russian soil and there never will be!"

Such insults and sarcasm made him many enemies. He was widely condemned. Although the poet was saddened by a lack of understanding of his thoughts and feelings, he continued to do what his opinions required and drafted poems and novels in an uncalculated manner.

27 ٢٧

However, he became enraged due to the injustices he faced.

Upon instructions from Tsar Nicholas, in 1826 Pushkin was released from exile in the Caucasus and brought to Moscow. His Majesty personally received him and spoke to him at great length, following which he told those present: "Today I spoke to the cleverest man in Russia". The fatherly and kind treatment of the Tsar left a favourable impression in Pushkin's heart, after which he drafted a nice poem.

28 ٢٨

Written in an admirable and attractive style, this poem described the power and grandeur of the great Tsar, the inspiration behind Russian reforms.

In 1826 the imperial court moved to Moscow and a circle with members of the nobility who enjoyed entertainment was gathered in the city making Pushkin return to a life of pleasure and fun. Yet before long he realized the banality of this group and became tired of balls and empty chatter. His life felt heavy, and he felt an unbearable boredom. In 1828, he wrote the ode entitled "Battle of Poltava".

29 ٢٩

This ode described the battle between Peter the Great and the Swedish king Charles XII, one of the major events that took place in Russia.

1830-1833, during this period Pushkin resided in Akneevo and wrote lyrics, many legends, and a few little tragedies as well as comedies. *The Covetous Knight* is a monologue, in other words, an article. In this work, Pushkin describes the well-known conditions and behaviour of knights and refers to the corruption in their lifestyles.

30 ٣٠

He explains some of their heroic deeds as well as their vanity and pomposity and the resulting misery and squander they suffer, leading them to borrow money from Jewish brokers with exorbitant interest rates and throwing themselves into unpayable debts. In this work, Pushkin offers lessons in good morals.

Mozart and Salieri show the difference between good morals and the bad morals of the latter and the blessings of the virtuous against the unvirtuous. Although Mozart had reached an elevated level in his art, it was also the simplicity, naivety, and good intentions in his nature, which received the favours of many great men. His closest and most loyal friend Salieri envied poor Mozart and plotted to destroy his happiness by poisoning him.

31 ٣١

At the time that great master Mozart reached the peak of his happiness, Salieri put his evil plans into action and managed to destroy Mozart's body; yet this action made the entire world vilify Salieri and Mozart's famous name is remembered with respect by everyone. When the work is studied in its entirety, a certain idea emerges. It is that those with intelligence always have many that envy them; enemies that will cheat and deceive the intellectual person at every opportunity.

32 ٣٢

Also, Pushkin's prowess comes through expressing the effects of all sciences, arts and particularly the science of music that honour the feelings and souls of people through Mozart's speech, and this is one of the things that make this work valuable.

In 1831, Pushkin married a beautiful and reputable girl by the name of Natalya Goncharova. During this time Pushkin started to collect the materials required to write the history of Peter the Great and thus travelled to important sites in Russia. As he passed through Kazan and Orenburg, he wrote two wonderful chronicles titled "A History of Pugachev" and "The Captain's Daughter" based on old legends that still lived on in the accounts of the people of the region.

33 ٣٣

In the last days of his life, Pushkin authored several heroic poems and engaging stories, and this revealed his tendency for philosophical thought at the height of his maturity. These works strike one with the variety they display; these include imitations of ancient Roman writers, western Slavic songs and Russian folk stories, historical legends, and historical and scientific articles.

The Captain's Daughter is based on events that took place during the time of Pugachev. Both the subject matter and the style in which the event is told are worthy of attention.

34 ٣٤

His account gives an impression of the patriarchal rule of the government in Orenburg and the gullibility and kindness of the people of the time. This work deserves to be acknowledged due to the naturalness of its language, its elegance and grace.

He wrote the history on Pugachev's circumstances and actions based on his own time. His objectivity and the accuracy of detail he relayed in his historical writing gained him the favour of the Tsar and he was given a high-ranking title in the Imperial court as well as 20.000 roubles to meet the book's publication costs.

35 ٣٥

In 1836 [e] Pushkin published a periodical journal titled *Sovremennik*, i.e. "*The Contemporary*", dedicating a great deal of space to objective criticism. Unfortunately, he was only able to publish four issues of this journal.

At this time, circumstances arose which led to the great poet's decline. Slanderous rumours that targeted his wife's dignity and honour led to a duel with the son of the Dutch ambassador (D'Anthès) where Pushkin was wounded and died after two days. This saddened everyone since then his competence and prowess were at their height.

---

[e] This date is mistakenly given as 1863 in the original text. 1836 is the correct date.

THE POET PUSHKIN

36 ٣٦

Three of the best narrative poems Pushkin authored during his time in Caucasus were *The Prisoner of Caucasus*, *The Fountain of Bakhchisaray* and *The Gypsies*. Let as review some of the famous works by the poet.

Poltava

In this narrative poem, written in 1828, Pushkin concentrated on the time when one of the most important incidents in Russian history took place in the form of a battle between Peter the Great and the Swedish King Charles XII. Other events described and reported are secondary to this major event and serve to offer the readers an idea about the qualities and skills of Peter the Great.

37 ٣٧

The *Poltava* narrative poem is divided into three sections and an epilogue has been added. The first section opens with Vasily Kochubey who has a big fortune and his dear daughter Maria whom he treasures. The Cossack Hetman Mazepa asks Maria's hand in marriage but is insulted and turned down by her mother who does not share her daughter's beauty. The girl agrees to elope with Mazepa and her father prepares to violently avenge himself for this great humiliation.

38 ٣٨

As this story is told, the poet gives an apt account of the efforts shown and the difficulty of the challenges faced by Russia in gaining itself an important political position among European states and in supporting the works of the new civilization imported into the country.

The work describes how the Ukrainian Cossacks demanded to advance to Moscow to free themselves from Russia's yoke during the attack of Charles XII on Russia. However, their chief Hetman

Mazepa becomes afraid and resists making a move, and this causes a great deal of excitement among Cossacks.

39 ٣٩

Although Mazepa appears to be loyal to the Tsar, he is in fact a supporter of Charles XII with the motif of breaking free from Moscow's yoke. The narrative poem describes the circumstances of Mazepa, and the plot Kochubey has designed to take revenge upon Mazepa. As Kochubey had disclosed his ideas to Mazepa during a conversation before their breakup, he thought this a good opportunity to take revenge from Kochubey. He joins forces with Colonel Iskra, commander of Poltava and informs the Tsar about the situation and writes to him about Mazepa's betrayal and treason to ensure his assassination and execution.

40 ٤٠

However, while they are busy informing the Tsar, Mazepa acts and gains the help of Sweden, Poland, and the Don Cossacks, secretly, knavishly, and cautiously preparing for a battle.

As Mazepa's aide Orlik was scheming to control the situation with great skill and mastery, and Mazepa gained the favour of the Tsar with trickery and quick-wittedness, Peter does not trust the news he has received from Kochubey and the Colonel and turns them over to Mazepa suspecting both to be slanderers.

41 ٤١

Mazepa is thrilled that he has captured his enemies by luck and decides to publicly execute them to kill them. In the meantime, Maria is not aware of any of these events.

The second section depicts a conversation between Mazepa and Maria:

On a moonlit night, Maria waits for Mazepa's arrival in the garden and as soon as she sees him, she welcomes him with kindness and sadness. She reveals the worries and concerns she has kept within her until that day and asks Mazepa why he leaves her so often and disappears. This proves that he has lost his love for her, she reproaches.

42 ٤٢

The treacherous Mazepa tells Maria about his aim, in other words, his plot against the Tsar to put an end to her concerns. He tells her that if he succeeds in his ploy, he will become the king of Ukraine. Upon hearing this happy news, innocent Maria goes down on Mazepa's knees with joy and tells Mazepa how much she worships him. After Maria compassionately tells Mazepa that she would sacrifice her father, mother and homeland for him, this section of the narrative moves on to an account of the arrest of Kochubey, the terrible conditions of the tower where he is imprisoned and the tragic story of his decline.

43 ٤٣

Mazepa's aide Orlik visits the tower to ask Kochubey about where he hid his treasure, but when he is not satisfied with his answers, this results in inflicting severe torture on Kochubey.

In the morning Maria's mother comes to her to tell her about the disaster that has struck her father. She asks her daughter to intervene and help in securing an amnesty and release for her husband. Upon hearing this tragic news, grief-stricken Maria faints and when she gains consciousness, she decides to leave Mazepa's house forever. Her father is to be executed by Mazepa the next day. Accompanied by her mother, Maria runs to the field where her father will be executed with the hope of rescuing him, but alas, she arrives too late

44

and the unfortunate men who have sacrificed themselves for truth and loyalty are already hastily executed.

In the third section of the narrative poem, Hetman Mazepa is seemingly taken ill suddenly. Yet with the arrival of the army of Charles XII in Ukraine he recovers from this pretended sickness and attacks Tsar's army in collaboration with Charles's forces. However, both Charles and Mazepa are defeated by Russian troops in Poltava and must flee. This makes Peter the Great find out Mazepa's treason and suffer from great remorse for having Kochubey executed unjustly. Maria becomes mad with grief and her image stays with Mazepa, torturing his conscience.

45

The epilogue is a repetition of the events by way of summary.

The Bronze Horseman

The narrative poem the *Bronze Horseman* is composed of an introduction and two parts. The introduction depicts the desolate and melancholic views of the banks of the Finnish strait before the founding and development of the city of Petersburg and describes the effect of the swamp and forest uninhabited by humans but a few fishermen that he refers to as "orphaned nature'.

46

It reveals the thoughts and concerns that pass through Peter the Great's mind about the importance and value of the future capital for Russia in terms of commercial relations and current politics. Following this, the poet moves one century forward, and lays bare the beauties the city of Petersburg has since acquired, in the form of tall buildings, charming gardens and orderly piers and offers a comparison with Moscow, the old capital for the readers. After this, the poet talks about his own sentiments and describes, among others, the elegance of Petersburg and the pure light that particularly becomes visible on summer nights and the beautiful views of the great currents of the river Neva, as well as the daily lives and characteristics of the residents of the city and the shiny uniforms of the imperial guards.

47 ٤٧

Pushkin then describes a scene from the great flood that occurred in 1824 by relaying the story of a poor, small civil servant by the name Evgenii. He depicts the difficulties he suffers in poverty and shows the grief and excitement he feels after being flooded by rising waters in his hut. Evgenii is separated from his fiancée for a few days and feels the pain of not knowing how she is. Once the waters that rose to four yards and destroyed many bridges and houses recede, he goes to his fiancée's neighbourhood in a boat where he sees nothing but ruins. Grief-stricken he becomes mad and takes his life. His dead body is seen in the middle of the ruins on the riverbank.

48 ٤٨

The first part of the work is a statement of gratitude addressing Peter the Great, praising the worth and value of the great emperor for the efforts and progress he has mobilized in Russia for the importation of European civilization, sciences, and fine arts.

However, the second part depicts a specific event, from the perspective of ordinary people: by describing the troubles and disasters suffered and the turmoil faced, it promotes tolerance and patience as well as forgiveness and compassion.

49 ٤٩

The Captain's Daughter

The Captain's Daughter is composed of fourteen chapters and an epilogue. The first five chapters tell a true story as given below:

The story tells about the education received by the protagonist of the story, Pyotr Grinyov, from his family and his entry into military service with the Orenburg army. During his journey, Grinyov stops at a teahouse in the city of Simbirsk and there he comes across an officer with whom he plays cards and as a result loses all his money. Deeply worried, he continues his journey and gets caught up in a blizzard.

50 ه.

Fortunately, in the middle of a terrible storm a kind man appears and shows Grinyov the way. Grinyov wants to give his thanks to this kind man, but since he had gambled away all his fortune, he gives him the plain lamb skin he wore on his back. Thanks to him, Pyotr arrives in Orenburg unharmed and goes to the fort Belogorsky where he will serve his military duty. At this point, the poet describes the position and condition of the fort and the family of the commanding captain Mironov. The commander's daughter Maria and his wife make up his household, in addition to a young officer who was sent there on a military exercise.

51 ه ا

Grinyov is well received by this family and their relation grows stronger through the commander's daughter and finally he asks to marry her and requests his father to put his plan into action.

The young officer who was named Shvabrin becomes jealous of the romantic affair between Grinyov and Maria; this worthless man says ugly things about innocent Maria. Naturally, this leads to hostility between the two men, and they decide to resolve it by a duel. The duel takes place and poor Grinyov is wounded.

52 ه ٢

However, Maria treats him and helps him recover upon which he writes a letter to his father, asking for his permission and consent to marry. In his reply, his father does not give his consent, and on

THE POET PUSHKIN

the contrary, warns him and denies his request. The commander's family is taken by despair. A series of unexpected events that take place in the meantime reinforce and strengthen Grinyov's nature and resolve.

The seven chapters in the middle of the narrative deal with the conditions that led to the battles of the Yaik Cossacks. Here is a summary:

53 ٥٣

The commander of the Fort Belogorsky receives the news that there is a Cossack by the name Emilian Pugachev who served at an outpost and gathered an armed band to loot and destroy towns and villages on their way. The fort is at once taken under protection. Pugachev attacks Fort Belogorsky and kills the commander, his wife and nearly everyone there. His daughter Maria takes refuge in the priest's home and saves her life by introducing herself as the priest's niece. The previously mentioned Shvabrin defects the army in betrayal and joins Pugachev's band. Pugachev appoints him the guardian of Fort Belogorsky. Just as they put a rope around Grinyov's neck and prepare to end his life, his life is saved when it is revealed that he is the officer who gave a lambskin to Pugachev unaware of his identity.

54 ٥٤

When he speaks to Pugachev, he gives Grinyov permission to travel anywhere he likes. Grinyov leaves the fort for Orenburg, but Pugachev arrives before long and raids the place. In the meantime, Shvabrin forces Maria, Grinyov's fiancée to marry him. The girl writes to Grinyov to inform him of the situation right away. As soon as Grinyov receives the letter he immediately goes to Pugachev and tells him the full story, Pugachev is touched by the situation and travels to Fort Belogorsky with Grinyov.

55

He surrenders his fiancée to Grinyov and allows them to travel wherever they wish. He reprimands Shvabrin for his action.

The final two chapters consist of an account of the disasters that strike Grinyov following his departure from Belogorsky. On his route, Grinyov encounters a troop of Hussars who are following Pugachev. When he is brought before the major commander of the troop it is understood that the major is none other than the officer whom he gambled and lost his money to in Simbirsk. They recognize each other. Grinyov is reluctant to disclose who Maria is, so it is decided that he will be sent to Kazan with a guard to be interrogated.

56

Grinyov sends Maria to his father with his servant Savelich. Before the arrival of Maria, Grinyov's father was naturally unaware of the true situation and was grieved with the thought of his son collaborating with bandits. Maria arrives and explains him the situation, and she decides to travel to Petersburg and go down on the knees of the Empress and implore her to spare Grinyov from danger. With this decision, she leaves for Petersburg and with the help of luck, sees Catherine in the garden and at once goes down on her knees. She tells the empress the misfortunes of her fiancé and manages to influence her, winning her compassion and pity.

57

The Empress responded to her pleas with mercy and compassion and sent Grinyov's father a hand-written letter, praising the sacrifices Maria has made to save her fiancé and her pure love for him. The family who received that letter showed it great respect and veneration.

THE POET PUSHKIN

As can be gathered, this story is based on historical events. It depicts the morals and manners of the gentry, their ideas on the general state of affairs and services

58

and the misgovernance of Russia's south-eastern territories and particularly the wretched state of the city of Orenburg and the evils of the military guards in the city. The details of the story about the Pugachev rebellion are presented from the perspective of historical events.

In terms of its literary merits, the work is written in elegant, fluent, and modern language, free from unfamiliar foreign terms and words; so, it is pleasant to read and study. It does not display the confusing pretentious and complicated style of previously written works.

59

Boris Godunov

Pushkin's eponymous tragedy was published in 1831. The substance of the play is the life story of one of Russia's former tsars, Boris Godunov and the significant national events that took place during his reign. Pushkin did not rely on the old, so-called "classical" style, and adopted Shakespeare's tragedies as a model. He followed his own extraordinary inherent strengths while creating this work. The tragedy is composed of two parts of different lengths. The first part is about the events of 1598, while the second part relays the events of 1603 and 1605.

60

The first part is an introduction where the author identifies the reasons giving rise to the conditions and events told subsequently in the second part. This tragedy was not written to be performed on the stage. It was only written to be read. That is why instead of twenty-four theatrical scenes, it is composed of twenty-four chapters which each depict quite distant and distinct matters.

Part One describes Boris Godunov's ascension to the throne of tsardom. During this time, Prince Shuyskiy from one of the oldest families in Russia, and Prince Vorotynsky vote to reject Godunov but cannot stop the ascension to the throne of the new tsar. Five years after this introduction, the author relays a conversation in the Chudov Monastery between priest and chronicler Pimen and a young apprentice priest Grigory.

61 ז׳א

Tsar Ivan declares his son Dmitri as his heir to the throne, Boris has a son called Fyodor and when he grows up, Boris disposes of Dmitri to make his son the Tsarevitch. People are suspicious about what became of Dmitri. When Grigory receives this news from Pimen, he ventures to present himself as Dmitri the Tsarevitch. The abbot in the monastery tries to detain Grigory to force him to abjure and to repent but Grigory flees to Lithuania.

62 ז׳ב

The subsequent chapters of the play show Boris in his family. He speaks sweetly to his daughter Ksenia. He looks at the map of Russia Fyodor has drawn and praises it. He takes the opportunity to point out the use and importance of sciences and arts for everyone. At that point he is given the news that an impostor by the name Grigory has surfaced in Poland as Tsar Dmitri. He starts preparing for war. In the next chapter the false tsar falls in love with Marina Mniszech, who is known for her beauty and is also the daughter of a gentleman from the Polish nobility.

63 ז׳ג

The false tsar and his beloved get together. As Marina knows of his love for her, she does whatever it takes and makes her lover admit his scheme.

Following this, the subsequent chapters describe the battles between the false tsar and Boris. Both parties take turns winning and losing. Boris reacts violently against the supporters of the false tsar. However, before he defeats his opponent, he suddenly becomes ill and dies on the first day of April 1605. The winning troops of his opponent join Moscow.

Historians have disagreed considerably about these events.

64

Nevertheless, Pushkin relied on Karamzin's account and penned his work accordingly. The main characters in the play are Boris Godunov and the false Tsar Dmitri, while secondary characters are Prince Shuyskiy and the false tsar's lover Marina. Pushkin made all these characters speak in a convincing fashion and this made his work a success. He wrote wise words, spoken by Boris, about the philosophy of governance. Boris praised and recommended education and the arts with great insight.

In the play, Pushkin creates Prince Shuyskiy as a model courtier, articulate and intelligent.

65

However, the prince only looks after his personal interest and does not hesitate to pull tricks or contrive. This man could put up with any kind of insult or hypocrisy. Events that upset others did not affect him in the least.

Even though she did not at all love the false tsar, she went along with him with the hope that she would become the tsaritsa if became the tsar. Although the false tsar was deeply in love with her, she did not agree to marry him then and informed him that she would only consent to marry him after he becomes the tsar. This girl is the model of a woman who is intelligent and quick-witted, fond of fame and reputation, and unbelieving of love and affection.

66 ٦٦

Boris Godunov may well be considered Pushkin's most famous work. To write the play, Pushkin researched the Russian language spoken at that time, and not only did he make the language appropriate for that period, but also produced ideas and morals in the spirit of the old times.

Addendum

Although Pushkin was considered an important writer during his time, his significance increased among Russians even further after his death. Pushkin's significance has also grown in Europe where he has become well known. Operas and plays adapted from his works have appeared on European stages.

67 ٦٧

Furthermore, the French have been interested in Russian literature for some time and translated many works. Pushkin is among those Russian authors who are favoured by the French.

The End

MUSLIM WOMEN AT THE TIME OF THE CALIPHS (1899)

The Proceedings of the Rome Congress of Orientalists published a summary of the Muslim Women at the time of the Caliphs given by Olga de Lebedeff in 1899. [735]

> In this period Muslim women received the same education and had the same rights as men. They even had considerable influence in public life where they sometimes took a lead. Islam is not at all against the intellectual freedom and education of women. It even encourages this freedom. It is the fanatical and uneducated lawmakers who are against this freedom. Dynastic quarrels and religious wars are the only reason for the decline of Arab civilization.
>
> The Caliph al Qadir b'illah (991) was the first to stop Arab progress. Eastern women are beginning to awaken from several centuries of intellectual apathy and women authors are beginning to be published. Some Eastern feminist writers are working on the emancipation of women and want to return them to the important social position they used to have. The only way to attain this goal is to wake up the East from its sleep, and to let it into our

civilisation. For that to happen the peoples of the East must be willing participants; if not, like determined barbarians, they will be engulfed by the civilization of modern European countries.

Here she was not alone to report on this subject, as recorded in the congress report:

> This was followed by some information from Mr Arnold about the emancipation movement for women in India, a parallel movement to that in Turkey and Egypt.[f] He mentioned a book in Hindi by Mawlawi Mumtaz Ali, called *Huququ-n-Niswan* [*The Rights of Women*]', where women's emancipation is analysed in detail through the same verses of the Quran and the same hadiths which are ordinarily cited to maintain the social exclusion of women from public events.

---

[f] The orientalist Thomas Arnold, (1860-1935) taught philosophy at Government College in Lahore.

On the Emancipation of Muslim Women (1900)

Preface

[Preface written by **Marie de Besneray**, Officer of the Academy, Member of the Society of People of Letters].

It is always with a lively interest that we follow, both in France and abroad, the growing progress of women in literature, the arts and science. Today, as it concerns an eminent woman and compatriot famed for her learning and high intelligence, I am happy to offer her the tribute of my deepest respect. Madame Olga de Lebedeff, who is a talented historian and convinced zealous spokesperson about the emancipation of Muslim women, is not only appreciated in Russia, her native country, but also very well-known in the East. Speaking many languages, including Turkish, Arabic, and a student of Sanskrit, she has skillfully traced a thousand precise and charming pictures of these countries about which we know so little. She has opposed prejudices and mistakes, has refuted erroneous stories, and like Aliye Hanum - a great lady from the East – she has shown us the world of the Ottomans in a more accurate light. We hope that in France this work by Madame de Lebedeff receives the success that it merits by virtue of the authority of its author. To enable women of all nationalities to care about ideas, to teach them moral truths, and the eternal rights of conscience, will always be the worthy task of a great mind. Women work everywhere. Most have learnt that once they have a pen, it is not just for playing with empty words and phrases like a small bell, that there is no sense in just entertaining the idle rich, but that a piece of work, even a purely literary one, is an important activity which is only of value through the moral power it contains. A considerable number of people are echoing this belief of ours. Since we have the ambition to trace a new path through the useless undergrowth of dead wood, let us make it a straight and beautiful one, luminous and free.

***

[*On the Emancipation of Muslim Women* by **Olga de Lebedeff**, with page numbers referring to the original]

At the twelfth Congress of Orientalists held in Rome, I outlined my views on the emancipation of Muslim women. Owing to the brevity of the allotted time, I was unable to expand my views fully in that lecture. This important topic needs to be developed further so that we can see how Muslim women can escape from their present, slave-like, condition. There are many uneducated or fanatical people in the East who believe that Islam has excluded women from social life and that an education equal to that of a man is forbidden - a view shared by certain Europeans too. (p. 2) It is important to fight against this prejudice.

Looking at Arab women's position in society at the height of the Arab civilization, we can see that Islam had never prevented women from receiving the same education and the same rights as the men.

This is in fact what happened in Baghdad in the era of the Umayyads and the first Abbasids up until the reign of the Caliph al-Qadir Billah, who was the first to stop progress in Muslim society [991 AD but quoted as 921 in the text /CH].

ON THE EMANCIPATION OF MUSLIM WOMEN

It is said that in the time of Mansour [8th century], two female cousins of this sovereign went to the Byzantine war dressed in chainmail. Under of the reign of Rashid and Meemoun, women discussed with intellectuals, took part in poetry competitions and enlivened society with the grace and subtlety of their minds. Young Arab women fought on horseback and commanded troops. Meetings in high society only ceased in the reign of Mutewwekil [847-861 AD]. The mother of Mouktedir Ktrun-Neda, presided over the deliberations over the high court of justice, gave audiences to foreign dignitaries and ambassadors, summoned the judges and notables, signed and published State edicts. (p. 3)

The Empress Zubaidah, wife of Harun al-Rashid[736], was a woman of exceptional mind and an excellent poet. At her own cost, she had the great aqueduct of Mecca constructed, and rebuilt the city of Alexandria which had been destroyed by the Greeks. Bourane, her daughter in law, the wife of Meemoun (826 A.D.) [al-Ma'mun] was remarkable for her beauty, her mind, her erudition, and her virtues. She founded several colleges and women's hospitals in Baghdad.

Sukeina, the great granddaughter of Mohammed by his daughter Fatima, was a prodigious learner; she collected all the illustrations of her time in her living room. The poetess Fadl lived at the time of Mutewwekil. Her poems rival those of the greatest poets. In the 12th century A.D. Sheika Choukhda lectured in Baghdad on literature, history, and rhetoric. Zeineb Unun-ul-Moueyed had a Diploma as a Professor of Jurisprudence. In Saladin's reign [1174 – 1193], Takiyek, daughter of d'Abou'l Faradj, lectured on Hadis (traditions) and besides was a distinguished poet. (p.4) Umm-ul-Khair Fatima and Umm-Ibrahim Fatima Yezdani taught Theology.

Seida Nefisse was a teacher of Sheikh Chafei: she spoke the funeral prayers at his death as if she were carrying out the functions of a mullah. Similarly in Granada, ancient authors notably Ahmed

Makri in his *Nefhouttybi* (or *Scented Breath*), tell us about a constellation of distinguished women.

The Nazhoun, Zeineb, Hafsa and Safia and so many others shone with an inextinguishable brilliance by the brightness of their minds. In these cases, as in Baghdad, they studied all branches of science and the arts.

Among the disturbances of the twelfth century, when the social and political structure of Western Asia was on the point of collapsing, Muslim women were still the object of chivalrous customs and the most delicate attention. Marriage was a solemn act, the domestic hearth a sanctuary and the birth of children a blessing from God.

Before being passed to other tutors, the children were first taught by their mother. Girls were brought up with the principles of virtue and purity so that they might become in the words of *Kitab-ul-Iytibar*, 'the mothers of men'. (p.5)

Women of the highest rank practised music, which had not yet been placed on the index [banned] by Islamic lawmakers. Rashid's sister, Princess Olayah, was an accomplished musician; her compositions are mentioned in the Kitab-ul-Aghany (book of songs) of Abou'l Faradj-el-Isphahany. The daughter of this princess had the same talent. A passage from the same book describes Obeida, who lived in the reign of Meemoun and Moutassine, as a woman of great beauty, virtue, and talent; her voice was melodious and the skill with which she accompanied herself on the tambourine gave her the nickname of 'Et-Tambouriyeh'.

Princesses and grand ladies gave musical evenings called Noubat-el-Khatun, with orchestras composed of a hundred musicians led by skilled conductors.

The Timourid Sultans who brought many innovations to Persia, introduced among others the custom of organising at Persian New

Year a big 'charity sale' where princesses and great ladies sold in elegant premises all sorts of beautiful things which the Sovereign, princes and the nobility came to purchase while admiring the beauty, graciousness, and the minds of these brilliant women. This sale was called the 'Mine-Bazaar'. (p.6)

Many women have reigned over different Muslim peoples. I shall only name the most famous, because they are so many in number, that I should be afraid to tire my readers by mentioning them all. Turkhan-Khatun, widow of Saad II, Atatek of Shiraz, and Aisha-Khatun, they were distinguished by their erudition and their taste for architecture and embellished Shiraz with splendid buildings.

In Cairo, the wise sister of Sak-Him bi-emri Illah, known as Sitt al-Mulk, was Regent after the death of her brother, with the title of 'Queen of the Muslims'.

In India, Begum Razia ['Razia Sultan'], daughter of Sultan Altemeh was promoted to the throne of Delhi after her brother had been deposed.

Nur-Jahan, wife of Jahangir, was so adored by her husband that he allowed her to reign in his place and had coins minted with her effigy. It was this charming princess, who was praised by Moore[737] under the name of 'Lalla Rookh'. The ruins of her mausoleum can still be seen in Lahore.

Thus, Muslim women enjoyed complete liberty; they had the same education as men, the highest places in society and played a preeminent role, not only in the family, where the education of youth was entrusted to them, but also in public affairs, the sciences, and arts. (p.7) They could make immense progress in intellectual culture and social liberty: Islam was not against it.

Unfortunately, the subservience of Muslim women was introduced by the unfolding of the following events: the false interpretation of the principles of Islam and the development of customary laws[738] of an unrefined society.

During the deadly struggle of the crusades, Muslims turned their thoughts to a single aim - personal survival: *"Primum vivere, deinde philosophari"* - meaning "Live first, then philosophise". The victories of Zendjy, Noureddine and Saladin barely saved them from the attacks of the Franks, before the wave of Tatar hordes came to sweep away all the civilisation of the Orient and to prepare the subjection of women.

It is certain that a civilised society cannot exist without educated women. "To want to limit women to managing their home, and only educate them for that is to forget that from the home of every citizen come the errors and prejudices that govern the world". This is how [Louis-] Aimé Martin[739] puts it and he adds: "the spirit of peoples, their virtues rest on the maternal breast - in other words - the civilisation of humankind."

The forward progress of Muslim women ceased entirely[g] due to political disputes, religious and dynastic struggles, and civil disturbances: it took a step backwards at the time when western civilisation was starting to develop. At the same time women were increasingly subjected to the whims of men; the latter energetically persuaded them through despotic jealousy, quite wrongly, that Islam forbade them from educating themselves and having the same rights as men.

In this regard they would have remained as servants up until today if European influence had not come to rouse them from their passivity. France has played an active role in improving the situation of Muslim women. Mr Edmond Groult, founder of some local museums in Lisieux (in the Department of Calvados), tells us that Girls Schools are being founded in Algeria and Tunisia.[740] (p.9) There some courageous French women, devoted to improvements for their Muslim sisters, instruct them - besides Arabic and French - in some basics of science and art, particularly

---

[g] Under **errata** amended : 'Furent donc les causes **uniques** de l'arrêt de cette marche en avant et amenèrent un mouvement rétrograde au moment où la civilisation occidentale commençait à se développer'

cooking and sewing. He goes on to say that "the young ladies who leave these schools are highly valued by their Muslim suitors (care having been taken not to undertake any religious proselytism). Sometimes, a remarkable thing happens; as the young girls have got used to tidiness, cleanliness, and personal dignity, which they cannot then do without, they impose certain conditions on their suitors - which the latter look kindly on and accept extremely eagerly. They demand to have a bed to avoid lack of privacy with farm animals, with which too many Muslim women are still obliged to live in close quarters. They require a table and chairs to be able to sit down and eat with their husbands, and with their future children.

These girls are sometimes bold enough to request that they be excused from wearing the veil, for most Oriental women cover themselves up, as if with a shroud. One knows, of course, (p.10) that the Quran itself did not impose this barbaric custom on them, and that the women of several Muslim tribes have never resigned themselves to it. In short, they compel their husbands to live in European-style houses, or to make big windows in their shacks, to let in light and fresh air, needed for good health, essential for cleanliness, necessary to the attractiveness and happiness of the family home; benefits which are at present unknown in many Muslim countries.

Moreover, France has granted to its Muslim subjects two valuable improvements, which are producing the best results. From 1863 to 1868, laws granted to both sexes the right to private property, the best stimulus for work and making savings and, in turn, the best means of developing public and private wealth; plus, the only one which guarantees personal freedom. The law of April 1882 gave them patronymic and family names – the distinguishing marker of their individuality.[h] Finally, a draft law is being made to give political rights to Muslims (or to some of them) for their

---

[h] [Senatus Consulte - April 22, 1863: Organization of the status of landed property. In Algeria, division of land according to different types of ownership. This was completed by imperial decree on 9 May 1868 / CH].

gradual assimilation with the French." (p.11) As can be seen, in France the matter of emancipation of Muslim women is entering the realm of reality: civilised societies can only approve.

The education of women is also occurring in Syria, thanks to girls' schools being established by Europeans, run mostly by French nuns. Egypt and Tunisia have imitated Syria's example but less enthusiastically.

We are delighted to say that one can already read Arab and Turkish journals, such as the *Mouktataf* and the *Hilal* in Cairo and the *Lican-ul-Ilal* in Beirut, which publish a mass of novels and thoughtful articles written exclusively by women. I would like to mention Princess Tchechmi Afete in Cairo, who has authored some fine poems. Charitable as well as cultured, she founded in this city a school for young girls and a refuge for the blind. I should also mention Aiche Taimouriyeh [Aisha Taymur 1840-1902], a distinguished poetess, and Zaynab Fawwaz, the author of a large biography of Muslim women entitled: '*Ea-dour-el-manthour fi talakkate rabbate el houdour*', that is to say, 'Scattered pearls of the fair sex'. Finally, another excellent writer of prose is Marian Halil [Maryam Khalil]. (p.12)

In Constantinople, the famous and erudite Fatima Aliye Hanum has composed several novels and numerous articles on philosophy. Makbule Leman Hanum [1865-1898] is known for her philosophical letters. The writings of these two ladies appeared some ten years ago in the journal *Tercüman-ı Hakikat*, when it was produced by the learned, and immensely popular, Ahmed Midhat Efendi. At that time, it was not yet permitted for Muslim women to write their works in their own name.

This movement of emancipation – although simply intellectual – has gained new impetus since Oriental women have themselves founded journals such as *Imra'ate* & *Fetate* in Egypt, and *Hanumlara Makhcons Gazetassy* in Constantinople, led by the consummate poetesss Nigar Hanum. These journals, aided by other feminist writing, are stimulating the intellectual life of Muslim women. They strive to make every out-dated custom - which has kept women under male guardianship redundant - and to return women to their erstwhile status, when long ago Islam was civilised.

Let us also mention that in recent times there have been several prestigious Muslim writers who have written various works in favour of freedom for women. It is to be hoped that their standing will win over many of their fellow believers. (p.13) Of these a mention of two of these will suffice as they are both remarkable for their broadmindedness: the *Takhrir-el-Imraate* by Kassime Emine [*Tahrir al-mar'a* by Qasim Amin, The Emancipation of Women], President of the Court of Appeal in Cairo and the *El-Imraate-fich-Chark* [al-Mar'a fi al sharq, meaning Woman in the East] by Wacif, an Egyptian government official; also worthy of attention is the article called *Ene-niça fil-Islam* by the famous Muslim author from Calcutta, Syed Ameer Ali.

We are seeing the dawn of a new age and can say with the poet (Virgil): '*Magnus ab integro nascitur ordo*' [The great order of the ages is born afresh'].

But if the aim of this grand task is to be the rekindling of Oriental culture, we too have a duty to participate. In the past we have borrowed so much from it that our present civilisation has a duty to share the benefits of our insights. Let us awaken the East from its slumber!

To this end let us propagate as much as possible the societies of Orientalists to teach us about the ethics and cultural needs of these [Eastern] peoples. We can also establish lasting relations outside of any religious or political concerns between the two worlds of East and West. (p.14)

I conceived of this idea after a protracted stay in the Orient [Middle East] and have been campaigning for three years; we hope to see a Society of Orientalists organised shortly in Russia.[741]

Some eight years ago, we drafted a paper in Turkish, French, Russian, English, German, and Arabic, in which we set out the necessity to reject all petty feelings of nationalistic or religious enmity and to extend the hand of friendship to the peoples of the East. To go forward with them towards a truth proved by reason and lit up by science, which bring us enlightenment in its fullness.

We are happy to point out that these same ideas have been conceived and put into practise in France by the admirable *Society of Allied Eastern and Western Women* whose aim is 'the progress of friendly relations between all nations and the establishment of permanent peace'. The President of this society is Madame Hyacinte Loyson in Paris[i] and the honorary President Her Highness Princess Nazli of Cairo.

The aim of the alliance is laid out in a letter - Madame Loyson[742] has been good enough to send us an explanatory letter. (p.15) Here are the principal points:

1) To create mutual assistance between East and West based on charity, goodwill, and prompt action in everything affecting social and domestic life. Send to the East experienced, intelligent, and truly Christian female teachers who will have a good moral influence on young Muslim girls without the least religious proselytism, but on the contrary cooperating with kindness in the religious life of the host family in which they will be.

2) To found houses in Paris, Constantinople and Algiers, where the teachers would be able to learn at least some vocabulary of the language which they would need to use and acquire other

---

[i] 29, Boulevard Inkermann, Parc de Neuilly.

ON THE EMANCIPATION OF MUSLIM WOMEN

knowledge. They would teach according to need, French, English, German, Italian or any other European languages.

3) To publish in Eastern languages some suitable and useful books for Oriental peoples [j]

4) To make every effort in France or elsewhere to develop charitable views and cordial relations between all peoples; to treat different races, cultures and religion with consideration and respect by avoiding pointless discussions; seeking rapport rather than disputes and encouraging good ethics, etc. (p.16) By opening the doors of Western civilisation to Muslim women and bringing them humanitarian ideas, this 'Alliance of Women' will help [Muslim women] to gradually obtain equal rights to those of men.

The emancipation of Muslim women trails behind that of Europe, as it is tightly bound up with society in general in the East, but this should not be alarming to Muslims. The Sheiks-ul Islam of Cairo and Constantinople should emulate the Sheik-ul Islam of Tunis, who has expressed his sympathetic support of the Women's Alliance, by approving the idea set out in our above-mentioned statement. (p.17)

We dare to hope that influential personages in the East will want to help us fulfil these ideas, which are precursors of the civilisation we are bringing to the East. The relentless events of history and advanced social living conditions prove to us the urgency of this, as in the contrary case, one will see the phenomenon of the Tatar

---

[j] 'To this same end, eight years ago I published some translations of several famous Russian authors in Turkish language(s), including their biography.'
Pushkin: The Snowplough [sic.], The Queen of Spades
Lermontov: Demon
Count Leo Tolstoy: What Men Live By; Two Old Men; Ilyas, Family Happiness; Master and Man
Mullah Bayazitov: In Refutation of Renan
O de Lebedeff's Article: The Tribe of the Chuvashes in Russia
Also, by O de Lebedeff: Abbreviated History of Russian Literature, which includes the biographies of the most famous authors

invasion being recreated, but in the opposite direction; whereas at that time it was barbarism that swept away civilisation, now, civilisation will swallow up barbarous customs!

The most benefit for the East, would be to take our outstretched fraternal helping hand. Let us work together! The future is marching on, so let us help it quicken its pace. This is the way to accelerate a renaissance for which we hope and pray, the early signs of which we have just outlined, and for which we have been waiting for so long.

It is now said by a great poet that 'our human spirit has come of age.' In fact, everywhere the future promises to be brighter. The fervent spirit of charity and brotherhood knocks over barriers and unites hearts. (p.18)

May our heartfelt hopes be realised! We trust that our modest efforts will not be fruitless, so that at the dawn of this new century, East and West may unite in harmonious understanding! *

Olga de Lebedeff, Rome

December 1899

* The Russian translation elaborates on the French in the last phrase: 'the cultures of East and West may merge in one harmonious accord'.

ON THE NEW RIGHTS OF MUSLIM WOMEN (1902)

Les Nouveaux Droits de la Femme Musulmane, as recorded in the *Proceedings*

XIII International Congress of Orientalists
8 September 1902

Fig. 99
Ignace Goldhizer

The following is a translated transcript of the address by Her Excellency Olga de Lebedeff at the congress in Hamburg. It was first published in Arco in 1902. The report was read aloud at the congress by Ignace Goldziher, the eminent Islamic scholar.[743]

"Ladies and Gentlemen! At the 12th Congress of Orientalists, which you held in Rome, I had the honour to speak to you about the need to focus on the rights and the social positions of Muslim women. For that I had recourse to history and I informed you of the privileged situation of Arab women in now distant times when the Islamic civilization was at its peak.

Today I wish to speak to you of the intellectual advances made by Muslims themselves regarding the emancipation of their women; and it is this which in my humble opinion represents a much more important occurrence than the chance appearance in the Muslim world of a 'civilized and literate' woman.

'Today Egypt can be said to be the most enlightened Muslim country. It has become the religious centre of Muslim countries thanks to its famous al-Azhar Academy [University] which attracts many students from all over the East. It can claim to be the intellectual centre of all the eastern countries thanks both to the English influence and the use of Arabic, the mother tongue of all eastern learned people. The natural result is that all attempts at reform in Muslim legislation come from the country of the Pharaohs.

Without dwelling on all the means tried up till now, I will confine myself to saying a word about recent attempts which have been the most effective and about changes that have happened in the legislation itself to bring Muslim women out of their truly servile position.

I want to talk about the efforts of Qasim Amin Bey, who has become an important name in Muslim legal affairs and who is working towards the same goal as ourselves - the emancipation of Muslim women. We hope that his latest book entitled *The New Woman* will be a means of improving the position of women and thus bring about progress in Muslim society. Qasim Amin Bey has attempted to free women from the ignorant servile state in which they now slumber and to bring the concept of the family closer to that held by the Europeans. To this end he has formed a group of enlightened Muslims who are helping him to spread his ideas. He has published several brochures devoted to this theme and papers which popularize the completely new concept he has of women and their duties towards family and society. According to him, the pitiable position of women in society is due to Muslim law which hardly gives women any human rights. As you know a married woman is entirely dependent on her husband and a daughter is in a serf-like position in relation to her father and elder brothers. Therefore, a Muslim woman is never free at any moment of her life. Muslim laws have made her a slave and she remains in this state.

Qasim Amin Bey claims that Muslim law has never known the true sense of the word 'family' and has never understood the key role that family ought to play in society and the state. Take any book of Muslim law, he says, and you will not find a single word about the family and the place it should take in building society.

The famous '*Preface*' of Ibn Khaldun himself is silent on this subject. As if denying that the family is the foundation of all societies!

The result is that Muslim law is far from reaching perfection and on that, moreover, our lawyers and enlightened Muslims agree.

Our author adds, 'if Muslim civilization has come and gone before the discovery of the true principles of modern science and before the birth of social science, how can we imagine that this sort of civilization can achieve a perfect social ideal? How dare we claim that we Muslims have nothing to borrow from Europeans? We do not want to diminish in any way the ancestors or the progress they have made in knowledge; but it would be unforgivable to continue with these mistakes and to believe that the early Muslims had attained perfection. Let us remember the verse of the famous

Motennebi: *"The worst possible fault is the one that could have been rectified and was not"*.

'Every Muslim', continues Qasim Amin Bey, 'should study the history of our ancient Muslim culture as it is a base for our contemporary civilization, but it is only right to agree that many principles of this ancient culture are out of date and do not fit in with the conditions of modern life and that even many of our institutions are based on wrong ideas. If we look back at the family life of our ancestors, we will see that there have always been abnormalities. For example, to conduct a marriage the husband only needs two witnesses; to divorce on the other hand he does not need a single witness. He can get rid of his wife without a single valid reason, and he could remarry as often as he wanted without conforming to the relatively simple demands of the Quran.

That was done at the outset of Islam and the practice continues to the present day, but not a single administrator or lawyer considers ending this disgusting evil, which causes a Muslim family to be dispersed and destroyed.'

Qasim Amin Bey concludes that European Christian laws concerning the family and the very European Christian family are at an incomparably more advanced stage than the Muslim family and its legislation. Muslims should direct all their efforts towards this ideal of the contemporary European family if they want to acquire independence in the future.

Qasim Amin Bey is brave enough to promote this bold idea in his book 'The New Woman' which has scandalized all 'orthodox' Muslims, but he does not stop at this. He claims that Muslim law has no idea of woman's role and moreover it is hardly surprising that women have been so harshly treated since the law has not had a better understanding of certain other aspects of life.

As he develops his ideas about the faults in Muslim law in general and the injustice towards women, Qasim Amin believes it is necessary to modify and even, if necessary, to do away with the section of the Islamic code which concerns women if the Muslim empire, society, and family are to be saved from ruin. To achieve that, Muslim women must be given a similar education to that of European women and remove the veil which for her is a shroud and a sign of servitude. The criticism that the writer makes of this barbarous custom and the audacity of his ideas are signs of a conviction, never seen till now in Islamic history.

It is hardly surprising that any Muslim who considers himself a guardian of traditional values should protest these novel ideas of Qasim Amin Bey and have accused him of heresy. One of these unenlightened fanatics, who hates this reformer, published an article in a newspaper that the emancipation of Muslim women is one of the most eagerly pursued goals of Christians who only want to destroy the Muslim religion and that any Muslim who shared such ideas would cease to be an orthodox believer.

It is obvious that our reformer is only strengthened in his opinions by this kind of criticism. Moreover, fortunately for him enlightened Muslims have been happy to receive his ideas. The Egyptian prime minister sent Qasim Amin Bey an open letter showing his sympathy for these latest ideas saying they should be widely spread to the public. The mufti of Egypt and Sudan Mohammed Abdou and more importantly the rector of the Muslim theological college El-Ezhar [al-Azhar University], Selim El-Bichri, show deep sympathy for his emancipated ideas.

These demonstrations of approval are important for the future and mark the beginning of a new era in the Muslim world.

On this note, I am delighted to announce that the religious chief of Egyptian Muslims has given his approval to the innovations of Qasim Amin Bey so that reforms have passed from the written word into the realms of reality. He has formed a commission of which he is president, which aims to find ways of improving the precarious position of Muslim women by giving them some rights.

The work of this commission has resulted in the drafting of eleven laws, which have been approved by the government and are already in force. I hope you will allow me to mention a few of them here:

1) A husband cannot refuse to maintain his wife if he has the means; but if he has neither the means nor the wish to do so the judge will immediately issue a divorce decree. In a case where the husband pretends that he is poor, the same thing will happen. But if on the other hand he can prove that he really does not have the means of keeping his wife, he will be given a period of four months and if at the end of these four months he is not able to maintain her divorce is granted.

2) If through sickness or imprisonment the husband refuses to maintain his wife, the judge will give him sufficient time either to be cured or to finish his prison sentence. If at the end of this time the husband is still incapable of maintaining his wife, divorce is declared.

6) In the case that the husband disappears, the wife has the right to call upon the minister of justice to instigate a search for him; if he is not found the wife is permitted to remarry after four years, four months and nine days without further recourse to the judge.

10) If there is a dispute between the spouses and if the means shown in the Quran to settle the case are fruitless, the matter is brought before the judge. The judge will then choose two arbiters from the relatives or neighbours of the two spouses, and he sends the spouses back to these arbiters for them to try to bring about reconciliation. If they fail, divorce is declared.

11) Any woman has the right to ask her for a divorce if her husband ill-treats her, if he leaves her for no reason, if he treats her with undeserved harshness, and in this case the woman is only obliged to prove the truth of her claim.

These new measures of the law, which at last bring a ray of light into the dark world in which the Muslim woman has lived up till the present day, are worthy of the votes of all educated Muslims both in Egypt and in other Islamic countries.

Ladies and gentlemen, we will all rejoice about this together; but you will also join your voices with mine to make the lawmaker understand that like Lucan's [satirical] hero that: 'he has done nothing because it all still remains to be done' (*nihil actum reputans, is quid superescet agendum*)[k]: and we all hope that these reforms are only the first steps on the path and at the culmination of which wives will finally have equal rights to those of the men who are still today their masters."

---

[k] From a Latin poem "Pharsalia") by Lucan. Believing that nothing had been done if there was still something to be done. Mark Anneo Lucano

Speech at the Algiers Congress (1905)

XIV International Congress of Orientalists

The following speech - '*Discours*' - is taken from the *Proceedings* of the XIV International Congress of Orientalists.[744] This was also published in Russian by *Imprimerie Trenke et Fusnot* in St Petersburg in 1905, and is translated here as follows:

> Mr Governor General, Ladies and Gentlemen.
>
> The recently formed Russian Society of Oriental Studies, which I have the honour to represent here with Messieurs Professors Knauer and Stréboulayef, is happy to participate in the fourteenth International Congress of Orientalists. Our society has charged me with transmitting to all the illustrious members of this congress, all their most sincere wishes for their success in furthering knowledge and for the work we have undertaken in common for bringing together East and West.
>
> As for myself, I have always been personally devoted to the cause of emancipation of Muslim women - within the limits indicated by their Prophet - who founded a religion, which is perfectly compatible with all modern advances, on condition that it is correctly interpreted and understood. As for myself, I must say

that I feel doubly happy to find myself in this beautiful colony, an extension of France, which we all love and admire; a free country of grand ideas, always prepared to talk of emancipation and breaking the shackles of obscurantism!

It is in this beautiful country where beloved and accomplished Muslim women have already entered on the path of progress following their elder sisters in Europe with whom they will soon catch up. Let us hope that they will have the wisdom to just absorb the good examples, above all striving for their own intellectual advancement, which will enable them to bring up good sons for their homeland and virtuous daughters, destined to become their faithful and educated companions.

But progress is like a double-edged sword - it might therefore become harmful if it is not based on emotional development and on the principles of the highest morality.

In the interest of their own happiness, I therefore wish for my beloved Eastern sisters to never let themselves be seduced by the frivolous sides of an over-refined society which would not correspond to their ideal, and would only bring them, on the contrary, disappointment and unhappiness.

Finally, I express the wish that they may have the wisdom to find themselves in a right environment, corresponding more closely to their legitimate hopes towards a higher status, in order to always better fulfil on earth, the role of companion and comforter of man:[745] a role for which they have been created and which should be a woman's most noble attribute in every latitude and civilization!"

An Appreciation: On the Conversion of the Georgians to Christianity by the Patriarch Macaire

AN APPRECIATION BY MARILYN BOOTH

Histoire de la conversion des Géorgiens au Christianisme
Trans. Mme Olga de Lébédew [1] (Arabic to French)

In 1905, de Lebedeff published a translation of a short seventeenth-century manuscript, held at the Vatican, penned by the then-Patriarch of Antioch, Macaire or Macarius III (d. 1672). The translation, with a text edition of the Arabic, was published in Rome and offered in homage to the 14th International Congress of Orientalists, to be held in Algiers. [746]

The reader immediately confronts a scholarly apparatus, describing the manuscript's appearance and provenance; it was copied

---

[1] Patriarche Macaire, *Histoire de la conversion des Géorgiens au Christianisme*, trans. Mme Olga de Lébédew (Roma : Casa Editrice Italiana, 1905). The title page labels this Codex 689 du Vatican. The Arabic text : *Nabdha fi akhbar al-Karj*.

in Rome in 1756, and this publication is said to be a faithful rendering of a text bearing 'formes souvent vulgaires et incorrectes.' The translator's preface explains that it is part of a longer text written by the Patriarch's son during their expedition to Russia (c1669-71); the son died in Georgia on the return journey and so this section was composed by the Patriarch. The larger manuscript, minus this, had been translated into Russian and English; the translator explains that she learned of this manuscript from Professor Ignace Guidi, and that she has translated it for its lively narrative of the religious and political state of the Georgians 'in a period when this land was almost unknown to us.'

The Arabic text is indeed both colloquial and lively; the Patriarch does not mince words on religious and social practices that he clearly found appalling and in which—he relates—he tried to intervene. The worst of it was that these practices were followed and encouraged by the clerisy at all levels. These practices included enslavement and selling people into slavery; separating married couples; alternatively, not practicing the sacrament of marriage at all; ignoring the sacrament of baptism; failing to instil even a minimum of religious instruction in the populace; and so forth. In a shorter section, the author outlines the merits and 'fine deeds' of this people, which mostly comprise the wealthier households' pious practices.

One feature that may have sparked Lebedeff's interest in the text is that it details marriage customs, women's pious practices, and other aspects of family and women's lives, with great sympathy. The 'villains' in this narrative are the senior clergy, faulted as very poor role models and criticized for ignorance, greed, nepotism, in-fighting, and generally selfish and reprehensible behaviour.

Lebedeff's translation generally adheres closely to the original and preserves a rather informal tone. Clearly, this was a work of research: she provides several lengthy footnotes to supplement mention of various historical figures. Quite often, though, she 'fills in' what is a terse and unadorned narrative. Where the author uses the imperative *i 'lam* (know, learn) to start each distinct thematic section, she makes an addition:

'Apprends, ô lecteur' (9 and later; Ar. 3),[747] [m]which nicely conveys the colloquial tenor. In that same sentence, she clarifies, translating the unspecified *fi al-sabiq* (previously, earlier 9; Ar 3) as 'dans les premiers temps du Christianisme'. Such explications and expansions are most evident in the historical section, less so in those describing contemporary practices.

Sometimes, her translation is more strongly specific in description; thus, for *marad sa'b* (a difficult disease) she uses 'une maladie inguérissable' (10; 3). Telling the story of what was thought to be the original conversion in the area—a queen and finally, her spouse—Lebedeff translates 'he did not obey her' (*lam yuti'ha*) as 'ayant refusé d'embrasser le Christianisme' (10; 3). For the original's laconic 'he [the King] did that', she gives: 'Le Roi s'étant conformé à la demande de la sainte …' (10; 4). What is simply 'this news' (*hadha al-khabar*) in Arabic becomes 'la nouvelle de ce crime' (18; 11). And the bishop simply 'saves' this queen (after she has provided many gifts including a young woman), whereas in the French, he saves her 'from the anger of the people who wanted to kill her' (18; 11).

Where it is decided that a representative of Antioch must come each year to 'examine the errors of the head priests' [*li-yafhas ghalatat ruasa* [sic] *al-kahana*), she uses the more euphemistic 'chargé de contrôler les faits et gestes du clergé' (12; 5). Where the author refers to the Georgians as a 'tribe' (*qabila*), she uses 'peuple', reserving *tribu* for more specific groupings (13: 6). Occasionally, though, she is less specific: a 'school to teach them reading and the branches of knowledge' becomes 'une école pour les y élever' (13; 6), and 'her niece' (*ibnat akhiha*) is simply mentioned as (her husband's son's) fiancée (17; 11). 'More cruel /evil than the barbarians' (*asharr min al-barbar*) becomes 'avec la plus grande cruauté' (20; 13).

But as can be seen from these few examples—and more could be adduced—this is a close translation and the occasional expansions or rarer omissions of the translator do not alter the text in theme, approach,

---

[m] I have given the French page numbers first and the Arabic second, even when I mention the Arabic before giving the French—for no reason, except that in the volume, the French precedes the Arabic; they are paginated separately.

or tone. In fact, Olga de Lébédeff has produced a lively and readable text of her own.

Famous Women: Gülnar Hanım, or Mme Olga de Lébédef (1907, Cairo)

Translation from the Arabic to English by Marilyn Booth

Fatat al-sharq 1: 7 (15 April 1907): 193-201.
Shahirat al-nisa: Jullanar Hanım, aw al-sayyida Ulgha di Labidaf, Mme Olga de Lébédef [name given in both Arabic transcription and Roman letters].

[First page, masthead of the issue, is her picture with the title beneath, p.194]

From earlier issues of this magazine, it will be apparent to readers that we have devoted its leading feature to publicizing histories of famous Eastern women. Thus far, we have not published any Western woman's history. We had resolved to adhere to this approach, wanting to give the subject its full due, bringing to it all the material our research could excavate. We would not insert the history of a famous Western woman before emptying our quiver of histories of Eastern women. However, we request readers' indulgence in offering the biography of Mme Olga de Lébédef before we have exhausted the subject of Eastern women's histories. This is because she came to Egypt this past winter and was among us, and she was warmly welcomed. Having the good fortune to become acquainted with her, we found her a very fine lady of considerable learning and knowledge, very widely read. This has led us to contravene our initial plan, as we wished to display her merit and service to East and West and her excellence in the world of civilized exchange and refinement.

This fine woman was born in the city of [St] Petersburg, capital of Russia, in 1853 AD, to a family of age-old glory and lineage. She was born in the home of her father, Serge de Barstschof [in Arabic: Sergius], who was an army officer at that time. Her godfather was His Majesty, Emperor Alexander II.

As for her mother, Countess Koutaissof [in Latin and Arabic characters], in her youth she was the paragon of goodness and beauty, and was adorned, moreover, with refinement and the greatest accomplishment. She had been born to a Russian father, with a Turkish grandfather from the city of Coutaiss [sic, in Latin characters] in the Caucasus [lit., Caucasia]. During the war that flared up between Russia and the Ottoman State in the era of Empress Catherine [II], the city of Koutaiss [here in Arabic only] fell into the hands of the Russians, and they plundered it. Prince Potemkin, the most senior general in the Russian army, noticed this Turkish grandfather. Admiring his handsome appearance and his intelligence, he took him to Petersburg and presented him to Empress Catherine. He was an orphan, no more than thirteen years old, and so the Empress took him into her household. She had him baptized and raised him with her son, Duke Paul [Boulus], who was [made] a godfather to him at the time of baptism. She called him Yuhanna ibn Boulus [John son of Paul] and granted him the title and name of Count Koutaissof [only in Arabic; a typo, Kunaysuf].

When Duke Paul assumed the throne, he elevated him, appointing him to a senior post in his government, and marrying him to a daughter of the nobility. He had two sons, the oldest of whom died—his name was Alexander—in the Battle of Borodino in 1812.[n] There was much grief at his death, for he was a courageous and intelligent individual. He was elegized by Lermontov [*limontof*], the famous poet. The second son, named Boulus, married after his father's death. He had many children [or sons]. We mention only one, Hippolyte, because he was the grandfather of this biography's subject.

Hippolyte married Princess Urusov, who was from a Muslim family in the Tatar region. She gave birth to a daughter who was the mother of Mme Olga de Lébédef. And so, the subject of the biography grew up with a natural fondness for the Turks and Islam. She was her mother's only child. From childhood, she had a penchant for studying languages, drawing and music, and because she liked them, she was resoundingly successful at all these subjects.

Aged seven, she travelled with her parents to many places, accompanied by an English governess on all her travels, as well as instructors with whom she studied the various branches of knowledge, and the languages of wherever she happened to be at the time. With her capacious intelligence and strong memory, within a month she would have learned the language of the country where she was residing.

After a lengthy period of travel, she returned with her parents to St Petersburg. There, she was unable to continue studying and reading, for she was married, at the age of sixteen, to the son of General Dlotovsky, at the time working as a public prosecutor in the Russian government. After her marriage, she focused on studying languages on her own. She studied Italian and drawing [or painting], and she played the piano in private charity

---

[n] A battle fought during the Napoleonic Wars, in France's invasion of Russia, on 7 September 1812.

association gatherings. Her fine playing softened people's hearts, and she charmed their minds with her eloquence and refined clarity of expression. She took unusual pleasure in serving invalids, aiding the troubled, and coming to the rescue of those in need. She read the Holy Book to female prisoners and consoled them for the calamities and afflictions they had suffered, with her sweet words and delicate way of speaking.°

A few years later, her husband was appointed to the court of the state of Kazan. She travelled there and lived with her husband for ten years replete with discord and woe. She was forced to request a divorce, which was granted. With him she had had four children. Immediately, she married Alexander de Lébédeff, who was from one of the most venerable, notable, eminent, and wealthy families [there]. He is now amongst the emperor's chamberlains. She took her children with her and lived a happy life with her second husband. She devoted herself to studying the arts of singing, drawing, and musical instruments, and her achievements were splendid. Since, as we said, she was inclined by nature to help the wretched, and to serve invalids and those in need, she studied most of the available medical manuals, and learned the Tatar language in a short time, enabling her to become acquainted with the needs of people in trouble and those serving in her husband's properties. She did not stop with that; she mounted many musical soirees in aid of the poor. None of this deflected her from her determination to continue studying, reading, and writing.

Her first written work was a book she translated from the Tatar language [into Russian]. In Persian, it is called the *Qabus Nameh* [*kabus na'ma*]. The translation was so strong that she won a

---

° There seems to be a typographical error: *ibtalaynā* [we suffered] for *ibtalayna* [they (fem.) suffered].

valuable prize from Mr. Schefer, director of the Schools of Living Eastern Languages in Paris. [p] It is a valuable Persian work.

After that, she travelled to Stockholm, capital of Sweden, where she attended the [International] Congress of Orientalists[q] in 1889 and became acquainted with Ahmed Midhat Efendi, delegate of the Ottoman state. She presented him with a small book on history which she had translated. Midhat Efendi received it with great pleasure and admiration and praised her for her strong understanding. He entreated her forcefully to visit Istanbul so that she could perfect her Turkish. She travelled there in 1890, taking her children, and she devoted herself to studying that language for six months with the learned Ahmed Cevdet Efendi, formerly a writer at the *Tercüman-ı Hakikat* newspaper and currently proprietor of *Iqdam* newspaper. She translated many books, which she dedicated [or presented] to His Majesty, Mawlana [our lord] the Sultan 'Abd al-Hamid Khan. He—may God ever strengthen him—graciously condescended to have his secretary, *Dawlatilu* Thurayya Pasha write to her, conveying a letter comprising expressions of attachment and bestowing favour upon her, conferring the Order of the Shefakat second class [for women] upon her. She began going to Istanbul every winter, spending ten hours of every day studying the Persian and Arabic languages until she had delved into them thoroughly. Here is one indication of her strong determination and persistence in work. She took her daughters with her on all of her travels to implant in them the love of inquiry and to increase their experience and knowledge.

Residing in Istanbul, she got to know the greatest men of state and the most eminent notables and scholars, among them Ahmed

---

[p] L'École nationale de langues orientales vivantes, founded under another name and apparently known as this when this biography appeared, although this was not its formal name until 1914. Charles Schefer (1820- 1898) was the director (Ecole des languages orientales, 1867-98); (President of the Congress of Orientalists in Paris 1897), diplomat and Professor of Persian.

[q] Lit., the somewhat awkward 'Congress of Orientalist Languages', *mu'tamar al-lughat al-mustashriqa*.

Tevfik Pasha, former governor of [B-r-u-s-ah – Prussia?]ʳ, famous for his knowledge and writings; and Ahmed Cevdet Pasha, the linguist and historian of great repute, and al-Muʿallim [the teacher or master] Naji, the famous poet, as well as others whom the magazine does not have space to enumerate. Among her female friends was the famous poet known as Nigar Hanım, and Fatima Aliye, the daughter of Cevdet Pasha and very famous writer. (Her life history was told in this magazine's previous two issues).

In 1904 [sic], the subject travelled to Naples, Italy, where she spent the winter season. She returned to Petersburg where she founded an association, that she called Société des études orientales. Its aim comprised the study of everything connected to the East: languages, religions, history, customs, exports and imports and crop yields [sic],ˢ and other matters concerning the East and Easterners. It restricted itself to the teaching of the Japanese, Persian, and Turkish languages.ᵗ She [or it] translated many writings from Russian to the Eastern languages with the aim of circulating among Easterners the customs of Russia, and likewise from the Eastern languages into Russian everything that the Russians enjoyed knowing about the East and its peoples. She [or it] founded two schools of commerce in the East, along with commercial establishments displaying samples of Russian merchandise: and many associations in Bukhara, Samarkand, Ashkabad, Tabriz, Tehran, Tiflis, and most famous cities of the East. She now lives under the patronage of [lit. as a subject of or

---

ʳ 1845 –1936, known as Ahmet Tevfik Okday following the 1934 Surname Law of 1934. Of ethnic Crimean Tatar origin, he was the last Grand Vizier of the Ottoman Empire.

ˢ *Mahsulat*, which can mean 'crops' or 'produce' or 'harvests' but also yield in the sense of income.

ᵗ The meaning is ambiguous as the fem. verb could refer either to the association or to Lébédef: if the latter: she restricted it to teaching…. She seems to be the referent of the subject of the next sentence: she translated rather than it [had] translated.

under the care of] Duke Michael, uncle of his Majesty the Emperor of Russia Nicholas II; and her circles in Russia are comprised of elites and nobles.

As for the Société des études orientales, which she founded and whose honorary president she is, its current president is the esteemed General Schwedoff [in Ar., Shafaydun]. It has made great advances and has been hugely influential in strengthening relations between Russia and the Near and Far East, deflecting attention away from the religious and political factors that cause division between one nation and another, one kingdom and another.

In recent years, the subject of this biography attended the Orientalist Congress in Rome, Hamburg, and Algiers, and presented some of her writings to their members. She spoke on one occasion about the 'Emancipation of the Muslim Woman'. She has [written] many speeches and articles in all subjects, and we will give details at the end of this essay. As for the languages that she has studied to an advanced level, they are Russian, French, English, German, Italian, Spanish, Greek, Tatar, Turkish, Persian, and Arabic. She also has a broad grasp of Latin, Sanskrit, and Hebrew. She came to Egypt this winter to complete her study of Arabic with a shaykh at al-Azhar. Here are her writings ...

[The list gives titles in Arabic and the original, in the following categories: translations from and to Turkish/Russian; her original writings; some of her translations into Russian; books translated from Arabic into French. [This does not mention the Aliye translation, interestingly.]

In addition to these, she has published many articles in newspapers in various languages.

The subject of the biography has received the Palme [d'Or] Order from l'Academie française and a gold medal from the Romanian Scientific Academy. On one face is the image of the King of

Romania, and on the other, this expression: *Bene Merenti*—that is, 'for the one who deserves it'. She has received the Serbian Star [l'Étoile] medal from the King of Serbia [*malik al-sirb*], a decoration that she is the only lady to have received; and the Order of St Saba also from the King of Serbia [*malik sirbiya*] also, as well as the Order of the Red Cross from the State of Russia and the Order of Shefakat second class from his Majesty, Mawlana the Sultan.

This is the information we have been able to establish concerning the legacies and works of this fine woman. This is not a little of her excellent attributes and her superb cultural/literary/moral refinement. We will provide [in future] some snippets of her news and conversations to indicate how much knowledge and excellence she has accrued.[u]

Translated by Marilyn Booth
Arabic text from the private collection of Marilyn Booth

---

[u] I have not seen any further news of her in this journal though I have not looked exhaustively for it.

Appendix: A Short History of Ivan Kutaisov (Koutaissoff)

> La Russe est une puissance européenne.
> Catherine the Great [748]

Taking foreign slaves as 'gifts of war' was not uncommon, even fashionable, in both the Muslim and Christian worlds. Peter the Great was given an African slave procured in Constantinople who would become a great Russian statesman in his own right and was the great-grandfather of Alexander Pushkin. Catherine the Great received an Ottoman boy as a prize of war in 1770 and gave him to her son Paul.[749]

This boy, renamed Ivan Kutaisov, was to become a favourite of Paul I. He was an ancestor of Olga de Lebedeff, a great-great-grandfather on her maternal side. The origins of Ivan Kutaisov are also the stuff of legend and as Ivan's story appears to be little known to Anglophone readers, I would like to introduce him and his family.

Ivan was brought to Russia as a child of ten or eleven after the siege of Bender, now Moldova. It is believed that he was born in 1759 in the city of Kutaisi in the Caucasus, however Russians referred to him as a Turk because he had been captured in Ottoman lands, though the Ottoman empire was comprised of many nationalities.[750]

Unconfirmed Georgian sources state that Kutaisov's father was the governor of Kutaisi, and his name was Simon Kikiani.[751] As Simon converted to Islam and supported the Ottomans, he was given the name

APPENDIX: A SHORT HISTORY OF IVAN KUTAISOV

of Hasan Pasha. During Russo-Turkish wars (1768-1774) Hasan Pasha was the governor of Kutaisi and it was his son who was bought for a ransom.

Catherine then gave the boy to her son Grand Duke Paul to improve their difficult relationship. Crown Prince Paul was made Ivan's godfather. The heir to the throne was only about five years older than Ivan and over time he became reliant on his new servant, who had a ready smile and was keen to please. Paul took good care of him. The newly christened Ivan was transformed into a Russian citizen carrying the patronymic name of his godfather Paul ('son of Paul'): Ivan Pavlovich Kutaisov (or Koutaissoff), a name that means 'from Kutaisi.'

Thus, Ivan was the first member of the Kutaisov family. In 1779, aged twenty, he married Anna Rezvaya, the daughter of a wealthy St Petersburg merchant. Together, over sixteen years, they had five children.

Crown Prince Paul sent Ivan Pavlovich to Versailles and Berlin to become a barber and trained in first aid. Thus, on his return Ivan worked as the Crown Prince's valet and barber. As the years went by, Ivan Kutaisov became Paul's most trusted and loyal servant.

The Favourite

In 1799, once Paul (Павел I) was on the throne, Ivan was rapidly promoted at court and rewarded for his loyalty. First, he was made a baron and, very shortly after, a hereditary Count of the Russian Empire.[752] The new Kutaisov coat of arms carried the phrase «Живу однимъ и для однаго» 'By one I live and for him alone' – a phrase of loyalty to his benefactor the Tsar. He accrued much wealth and was gifted substantial lands in Courland, owning more than five thousand serfs.[753]

Ivan was discreet about the Tsar's private life, yet in time, manipulated court intrigues. One of his main rivals for the Tsar's trust was the Tsarina. Maria Feodorovna was Paul's faithful wife and mother of his ten children. To weaken her strong influence, Ivan organised the introduction one by one of two young women to Tsar Paul who each in turn became his mistress: Katya Nelidova and Anna Lopukhina.

Meanwhile, Ivan's rise to power and influence was also not a matter of indifference to the aristocrats and Russian nobility. They looked down upon the foreign Ottoman origins of Ivan Kutaisov. He was often referred to a Turk, then almost synonymous with the breakdown of orderly things. The term 'Turk' had historically invoked suspicion both in Russia and Europe. Turks and Moors were seen as 'faithless' and mistrustful from representations in Shakespeare's Othello, to inherent loathing of fearsome Mongols khans who imposed the autocratic Tatar yoke on their land so many years ago.

Fig. 100
Count Ivan Kutaisov (1759-1834)

Those in the military and Russian aristocracy who mistrusted Ivan Kutaisov caricatured him as a 'mushroom count'. A story along these lines first appeared in the British press in 1843 and was still being published in 1887 in various US states from New York to Boonville in Kansas, Indiana, and California. The tale quoted Prince Dolgoruki's *Handbook of the Principal Families of Russia* where the famous General Suvorov upbraided Ivan Kutaisov for his titles despite his lack of military or other distinguished service.[754] *The New York Tribune* commented as follows: "The upstart nobility of Russia is not held in high esteem by the

APPENDIX: A SHORT HISTORY OF IVAN KUTAISOV

old families with ancestors. It is said of Suwaroff, the great campaigner, that he once 'took down' one of these mushroom counts in a way that has become a tradition at St Petersburg…he was a menial…but now he is a master of the czar's stables and a count into the bargain'."[755] However, even Suvorov, 'Russia's invincible hero,' was also outspoken to Tsar Paul and was at one stage sent into exile.[756] In fact, Suvorov was also a good friend of Ivan Kutaisov's brother-in-law, Dmitri Petrovich Rezvoi, a military man who fought in many foreign campaigns.

Whilst for many years Tsar Paul prized the loyalty of Ivan Kutaisov in contrast to the hostile nobility, in the end their own ambitions got the better of them both.

Tsar Paul's reign consisted of four short years. He brought in unpopular reforms at court, such as increased peasant rights and checks on the corrupt treasury. His first year saw 48,000 new decrees.[757] He maintained a largely peaceful diplomatic foreign policy at a time of war, ending his alliance with Britain by leaving the Second Coalition against Napoleon in 1799.[758] At the time, Paul's reversals of many of Catherine II's policies were seen as absurd and pernicious and brought about scheming against him by the nobility whose rights were curtailed, and for whom corporal punishment had been reintroduced in 1798. The threat of humiliation for nobles hung in the air, either with banishment to Siberia or being stripped of one's rank. Paul, in turn, feared and suspected scheming from the nobles and began a campaign against 'depravity' in the Guards and at court.[759]

The fear of assassination became paranoia and got the better of Paul I. The suddenness of neurotic decision-making fuelled his unpopularity and the inglorious nickname of 'Mad Tsar' was attributed to him. The plotting and his eventual assassination on 11th March 1801 (Julian calendar), 'that day of horror' as Alexander II put it,[760] was no random act.[761] In the 'Memoirs of the Reign of George III,' William Belsham explains it this way:

> The oppression and caprice of Paul's government had left him no friends. The latter of those qualities was still more fatal to him than the former. The favourite of today knew that he might be the victim of tomorrow. [762]

The Unopened Letter

Ivan Pavlovich Kutaisov was aware of the Tsar's fears in the days leading up to the assassination because they had talked about various potential scenarios. The emperor's obsessive fears and mistrust were nothing new. This time, Kutaisov had been hoodwinked and circumvented by the colluders, so in the end, he did not hear of the actual plot conspiracy until it was too late.

He nearly died of shock with the news of the Tsar's murder, particularly as he belatedly read an unopened warning letter the next morning, which had been in his pocket. He is described as having a 'limitless devotion' to the emperor. But in recent times he had neglected his duties; one of his favourite sayings was 'business tomorrow'.[763] This was on account of Ivan's resentment that the Tsar had become infatuated with Ivan's own mistress, Madame Louise Chevalier.

Louise Chevalier was a twenty-five-year-old actress and singer, with whom Kutaisov had fallen madly in love and fathered a daughter.[764] His passionate feelings for his Madame Chevalier had caused Ivan Kutaisov to lose all reason. His despair on both counts is described in the memoirs of Madame Vigee-Lebrun (1755-1842), a member of the Academy of Fine Arts of St Petersburg.[765] Following the Tsar's assassination in his newly built St Michael's castle, Ivan Kutaisov was arrested for a short time.

Accounts vary as to his temporary exile in Europe. What is sure, is that he departed St Petersburg and moved to his country estate of Rozhdestveno near Moscow with his wife and two daughters. There between 1810-1823 he built a new manor house and a stone church called 'The nativity of Christ' in honour of John the Baptist, St Peter, and St Paul. He lived out the rest of his life here; he enjoyed considerable success in agriculture producing linen and cloth. Just occasionally he would return to the high life of Moscow or St Petersburg.[766]

The Kutaisovs had four surviving children: Paul, Alexander, Maria and Nadezhda. The young men were employed the service of the Imperial government and army and the ladies married into the aristocracy.

APPENDIX: A SHORT HISTORY OF IVAN KUTAISOV

Fig. 101
'The nativity of Christ'

Olga's Great Grandparents

In 1800, Ivan's eldest son, Paul Kutaisov, married Prascovia Lopukhina (the younger sister of the Tsar's mistress Anna Lopukhina); they are the great grandparents of Olga de Lebedeff.

Their son Hippolyte (1806 -1851) was Olga's grandfather. Olga de Lebedeff knew 'grand-maman' Prascovia Lopukhina, who died in 1870. One treasured photograph, now lost, portrayed seven generations of women in the family; a testament to the fact that they were all married so young.

Paul Kutaisov (1780-1840) trained in the army from age seven but was not cut out to be a military man. He rose to the highest ranks of government from chamberlain to the Privy Council and the Senate in 1817. Like his father he was a commander of the Knights of Malta and a Knight of the Order of Alexander Nevsky. He served as member of the Committee for the construction of St. Isaac's Cathedral, the grandest construction during the reign of Nicholas I. As a senior statesman, in 1826 he was appointed to the Supreme Criminal Court charged with prosecuting the Decembrists. Despite the latter role, he had a genuine appreciation for the arts, and he was known as a patron of painters and the theatre; he was also on friendly terms with Alexander Pushkin (despite the latter's liberal views).

OLGA DE LEBEDEFF – A LIFE ACROSS EMPIRES

Fig. 102
Prascovia Petrovna Lopukhina (1784- 1870) married at sixteen to Paul Kutaisov

Consequent to these artistic interests there are many oil portraits of Paul Kutaisov's family which survive to this day in the Hermitage Museum. He was of shy character, charming though. Gentility in manners and behaviour were generally regarded favourably: 'womanishness was by no means accounted shameful, and affectations of a kind which might be unpleasant to witness in women, were considered the height of worldly refinement'.[767]

Paul Kutaisov and Prascovia Lopukhina had four children who reached adulthood: Anna (1800-1868), Ivan (1803-1868), Alexandrine (1804-1893) and Hippolyte (1806-1851).

Their eldest daughter Anna Kutaisova, once a lady in waiting to Nicholas I's wife Alexandra Feodorovna, married into the Georgian royal family. Her husband the Crown Prince of Georgia, Okropir Gruzinsky, lived in exile in St Petersburg, Kostroma, and Moscow, having been forbidden from settling in Georgia following Russia's annexation of Georgia in 1800. Okropir and Anna carried the title of His/Her Serene Highness.

Upon her death, the Moscow journals announced that 'the deceased was well known for her great erudition and benevolence. She was acquainted with all the remarkable personages of the 19th century;

APPENDIX: A SHORT HISTORY OF IVAN KUTAISOV

was a pleasing writer, and so excellent a composer that Meyerbeer, in speaking of her songs, said- "I should like to have produced them."[768]

Ivan Kutaisov's second son Alexander (1784-1812) had a military career, distinguishing himself as a brave commander in the battle of Friedland, at Ostrovno and Smolensk. Many consider his battlefield prowess to be inherited from his uncle, Major General Dmitry Rezvoi, who was his commander in 1803 in the second artillery regiment. At age twenty-eight, he led the charge of the artillery cavalry during a counterattack on General Raevsky's battery in the famous Battle of Borodino against Napoleon in 1812. Alexander thus died a hero. His name was eulogised in a poem by poet Vasily Zhukovsky (later the tutor of Alexander II). His portrait painted by English portraitist George Dawe, hangs in the Military Gallery of the Winter Palace (Hermitage). Not forgotten on the two hundredth anniversary of his death, a coin was minted featuring his portrait. It is said that he spoke several languages, including Turkish.

Ivan's daughter Maria (1787-1870) was a lady-in-waiting to Tsar Paul's wife Maria Feodorovna and married a Count Vasiliev in 1805. The youngest child Nadezhda Kutaisov (1796-1868) married Prince Alexander Golitsyn in 1821, a prince from one of the most ancient aristocratic families in Russia. Nadezhda adored her father, calling him her best friend, truest support and mentor.[769]

The head of the family, Ivan Pavlovich Kutaisov lived up to his seventy-fifth year. It was said he never forgot Louise Chevalier, because right up to his death in 1834 he carried a miniature, a watercolour portrait of her on his person.[770] Ivan's wife of fifty-five years, Anna Rezvaya, a steadfastly devout woman, died fourteen years later. Both husband and wife died during the dreaded cholera epidemics, then a new contagious disease which had originally arrived from Mumbai (Bombay) in British India. They were buried at the church they had built. Their youngest daughter Nadezhda inherited the estate of Rozhdestveno, and with it a large library of rare books.[771] Their elder daughter Maria Ivanovna Vasilieva eventually inherited their three-storey mansion at 24 Palace Embankment in 1849.

Though I have not found a detailed biography about him to date in English, information in Russian about Ivan Kutaisov is featured in the Russian Biographical Dictionary. Modern day bloggers still depict Ivan

Kutaisov 'worthless' or as a 'rascal;' previous caricatures include his 'oriental' eyes (though his portrait in 1800 by E. de la Sell portrays him with blue eyes). All aristocrats and royals had barbers and valets, but Ivan Kutaisov has also been likened to the valet-barber Figaro in the comedy 'The Barber of Seville,' written in 1773 by Beaumarchais.

Kutaisov himself was just a teenager at the time that this censored and comic play was written. Ivan was an extraordinary survivor, forcibly abducted in childhood, who skilfully adapted to new circumstances in a gilded cage of court intrigues, which he in part manipulated.

His master has generally been given unsympathetic short shrift. Catherine II and her favourites humiliated Paul for many years, but the historian Norman Davies describes Paul I as 'a would-be reformer-Tsar'. He adds that the Tsar 'was long held to be mentally unbalanced by official historiographers, obviously for being sane'.[772] Russian historian Yevgeny Anisimov noted: What occurred bore out what Paul himself had written in his youth, condemning tyranny: "Despotism, swallowing everything, finally destroys the despot himself."[773] In contrast with his more famous predecessors on the throne, Paul I was a relatively good parent, produced several potential heirs who lived to adulthood and produced an official line of succession.

From the time of Ivan's capture in 1770, the fate of the descendants of Ivan Kutaisov was tied to serving the Russian state or the army. The history of the later generations - and in particular the female descendants - proved much more elusive to uncover.

The last Kutaisovs

Son of Hippolyte and sibling to Prascovia Hippolitovna Barstchoff, Pavel Ippolitovich Kutaisov (1837-1911) was a military man who during his career had all kinds of interesting assignments and postings including in government. One of his first expeditions from 1863 to 1865 was as assistant to the military commander in Kutaisi in the Caucasus.

He spent two years in London as military attaché (1871-1873), attending royal and diplomatic functions. In 1877 he was governor of

APPENDIX: A SHORT HISTORY OF IVAN KUTAISOV

Nizhny-Novgorod, where his wife founded an orphanage. He was author of the 'Kutaisov papers' (1881-1882) in his role as chief state appointed investigator of the causes of the Jewish pogroms.[774] For some years he was a member of the Ministry of the Interior and a member of Alexander III's secret police. He eventually became General of the Infantry and Governor of Irkutsk, Siberia.

Pavel's four children were a similar age to Olga's own: Alexander (1869-1927), Vladimir (1871-1920), Elizaveta (1875-1916) and Konstantin Kutaisov (1878-1918). The eldest, Alexander, moved to England after the revolution. One of his two daughters, Elizabeth who never married, became a professor of Russian at Birmingham, and was also known as 'Princess Koutaissoff' by some of those who knew her.[775] Elizabeth Koutaissoff became an authority on Russia publishing two book reviews in the magazine Political Science in 1968 and 1969 and her own book 'The Soviet Union' in 1971. Elizabeth is the last known Kutaisov to carry that name as far as I know; she was my great-grandmother's second cousin.

Fig. 103
Pavel Hippolitovich Kutaisov (1837-1911) and one of his sons

Author's Notes

Calendar Dates

In Imperial Russia, dates followed the Julian calendar up till 31 January 1918. In the nineteenth century, the Julian calendar days were twelve days behind the Western European Gregorian calendar. In some correspondence, dates were written in with both variants, for instance: 2 / 14 August 1899; this can account for differences in birthdates and so on and might be referred to as **Old Style** (O.S. Julian) or **New Style** (N.S. Gregorian).

Dates officially recorded in Late Ottoman journals were recorded in a completely different manner, according to the solar financial Rumi Calendar or the lunar Islamic religious Hijri Calendar. Both dating systems were commonly used.

Variations in Spelling of Names & Places

Spelling transliterations of people's names and places from other languages into English have their widely diverging variations and conventions which change over time. There is no universal standard for transliterating the Russian names written in Roman script. There are also fashionable and period variations or interchangeable spellings, such as, for instance: Dlotovsky or *Dlotowskii*; Lebedeff or *Lebedev*; Koutaïssoff or *Kutaisov*; Ouroussoff or *Urusov*, Czar or *Tsar*.

AUTHOR'S NOTES

These are not the only spellings of these names in the text, especially where they are quoted by another author. There are eleven variations to be found online in Roman alphabet and Russian Cyrillic script for the subject of this book:

Olga de Lebedeff
Olga Lebedeva
Olga de Lébédeff
O. de Lébédew
Olga dö Lebedef
Madame de Lebedeff
Dolebedof
Labedeff
Ol'ga S Lebedeva
О. С. Лебедева
Лебедева Ольга Сергеевна.

Under Olga's Tatar-Turkish and Arabic pen name of *Gülnar* there are various versions too: *Madame Gülnar (French), Gülnâr Hanım (Turkish), Jullanur (Arabic)* and *Gjul'nar chanum (German).*

Tatar names also vary in Latin script according to how they are pronounced, or when and by whom they were published: Kaium or Qayyum, Shihabetdin Marjani (English usage) or Shigabutdin Mardzhani (Russian transliterated spelling), Gaspirali (Tatar usage) or Gasprinsky (the Russian usage). The same is true of Turkish names transliterated into Russian, French or English.

Olga's maiden name is pronounced "Bar-sch-**choff**" - with the accent on the last syllable. In the nineteenth century they spelled it in Roman script either *Barstchoff* or *Barstchow*. It has also been written as Borshoff or 'Borschtchova'. But later during the mid-twentieth century, it became *Borschov* in Latin script or just *Borshov*.

In Russian versions there were also *interchangeable* variations, most commonly 'Борщов', 'Барщев' or 'Борщёв'. Though they look different, there is one last explanation: the first syllable is soft, and the vowel sounds like an 'a' even if it is written with an 'o'; the last syllable carries the accent and the clear 'o' sound.

One reason there is fluidity with transcription is that different people speak the same thing in a different way. If you say it in English, it sounds different to when you say it in Russian. Take the word 'Lebedev', in Russian it sounds more like: 'Lye-bye-dy-eff'.

It was usual in the late nineteenth and early twentieth centuries for the Russian surnames ending '-ov' to be written as '-off', which is how it sounds.

Strictly speaking in Russian, a woman's family name takes a feminine ending with the addition of the letter 'a' (Barshchova), but the European versions of the name did not adopt that ending.

Place names: With historical change, often place names change. Here, most cities are described in their pre-revolutionary (or pre-1991) forms, such as Kovno not Kaunas. This is to reflect how places were known within the context of the time, and not to discount the validity of more recent historical changes for instance in modern day Ukraine where Kieff or Kiev is now Kyiv, or formerly Odessa is now spelt Odesa. Of particular note, the Ottoman capital referred to here is Constantinople, not Istanbul, as referred to by contemporaries and Ottoman diplomats.

Olga de Lebedeff or Olga Lebedeva?

In Russia, Olga is referred to as Olga Sergeevna Lebedeva (*Ольга Сергеевна Лебедева*).

Her published identity in Europe was Olga de Lébédeff or Lébédew. Here, I will use this version in Anglicized form (without é).

Olga's family spoke mostly French together. Their nicknames are mostly written French-style as I have found them in letters and on photographs: 'Micha' is the diminutive of Michel (the 'ch' is pronounced 'sh'), and 'Sacha' of Alexander. Like those names, endings of male nicknames in Russian often end in 'a', others in this text are Volodya and Valya.

AUTHOR'S NOTES

The young Olga was nicknamed 'Olishe' (written in French as Oliche). Another diminutive form of the name Olga in Russian would be '*Olichka*', or '*Olya*', both with the emphasis on the 'O'.

Patronymics

The patronymic is the father's name which follows the Christian name and comes before the surname; a system traditionally used in Russia (as well other societies such as Welsh or Icelandic who had no need for family names).

There were five other members of Olga de Lebedeff's family who were also called Olga, and this is where the 'patronymic' comes in useful to distinguish them all. Starting with our subject, for example:

- **Olga Sergeevna Barstchoff, later Olga de Lebedeff (1852 - 1933)**, whose father was Serge.

- **Mother**: Olga Hippolitovna Barstchoff-Koutaissoff (1835-1900), whose father was Hippolyte, her patronymic in Russian is pronounced '*Ippolitovna*'. Christened Prascovia, to avoid confusion in the narrative, we use this name **Prascovia Hippolitovna Barstchoff**.

- **Daughter**: Olga Alexandrovna Lebedeff (1880-1962), whose father was Alexander. She was christened Evfrosinia (or in French: Euphrosyne).

- **Granddaughter**: Olga Vladimirovna Gorloff (1907-?) whose father was Vladimir. She was christened Elena.

- **Great granddaughter**: Olga Sergeevna Bobrovsky (1919-1920), whose father was called Sergei; christened Maria Magdalena.

Of them all, only one was christened Olga, and that was Olga Sergeevna Barstchoff (de Lebedeff). The others all had other given names for their christenings but had the nickname of 'Olga'.

Questions and Debates of the Period

Studying Olga de Lebedeff in her time has meant considering some of the big social issues or political questions. I characterise these background debates of the era in the following manner:

- **The Eastern Question** - political jostling by the European powers in Eastern countries near the Russian Empire and was a term used in diplomatic and historical writing.
- **The Pan-Slavic Question** - how Russians viewed their own history. Eastern lands in their Empire were not considered 'colonial' acquisitions. Rejection of Europe as a superior model, connected to the rise of a national consciousness and pride in a national Russian identity that could embrace all the Empire from Vilnius to Vladivostok.
- **The Woman Question** – this was a social question. The position of women in the family and society: that they could have a voice and rights (beyond being a man's comforter or helpmeet), was widely debated. Themes concerned the condition of women which included the subject of education and the law, women in colonies, and the status of Muslim women.[776] The status of women was the most complex issue in East West comparisons.[777]
- **The Muslim Question** and the **Pan-Islamic Question** were separate but connected concerns in the Russian Empire. How to manage the Muslim population and build allegiance to the Russia? How to avoid religious 'fanaticism' or allegiance to the Ottoman Sultan?

These cross-cultural Questions concerned topical issues of the day that in one way or other shaped the life of Olga de Lebedeff and are themes arising in the course of the narrative.

AUTHOR'S NOTES

Orientalist and Orientologist

The terms for the words Orient, Eastern, European and Orientalist have changed over time and are frequently considered geopolitically sensitive. If they are used here, it is within the context of how they were used in the late nineteenth and early twentieth centuries before the Russian Revolution of 1917.

In those times being an Orientalist described someone who made special studies of the languages and cultures of the societies in the Middle East (alternately named Near East or Western Asia) and Asia. They presented or published works on the subject. Further discussion on that term, which has provoked controversy in more recent years is presented below and during the narrative.

A later polemic has arisen postdating Olga's life - **The Orientalist Question** - which examines the motivations of Oriental scholars and the influence of power and colonialism on them and their works. This discourse arose first amongst Russian and French Marxists. In part their 'anti-Orientalist' and anti-bourgeois rhetoric is said to have inspired Edward Said. His book *Orientalism* introduced a shift away from classical Oriental Studies by exploring the exchange between individuals and large political concerns related to the empires of Britain, France and later America, highlighting the dynamic between rulers and subject races, the strong and the weak.[778] In focussing on the empires of the high imperial age, he excluded the German, Russian, Dutch, Greek and Italian Orientalists.

Due to the imperialistic thesis by Edward Said about the term 'Orientalist', this name is now hardly used to refer to Oriental scholars, i.e., a scholar of the Middle East (previously Levantine or Ottoman studies) or of East Asia. The term 'Orientologist' is now used in its stead.

By contrast, in his book *For Lust of Knowing*, writer and historian Robert Irwin imparts that this is regrettable. He counters Said's assertions about Orientalists and a monolithic discourse, saying that Orientalist scholars themselves had a nuanced range of approaches and different agendas, but shared a passion for knowledge across ideologies. Although they corresponded and co-operated there was hardly an Orientalist type or a common Orientalist discourse.[779]

Later exceptions to this were Soviet Orientalists who took a destructive approach to Islamic history; [780] essentially everything was obliged to be examined through the ideological lens of communism. Before them, the doyen of Russian Imperial Orientalism Baron Viktor Rozen (1849-1908) denounced Eurocentric ways of looking at world history[781], presumably based on his detailed knowledge of the Arab world and its culture rather than because of any enforced ideology.

In Russian, one of the loan words used for an Oriental scholar in Olga's day was also 'Orientalist.' Thus, Olga de Lebedeff was referred to as 'Orientalistka.' [782] Then, as today, another term also used was *востоковед* (or 'Vostokoved') which denotes that a person is a [professional] specialist in Eastern languages and, or religions; an academic on the combined sciences of Eastern countries. The first part of the word 'Vostok' means the horizon or East, but also from where the sun rises (in its Latin verb equivalent, *Orior* comes from to rise or arise [of the sun], from where we arrive at *Oriente* or *Orient* – and Orientalist). The second part of the word 'ved' comes from an ancient form of the Russian verb to know (which stems from the Sanskrit word *Veda* meaning knowledge, wisdom, science or vision).

Illustrations

Most illustrations in this book, unless otherwise stated in the End Notes or Acknowledgements, are from the family collection. They were inherited from Olga's grand-daughter Nina Bahache de Bobrovsky, known in her family as Ninette. Huge thanks to my mother, Veronica, for entrusting these to me, as custodian of the stories of her ancestors.

Portraits of N. Borschova, Prince Gorchakov and Ivan, Paul and Praskovya Kutaisov and the Urusov sisters are in the public domain, as are those of Qayyum Nasyri, General Schwedow, Ignace Goldhizer, Fatma Aliye and Nigar Binti Osman.

AUTHOR'S NOTES

My Great-Great-Grandmother:
Olga de Lebedeff, née Olga Sergeevna Barstchoff

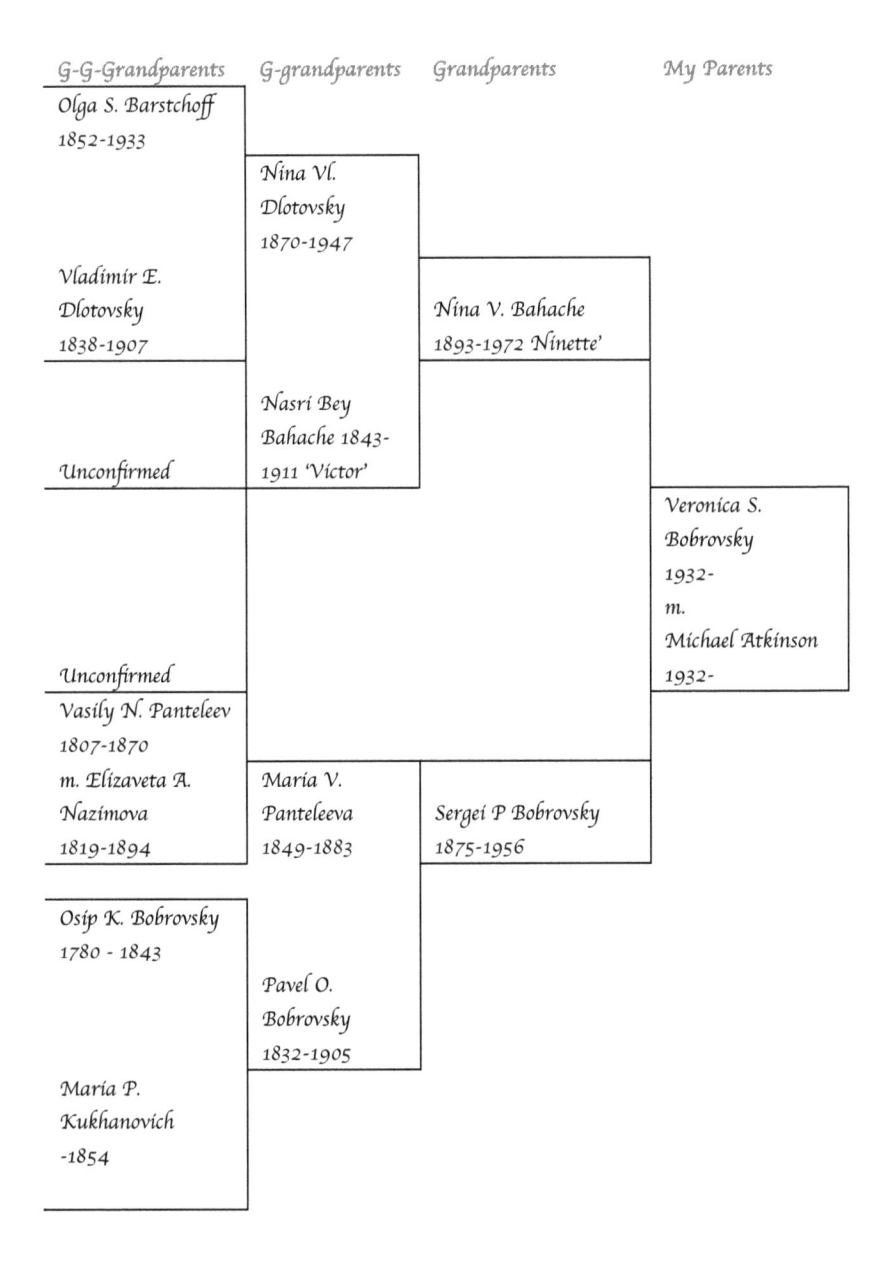

G-G-Grandparents	G-grandparents	Grandparents	My Parents
Olga S. Barstchoff 1852-1933			
	Nina Vl. Dlotovsky 1870-1947		
Vladimir E. Dlotovsky 1838-1907		Nina V. Bahache 1893-1972 'Ninette'	
Unconfirmed	Nasri Bey Bahache 1843-1911 'Victor'		
			Veronica S. Bobrovsky 1932- m. Michael Atkinson 1932-
Unconfirmed Vasily N. Panteleev 1807-1870 m. Elizaveta A. Nazimova 1819-1894	Maria V. Panteleeva 1849-1883	Sergei P Bobrovsky 1875-1956	
Osip K. Bobrovsky 1780 - 1843	Pavel O. Bobrovsky 1832-1905		
Maria P. Kukhanovich -1854			

Timeline and Family Tree

1852 Birth in St Petersburg
1860 -1861 A grand tour of Europe and year in Paris
1869 Marriage to Vladimir E. Dlotovsky (1838–1907) and move to Kovno.
1870 Birth of daughter Nina (1870–1947)
1871 Birth in Kovno of daughter Vera (1871–)
1873 Birth of Son Vladimir (1873-?) he died young or in infancy.
1876 Birth of second son named Vladimir (1876–1907)
1878 Divorce. Marriage in Kazan to Alexander Lebedev (1843–1910)
1880 Birth of Alexander in Pau, France (1880-1937)
1881 Birth of Olga Alexandrovna (1881-1962)
1886 Birth of son Mikhail Lebedev (Micha) in St Petersburg (1886-1947)
1886 Publication of the prizewinning translation *Qabus Nameh*
1888 Death of father, Sergei M. Barstchoff
1888 First journey to Constantinople to request publication of translations.
1889 Stockholm: International Congress of Orientalists (September)
1889 Tour with Ahmed Midhat: Gothenburg, Helsinki, Berlin, Aachen, Paris
1890 Arrival in Istanbul: 13 October till May 1891 at Hotel De Belle-Vue
1890 First publication in Constantinople: *The Blizzard (Metel')* by Pushkin
1891 Two translations of the Mufti of St Petersburg:
  - *Refutation of Renan: Islam and Science*
  - *The Relations of Islam with Science and the Adherents of Other Faiths*
  - *Demon, An Eastern Legend* by Lermontov (March /April)
  - *The Poet Pushkin (Şair Pushkin)* in Ottoman (see Book Two)
1890 - 1891 Ottoman decoration Order of Compassion 'Nisan-ı Shefakat'
1891 Article in praise of Madame Gülnar, Servet-ı Fünûn (June / July)
1891 Return to Constantinople (October –April 1892)
1892 Published Translations:
  - *Family Happiness*, Tolstoy, (February)
  - *Who is a Good and Happy Person?* VA Zhukovsky (March)
  - *Two Old Men*, Tolstoy (April)
  - *The Death of Ivan Ilych*, Tolstoy (April)
  - *What Men Live By*, Tolstoy (May)
  - *The Queen of Spades (Pikovaya Dama)*, Pushkin.
  June: Marriage of daughter Nina Dlotovsky to Nasri Bey Bahache
1893 Return to Constantinople
  Rift with Ahmed Midhat in January

SOURCES AND ACKNOWLEDGEMENTS

Birth of Granddaughter Nina Bahache 10 March
Journal *Servet-ı Fünûn* separate publications:
- *Ilyas* by Tolstoy
- '*The Poet Pushkin his life, his art*'
- The City of Kazan [*Kazan Sehri*] 25 March

1893 Nov. returns to St Petersburg - petition for Russo-Tatar paper
1894 To Constantinople till April
Correspondence with Leo Tolstoy on 23 June, 1 August, 18 August, 12 September; from Leo Tolstoy on 4 & 22 September
1893 -1894 Published (Hijri calendar 1311)
- *Rus Edebiyatı* - A History of Russian Literature (132 pages) under pseudonym Madam Gülnar Olga de Lebedef
1895 Article in Journal *Ikdam*, in praise of Gospoja Lebedeva
1895 Translated *Master and Man*, L.N. Tolstoy
1896 French translation of Fatma Aliye's *Nisvan-i Islam: Les femmes Musulmanes* {*Women in Islam*], pub.Paris.
1898 First visit to Cairo
1899 International Congress of Orientalists in Rome (3-15 October)
- *Abrégé de l'histoire de Kazan* [*An Abbreviated History of Kazan*]in French
- Address: *Muslim Women at the time of the Caliphs*
1899 She finished writing *De L'Emancipation de la femme Musulmane* [*On the Emancipation of Muslim Women*] in Rome in December
1900 Published in Lisieux, France and St Petersburg:
- *De L'Emancipation de la Femme Musulmane*
1900 Death of mother in Arco, Olga inherits Villa Lubiana
1900 Founded the Russian Society of Oriental Studies in St Petersburg, International Congress of Feminine Works and Institutions, Paris
1902 International Congress of Orientalists in Hamburg
- Speech : *Les nouveaux droits de la femme musulmane : mémoire* [*The New Rights of Muslim Women*].
- *Récits de Voyages D'un Arabe*
1903 Award: Officer of the Academy by the University of France (9 March)
1905 International Congress of Orientalists, Algiers.
- *Histoire de la conversion des Géorgiens au Christianisme* from Arabic to French

	-	Speech: *Serving the idea of the emancipation of Muslim women within the limits that were indicated by the Prophet.*
1906		- 1912: Study of Arabic in Cairo
1907		Death of 1st husband Vladimir Dlotovsky in January, and their son Vladimir
1908		Founder of new Theosophist Lodge in Cairo.
1910		Death of Alexander Lebedeff in Kazan
1911		Publication: *Treatise on Sufism* offered to Athens congress: *Traité sur le Soufisme de l'imâm érudit Abou 'l-Kâsim Abd'Oul-kerim Ibn Hawazin el Kochâïrî.*
1912		International Congress of Orientalists in Athens (April)
1915		In Kazan, Russia
1918		To Arco, Trentino, Italy
1928		To France
1933		Death in Menton, Alpes Maritime (France)

Sources and Acknowledgements

Along with my own journey of discovery, the narrative introduces a slice of life rarely seen, via private letters, which fill in some cultural detail. The two articles I had found by Turcologist scholars J. Strauss and C.V. Findley, immediately shed light on my once famous ancestor.

Here I read that Olga de Lebedeff had represented a 'new type' of woman in Ottoman circles; one who challenged the nineteenth century stereotype of what a woman could achieve in the public and intellectual sphere. I then learned that Olga had also been an international advocate for Muslim women's rights.

To find out more, I struck up some correspondence with Professor Türkan Olcay from Istanbul University and translated the professor's Russian essay, which was subsequently entitled: *Olga Lebedeva (Madame Gülnar): A Russian Orientalist and Translator Enchants the Ottomans.*[783]

My research was enriched from correspondence with Russian independent scholar, Victor Dzevanovsky-Petrashevsky and his access to Russian archives. His interest in the biographies of Imperial Oriental scholars originated in a comparable way: he had found the archive of the Iranist Valentin Alexeevich Zhukovsky (1858-1918), who knew Olga, in his own family's possession.

I am greatly indebted to Marilyn Booth, Professor of Arabic and expert of women writers in Ottoman times. Marilyn's support of my research and her two contributions to this book as an Arabist have been invaluable. They helped unravel a new understanding of Olga's stays in Cairo and her impact on women writers there.

Who really was Olga de Lebedeff?

Finding Olga's date of birth in the archives in St Petersburg provided with a fresh perspective into her social background. Then, instead of a single archive, I found archival material in Russia, Italy, France, and Turkey and the USA containing scattered fragments of her story.

I am so grateful to all those who helped and guided me; each person providing a piece of this puzzle. I would like to acknowledge the following libraries, archives and individuals:

Archives and Libraries:

- The National Museum of the Republic of Tatarstan in Kazan: Fliura Kaiumovna Daminova and the General Director of the museum G.R. Nazipova, who explained the literary record of OSL in the early days of my research.
- The National Archive, Republic of Tatarstan (Kazan)
- The National Library, Republic of Tatarstan
- Kazan Federal University, Elmira Amerkhanova for drafted correspondence between AA Lebedev and Olga S Lebedeva, Ottoman poem translations in Professor Gottwald's archive
- The State Museum of Leo Tolstoy, Moscow and Valentina Bastrikina (for copies of correspondence dated 1894-1895)
- The Moscow State Archives of the Russian Federation (GARF) for letters dated 1857-1861)
- State Archive of Yaroslavl Region (GAYAO)
- Central State Historical Archive, St Petersburg (CGIA)
- St. Petersburg Branch of the Archive of the Russian Academy of Sciences (SPB ARAS), Elena Annenkova (Olga's letters to academicians Baron Viktor Rozen in German and Russian and to I Krachkovskii)
- Institute of Oriental Manuscripts, St Petersburg
- Pushkinski Dom, Institute of Russian Literature
- Russian Academy of Sciences (IRLI RAN) Manuscript Department: Letters to Koni 1908 (F 134), & correspondence with Isabella Grinevskaya (F 55) including Olga's biography in the archive of literary historian Semyon Vengerov (F 377)

SOURCES AND ACKNOWLEDGEMENTS

- Lithuanian State Historical Archive
- Salt Research, City, Society and Economy Archive, Istanbul: Photo credit, Ahmed Midhat
- National Archives – Pierrefitte-sur-Seine, Paris : Département Éducation, Culture et Affaires sociales
- OFPRA Mission Histoire, Paris
- Bibliothèque Nationale de France (online - Gallica) BNF
- Archive of Arco Comune, Trentino
- Biblioteca Nazionale Centrale (BNCF) Firenze: Credit of images from the correspondence of De Gubernatis 78.48a, reproduction by permission of the Minister of Culture / Biblioteca Nazionale Centrale, Firenze (Florence), further reproduction or duplication of these images by any means is prohibited.
- British Library
- Archivio Russo di Merano (Russisches Zentrum Borodina)

Special Thanks to the Following Individuals:

- Marilyn Booth, Professor Emerita, Khalid bin Abdullah Al Saud Chair for the Study of the Contemporary Arab World, Faculty of Asian and Middle Eastern Studies, & Professorial Fellow, Magdalen College, Oxford 2014-23. Marilyn has encouraged me with this work, not only contributing to this volume with a) a translation from Arabic of Olga's biography, and b) an appreciation of Olga's translation from Arabic, but also proofreading my manuscript through its different stages. In addition, thank you Marilyn for your two contributions to this volume.
- Türkan Olcay, Professor in Russian Language and Literature at Istanbul University, for her insights into Olga's influence on the Ottomans and her association with Ahmet Midhat, as well as for giving me the opportunity to do a translation into English of one of her articles in Russian on the subject in 2015.
- Victor Dzevanovsky, independent scholar and Associate of the Hermitage Museum, whose insights to Russian Orientalism and research into Olga's family have been invaluable.

- Johann Strauss, then Professor at Strasbourg University, for sending me his article on *Gülnâr Hanım*.
- Şehnaz and Aykut Gürçağlar, translators of *Şair Puşkin* (The Poet Pushkin) from the Ottoman Turkish script. Şehnaz is associate Professor at Bogazici University, Istanbul, and at York University, Toronto.
- Hülya Arslan of Okan University, Istanbul for her article translated into in English: *Olga Lebedeva, An Exemplary Translator in the Field of Intercultural Communication.*
- Jelena Orlova, for her work in the Lithuanian State Historical Archive
- In Russia: Tatiana Smirnova, historian and author, whose grandmother was first cousin of Olga S Lebedeva; her books provided background information on the Borshov (Barstchoff) family. Also, Mr. Michael Talalay, Mikhail Bashkanov, Mikhail Druzin, and Anna Kommisarova, Sanya Safina, Andrei Golitsyn.
- In Italy: Don Walter Sommavilla, Arco parish records; Selenio Ioppi, historian and Paolo Boccafoglio at journal Il Sommolago, Arco. Ivana Bonora for her kindness in helping us find Villa Lubiana.

In the UK: Anna and David Leedham for advice on the Russian internet and contacting Russian archives. Taisia Lukhnitskaya and Julia Aliseyko for help translating Madame Gülnâr by Gazinur Murat from Russian version. Olga Pokrovskaya O'Connell for transporting letters from the Tolstoy Museum in Moscow.

My grateful thanks for further editorial advice: Jeff Chambers, Roger Keys, Nick Atkinson, Tessa Boase, Clare Thurlow, Ivan Hutnik and Carol Ermakova.

- Brenda Nisbet for editing *On the New Rights of Muslim Women* and *On the Emancipation of Muslim Women at the time of the Caliphs* (in March 2018 whilst receiving cancer treatment) and to Michael Gittins for further revisions of the same.
- My late uncle and aunt Sergio Bobrovsky and Tania Bobrovsky-Romaní for their inspiration.
- Nina Ladoux, Carlos Bobrovsky, and Paul Atkinson for enabling the transfer of the family archive to the UK.

SOURCES AND ACKNOWLEDGEMENTS

- Marian Hamilton for her support on the project including our special visit to Arco and the Butler Library at Columbia University.

- Huge thanks to my parents Michael and Veronica Atkinson who helped decipher manuscripts, translations, and inscriptions, and supported this project all the way.

- The biggest debt is to Jamie, Luke and Daniel Hamilton for letting me hang out 'in the archive' and for their advice with my title. Thanks, in particular, to Jamie – source of many insights, who believed in this project from the beginning and provided essential support both in editing and publishing.

BIBLIOGRAPHY

Afanasev, 'Jurors and Jury Trials in Imperial Russia 1866-1885', *Russia's Great Reforms 1855-1881*. Translated by Willard Sunderland. (Eds. Elkof, B, Bushnell, J., and Zakharova, L.) Indiana University Press, 1994.

Aksai, Kh., Khaldyz, O., Arslan, H. *Istoria Druzhby myezhdu solntsem i snegom*, Litres, 2022.

Akün, Ömer Faruk, 'Gülnar Hanım' *TDV İslam Ansiklopedisi*, C 14, TDV Yayınları,
İstanbul, 1970.

Algar, H. Introduction to Al-Qushayri's Principles of Sufism. Academia.com, 1992.

Almanach de Gotha, Justus Perthes, edition 1880

Anisimov, Y. *The Rulers of Russia*. Golden Lion Publishing House, St Petersburg 2012

Annuaire Almanach du commerce, de l'industrie, de la magistrature. Paris : 1873.

Arslan, H. *Olga Lebedeva, An Exemplary Translator in the field of Intercultural Communication*. (Published in Turkish: Kültürlerarası İletişimde Örnek Bir Çevirmen Kimliği: Olga Lebedeva // Cilt, 16 Haziran 2005)

Artamonov, B. 'Russkoe komandovanie v Krimskoi voinye', *Zapadnaya Rus*, 11. Jan.2014

Bassin, M. 'Russia between Europe and Asia: The Ideological Construction of Geographical Space', *Slavic Review*. 1991.

Batchelor, S. The Awakening of the West, The Encounter of Buddhism and Western Culture. Parallax Press, California. 1994

Beable, W. Russian Gazetteer and Guide, London. 1919.

Bekiroğlu, N. 'Unutulmuş bir Müsteşrik : Olga dö Lebedeva / Madam Gülnar.' *Dergâh*, nr. 46, İstanbul 1993, s. 8-10

de Bellaigue, C. *The Islamic Enlightenment*. Vintage, 2017.

BIBLIOGRAPHY

Bobrovsky, P.O. *Istoria Leib-Gvardii Ee Velichestvo Gosudarni Imperatritsi Aleksandri Fyodorovni Ulanskovo Polka*. St Petersburg, Vol. 1 & 2. 1903.

Boer, I. Haerkotter, R., Kappert, P., (Eds.) *Turken in Berlin 1871-1945*: Eine Metropole in den Erinnerungen osmanischer und türkischer Zeitzeugen. Walter de Gruyter, 2002 & 2012.

Bogdanovich, A.V. *Memoirs*. Russian State Historical Archive. 1888.

Booth, M. *May her Likes be Multiplied, Biography and Gender Politics in Egypt*, University of California Press Ltd, 2001

Booth, M. 'Introduction: Translation as Lateral Cosmopolitanism in the Ottoman Universe.' *Migrating Texts: Circulating Translations around the Ottoman Mediterranean*, edited by Marilyn Booth, Edinburgh University Press, Edinburgh, 2019.

Booth, M., & Savina, C. (Eds.). *Ottoman Translation: Circulating Texts from Bombay to Paris*. Edinburgh University Press, 2001.

Booth, M. & Gorman, A. (Eds.), *The Long 1890s in Egypt: Colonial Quiescence, Subterranean Resistance* (pp. 365–398). Edinburgh University Press.

Brendemoen, B. 'The Eighth International Congress of Orientalists, Held in Stockholm/Uppsala, and Christiania (1-14 September 1889), and its Echo in Turkish Literature'. Chapter 10 in *Turcologica Upsaliensia: An Illustrated Collection of Essay'*. Brill, Leiden, 2021.

Brower, D. 'Islam and Ethnicity: Russian Colonial Policy in Turkestan'. *Russia's Orient, Imperial Borderlands and Peoples, 1700-1917*. Indiana University Press, 1997.

Boyar, E. 'The Press and the Palace: The Two-Way Relationship between Abdulhamid II and the Press (1876-1908)'. *Bulletin of the School of Oriental and African Studies*, University of London, Vol. 69, No 3, 2006.

Carlson, M. *No Religion Higher than the Truth: A History of the Theosophical Movement in Russia 1875-1922*, Princeton University Press, copyright date 1993, published 2016.

Çelik, Z. 'Speaking Back to Orientalist Discourse at the World's Columbian Exposition' *Noble Dreams Wicked Pleasures, Orientalism in America, 1870-1930*. Princeton University Press, 2001.

Cheikh, Y. *L'Emancipation de la femme Musulmane* [Le guide honnête pour l'éducation des filles et des garçons] Dar Al Bouraq, Beyrouth, 2000.

Chicherin, B. *Vospominania*. Vol.1 Moskva sorokovix godov. Putyeshestvie za granitzu

Christian, R.F. *Tolstoy's War and Peace, A Study*. Clarenden Press Oxford, 1962

Christian, R.F. (ed.) *Tolstoy's Letters*. Vol. 02, Selected, edited, and translated by RFC. Faber and Faber, 2010.

Clay, C. M. *The Life of Cassius Marcellus Clay Memoirs, Writings and Speeches* Vol.1 Published in Cincinnati by J. Fletcher Brennan & co.,1886.

Clark, T. (ed.), *The Russian Chronicles*, Garamond Publishers Ltd, 1990.

Colak, B. Portraits of Women in the late nineteenth century Ottoman Empire from the pen of Ahmed Midhat Efendi, Bilkent University, 2002.
Coufopoulous, D. *A Guide to Constantinople*, London 1895 & 1899
Crews, R.D. For Prophet and Tsar, Islam and Empire in Russia and Central Asia. Harvard University Press, 2006.
Davies, N. *Europe – A History*. O.U.P. 1996.
Dowler, W. Classroom and Empire: The Politics of Schooling Russia's Eastern Nationalities, 1860-1917. McGill-Queens University Press, 2000.
Dukhovskaya, B. *The Diary of a Russian Lady*. John Lang, London. 1917.
Esposito, J. L. (ed.), *Oxford Dictionary of Islam*, Oxford University Press, 2003.
Findley, C.V. 'An Ottoman Occidentalist in Europe', *The American Historical Review*, Volume 103, Issue 1, February 1998.
Frankopan, P. The Silk Roads, A New History of the World. Bloomsbury 2015.
Furtado, P.(ed.) *Great Cities through Travellers' Eyes*. Thames & Hudson, 2019.
Galeotti, M. A Short History of Russia, How to understand the world's most complex nation. Penguin, Random House, 2021.
Gordlievsky, Vl. *Ocherki po novoi osmanskoi literatur*. Tipografia Krestnovo Kalendarya, Moscow 1912.
Gasprali, I. *French and African Letters*, Annotated Translation, and Introduction by Azade-Ayse Rorlich, The Isis Press, Istanbul, 2008.
Geraci, R. Window on the East, National and Imperial Identities in Late Tsarist Russia. Cornell University Press, 2001.
Gousseff, C. *L'exil russe*. CNRS éditions, 2008.
de Gubernatis, A. Dictionnaire international des écrivains du jour. Vol. 1, Florence, 1888.
Grazioli, M. (ed.), La Vita del Kurort, ARCO: la memoria, i luoghi e le persone della città di cura nella fotografia (1866-1915), 1994
Harcave, S. (ed.) *The Memoirs of Count Witte*, pub. M.E. Sharpe, 1990.
Harmsworth, The Harmsworth Universal Atlas and Gazetteer: 500 Maps and Diagrams in Colour, with Commercial Statistics and Gazetteer Index of 105,000 Names. Nos. 97-98 Central & South Russia (George Philip & Son Ltd, The London Geographical Institute)
Hawksley, L. *March, Women, March*. Andre Deutsch Ltd, 2013.
Hollingsworth, B. 'Arzamas: Portrait of a Literary Society'. *The Slavonic and East European Review*, vol. 44, no. 103, 1966.
Hourani, A. *A History of the Arab Peoples*. Faber and Faber Ltd 1991 & 2013.
Hutton, M.J., Russian and West European Women, 1860-1939. Dreams, Struggles and Nightmares.Roman & Littlefield Publishers, Inc. New York, Oxford, 2001.
Idris, M. 'Colonial Hesitation, appropriation, and citation: Qasim Amin, empire, and saying 'no'.' *Colonial Exchanges. Political theory and the agency of the colonized*. (Eds.) Hendrix B.A. and Baumgold, Manchester University Press, 2017.

BIBLIOGRAPHY

Ikonnikov, H.F. *Dvoryanstvo Rossii*, 2nd edition. T.Y. Paris, 1965.
Ioppi, S. *Di Villa in Villa*, Il Sommolago, Arco, 2004.
Irwin, R. For Lust of Knowing. The Orientalists and their Enemies. Allan Lane, 2006.
Jarman, C. *River Kings*. William Collins, 2021.
Jordell, D. (ed.), *Catalogue General de la Librairie Française* (Continuation de l'ouvrage d'Otto Lorenz), Paris, 1905, Vol. 16
Karaca, I. 'Ahmet Midhat Efendi ve Madam Gülnar'. *Türk Dili ve Edebiyati Dergisi Cilt/SayiXLVI*. Istanbul University, 2013.
Karimullin, A. 'O.S. Lebedeva - Gülnar Hanum'. *Narodi Asii i Afriki* (Peoples of Asia and Africa), 1977
Karimullin, A. *Knigi i Liudi*, , Tatarskoe Knizhnoe Izd., Kazan. 1985.
Kelly, C. A History of Russian Women's Writing 1820-1992. OUP / Clarenden Press, 1994.
Kelly, C. Russian Literature A Very Short Introduction. Oxford, 2001
Kennedy, H. *The Caliphate*, Pelican, 2016.
Khalid, A. 'Representations of Russia in Central Asian Jadid Discourse'. Ed. Brower & Lazzerini: *Russia's Orient, Imperial Borderlands and Peoples 1700-1917*, Indiana University Press, 1997.
Kleinmichel, M. *Memories of a shipwrecked world, being the memoirs of Countess Kleinmichel*, Translated by Vivian Le Grand, Brentano's, New York, 1923
Knowles, E. (ed.), The Oxford Dictionary of Quotations, Fifth Edition, Oxford University Press, 1999
Koblitz, A. H. 'Science, Women, and the Russian Intelligentsia: The Generation of the 1860s'. *Isis*, 79 (2), 208–226. 1988
Kuskov, V. N. *Sud'ba no imeni zabod*, Svet, Mozhga, 2016
Langdon-Barber, J. Mediterranean Mosaics; or, the Cruise of the yacht Sapphire, 1893-1894. 1895
Lindenmeyr, A. 'The Rise of Voluntary Associations During the Great Reforms: The Case of Charity.' *Russia's Great Reforms, 1855-1881*, B. Eklof, J. Bushnell & L. Zakharova, (Eds.), Indiana University Press, 1994.
Lotman Y. & Pogosan, Y., *High Society Dinners, Dining in Tsarist Russia*, Prospect Books, 2014.
Lubenow, W.C. 'Only Connect' Learned Societies in Nineteenth Century Britain. The Boydell Press, 2015.
Mackenzie Wallace, D. *Russia*. Vol.1, Cassell Petter & Galpin, London Paris and New York, 1877.
Makeev, A. 'Poslanitsa Russkoi Kulturoi.' *Russkii Mir*, 1.2.2016.
Mikhailova, S.M. Razvitie Orientalistiki v Kazanskom Universitete v XIX veke. Kazan', Moskva, Peterburg: Rossiiskaia imperiia vzgliadom iz raznykh uglov [Kazan, Moscow, St. Petersburg: Multiple faces of the Russian empire] / ed.

by B. Gasparov et al.]. Moscow, OGI Publ. 414 p. Pp. 275–301. (In Russ.) 1997

Mills Patrick, M. *A Bosporus adventure*; Istanbul (Constantinople) woman's college, 1871-1924, Stanford University Press, 1934.

Morissey, F. A Short History of Islamic Thought. Head Zeus, 2021.

Obolensky, C. *The Russian Empire*. Jonathan Cape Ltd, 1980.

Olcay, T. *Olga Sergeevna and her input to Russian-Turkish Literary Connections*, Moscow State Psychological Pedagogical University, (in Turkish). 2010.

Olcay, T. Lev Tolstoi v dorespublikanskoi Turtsii: istoria perevoda, retseptsia, L. Tolstoi v Turtsii, KPFU, 2016.

Olcay, T. 'Olga Lebedeva (Madame Gülnar): A Russian Orientalist and Translator Enchants the Ottomans'. *Slovo*, Vol. 29, 2. Summer 2017.

Özgür Tuna, M. Imperial Russia's Muslims: Islam, Empire and European Modernity, 1788-1914. Cambridge University Press, 2015.

Özgür Tuna, M. 'Pillars of the Nation, The Making of a Russian Muslim Intelligentsia and the Origins of Jadidism', *Kritika*, 2017.

Özgür Tuna, M. 'Gaspirali v. Il'minski: Two Identity Projects for the Muslims of the Russian Empire', *Nationalities Papers*, Vol. 30, No. 2, Carfax Publishing, Taylor & Francis Group, 2022.

Pleshakova, O. *Knizhnie Znaki – v Sobrannii Politechnicheskoi Biblioteki*, Politechnicheski Muzei, Moscow, 2015.

Pritsak, O. 'The Pogroms of 1881', *Harvard Ukrainian Studies* Vol. XI June 1987.

Pushkin, A. *Novels, Tales, Journeys The Complete Prose*. A new translation by Richard Pevear and Larissa Volokhonsky, Penguin Random House, 2017.

Richardson, H. E. *Cassius Marcellus Clay: Firebrand of Freedom*. University Press of Kentucky, 1976.

Rieber, A. 'Interest Group Politics in the Era of the Great Reforms', p.62-76 *Russia's Great Reforms 1855-1881*. Ekloff, B., Bushnell, J., & Zakharova, L. (eds). Indiana University Press, 1994.

Ross, D. Tatar Empire, Kazan's Muslims and the making of Imperial Russia. Indiana University Press, 2020.

Said, E. *Orientalism*. Penguin Random House, 2003.

Safina, S. Zhivite, Moi Lubyantsi ! Kazan 2005.

Safina, S. Lubyani, Rodina Lesovodov. Kazan 2011.

Schimmelpennick van der Oye, D. 'The Curious Fate of Edward Said in Russia'. *Études de lettres*, 2-3. 2014.

Schimmelpennick van der Oye, D. Russian Orientalism: Asia in the Russian Mind from Peter the Great to the Emigration. Yale University Press, 2010.

Sebag-Montefiore, S. *The Romanovs*, Weidenfeld & Nicholson, 2016.

BIBLIOGRAPHY

Sevinç, A., Fazlıoğlu, G. 'Turkish Participation to 1893 Chicago Exposition', *The Turkish Yearbook of International Relations*, Vol. 31, Ankara University, 2000.

Shifman, A.I. *Lev Tolstoy i Vostok*, Moscow, 1971.

Shrimpton, J. Tracing Your Ancestors through Family Photographs, Pen & Sword, 2021.

Shissler, A.H. 'Haunting Ottoman Middle-Class Sensibility: Ahmet Midhat Efendi's Gothic.' *Migrating Texts: Circulating Translations around the Ottoman Mediterranean*, edited by Marilyn Booth, Edinburgh University Press, Edinburgh, 2019.

Şimşek, Z. Nur, 'Reconstructing Madam Gülnar Through Fatma Aliye's Letters', *Yeni Türk Edebiyatı Dergisi*, 21. sayı. Nisan, "Fatma Aliye'nin Mektuplaşmaları Üzerinden Madam Gülnar'ı Yeniden Kurgulamak", Yeni Türk Edebiyatı: Hakemli Altı Aylık İnceleme Dergisi, S 21, 2020, s. 147-159. (Accessed translation through Academia.edu)

Sixsmith, M. Russia, *A 1000-year Chronicle of the Wild East*, BBC Books, 2012.

Smallwood, V. Women's education in Turkey (1860-1950) and its impact upon Journalism and Women's journals, SOAS (PhD), 2002.

Smirnova, T.V. *Otkrivaya starinnii albom*. Sergeev Posad, 2016.

Smith, D. *Former People: The Last Days of the Russian Aristocracy*. Macmillan / Farrar, Strauss & Giroux, 2012.

Smith-Peter, S. 'Enlightenment from the East: Early Nineteenth Century Russian Views of the East from Kazan University.' *Znanie, Ponimanie, Umenie*. No1. Moscow. 2016

Stone, N. *The Russian Chronicles*. Garamond Publishers Ltd, 1990.

Strauss, J. Olga Lebedeva and her works in Ottoman Turkish. Simburg, Istanbul, 2002.

The Theosophist, 10 July 1908 (New York Public Library).

Tolstoy, L. *War and Peace*, OUP, 2010.

Tolz, V. *Inventing the Nation*, Arnold, 2001.

Tolz, V. 'European, National, and (Anti-) Imperial: The Formation of Academic Oriental Studies in Late Tsarist and Early Soviet Russia'. *Kritika: Explorations in Russian and Eurasian History*, vol. 9 no. 1, 2008.

Tolz, V. *Russia's Own Orient*. Oxford University Press, 2011.

Troyat, H. *Pushkin: His Life & Times*. Gollancz, London 1951.

[a] Turan, N.S. Yüzyılda Rus Şarkiyatçılığın Bir Dalı Olarak Türkoloji'nin Gelişimi, Türk Dünyası Belediyeler Birliği (TDBB) Yayınları, No: 29, Istanbul, 2020

Turnerelli, E. Kazan the Ancient Capital of the Tatar Khans, Vol. 2, London, 1854.

Volpi, J-C. 'Menton, Une Exception Azuréenne ou 150 ans d'Histoire du Tourisme (1861-2011)', *Alpes Maritimes et Contrées Limitrophes*, No.200. 2011

Whitman, S. *Turkish Memories*, William Heineman, London, 1914

Wood, E.A. The Woman Question in Russia: Contradictions and Ambivalence, Massachusetts Institute of Technology, 2020

Wortman, R. Visual Texts, Ceremonial Texts, Texts of Exploration: Collected Articles on the Representation of Russian Monarchy. Academic Studies Press. 2013.

Zaytsev, I. 'Olga de Lebedeff and her translations of Ottoman poetry into Russian', *Dve turetskie pecni v perevode O.S. Lebedevoi*. Moscow, 2018.

Endnotes

[1] Carter Vaughn Findley: C. Vaughn Findley, 'An Ottoman Occidentalist in Europe', *The American Historical Review*, Volume 103, Issue 1, February 1998, 15-49, here p. 33.

[2] Carter Vaughn Findley (see above) and Johann Strauss: J. Strauss, *Olga Lebedeva, and her works in Ottoman Turkish*, Simburg, Istanbul, 2002.

[3] Russian, Tatar and Turkish sources are cited in the Bibliography: Akhunov, Karimullin, Safina, Shifman, Smirnova, Zaytsev; Akün, Arslan, Bekiroğlu, Karaca, Olcay, Özgür Tuna, Şimşek, Turan.

[4] D. Smith, *Former People: The Last Days of the Russian Aristocracy*, Macmillan / Farrar, Strauss & Giroux, 2012. As Anna Leedham told me in 2024, much later in the Soviet Union being classed as 'former' could carry some element of nostalgia or respect as a comparison 'not like us proletarians'.

[5] C. V. Findley, p. 31. Footnote 70, Ahmed Midhat spoke of *Madame* Gülnar, reflecting Olga's non-Ottoman-Islamic identity.

[6] M.J. Hutton, Russian and West European Women, 1860-1939. Dreams, Struggles and Nightmares. Rowman & Littlefield Publishers, Inc. 2001, pp. 62-66. This did not stop dedicated women from the clerical estate from travelling great distances to study and Russian radical writers spoke of a woman's obligation 'to serve the people'. By 1897, 4300 noblewomen had obtained university and higher education, most had journeyed to Swiss, French and German universities, after Russian universities were closed to them in 1863.

[7] N. Davies, *Europe – A History*, Oxford University Press, 1996, p.557.

[8] https://baza.vgd.ru/1/58316/ accessed 11 Jan 2022 / Vasilii Andreyevich, Andrei Vasilyevich, and Matvei Mikhailovich.

[9] The wife of S.S. Barstchoff was Alexandra Dubyanskaya (1769-1798) whose ancestor Archpriest Feodor Dubyansky was confessor to Empresses Elizabeth and Catherine.

[10] St Petersburg Historical Archive Fond Numbers 262, 190 and 921 detail some of the villages owned by Sergei Borshov's father M.S. Borshov in the Schlisselburg District outside St Petersburg: Khandrovo, Krutoi-Ruchey, Malaksa, Berezovka, Lodva-Luchikovskaya, Mikhailova, and Voronova including arable land as well as his properties in St Petersburg (136 Fontanka Embankment & on Troitsky Prospect and 32 Lermontovsky Prospect and Zagorodny Prospect). There appear to have been other manors and dachas with arable land indicated in the archives: Koltushi at (Poretsky), dacha Dubki and in the village of Turovo.

[11] One of three palatial mansions built by the general senator S.S. Barstchoff. Another was called *Dom Borshov* in Kostroma on the Golden Ring near Moscow, which still survives to this day.

[12] The Harmsworth Universal Atlas, Nos. 97-98 Central & South Russia *The Harmsworth Universal Atlas and Gazetteer: 500 Maps and Diagrams in Colour, with Commercial Statistics and Gazetteer Index of 105,000 Names.* (n.d.). United Kingdom: George Philip and Son Ltd, Amalgamated Press.

[13] In Russian it was called the 'Krestovozdvizhenskaia Obshchina'

[14] T.V Smirnova, *Otkrivaya starinnii albom*, published in Sergeev Posad, 2016, p.13 & 117 (though a letter dated 1855 shows that Sofia's death in the above book is incorrect. Elena and Sofia died aged in their early twenties).

[15] J. Shrimpton, *Tracing Your Ancestors through Family Photographs*, Pen & Sword, 2021, p. 69; the mutton-chop whiskers were not only fashionable amongst Victorian men, but also those living in far-away Kazan and St Petersburg.

[16] P.O. Bobrovsky, *Istoria Leib-Gvardii Ee Velichestvo Gosudarni Imperatritsi Aleksandri Fyodorovni Ulanskovo Polka*, St Petersburg, 1903, Vol. 1 p. XXII. Further reading about Pavel Osipovich may be found in his biography by Oleg Xazin *General ot Infanterii Pavel Osipovich Bobrovsky*, Moscow 2007; P.O. Bobrovsky also wrote a history of Peter the Great.

[17] T.V Smirnova, 2016, p.13.

[18] Moscow State Archive (GARF): Gosudarstvennii arkhiv Russkaya Federatsia GARF, Fond 109, Op. 214, D. 197, p. 114.

[19] A. Pushkin, Novels, Tales, Journeys The Complete Prose, A new translation by Richard Pevear and Larissa Volokhonsky, Penguin Random House 2017, The Shot, p.39.

[20] T.V. Smirnova, p. 13. According to the reminiscences of Tatiana Smirnova's grandmother. Also, in the letters stored at GARF, F. 109. Op. 214 (p. 28 is a possible reference to this event).

[21] GARF, Fond 109, Op 214, D.197, p.3.

[22] B. Chicherin, Vospominania. Moskva sorokovix godov. Putyeshestvie za granitzu. Vol.1.

[23] Alternate spelling is Prascovia Hippolitovna Barstchoff-Kutaisoff. Though she had been given the name Prascovia (after her paternal grandmother

ENDNOTES

Princess Prascovia Petrovna Lopukhina), we know from family letters that she called herself 'Olga'. Her full name in Russian was 'Olga or Prascovia Hippolitovna Kutaisova' (in Russian the 'h' is not written or pronounced in 'Hippolitovna'). Her father's name Hippolyte demonstrates the use of Greek names, popular in Russia at the time. Prascovia is an ancient Russian name derived from the Greek, which has many variations including 'Paraskieva' and means 'Preparation'.

[24] My grandmother wrote that Prascovia Hippolitovna had another brother Ippolit Ippolitovich Kutaisov, but of him there is no further record to be found.

[25] B. Chicherin.

[26] F. 37 Ukraina. Odessa, Pokrovsky Church Op. 3 Ed. Khr. 1036, pp. 174 - 175; also, State Archive of Yaroslavl Region, GAYAO F.213 op.1, d.980.

[27] GARF, Fond 109, Op. 214, D.197, p. 31.

[28] P.O. Bobrovsky, *Istoria Leib-Gvardii Ee Velichestvo Gosudarni Imperatritsi Aleksandri Fyodorovni Ulanskovo Polka, St Petersburg*, 1903, Vol.2, pp.364, 386 & 388 The history of the Ulansky regiment (1803-1903) was published in 1903 in three volumes by another paternal great-grandfather of mine: the senator, General of the Infantry, military jurist, and historian Pavel Osipovich Bobrovsky. Detailed sections of this regiment's history during the period of the Crimean War unfortunately appear to be absent, but I was happy to find details of Serge's military service. His younger brothers Alexander and Mikhail followed him in that regiment a few years later, after attending the Nikolaevsky Military Academy.

[29] Y. Anisimov, *The Rulers of Russia*, Golden Lion Publishing House, St Petersburg 2012, p.153. Whether the ships could have reached Kronstadt is uncertain.

[30] B. Artamonov, 'Russkoe komandovanie v Krimskoi voinye', *Zapadnaya Rus*, 11. Jan.2014 https://zapadrus.su/rusmir/istf/933-russkoe-komandovanie-v-krymskoj-vojne.html accessed 5 October 2020. The author remarks that Russian forces were overwhelmed due to the 'industrial revolution of capitalist governments.

[31] The military reforms of the 1860s-1870s were organized by Dmitry Miliutin. These reforms resulted twenty-two years later in a military victory for Russia in 1877-78 against the Ottomans - a war that Russia considered to be a resolution of 'the Eastern Question'.

[32] 'History of Pre-revolutionary Russia according to diaries and memoirs' Vol. 3. Section 2, 1857-1894; – *Istoria dorevolutionnoi Poccii v dnevnikakh i vospominaniakh* 1857-1894, vol.3. Part 2 pub. Kniga, Moscow 1980

[33] Signature on the 'Erast Konstantinovich Dlotovskii papers 1826-1879' sent to Columbia University in 1953, Bakhmetev Collection by my grandmother Nina Bahache. Original documents of the General's promotions and decorations.

[34] Countess Kleinmichel, *Memories of a shipwrecked world*, Brentano's New York, 1923, p. 110. Translated by Vivian Le Grand,

[35] St Petersburg Historical Archive Fond Number 190, op. 4, delo 324

[36] R.I. Ermerin. (either : La Noblesse Titree de l'Empire de Russie avec la description de ses armoiries or Annuaire de la noblesse de Russie, St Petersburg), II, 170, No. 84. Grateful thanks to Andrei Golitsyn.

[37] Notes from Underground (1864), pt. 1 ch. 2, (transl. Andrew R. McAndrew), from The Oxford Dictionary of Quotations Ed. Elizabeth Knowles, Oxford University Press, 1999, p.276, 7.

[38] Gosudarstvennii arkhiv Russkaya Federatsia, GARF, Op. 214, D. 197, p. 3, a letter to Monsieur de Barstchoff signed by a debtor named Skirov.

[39] I had learned about Olga's maiden name of Barstchoff from my grandmother, but I needed to find out more from the archives. There was no information at the archives in Kazan or Yaroslavl, but at the latter I was pointed in the direction of the St Petersburg Historical Archive. There, the details of Olga de Lebedeff's christening certificate were unearthed for me and this is how I learned about her parents.

[40] According to the Julian calendar. If you calculate Olga's birth by the Gregorian calendar twelve days later at that period, her birthday would have been 22 December (Capricorn).

[41] Central State Historical Archive of St Petersburg, Fond 536, Op. 6, D.2682, p.10; Also, the records of the church of the Ismailovsky Regiment from 1852, No. 46.

[42] Y. Anisimov, *The Rulers of Russia*, Golden Lion Publishing House, St Petersburg 2012, p.120.

[43] N. Stone, *The Russian Chronicles*, Garamond Publishers Ltd, 1990, p.184. A ducat was a gold coin.

[44] Y. Lotman & Y. Pogosan, *High Society Dinners, Dining in Tsarist Russia*, Prospect Books 2014. Her name as 'Mme B-K' has a mentioned in the diaries of Pyotr Pavlovich Durnovo of 1857/8. Her sister Sophie borrowed her headed paper in a letter to Serge from Helsinki in1857; the letter is stored in the Moscow State Archive. In some circles the double-barreled surname was common practice.

[45] According to the August 1857 register of the St Petersburg nobility, Yaroslavl Historical and Genealogical Society.

[46] GARF. F109. Op. 214. D. 197, pp.28-45. All translations from this archive are by C. Hamilton.

[47] Y. Lotman & Y. Pogosan.

[48] Gosudarstvennii arkhiv Russkaya Federatsia GARF. F. 109, Op. 214. D. 197. pp. 42-43.

[49] GARF, Fond 109, Op 214, D. 197, pp. 1-2

[50] Borshov, Mikhail, son of the colonel, buried 1857 (Novodevichy monastery – S. Snessorev. St Peterburgskii Voskresenskii zhensii monastir, part 111, St

ENDNOTES

Petersburg 1887 Prilozhenia. № 286). Peterburgskii nekropol', Tom 1 St Petersburg, 1912, pp. 274-275.

[51] *The Life of Cassius Marcellus Clay Memoirs, Writings and Speeches* Vol.1 Published in Cincinnati by J. Fletcher Brennan & co.1886 pp.442/3.

[52] H.E. Richardson, *Cassius Marcellus Clay: Firebrand of Freedom*, pub 1976 Univ Press of Kentucky, pp. 89, 90, & 97.

[53] *The Life of Cassius Marcellus Clay Memoirs, Writings and Speeches* Vol.1, Published Cincinnati, J. Fletcher Brennan & Co. 1886, pp. 448/450

[54] According to Alla Videneeva, a local historian.

[55] H.E. Richardson, p. 139.

[56] This large collection is remarkably preserved at the State Archive of the Russian Federation in Moscow. Olga (Prascovia) Hippolitovna Barstchoff wrote to her husband Serge Barstchoff in French; seven letters are from the young Olga. Moscow State Archive of the Russian Federation (GARF) Fond 109, Op. 214. In the absence of anything indicting, it does not feel like a betrayal of confidence to share the letters. For this discovery I must thank Russian historian, Victor Dzevanovsky-Petrashevsky.

[57] C. Kelly, *A History of Russian Women's Writing* 1820-1992, OUP / Clarenden Press, 1994, p.61 / Literary and political monthlies published debates on women's rights from the late 1830s.

[58] Letters in the Moscow State Archive mostly written from Prascovia to Serge are dated 1855-1861, the majority being from 1860.

[59] GARF, Fond 109, Op. 214, D. 197, p. 46

[60] On the Continent the English had a reputation for being rather stiff, conceited about their language, or not so agreeable, such as reported in *Eastern pilgrims, The Travels of Three Ladies* by Agnes Smith, 1870.

[61] Salvatore Rosa (1615-1673) was an Italian landscape painter, with wide subject matter including allegories and scenes of witchcraft. He was considered a hero by painters of the Romantic movement. Quote from Gosudarstvennii arkhiv Russkaya Federatsia GARF. F. 109. Op. 214. D. 197. pp. 55-56.

[62] G. Krätzer & Fillmore, M. (1860) *Das Rheinland von Basel bis Rotterdam: nebst denen zunächstliegenden Städten, Strassen und Eisenbahnen.* [Mainz: Verlag von Jos. Halenza, ?] [Map] Retrieved from the Library of Congress, www.loc.gov/item/2015591075/. Section of the full map

[63] Wikimedia Commons: Fonte nl.wiki. Koninkrijk Sardinië - kaart gepubliceerd in 1856 door Charles Desilver, Philadelphia - public domain wegens ouderdom.

[64] Gosudarstvennii arkhiv Russkaya Federatsia GARF F. 109. Op. 214. D. 197. p. 75.

[65] GARF. F. 109. Op. 214. D. 197. p. 81

[66] GARF. F. 109. Op. 214. D. 197. p. 66.

[67] GARF. F. 109. Op. 214. D. 197. p. 71.

[68] GARF. F. 109. Op. 214. D. 197. p. 76.
[69] The wines cost a total of 412 roubles and 72 kopeks; Gosudarstvennii arkhiv Russkaya Federatsia GARF .F. 109. Op. 214. D. 197. pp. 1-2.
[70] GARF. F. 109. Op. 214. D. 197. p.90.
[71] GARF. F. 109. Op. 214. D. 197. pp. 13 & over
[72] GARF. F. 109. Op. 214. D. 197. p.81
[73] GARF. F. 109. Op. 214. D. 197. pp. 16, 17 & over
[74] GARF. F. 109. Op. 214. D. 197. pp. 20-21
[75] GARF. F109. Op. 214. D. 197. pp. 106-107.
[76] GARF. F. 109. Op. 214. D. 197. P. 11
[77] www.getty.edu/art/collection/object/107E57.
[78] GARF. F. 109. Op. 214. D. 197. p.126.
[79] GARF. F. 109. Op. 214. D. 197. p. 88.
[80] GARF. F. 109. Op. 214. D. 197. p.116 (p.96).
[81] GARF. F. 109. Op. 214. D. 197. p. 227
[82] Written 1/13 July 1861. GARF, F. 109, Op. 214, D. 197, pp. 18 & 19.
[83] GARF F.109. Op. 214. D. 197. p. 267.
[84] From the memoirs of Prince A.F. Orlov, No5, pp. 417-422 1905, (2357. Борщов С. М. *Из воспоминаний о князе А. Ф. Орлове.* - РС, 1905, т. 122, № 5, p. 417–422. Борщов Сергей Михайлович, полковник, член Петербургского губернского комитета об улучшении быта помещичьих крестьян, в 1861 г. - чиновник особых поручений при наместнике Царства Польского.   Конец 50-х гг. Записка автора о поземельном устройстве крестьян. Отношение к ней председателя Государственного совета и шефа жандармов А. Ф. Орлова). http://uni-persona.srcc.msu.ru/site/research/zajonchk/tom3_2/V3P22360.htm. Accessed 18 April 2023.
[85] GARF. F. 109. Op. 214. D. 197 p. 65; M.S. Barstchoff already suffered from alcoholism and subsequent dementia, his daughter in law wrote on 29 August 1860: 'I doubt he will remember that his daughter [Nadine] has been abroad'.
[86] H.F. Ikonnikov, *Dvoryanstvo Rossii*, 2nd edition. T.Y. Paris, 1965, p. 46. La noblesse de Russie : copie des livres généalogiques de l'Union de la noblesse russe, constituée d'après les actes et les documents existants, et complétés par le concours dévoué des nobles russes / publié par Nicolas Ikonnikov.
[87] L. Tolstoy, *War and Peace*, OUP, 2010, pp.1009-1010.
[88] J. Shrimpton, Tracing Your Ancestors through Family Photographs, Pen & Sword, 2021, pp. 30-57.
[89] T. Clark, *The Russian Chronicles*. pp. 54-57. The Primary Chronicle recounts that as well as being a great warrior, Vladimir had eight hundred concubines and 'was a lover of women like Solomon…. He was an uneducated man, but in the end, he found salvation.'
[90] An alternative spelling of Vladimir in German is 'Voldemar' or 'Woldemar'.

ENDNOTES

[91] From Serpeysk in the Kaluzhsky region.

[92] The first names of the Dlotovsky grandfathers are documented in family papers: Stanislav (1650), Mikhail, Pyotr, Bogdan, Konstantin, Erast.

[93] The Russian papers reported that he died at Tsarskoye-Selo on 25 July 1887 (According to the French newspaper La Liberté 2 Aug 1887). https://gallica.bnf.fr/ark:/12148/bpt6k4784298b / accessed 7 June 2022

[94] During the reign of Alexander II, he was involved in the ruthless treatment of the Polish uprising, as he was Military Governor of the Vitebsk region.

[95] Towards the end of his career Erast Konstantinovich was appointed General of the Infantry, the highest rank in the infantry; he only retired from active service in 1881 at the age of seventy-four and appears to have settled in St Petersburg with his wife. According to the 1881 Almanac of Gotha he held the post of President of the Supreme Military Tribunal, which he retained until his death. Justus Perthes, Almanach de Gotha, 1881 (p.903).

[96] For his bravery and determination in service, he was awarded many military honours from Nicholas I to Alexander II. The original certificates, sealed in wax with the imperial crest and signed by the Tsars and their respective military chiefs, are now archived at the Bakhmetev Collection at New York's Columbia University. These were sent there for safekeeping by my grandmother Nina Bobrovsky-Bahache in 1952; she was Erast Konstantinovich's great granddaughter.

[97] He achieved Distinction in Theology, Roman (Latin) literature, Russian History and Literature, General History, Slavic Philology, Pedagogics, Logic and Psychology, and French; in Greek Literature he scored 'Good.' This is detailed on his Diploma Certificate in the family archive. His history dissertation for his final exams was on 'The disintegration of Charlemagne's monarchy' is kept at the St Petersburg Historical State Archive: TsGIA SPB. F.14 Op.10 D.178 https://spbarchives.ru/infres/-/archive/cgia/14/10/178 (accessed 2 July 2020).

[98] In the family archive.

[99] C. Obolensky, The Russian Empire with an introduction by Max Haywood, pub. Jonathan Cape Ltd, 1980, p.16.

[100] I acquired this information from V. Dlotovsky's service records in my possession and from L'Année Géographique, January 1867, https://gallica.bnf.fr/ark:/12148/bpt6k96922306 accessed 7 June 2022. The latter mentions the border with the Kyrgyz.

[101] 4 April 1865, from his Service Records dated 1880 & 1886 (Each one is a 'Formuliarny spisok o sluzhbe').

[102] 3 March 1867, ibid and from an original document in the family collection

[103] Ministry of Justice chancery order No. 3084, dated 20 February 1867, in the family archive (he was appointed on 8th February 1867).

[104] G. Baranov (editor) *Kazanski okruzhnoi syd: 140 let*, 2010, p. 16.

[105] A. Afanasev, trans Willard Sunderland, Jurors and Jury Trials in Imperial Russia 1866-1885; *Russia's Great Reforms 1855-1881*, Indiana University Press, 1994, pp. 214-228.

[106] Library of Congress, Prints & Photographs Division, Prokudin-Gorskii Collection, www.loc.gov/pictures/item/2018680071/ Accessed 2 October 2023. Photo dates from 1912, photographer: Prokudin-Gorskiï, Sergeï Mikhaïlovich, 1863-1944.

[107] W. Beable, *Russian Gazetteer and Guide*, London 1919, p. 27

[108] According to diocese archives in Kaunas:
Nina 605/15/6 – 1870.
Vera 605/15/7 – 1871.
Vladimir 605/20/402 – 1873.

[109] *The Harmsworth Universal Atlas*, Nos. 97-98 Central & South Russia. The Harmsworth Universal Atlas and Gazetteer: 500 Maps and Diagrams in Colour, with Commercial Statistics and Gazetteer Index of 105,000 Names.

[110] *Fatat-al Sharq*, Famous Women, Biography translated by Marilyn Booth.

[111] The Memorial book of 1873, Vilnius archive.

[112] A. Lindenmeyr, The Rise of Voluntary Associations During the Great Reforms: The Case of Charity. *Russia's Great Reforms*, 1855-1881, edited by B. Eklof, J. Bushnell & L. Zakharova, Indiana University Press, 1994, p. 272 (P. Ariian, Zhenschchiny v istorii blagotvoritel'nosti v Rossii, Vestnik Blagotvoritel'nosti, 1901, no 9, 48).

[113] A. Lindenmeyr, *Russia's Great Reforms*, pp. 270-273.

[114] Memorial Book of the Kovno Governate for 1872; 378/o.o/1870/643; V. Dlotovsky's Service Record of 1886 in author's collection. The medal photographed is in the family collection. The date of 26 November 1866 on the medal commemorates the date when the reform law was passed for state peasants; they were allowed to retain ownership of lands in their use.

[115] Governor generals archive of appointments and transfers, 1874. Vilnius Historical Archive: 378o.o/1874/8. He was sent to section one of the fifth department.

[116] 'Si quelque fois, Monsieur Dlotoffski, vous jetez sur cette carte des regards fugitifs, vous verrez toujours des frais amicaux de votre très humble, dévoué et reconnaissant serviteur, qui, croyez m'en, ne cessera jamais de pleurer le jour où il a perdu en vous un chef bienveillant.'

[117] Vladimir Dlotovsky's service record 1880, in the family archive; also, his transfer to the Governing Senate is recorded in the Kaunas Archive, 'On the appointment, transfer and dismissal of civil servants in the department of the Ministry of Justice', 29 May 1874 document 378o. /1874/8, p. 54.

[118] Almanach de Gotha, Justus Perthes, edition 1880, p. 906 (population census 1870).
https://archive.org/details/almanachdegotha00unse_63/page/n947/mode/2u p / 23 September 2021 Edition 1885, pp.951-2. (Population census 1881).

ENDNOTES

https://archive.org/details/almanachdegotha00unse_65/page/936/mode/2up / 23 September 2021.

[119] Vladimir Dlotovsky's Service Record. A copy of this document in the family's keeping was presented for the boy's schooling in St Petersburg in 1886. The St Petersburg historical archive lists records that Vladimir Vl. Dlotovsky (1876-1907) was sent to the Gurevich Secondary School in St Petersburg aged 10; He also spent a period at the Imperial Corps of Pages.

[120] Translation by M. Booth of biography in *Fatat al-sharq* 15 April 1907.

[121] I found details of the divorce in each of Vladimir's 'Service Records' dated 23 September 1880 and 2 September 1886.

[122] Both Vladimir Dlotovsky's service records state this.

[123] The family of Olga's son in law, the Gorloffs kept a record of this date (confirmed in Alexander Lebedev's service record). An interview for *Fatat al-Sharq* reports that she had lived with V. Dlotovsky for 9 years; the year 1878 tallies with this.

[124] After a European folktale, The Hunter and the Swan Maiden: 'Михайло Потых и Лебедь'.

[125] Autobiography and Memoirs of Nikolai A. Melnikov p.212 http://feb-web.ru/feb/rosarc/rah/rah-198-.htm sourced 10 June 2020.

[126] E. Turnerelli, Russia on the Borders of Asia, London 1854, Vol 1, p. 163

[127] The diaries of A.V. Bogdanovich describe the visits of the Lebedeff couple to St Petersburg, see below.

[128] Memoirs of A.V. Bogdanovich, Russian State Historical Archive; РГИА. Ф. 1620. Oр. 1. Д. 238.pp. 40–41. 2 February 1888.

[129] Translation by M. Booth of biography in *Fatat al-sharq* 15 April 1907

[130] M. Druzin, Informal political institutes in Post-reform Russia: EV Bogdanovich, public figure of the post-reform period, 2020 (DOI: 10.31857/S086956870008275-3).

[131] Memoirs of A.V. Bogdanovich, Russian State Historical Archive; РГИА. Ф. 1620. Op. 1. Д. 238. pp. 33–34 (page 33 reverse side). Dated 1 February 1888/ thanks to Mikhail Druzin from the St Petersburg Institute of History (Russian Academy of Sciences), a researcher into the memoirist, for this source. He explained that the memoir omits the Lebedeffs first names, but the author has given the Lebedeffs certain characteristics which tally with the period, identity of the Kazan delegate, two marriages, an eleven-year-old son, which all appear to confirm their origin.

[132] Ibid.pp.41-42 (RGIA Fond 1620, op.1. Doc 238, p. 41 reverse – 43, (*dated 4 May 1888*).

[133] V. N Kuskov, *Sud'ba no imeni zabod*, Svet, Mozhga, 2016, p. 23. Alexander's father was called Alexander Evgrafovich Lebedev (-1878); his grandfather was Captain or Berg-Hauptmann Evgraf Alexeevich Lebedev, rewarded for his patriotic service in the Decembrist uprising in 1825 and who married the Governor Strekalov's daughter.

[134] www.baza.vgdru.com/1/18697/all.htm. Accessed 28 August 2020.
[135] Furs, leather, metalwork, wheat, fish, tea, timber, and textiles were among the products sold at the Nizhni-Novgorod fair.
[136] Article from the Working Newspaper of Balakna, on the 400th anniversary of the factory: http://rabbal.ru/news/print.php?subaction=showfull&id=1468403817&start_from=&ucat=21&. Accessed 19 November 2020
[137] V. N Kuskov, p. 22. Governor Strekalov's position of Active Secret Advisor (*Deistvitelnii Tainii Sovetnik*) and presence in the Moscow District Senate, represented a civil post of the first or second rank.
[138] In his first year he published reports on the turnover capital of the Kazan Public Bank (1848-1883) and the state of the city's plumbing. В 173371 Zapiska ob oborotakh Kazanskovo obschstvennaya banka s 1848 po 1883 god / edited A. A. Lebedev, Kazan, 1883. Prilozhenia k zapiske Kazanskovo golovy A.A. Lebedev ob oborotakh kapitalov Kazanskovo obshchsestvennovo banka s 1848 po 1883, Kazan 1883 136264. 173648 AA Lebedev, *Zapiska o Kazanskom bodoprovode, sostavlennaya kazanskim gorodskim golovoi* Kazan, 1883, p. 137.
[139] He was honorary magistrate for Kazan province, was Chairman of the Trustees Committee for the poor, an honorary trustee of the Kazan real school, and a trustee at the School for Blind Children.
[140] *The Russian Chronicles*, (Ed. Director: Tessa Clark) Garamond Publishers Ltd, 1990, p.176.
[141] See: M. J. Hutton, pp. 61- 67.
[142] This is demonstrated by a postcard she sent to the Arabist Ignatii Yulianovich Krachkovsky, dated 9 January [circa 1915] at the St Petersburg branch archive RAN in which she has recommended a Professor Dogel (a zoologist) to Krachkovsky regarding help needed by the professor with some Arabic manuscripts. There is an elder professor of the same name, but my conjecture is that Olga would doubtless have put the younger of them in touch for being of the same generation.
[143] See Chapter 21, Note 702.
[144] The *ulama* refers to the collective body of Muslim Doctor of Law and interpreters of the Quran (plural of *alim* - scholar).
[145] J. Strauss, *Olga Lebedeva, and her works in Ottoman Turkish*, Simburg, Istanbul, 2002, p. 291.
[146] D. Mackenzie Wallace, *Russia* Vol.1, Cassell Petter & Galpin, London Paris and New York, 1877. p. 30.
[147] Women of the sixties were motivated to study medicine and science, not only for its own sake and to be educated but to be of use to those in the recently freed masses who had no idea about proper nutrition or sanitation or had never seen a doctor. See: Koblitz, A. H. (1988). Science, Women, and

ENDNOTES

the Russian Intelligentsia: The Generation of the 1860s. *Isis, 79*(2), 208–226. www.jstor.org/stable/233605.

[148] 'Famous Women', *Fatat al-sharq*, Cairo, 15 April 1907 (Translation by M. Booth, see Book Two).

[149] See: Karimullin

[150] During the times of the Tsars, the region where Lubiana was located was named Mamadishsky District of Kazan Province Later the region was renamed the Kukmorski in Tatarstan in 1965.

[151] The building of the Lubiana manor is thought to have started in 1882 after their copper smelting factory burned down in neighbouring Udmurtia and the Lebedeffs moved from their Bemizhsky estate; the Udmurtian lands had been originally land granted to Alexander's grandfather by Catherine II in recognition of his military service during the Turco-Russian war after 1777. www.iz-article.ru/promishlen.html Accessed 26 June 2020.

[152] S. Safina, *Lubiani, Rodina Lesovodov*. Kazan, 2011, p. 19.

[153] S. Safina, 2011, p15.

[154] *Documents of the National Archives of the Republic of Tatarstan on the history of manors.* www.archive.gov.tatarstan.ru/_go/anonymous/main/?path=/pages/ru/2nart/92vistupl/439_fedotova. Accessed 1 December 2019.

[155] Courtesy of Sania Safina.

[156] S. Safina, *Zhivite, Moi Lubyantsi!* Kazan 2005, p. 23.

[157] Letters dated 23 June 1894 & 12 September 1894 from Lubiana and another from Rome dated 155 March 1895 are kept at the Tolstoy Museum in Moscow; an envelope from Italy with postmark 21.8.95 (?) reads as stated.

[158] S. Safina, Kazan 2005, p. 17.

[159] This was told me by Victor Dzevanovsky- Petrashevsky in a letter dated 14 March 2021.

[160] An announcement in the newspaper *L'Indépendant des Basses-Pyrénées* : paraissant les lundi, mercredi et vendredi : www.gallica.bnf.fr/ark:/12148/bpt6k52632868 Accessed 23 February 21.

[161] OFPRA Historical Archives, Paris : Dossier n°122118 Olga GORLOF, née LEBEDEFF 27/04/1881, Box G99. OFPRA Historical Archives, 201, rue Carnot 94120 Fontenay-sous-Bois.

[162] The reforms Alexander II introduced were truncated by radical revolutionaries who assassinated him, following which the autocracy returned to repression and retreat (see *Russia's Great Reforms 1855-1881*, edited by Ben Elkof, p. viii).

[163] *Journal des étrangers,* syndicat de Pau, 1 Nov. 1882, https://gallica.bnf.fr/ark:/12148/bpt6k52213486 / Accessed 7 June 2022 or http://catalogue.bnf.fr/ark:/12148/cb32799645h Accessed 7 September 2022 Also, the *Pau-Gazette* dated 26 November 1882 http://catalogue.bnf.fr/ark:/12148/cb32834289r.

[164] This we know from the OFPRA refugee archives in Paris: Folder n°122118 of Olga GORLOF, née Lebedeff born 27/04/1881, box G99. Also, Victor Dzevanovsky advised that in a letter to Isabella Grinevskaya dated 1911 Olga describes that she had eight children in total (two died very young and six survived, four children from each marriage); here she also calls her daughter Olga Lebedev, 'Evfrosinia'.

[165] As per his christening document from the church archive. The Court Equerries' Church of the Holy Image was also famous because that is where Pushkin had had his funeral.

[166] R. Geraci, *Window on the East, National and Imperial Identities in Late Tsarist Russia*. Cornell University Press, 2001, p.170. No record of her formal membership has been found at the Federal State University Library of Kazan.

[167] Russian State Historical Archives, St Petersburg (RGIA). F. 1620. Op. 1. D. 239, pp. 50-52 reverse side. Her first name is never mentioned; the couple are referred to just by their surnames. From Alexander's position of mayor and other personal factors, it may be deduced with near certainty the identity of the couple. Academician Mikhail Druzin (RAN) is 95% certain that the Lebedevs from Kazan in the memoir relate to Alexander and Olga.

[168] See: Akhunov. A.A. Lebedef was replaced as mayor by S.V. Dyachenko on 17 May 1888 http://history-kazan.ru/kazan-vchera-segodnya-zavtra/istoriya-v-litsakh/zhzl-kazanskaya-seriya/17029-serega Accessed 7 April 2023.

[169] C. Vaughn Findley, pp. 32-33 He notes that she had a child-like submission to her mother and absent husband.

[170] The diaries of Alexandra Bogdanovich will in future be published in Russia.

[171] See below the memoirs of Countess Edith von Salburg, p.208. The Countess' married name was Baroness von Krieg-Hochfelden.

[172] O.S. Lebedeva (transl. from Tatar to Russian). *Qabus Name*, Kazan, 1886, p.132; 'Щедрость, знание, справедливость происходять оть ума. Самое высшее изъ этихъ трехъ – знаниие, учёность и мудрость, получаемая оть нихъ, потому что они подобны откровению Божему.' Translation to English by CH.

[173] Please see the full account in Book Two, in the translation by Marilyn Booth.

[174] Vl. Gordlievsky, *Ocherki po novoi osmanskoi literatur*. Tipografia Krestnovo Kalendarya, Moscow 1912. p.72. He describes the language as the 'kazansko-turketski yasik'. Vladimir Gordlievsky was Professor at the Moscow *Ecole des Langues Orientales*.

[175] J. Strauss, Olga Lebedeva and her works in Ottoman Turkish, Simburg, Istanbul, 2002, p. 291.

[176] J. Strauss, 2002, p. 292 quoting Avrupa'da Bir Cevelan, p. 174 by Ahmed Midhat.

ENDNOTES

[177] B. Dukhovskaya, p. 290.

[178] Peter Furtado (ed.), *Great Cities Through Travellers' Eyes*, Thames & Hudson, 2019, p.18.

[179] In Russian the name is transcribed as Гюльнар from Arabic, and usually written 'Гульнар' with a soft 'l' as also in the name Olga.

[180] H. Troyat, *Pushkin: His Life & Times*, Gollancz, London 1951, p. 69

[181] J. Strauss, p. 292.

[182] T. Olcay, 'Olga Sergeevna and her input to Russian-Turkish Literary Connections', Moscow State Psychological Pedagogical University 2010, pp. 1-2.

[183] O. de Lebedeff, *De L'Emancipation de la femme Musulmane*, Lisieux, 1900, p.12. Turkish women did sometimes use female pseudonyms as opposed to male ones.

[184] O. L. letter to Prof. J.F. Gottwald, Archive 2943, 86 at the Kazan Federal University Archive.

[185] National Library at Florence, De Gubernatis collection (Biblioteca Nazionale Central Firenze)

[186] SM Mikhailova, *Razvitie Orientalistiki v Kazanskom Universitete v XIX veke* [The Development of Oriental Studies at Kazan University in the Nineteenth Century], In: Kazan', Moskva, Peterburg: Rossiiskaia imperia vzgliadom iz raznykh uglov [Kazan, Moscow, St. Petersburg: Multiple faces of the Russian empire] / ed. by B. Gasparov et al.]. Moscow, OGI Publ. pp. 275–301. (In Russ.). 1997, pp. 290-291

[187] I. Zaytsev, 'Olga de Lebedeff and her translations of Ottoman poetry into Russian', *Dve turetskie pecni v perevode O.S. Lebedevoi*. Moscow 2018. The original poems were sent to me by Elmira Amerkhanova when she discovered them in the archive for the first time. Translations into English are mine.

[188] I. Karaca, 'Ahmet Midhat Efendi ve Madam Gülnar', *Turk Dili ve Edebiyati Dergisi Cilt*/SayiXLVI, Istanbul University, 2013, pp.55-72 (here p.58) https://cdn.istanbul.edu.tr/file/1CD58DF90A/D6D0215444C34D6CA836C25FF17B9F51?doi= Accessed 18 Nov 2020.

[189] I. Karaca, p. 56.

[190] See Endnote 187.

[191] D. Ross, Tatar Empire, Kazan's Muslims and the making of Imperial Russia. Indiana University Press, 2020, p. 117.

[192] D. Ross, p. 117.

[193] Ibid, such as Nikolai Ostroumov in Turkestan.

[194] Online article entitled (in translation): 'Orientology in Kazan and its outstanding figures'. https://studbooks.net/661995/kulturologiya/vostokovedenie_kazani_vyday uschiesya_deyateli. Accessed on 24 November 2021.

[195] O. de Lebedeff, Abrégé de l'Histoire de Kazan, p. 9

[196] R. Geraci, pp. 169-179.
[197] D. Ross, p. 117.
[198] R.D. Crews, For Prophet and Tsar, Islam and Empire in Russia and Central Asia, Harvard University Press, 2006, pp. 311 -316.
[199] M. Özgür Tuna, 'Pillars of the Nation, The Making of a Russian Muslim Intelligentsia and the Origins of Jadidism', *Kritika*, 2017 18(2): 257-81, (here p.10 and the essay of 1892 referred to in pp.16-17). https://people.duke.edu/~mt125/Documents/Pillars%20of%20the%20Nation.pdf Accessed 30 December 2023.
[200] I. Gasprali, *French and African Letters*, Annotated Translation, and Introduction by Azade-Ayse Rorlich, The Isis Press, Istanbul, 2008, p.20. The term *Terjuman* is the phonetic equivalent of *Tercüman*.
[201] I. Gasprali, ibid, p.114-115. Letter 37.
[202] D. Ross, p. 126.
[203] A. Karimullin, *Knigi I Liudi*, Kazan, Tatarskoe Knizhnoe Izd. 1985, p.244 Makhmudov had taught Arabic calligraphy at Kazan University and Tatar at the First Kazan Gymnasium. The other article by Karimullin is entitled: *O.S. Lebedeva – Gülnar Hanum*, Peoples of Asia and Africa (Narodi Asii i Afriki) 1977 n.3, pp146-152 under the chapter entitled: из историй востоковедения и африканистики.
[204] D. Ross, 2020, p. 115.
[205] R. Geraci, p. 178.
[206] https://islamansiklopedisi.org.tr/kayyum-nasiri / Accessed 26 September 2021.
[207] T. Olcay, 'Olga Lebedeva (Madame Gülnar): A Russian Orientalist and Translator Enchants the Ottomans', *Slovo*, Vol. 29, No 2 (Summer 2017), p.42; also I. Karaca.
[208] Tatar Internet Journal: «*Кара Аккош*» http://karaakkosh.com/gabdrahman-ilyasi-bichara-kyz.html. Accessed 23 June 2020.
[209] R. Salikhov: *Pioneers of the Tatar Renaissance*, 13/8/2003 www.e-vid.ru/index-m-192-p-63-article-3849.htm. Accessed 23 June 2020
[210] For instance, Azat Akhunov in his online article 2004 for *Tatarski Mir*, No 2. World without Frontiers (Mir Bez Granitz). Accessed 5/10/2015.
[211] Fond 977, op. fizmat d. 2048, p. 15.
[212] S. Whitman, *Turkish Memories*, William Heineman, London, 1914, p.17. This book was inscribed to the memory of Ahmed Midhat Efendi whom the author, the *New York Herald* correspondent, met when Midhat was Vice-President of the Imperial Ottoman Board of Public Health in Constantinople. Whitman recounts something of Ahmed Midhat's biography first in journalism and later in politics on p.35. The full epigraph reads : From the days of Darius, Alcibiades, and Justinian—when the corn-laden galleys from the Black Sea glided swiftly past the shore opposite

ENDNOTES

Seraglio Point—down to the present time, Constantinople has always been the object of desire of ambitious rulers of nations.

[213] O. de Lebedeff, *Récits de Voyages d'un Arabe,* Codex 286 du Vatican (1902), p. 64. The inscription of a talisman globe owned by the Sultan, to chase away enemies from the city: 'I conquered the world like this globe which I hold in my hand, but I have left it without having possessed any of it.

[214] *Hanım* pronounced 'Hanum' is used after the name, meaning Miss or Mrs. It also indicates respect, dignity and status for upper-class Ottoman women.

[215] *TDV Turkish Islamic Encyclopedia,* 1988, pp.243-248 / also see online version: https://islamansiklopedisi.org.tr/Gülnar-Hanım. Accessed 23 September 2021.

[216] Ahmed Midhat, *Avrupa'da Bir Cevelân,* Istanbul 1307 [1890], pp. 173-787, this account was first serialized in *Tercüman-ı Hakikat.* "Gülnar Hanım, Nâm-ı Dîger Madam Olga De Lebedef", *Servet-i Fünûn,* nr. 15 (20 June 1307), p. 170-173. "Ms. Gülnar. Gaspoja Lebedeva", *Ikdam,* no. 343, Istanbul 18 Muharram 1313 / 10 July 1895. [Abdullah Cevdet], "Gülnar Hanım. Madame Olga Dö Lebedef", *Kadin,* nr. 16, Thessaloniki 26 Kanunusâni 1324 [transl. from Rumi calendar January 1906], p. 7-9.

[217] I. Karaca, Ahmed Mithat Efendi and Madam Gülnar, Türk Dili ve Edebiyatı Dergisi, 2012, Cilt/Sayi: XLVI, 56 This article in Turkish contains many direct quotes from the original travelogue by A. Midhat.

[218] A.I. Shifman, *Lev Tolstoy i Vostok,* Moscow (1971) p.365; this is also quoted by A.N. Kononov Bibliograficheskii slovar otechestvennich turkologov, dooktiabrskii period (M,1974).

[219] Novoe Vremya (22 X / 3.XI, 1893) quoted from A. Karamullin: 'OS Lebedeva – Gülnâr Hanum'// Narodi Asii I Afriki (1977), N.3 p.146 [Каримуллин А. Г. О. С. Лебедева — Гульнар ханум // Народы Азии и Африки, 1977, N 3. According to Nazan Bekiroğlu in her online article *Unutulmuş bir Müsteşrik : Olga dö Lebedeva / Madam Gülnar.* Dergâh, nr. 46, İstanbul 1993, s. 8-10, the Russian Turcologist Kononov cites the date of Olga's first trip to Istanbul as 1888.

[220] Not to be confused with Ahmed Midhat Pasha. The Ottoman travelogue by Ahmed Midhat is called *Avrupa'da Bir Cevelân,* İstanbul, 1307 [1890], the section about Madame Gulnar is contained in pages 173-787.

[221] C. Vaughn Findley, An Ottoman Occidentalist in Europe, American Historical Review, February 1998, p. 20.

[222] J. Strauss, p. 290; "Gülnar Hanım Nam-I Diger Madam Olga de Lebedef", No.15; 170-173.

[223] E. Boyar, 'The Press and the Palace: The Two-Way Relationship between Abdulhamid II and the Press (1876-1908)', *Bulletin of the School of Oriental and African Studies,* University of London, Vol. 69, No 3 (2006) , pp. 429-432 www.jstor.org/stable/20182075. Accessed 29 Dec 2022.

[224] C. V. Findley, pp. 26-27

[225] A. H. Shissler. "Haunting Ottoman Middle-Class Sensibility: Ahmet Midhat Efendi's Gothic." *Migrating Texts: Circulating Translations around the Ottoman Mediterranean*, edited by Marilyn Booth, Edinburgh University Press, Edinburgh, 2019, pp. 193–210. *JSTOR*, www.jstor.org/stable/10.3366/j.ctvnjbgb3.14. Accessed 22 Feb. 2021.

[226] Ibid, p. 194.

[227] According to the memoirs of the Countess Salburg (see below)

[228] C. V. Findley, p. 33.

[229] I. Karaca p. 58.

[230] A. Midhat, *Avrupa'da Bir Cevelan*. pp. 173 & 174.

[231] T. Olcay, 'Olga Lebedeva (Madame Gülnar): A Russian Orientalist and Translator Enchants the Ottomans', *Slovo*, Vol. 29, No 2, (Summer 2017), p. 41

[232] This photo dated 20 March 1889 was taken six months before the congress in Stockholm at the studio of the award-winning photographer Francesco Pesce.

[233] In the collection of Angelo de Gubernatis, Florence: Biblioteca Nazionale Central Firenze

[234] I. Karaca, p. 58.

[235] Olga's translation of *Ilyas* by Leo Tolstoy was published later in Dec 1891-Jan1892. T. Olcay, 'Olga Sergeevna and her input to Russian-Turkish Literary Connections', Moscow State Psychological Pedagogical University 2010, p.123, and 'Olga Lebedeva (Madame Gülnar): A Russian Orientalist and Translator Enchants the Ottomans', *Slovo*, Vol. 29, No 2, (Summer 2017).

[236] Johann Strauss, 2002, p. 303.

[237] C. V. Findley, p. 33.

[238] C. V. Findley, p. 33 (footnote 79 from a letter to Fatma Aliye) But later, Midhat was somewhat bitter that her offer did not result in a publication for him: 'that she had agreed but not brought it off'.

[239] J. Strauss, pp. 304-305. This is a quote from Ahmed Midhat.

[240] C. Vaughn Findley, pp. 26-27.

[241] M. Booth, A.H. Shissler (Edinburgh, 2023), p. 372, footnote 18. From Chapter 8 'Fatma Aliye's Nisvan-ı İslam: Istanbul, Beirut, Cairo, Paris, 1891–6'.

[242] Booth, M. 'Before Qasim Amin: Writing Women's History in 1890s Egypt'. In M. Booth & A. Gorman (Eds.), *The Long 1890s in Egypt: Colonial Quiescence, Subterranean Resistance* (pp. 365–398). Edinburgh University Press. 2014, p. 382.

[243] Brendemoen, p.135 According to the account of a Norwegian journalist who wrote in *Aftenposten* on 8th September 1889.

ENDNOTES

[244] T. Olcay, 'Olga Lebedeva (Madame Gülnar): A Russian Orientalist and Translator Enchants the Ottomans', *Slovo*, Vol. 29, No 2, (Summer 2017), p. 44.

[245] B. Brendemoen, p.142 (see below).

[246] Many thanks for permission to use this photo go to 'Salt Research, City, Society and Economy Archive'. See C.V. Findley, p.27: The state dress uniform was decorated with decorations and worn with a ceremonial sword. His rank was Bala or *rütbe-i bala* [the highest rank after the vizierate awarded to many during the reign of Abdulhamid II.] Ahmed Midhat was referred to as *Votre Excellence*.

[247] I. Karaca.

[248] A. Midhat, 'Avrupa'da Bir Cevelân', *Tercüman-ı Hakikat*, Istanbul, 1307 [1890].

[249] Johann Strauss, Olga Lebedeva and her Works in Ottoman Turkish, Simburg, Istanbul 2002, p. 293.

[250] I. Karaca, p. 59.

[251] Turken in Berlin 1871-1945: Eine Metropole in den Erinnerungen osmanischer und türkischer Zeitzeugen, edited Ingeborg Boer, Ruth Haerkotter, Petra Kappert, Pub. Walter de Gruyter, 2002 & 2012 p. 40.

[252] I. Karaca.

[253] Turken in Berlin 1871-1945: pp. 37-39.

[254] I. Karaca.

[255] I. Karaca.

[256] N. Bekiroğlu in her online article: *Unutulmuş bir Müsteşrik: Olga dö Lebedeva / Madam Gülnar*. Dergâh, nr. 46, İstanbul 1993, s. 8-10.

[257] I. Karaca. Also, S. Whitman (p.36) writes that Ahmed Midhat met Victor Hugo and other literary notables on a visit to Paris, but it is not clear whether it was on this visit or there was a subsequent one.

[258] C. Vaughn Findley, An Ottoman Occidentalist in Europe, American Historical Review, February 1998, p. 32. Here, C.V. Findley speculates that possibly the [restrictive] nature of women's clothing of the time hampered Gülnar's outings and her ability to keep up with Ahmed Midhat.

[259] N. Bekiroğlu.

[260] C. Vaughn Findley, p. 22.

[261] J. Strauss.

[262] I. Karaca, p. 62 'Ahmet Mithat Efendi, Madam Gülnar'dan Rusların ve Rusya'daki Türk ve İslâm kavimlerinin, medeniyetin son gelişmeleri hakkındaki durumlarını sorar. Madam Gülnar ile konuşmalarından yola çıkarak Ahmet Mithat Efendi, Tatarların geri kalışını Rus hükümetinin hatası olarak görür... ileri gelen Tatarları bu yolda ikaz ve irşat eylemeleri lüzumunu anlattım."

[263] C. V. Findley, pp. 31- 34.

[264] C.V. Findley, p.32. Also, T. Olcay, Olga Lebedeva (Madame Gülnar): A Russian Orientalist and Translator Enchants the Ottomans, Slovo, Vol. 29, No 2, (Summer 2017), p.43.
[265] https://gallica.bnf.fr/ark:/12148/bpt6k45824822 Accessed 20 February 2022.
[266] N. Bekiroğlu (Avrupa'da Bir Cevelan p.779).
[267] C. Vaughn Findley, p. 33
[268] I. Karaca.
[269] C. Vaughn Findley, p.30. See Footnote 56, where Findley explains that Sufis used the term 'perfect person' [*insan-i kamil*] which elsewhere is translated as 'complete person', for a spiritual paragon.
[270] T. Olcay, Olga Lebedeva (Madame Gülnar): A Russian Orientalist and Translator Enchants the Ottomans, *Slovo*, Vol. 29, No 2, (Summer 2017), p. 45.
[271] C.V. Findley, p. 22
[272] A. Makeev, Poslanitsa Russkoi Kulturoi, Russkii Mir, 1.2.2016; https://rusmir.media/2016/02/01/lebedeva Accessed 14 Aug. 20; An interview with Türkan Olcay.
[273] J. Strauss, p.297.
[274] T. Olcay, 'Olga Sergeevna and her input into Russian-Turkish Literary Connections', Moscow State Psychological Pedagogical University, 2010, p. 123.
[275] A. Makeev, Poslanitsa Russkoi Kulturoi, Russkii Mir, 1. 2. 2016. https://rusmir.media/2016/02/01/lebedeva Accessed 14 Aug. 20. This is an interview for Russian literary journal 'Russkii Mir' with Türkan Olcay
[276] https://gallica.bnf.fr/ark:/12148/bpt6k50822119 Accessed 23 Feb 21; the newspaper is dated 14 October 1891.
[277] J. Strauss, Olga Lebedeva and her works in Ottoman Turkish, Simburg, Istanbul, 2002, p.294-5; Hotel de Blois (?); A. Makeev, vide supra (quoting Türkan Olcay); Bellevue is quoted by I. Karaca. Hotel Bellevue is mentioned in a travel guide dated 1840 (Murray, p.15), see: https://daneshyari.com/article/preview/1011877.pdf Accessed 6 Sept 2022.
[278] http://catalogue.bnf.fr/ark:/12148/cb327941766 Accessed 18 February 2022.
[279] General Blunt is not to be confused with Wilfred Blunt, a colourful figure and a former diplomat, who was married to daughter of Ada Lovelace, Lady Anne Noel, who espoused uncommon anti-imperialist views. For this he is mentioned by Edward Said, as an 'individualistic Victorian traveller in the East', one who did not express fear of the Orient or the 'traditional Western hostility' to it. E. Said, Orientalism, p. 237.
[280] S. Whitman, p. 55
[281] *Fatat al-Sharq* translation of Famous Women by Marilyn Booth (see below).
[282] I.Karaca.
[283] Quoted from İlber Ortaylı, "The Longest Century of the Empire" by Hülya Arslan in her article 'Olga Lebedeva, an Exemplary Translator in the Field

of Intercultural Communication'. p.2. (This paper was submitted to the "International Symposium of Issues Related to Translations and Translators" held on 11th - 12th October 2004 and organised by Sakarya University).

[284] T. Olcay, Olga Lebedeva (Madame Gülnar): A Russian Orientalist and Translator Enchants the Ottomans, Slovo, Vol. 29, No 2, (Summer 2017).

[285] Ibid.

[286] T. Olcay, Olga Lebedeva (Madame Gülnar): A Russian Orientalist and Translator Enchants the Ottomans, Slovo, Vol. 29, No 2, (Summer 2017).

[287] N. Bekiroğlu.

[288] I. Karaca, p. 65.

[289] J. Strauss, p.295; F. Alie 'Nisvan-i Islam : Les femmes Musulmanes', Paris 1896.

1891-2 in *Tercüman-ı Hakkikat*, re-published in Paris in 1896 and 1909 in Cairo. This will be further discussed in a subsequent chapter.

[290] Ertuğrul, Resurrection, Series 2, Episode 33 (Gümüştekin).

[291] Bibliothèque National de France [BnF], Gallica Istanbul, 23 May 1891, p.1 (Accessed 7 September 2022). This periodical also notes that Olga was staying at the Grand Hotel de Londres.

[292] Letter of H.P. Picot to S. Whitman, p. 277. Picot agrees with A. Vambery that: 'the real crux of Turkey's political problems is, and always was, Russia.'

[293] Booth, Marilyn. "Introduction: Translation as Lateral Cosmopolitanism in the Ottoman Universe." *Migrating Texts: Circulating Translations around the Ottoman Mediterranean*, edited by Marilyn Booth, Edinburgh University Press, Edinburgh, 2019, pp. 1–54. *JSTOR*, www.jstor.org/stable/10.3366/j.ctvnjbgb3.7. Accessed 7 Sept. 2020.

[294] https://arablit.org/2020/06/04/marilyn-booth-i-try-to-let-the-arabic-guide-me/ accessed 14 April 2021. (This is a point that M. Booth elaborates on further that 'the responsibility of the translator is to push back on stereotypes', https://sekkamag.com/2020/08/08/7862. Accessed 14 April 2021).

[295] A. Karimullin, Knigi I Liudi, Kazan, Tatarskoe Knizhnoe Izd. 1985, p. 246

[296] O. de Lebedeff, *De L'Emancipation de la femme Musulmane*, Lisieux, 1900, p. 15.

[297] This date is detailed at the end of the Russian edition: *Qabus' Name*, Kazan Imperial University Press, 1886, p. 143. It states the book was translated from the Turkish version translated by Ahmed bin Ilias, into Tatar by Abdul-Kaiom bin Abdul-Nasyri. Another translation of this work from another Turkish version of the text into French appeared in 1886, by the translator Amédée Querry; the latter worked on a manuscript from Kazan in 'turc orientale' by Abdel Courun de Chirvan (1882). Amédée Querry : drogman en Perse au milieu du XIXe siècle. See article by Florence Hellot-Bellier, https://core.ac.uk/reader/47715450. Accessed 13 May 2021.

[298] P. Frankopan, The Silk Roads, A New History of the World, Bloomsbury 2015, p. 120.
[299] I. Zh. Edijanov: The features of translation of religious texts in the works of K. Nasyri *Qabus Nameh* into Russian (Kazan Federal State University 2012).
[300] See biographical article Fatat al-Sharq in this volume. Schefer was familiar with Russian Orientology as he had attended the St Petersburg Congress of Orientalists in 1876 (Vol. 2, p. XIV of the proceedings).
[301] We can see from the photograph that she gave out copies to distinguished members of the intelligentsia, such as to Prof Kinsburg; also, in 1915 the letter to Isabella Grinevskaya mentions that she posted her a copy.
[302] J. Strauss, Olga Lebedeva and her works in Ottoman Turkish, Simburg, Istanbul, 2002, pp. 292 & 293.
[303] These are available to view at the Bibliothèque Universitaire des Langues et des Civilisations, Paris.
[304] The translation given by Johann Strauss is 'The Relations of Science and the Heterodoxes'.
[305] See translation by Sally Ragep (2011) p. 9: www.mcgill.ca/islamicstudies/files/islamicstudies/renan_islamism_cversion.pdf. Another refutation of Renan was made in 1883 by Jamal al-Afghani which describes the tensions between religion and philosophy, dogma and free-investigation. See: www.professorcampbell.org/sources/al-afghani.html Accessed 18 May 2023.
[306] It appears from Library of Congress that this was published again in 1893-1894 (1311). In his later work "Islam and Progress" (1897) Bayazitov asserted that 'the ultimate ideal to which humanity aspires, and the ultimate goal of its development on earth, is the unification of religion and science, these higher areas of the spiritual development of man".
[307] T. Olcay, 'Olga Lebedeva (Madame Gülnar): A Russian Orientalist and Translator Enchants the Ottomans', *Slovo*, SEES 2017, p. 20.
[308] J. Strauss, p. 303.
[309] J. Strauss, Olga Lebedeva and her Works in Ottoman Turkish, Simburg, Istanbul, 2002, p. 297.
[310] Ibid, p.310; A.I. Shifman, Lev Tolstoy i Vostok, Moscow (1971) p. 365
[311] T. Olcay, Olga Lebedeva (Madame Gülnar): A Russian Orientalist and Translator Enchants the Ottomans, Slovo, Vol. 29, No 2, (Summer 2017), p. 57. The novella is sometimes referred to as *Domestic Happiness*: R. Poggioli, *Tolstoy as Man and Artist*, Oxford Slavonic Papers, X (1962)
[312] Vl. Gordlievsky, Ocherki no novoi osmanskoi literatur', Moscow 1912, pp. 46-51.
[313] https://caroltranslation.com/2019/10/02/greatest-women-in-translation-marilyn-booth/ accessed 14 April 2021.
[314] T. Olcay, (Slovo), p. 57. Accounts vary as to whether it was serialised in 1890 or 1891.

ENDNOTES

[315] C. Kelly, Russian Literaturė A Very Short Introduction, Oxford, 2001, pp. 2-4.

[316] C. Kelly, 2001, p. 12

[317] 'Ruslan and Ludmila' (opera by Glinka); 'Eugene Onegin' (opera by Tchaikovsky); 'Boris Godunov' (opera by Mussorgsky).

[318] Gaspirali's Crimean newspaper was called *Terjuman* (transl. *The Interpreter*).

[319] J. Strauss, p. 304.

[320] J. Strauss; Quote from "Gülnâr Hanım," Servet-ı Fünûn, no 15: 172.

[321] J. Strauss, p. 301.

[322] B. Hollingsworth. "Arzamas: Portrait of a Literary Society." *The Slavonic and East European Review*, vol. 44, no. 103, 1966, pp. 308–309. JSTOR, www.jstor.org/stable/4205778. Accessed 17 Nov. 2020. In the above article, the author concludes that 'the significance of Arzamas in Russian literary history is in any case usually seen in its relation to its possible influence on the young Pushkin'. (p. 326). Incidentally Uvarov was the father of Olga's godmother Princess Alexandra Sergeevna Urusova.

[323] J. Strauss, p.297. Translated into Turkish and Tatar T.D.V. İslam Ansiklopedisi, 1996: 246.

[324] Famous Women, *Fatat al-Sharq*, April 1907, Cairo; transl. M. Booth.

[325] The second source comes from the biography Fatat al-Sharq (see above) and the later biography made by Isabella Grinevskaya.

[326] References to this work are found in *The Sun*, New York, Nov 27, 1895, p.6 and recorded in her essay *De L'Emancipation de la Femme Musulmane*, p.16 It was translated the same year that Tolstoy wrote it. A mention of this is found in the following article, stating a reference of the Russian newspaper *Nedelya* 1895: 1409. See: https://dergipark.org.tr/tr/download/article-file/2153269 Accessed 13 April 2023. A. Aykut, Türkiye'de Rus Dili ve Edebiyatı Çalışmaları Rus Edebiyatından Çeviriler (1884-1940) ve Rusça öğrenimi (1883-2006) Ankara University, 2006, p.7 . Ankara Üniversitesi Dil ve Tarih-Coğrafya Fakültesi Dergisi 46, 2 (2006) 1-27.

[327] T. Olcay (2017) , p.53 At the Alem Printing House (*Âlem Matbaası*. Ahmed İhsan).

[328] A. Akhunov, Senior Researcher at the Tatar Encyclopedia, Academy of Sciences, Tatarstan. 'Enlightenment,' 2003 www.tatworld.ru/article.shtml?article=151. Footnote 12: Poems translated by Madame Gülnar and Mustafa Resid were published in Şukufe-i İstiğrak, 1315, p.26 Another scholar, Türkan Olcay, first dates these publications to 1892.

[329] The above list of works is also referred to by T. Olcay, Olga Lebedeva (Madame Gülnar): A Russian Orientalist and Translator Enchants the Ottomans, *Slovo*, Vol 29, 2 (Summer 2017), p.53 and all the the works are listed in the TDV Encyclopedia article on Gülnar Hanım. This encyclopedia

was the first encyclopedia prepared and completed by Muslims (1983). Olga's translation of V.A .Zhukovsky was published in the Servet-ı Fünûn, Nr 56, March 1308, pp. 50-52. The historical novel *The Captain's Daughter* by A.S. Pushkin is also listed as a translation in I. Grinevskaya's biography of Olga, but it is not clear whether this was ever published.

[330] According to the Hijri calendar, the date 1311 is 1893-1894.

[331] H. Arslan, 'Olga Lebedeva, An Exemplary Translator in the field of Intercultural Communication;' paper submitted in Turkish in 2004 at the International Symposium of Issues relating to Translations and Translators at Sakarya University. Published in Turkish as: Hülya Arslan. Kültürlerarası İletişimde Örnek Bir Çevirmen Kimliği: Olga Lebedeva // Cilt, 16 Haziran 2005, s. 133.

[332] www.sabah.com.tr/sozluk/biyografi/Gülnar-Hanım-kimdir/. Accessed 26 September 2021, paragraph 18.

[333] J. Strauss, pp. 300-302.

[334] Dated 19/31 January 1897. Whereas N. Bekiroglu dates this letter to 19/31 January 1894, T. Olcay attributes it to 1897 (in her article dated 2017).

[335] Two Greek translations, written in the outline biography by Isabella Grinevskaya in the Pushkinsky Dom St Petersburg archive (see above). No other firm reference has been discovered, it is quoted here as one book *Starets Evstafii, vospitalelnaya Kniga Lva Melosa*. http://slovar.cc/ist/biografiya/2260691.html. Accessed 21 July 2022
One possible text was the only Greek reading book available in Constantinople in 1876 called 'The Teachings of an Old Man'. It included essays on morals, religion, social habits, and polite manners, intended for young people. See: M. Mills Patrick, A Bosphorus Adventure, Stanford, 1934, pp.60-61. Lastly the Arabic article Fatat al-Sharq article (see below) mentions a work entitled 'Irostathi' which may be the same.

[336] O. de Lebedeff, *De L'Emancipation de la Femme Musulmane*, Lisieux, 1900, p.16; the article was published in an unspecified journal.

[337] B.I Kolmakov (Federal University, Kazan) http://old.kpfu.ru/science/news/pushkin/p20.htm Accessed 26 June 2020. The Volzhskii Herald or *Волжский вестник*, was a Russian language newspaper printed in Kazan.

[338] As detailed in the newspaper Stamboul dated 14 Oct 1891, her arrival was 12 October 1891. https://gallica.bnf.fr/ark:/12148/bd6t524283d Accessed 18 February 2022, page 3, also A. Makeev, vide supra (quoting Türkan Olcay).

[339] B. Dukhovsky, *The Diary of a Russian Lady* (John Long, London 1917) p. 293.

[340] D. Coufopoulous, 'A Guide to Constantinople, London 1895 & 1899, p. 35

[341] J. Strauss, Olga Lebedeva and her works in Ottoman Turkish, Simburg, Istanbul, 2002.

[342] J. Strauss, p.314.

ENDNOTES

[343] There was a Nasri Bey first secretary to Chargé d'Affaires in Paris from 1873-1879 and served in Vienna as Consul General. Annuaire Almanach du commerce, de l'industrie, de la magistrature, Paris : 1873, p.21 https://gallica.bnf.fr/ark:/12148/bpt6k9762929c Accessed 14 April 2021.
(idem) 1875 https://gallica.bnf.fr/ark:/12148/bpt6k9763554c Accessed 14 April 2021, p.1669 (idem).
1877 p.21 https://gallica.bnf.fr/ark:/12148/bpt6k9677392n Accessed 14 April 2021.

[344] La Liberté 9 Dec 1875 https://gallica.bnf.fr/ark:/12148/bpt6k4780044v. Accessed 24 May 2023 See also: Almanach of Gotha 1884-1892, listed under Corps Diplomatique a St-Petersbourg. The spelling of his name varies as it is transcribed phonetically: Nasri Bakasch / Bakschasch / Bacache: the family used the spelling: Bahache. (Note that surnames were not much used at this time). https://gallica.bnf.fr/ark:/12148/bpt6k34481g?rk=21459;2 p. 951. Accessed 5 April 2023.

[345] Specific confirmation of the parentage of Nasri Bey Bahache is not yet available. Another Nasri Bey is son of Franco Nasri and sounds very similar but their surname is Coussa and not Bahache, moreover, he was a Greek Catholic. See : Bibliothèque nationale de France https://gallica.bnf.fr/ark:/12148/bpt6k5803783j p. 352.

[346] Paris: https://gallica.bnf.fr/ark:/12148/bpt6k9341813 p.21 Accessed 14 April 2021. In Vienna Almanach de Gotha. 1 Jan 1884, p.578 (CG = Consul General) https://gallica.bnf.fr/ark:/12148/bpt6k34478k p. 578 Accessed 14 April 2021. There is a chance this is another Nasri Bey (son of Franco Nasri) as he is only referred to as Nasri Bey there is cause for confusion. Other articles mention Nasri Bey, the son of Franco Nasri Governor of Mount Lebanon, a Syriac Greek Catholic.

[347] https://gallica.bnf.fr/ark:/12148/bd6t524048b / Accessed 18 Feb 2022.

[348] Bibliothèque National de France, Gallica, Stamboul, 25 July 1892 ark:/12148/bd6t523319b Accessed 9 March 2023.

[349] Owing to her mother's 'decisive objective', Nina's re-baptism took place at the Alexander Nevsky Church of the Paul Regiment Lifeguards: The National Archives, England and Wales, non-Conformist and non-Parochial registers, 1567-1970, Piece 0287.

[350] Nasri Bey had numerous official government contacts, including the Vali of Jerusalem [the governor-general of the vilayet was nominated by the Sultan] and the Governors of Mount Lebanon. As Secretary to the Sultan, in 1907 he arranged a festival to celebrate the Sultan's reign. He was on friendly terms with the Vali of Lebanon, Kiazim Bey who was later governor of Smyrna in 1909, and with the representative of the Syrian Bedouin tribes to the Ottoman Government at Aleppo, Ahmet Hafiz. Chakir Pacha under whom he had served in St Petersburg was also interim governor in Adana

and Inspector General of Anatolia. Nasri Bey was for the last years of his life based at Adana and Mersin.

[351] J. Langdon-Barber, Mediterranean Mosaics; or, the Cruise of the yacht Sapphire, 1893-1894, privately printed 1895, pp.136-138.

[352] Letter dated 1 August 1894. See below note about Hülya Arslan's article and translation.

[353] E. Cervantes, Address on the Education and Literature of the Women of Turkey, Pranava Books India p. 4.

[354] J. Strauss, pp. 294-5, corroborated by Turcologists, and by the Professor of Russian Language and Literature Türkan Olcay in her two articles.

[355] Beykoz Belediyesi: www.beykoz.bel.tr/sayfa/4/63/ahmet-mithat-efendi Accessed 6 February 2024.

[356] D. Coufopoulous, *A Guide to Constantinople,* London 1895 & 1899, pp.155, 169, 171.

[357] M.Siddiqui, Divine Welcome: The ethics of hospitality in Islam and Christianity, 29 July 2020, www.abc.net.au/religion/mona-siddiqui-hospitality-as-welcoming-in-gods-name/12503800 Accessed 9 March 2020

[358] M. Mills Patrick, *A Bosporus Adventure*, Istanbul (Constantinople) Woman's College, 1871-1924, Stanford University Press 1934, p. 21.

[359] N. Bekiroğlu.

[360] S. Whitman, p.36 https://louisville.edu/a-s/history/turks/Turkish%20Memories.pdf Accessed 14 August 2023

[361] http://tr.wikipedia.org/wiki/Muallim_Naci / Accessed 20 Aug 2020.

[362] S. Whitman, p. 243

[363] Turkish sources about this house are found online on sites about Beykoz: www.turanakinci.com/portfolio-view/beykoz-ahmet-mithat-efendi-yalisi/. Accessed 16 August 2023. https://kulturenvanteri.com/tr/yer/ahmet-mithat-efendi-yalisi/#18.26/41.136693/29.086129 Accessed 5 February 2024. https://beykozguncel.com/ahmed-mithatin-beykozdaki-hatirasi-gelinine-emanet/Accessed 5 February 2024.

[364] S. Whitman, p. 36

[365] S. Whitman, p. 223

[366] C. Vaughn Findley, 'An Ottoman Occidentalist in Europe', *American Historical Review*, February 1998, p. 21.

[367] A descendant called her 'Anjelik Melek', melek means Angel, the French version would be Angelique. She had a reputation for being deeply religious.

[368] B. Colak, 'Portraits of Women in the late nineteenth century Ottoman Empire from the pen of Ahmed Midhat Efendi', Bilkent University, 2002, pp. 98-105 / 'Henüz Onyedi Yaşında'.

[369] C. Vaughn Findley, p. 46.

[370] Library of Congress.

[371] R. Crews, pp. 326-329.

ENDNOTES

[372] *La Revue Diplomatique*, 25 Sept 1898 BNF ark:/12148/bpt6k5717211m Accessed 14 April 2021 (page 6). Nasri Bey became Governor of Mersin (as noted briefly https://gallica.bnf.fr/ark:/12148/bpt6k9341813 p.133 corroborated on my grandmother's wedding certificate). See also: https://gallica.bnf.fr/ark:/12148/bpt6k1269310h Accessed 18 February 2022. He was promoted to title of Oula Second Class in November 1893, a rare distinction. ark:/12148/bpt6k58064287 accessed 18 February. In addition, a glowing article describes his character : Journal de Salonique : publication bi-hebdomadaire, politique, commerciale et littéraire / directeur : Saadi Levy, 1910-07-07 : https://gallica.bnf.fr/ark:/12148/bpt6k1269310h Accessed 18 February 2022.

[373] Although there were to be visits back to Smyrna, Adana, and Mersin where Nasri Bey Bahache was assistant to the governor and Secretary to the Sultan Abdul Hamid II, Nina's schooling took place mostly in St Petersburg; in the holidays they travelled, and a favourite destination seems to have been Italy, as shown by photographs taken in Milan and Lake Como. Nina attended the boarding school of St Catherine's Institute in St Petersburg until 1910; she returned to Turkey in 1911 and stayed with her father and mother in Adana for several months until Nasri Bey died later that year; it just after his appointment as Governor of Smyrna had been confirmed.

[374] *Constantinople Messenger*, 'Ladies Class and Harem Education', Vol 1 No 29, 24th November 1880. V. Smallwood, p. 24 (see below).

[375] V. Smallwood, *Women's education in Turkey (1860-1950) and its impact upon Journalism and Women's journals*, SOAS (PhD), 2002 Published by ProQuest LLC 2017, p.24. https://eprints.soas.ac.uk/28570/1/10672729.pdf Accessed 9 Feb 2021.

[376] See: Olcay.

[377] www.dailysabah.com/portrait/2016/08/27/nigar-Hanım-cry-on-my-own. Accessed 6 April 2023.

[378] T. Olcay, p.46.

[379] Cağlar Demir. *The first woman novelist, Fatma Aliye and patriarchal social system*, Temmuz, 2016, p.180. https://dergipark.org.tr/tr/download/article-file/273714. Accessed 9 January 2023.

[380] T. Olcay, pp. 47-48.

[381] Tsar Nicholas I is believed to be the first to refer to Turkey as unwell in 1825: 'Turkey is a dying man. We may endeavour to keep him alive, but we shall not succeed. He will, he must die.' F. Max Muller (ed.) *Memoirs of Baron Stockmar*, 1873 Vol. 2

[382] Z. Çelik, 'Speaking Back to Orientalist Discourse at the World's Columbian Exposition', *Noble Dreams Wicked Pleasures, Orientalism in America, 1870-1930*, Princeton University Press, 2001, p.92.

[383] http://digital.library.upenn.edu/women/clarke/library/library.html. Accessed 9 May 2023.

[384] M. Booth, May her Likes be Multiplied, Biography and Gender Politics in Egypt, University of California Press Ltd, 2001, p.33.

[385] E. Cervantes, *Address on the Education and Literature of the Women of Turkey*, Pranava Books India, p.9. Information on the Arabic from Professor M. Booth.

[386] E. Cervantes, Address on the Education and Literature of the Women of Turkey, July 22, 1893.

[387] *Nisvan-i-Islam* 'Les femmes musulmanes' par Fathma-Alié traduit par Mme Olga de Labedeff (sic) connue sous le pseudonyme de Gülnar-Hanoum, Paris, 1896. A notice about this work was given on 15 May 1909 in *L'Orient* : revue franco-hellénique : organe spécial des intérêts grecs / N. Nicolaïdès, directeur-fondateur https://gallica.bnf.fr/ark:/12148/bpt6k57290535 / Accessed 23 Feb. 21. There appear to be a number of references to this work as outlined in the above notes.

[388] V. Smallwood, p. 112.

[389] Y. Lotman & J. Pogosjan, *High Society Dinners Dining in Tsarist Russia*, Prospect Books, 2014, p. 365. The Russian journal was called *Notes of the Fatherland*.

[390] A. Kirmizi, 'Authoritarianism and Constitutionalism Combined: Ahmed Midhat Efendi Between the Sultan and the Kanun-ı Esasi', p. 54 (Midhat caricatured over-Westernized men in his well-known fictive characters of Felâtun Bey and Sururi Efendi). C. Vaughn Findley calls Midhat a precursor of change in gender relations .

[391] The Oxford Companion to Women's Writing in the United States, ed. C. Davidson, L. Wagner-Martin, E. Ammons, T. Harris, A. Ling, J. Radway, Oxford University Press, 1995. Accessed online 13 December 2023 www.oxfordreference.com/display/10.1093/acref/9780195066081.001.0001/ acref-9780195066081-e-0581. This reference to the New Woman relates to the period 1890-1920.

[392] C. V. Findley, 'An Ottoman Occidentalist in Europe', The American Historical Review, Vol.103 Issue 1, Feb 1998. p. 46.

[393] C.V. Findley, p. 33. Footnote 80 explains, however, that standard nationalist historiography maintains that the emancipation of Turkish women began after the founding of the republic in 1923. By printing works by Gulnar and Fatma Aliye, Ahmed Midhat [and other publishers] had already started to give such women an important public voice (noting that learned and accomplished women had long been produced by great households).

[394] N.S. Turan, Yüzyılda Rus Şarkiyatçılığın Bir Dalı Olarak Türkoloji'nin Gelişimi, Türk Dünyası Belediyeler Birliği (TDBB) Yayınları, No: 29, Istanbul, 2020, p.171. Russia and Turkey Bilateral Relations in International Context Conference Book, Moscow Lomonosov State University and Istanbul University. Midhat is quoted here: 'Benim ona ehemmiyet verişim

ENDNOTES

şayet müsteşrikler meyânında İslâmiyetçe, Osmanlılıkça menâ'-i mukaddesemize vasıta-i hizmet olur ümidi idi'.

[395] C. V. Findley, p.33.

[396] C. V. Findley, (see below), p. 31 Footnote 70. A note follows that there were cases of women travellers in the Middle East who were sometimes treated as 'honorary men', in other words outside of the cultural norm.

[397] I. Karaca.

[398] N. Bekiroğlu; also Z. Nur Şimşek.

[399] A. Makeev, Poslanitsa Russkoi Kulturoi, *Russkii Mir*, 1.2.2016. https://rusmir.media/2016/02/01/lebedeva. Accessed 14 Aug. 20. This is an interview with Türkan Olcay for the Russian literary journal *Russkii Mir*

[400] I. Karaca.

[401] Z. Nur Şimşek, 'Fatma Aliye'nin Mektuplaşmaları Üzerinden Madam Gülnar'ı yeni den Kurgulamak', *Yeni Turk Edebiyat 21*, Nisan 2020, s. 147-159. Accessed 21 March 2023, Translated by Academia.com

[402] T. Olcay, 'Olga Lebedeva (Madame Gülnar): A Russian Orientalist and Translator Enchants the Ottomans', *Slovo*, Vol. 29, No 2, (Summer 2017), p. 54.

[403] Letter to Fatma Aliye dated 8 January 1894, quoted from C. Vaughn Findley, p.33, footnote 79.

[404] The reference comes from Z. Nur Şimşek, p. 154 (see above, 2020) who in translation quotes from Fatma Aliye.

[405] The memoirs of the Countess E. von Salburg. The bride's father was Vladimir Dlotovsky.

[406] T. Olcay, (Slovo), pp. 50-51.

[407] J. Strauss, Olga Lebedeva and her Works in Ottoman Turkish, Simburg, Istanbul 2002, p. 299.

[408] T. Olcay, (Slovo), p. 57. The translation of this work with 'a statement' by Midhat is included in this volume in Book Two.

[409] Z. N. Şimşek, p.155.

[410] Letter dated 1 August 1894, State Museum of Leo Tolstoy Manuscript Department. See below Hülya Arslan.

[411] S. Whitman, p. 35

[412] See Karaca, footnote 32: Mustafa Resid, Muharrerat-ı Nisvan, Istanbul 1313, pp. 3-8 (1895). See Akhunov.

[413] Gülnar Hanım, Gaspoja Lebedeva, *Ikdam*, nr. 343, Istanbul 18 Muharram 1313/10 July 1895, *TDV Encyclopedia of Islam*, Vol 14, p.248. The bibliography for the article about Madame Gülnar notes another similar title in Servet-ı Fünûn, no 15 June 20, 1307, as does another magazine *Kadin*, Salonika 26 Kanunusan 1324 (1906). In the Crimea, this article was originally published in *Tercüman* on 18 June 1895. Link accessed 2015 is no longer operational.

[414] Card to De Gubernatis, Christmas 1901. BNF, De Gub 74, 48a, 13. This shows a photo of Alupka.
[415] A sound in Russian unfamiliar in other European languages 'sh-ch' is also used in Turkish which shows how neighbouring countries can absorb elements of language from one another (e.g., *Hoşça kal* – 'goodbye' in Turkish).
[416] www.encyclopedia.com/topic/Tatars.aspx. Accessed 16 March 2016
[417] A definition made by M. Koeppen, author of Grande Carte Ethnologique de la Russie.
[418] D. Ross, p. 132.
[419] Catherine II brought an end to many of the harsh religious compliance laws. See: N. Fielding, Travellers in the Great Steppe, Signal Books Ltd, p.256
[420] Ibid, p.255-257.
[421] W. Dowler, *Classroom and Empire: The Politics of Schooling Russia's Eastern Nationalities, 1860-1917*, pp.12-17. This echoes the Russian saying that: 'An uninvited guest is worse than a Tatar'.
[422] D. Ross, 2020, p.157.
[423] D. Brower, 'Islam and Ethnicity: Russian Colonial Policy in Turkestan', *Russia's Orient, Imperial Borderlands and Peoples, 1700-1917*, Indiana University Press, 1997, p.120.
[424] R. Crew, 2006, p.331 Out of a total of 150 million tsarist subjects.
[425] R. Crew, pp. 1-4.
[426] D. Ross, p.88.
[427] M. Özgür Tuna, Gaspirali v. Il'minski: Two Identity Projects for the Muslims of the Russian Empire, Carfax Publishing, 2022, Nationalities Papers, Vol. 30. No 2, p.267.
[428] R. Crew, p. 330.
[429] R. Geraci, p.107, Gottwald was accused by Gordii Sablukov, head of the anti-Islam division at the Kazan Theological Academy during the years 1856-63 and author of the first translation of the Quran into Russian from Arabic. His Academy even offered a master's degree in anti-Muslim studies, or another description for this would be 'the refutation of Islam'.
[430] R. Geraci, p.110.
[431] M. Özgür Tuna, pp.269-273.
[432] R. Geraci, p. 95.
[433] R. Geraci, pp.116-140 the ministry made studies of efforts in British India and French Algeria.
[434] D. Ross, p. 87
[435] Ibid. p.154. Ross describes how young women and girls were educated in private circles, via the wife of the imam in the first half of the nineteenth century (p.79) and that by the 1850s female literacy in Kazan province was estimated to be as high as 70 per cent in prosperous villages.
[436] D. Ross, p. 143.

ENDNOTES

[437] O.de Lebedeff, *Abrégé de l'histoire de Kazan*, Societa Editrice Dante Alighieri, 1899, Rome : Tip. E. Voghera. Excerpts translated by C. Hamilton, p. 90.
[438] D. Ross, p. 79.
[439] O.de Lebedeff, Rome 1899, pp. 88-89.
[440] D. Ross, p.153.
[441] D. Ross, p.115. Also note that Geraci spells his name as Merjani (p.141)
[442] A. Karimullin, pp.258-259.
[443] Author of an unpublished 'History of Kazan' in Tatar-Turki. Marjani incorporated Faydkhanov's work into his own history of Kazan written in Tatar.
[444] R. Geraci, p.141.
[445] M. Özgür Tuna, p. 280.
[446] D. Ross, pp. 125-127.
[447] See above: A. Karimullin.
[448] See poem (2011) by Gazinur Murat which references her welcome to Karimov and mentions his son by name.
[449] In the Bugulminsky region, southeast of Kazan and Viatka (this was also near where the Dlotovsky family had an estate).
[450] A. Karimullin, pp. 259-260.
[451] D. Ross, p.147.
[452] D. Ross, p. 152.
[453] A. Rieber, 'Interest Group Politics in the Era of the Great Reforms', *Russia's Great Reforms 1855-1881*, Ed. B. Ekloff, J. Bushnell & L. Zakharova, Indiana University Press, 1994, pp. 62-76.
[454] I. Gasprali, *French and African Letters*, Annotated Translation and Introduction by Azade-Ayse Rorlich, The Isis Press, Istanbul, 2008, p.16
[455] M. Özgür Tuna, 'Gaspirali v. Il'minskii: Two Identity Projects for the Muslims of the Russian Empire'. *Nationalities Papers, 30*(2), 2002. pp. 265-289. doi:10.1080/00905990220140658. Accessed 26 April 2020. Gaspirali stopped publishing the Russian version after the Revolution of 1905. See: M. Özgür Tuna, 'Pillars of the Nation', p. 32.
[456] Other enlightened activists outlined by A. Karimullin, 'O.S. Lebedeva - Gülnar Hanum', p.149 included: I.I. Zapolsky, M.G. Nikolsky, others in the circles of N.G Chernishevsky, P.I. Pashino, Vl.S.Kurochkin; and amongst the Tatars were Qayyum Nasyri, M. Yakhin, T.Kutlyarov, G. Ilyasi, and Sh. Akhmerov amongst others.
[457] This correspondence is held at the Central State Historical Archive, Fond 776, op.8, d. 728, pp.60-64. See Karimullin, 'O.S. Lebedeva - Gülnar Hanum'
[458] M. Özgür Tuna, M. (2002).pp. 265-289. doi:10.1080/00905990220140658. Accessed 26 April 2021.
[459] R. Geraci, p.150.

[460] A. Akhunov, Senior Researcher at the Tatar Encyclopedia, Academy of Sciences, Tatarstan. 'Enlightenment,' 2003 www.tatworld.ru/article.shtml?article=151; this is a quote from A. Karimullin's article 'O.S. Lebedeva - Gülnar Hanum.'

[461] A. Karimullin, *Knigi I Liudi*, Kazan, 1985, p.247 (footnotes in my copy were missing for the exact year to be quoted). There are other separate mentions of Orientalist Mrs. Lebedeff in other publications in the period: *St Petersburg Vedomosti* 1896. 20.i (I.II) No. 19, Otd. Khronika, p.3, and *Volzhskii Vestnik*, 1896 25.I (6.II) No 23. Otd. Khronika, p.2

[462] www.muslim-spb.ru/index.php?page=gataulla-bayazitov accessed 27 Jul. 20 / In 1905 a Tatar newspaper named 'Nur' meaning "Light" was published in the capital.

[463] O.de Lebedeff, pp. 92-93.

[464] O.de Lebedeff, *Abrégé de l'histoire de Kazan*, Rome 1899, p.93 The authority of the Muftis in Russia was being kept in check to curb their influence; the first Russian mufti had expected the same status as the Orthodox Metropolitan. His powers were limited to religious matters. In the Ottoman empire the Hanafi muftis were elected by the government to interpret the law; at the head was the *shaykh al-islam* the mufti of Istanbul who acted as religious advisor to the Sultan and the Sultan used his power to uphold the *shari'a*. (A Hourani, A History of the Arab Peoples, Faber & Faber 1991, p.224).

[465] M. Özgür Tuna, M. (2002). pp. 265-289. doi:10.1080/00905990220140658. Accessed 26 April 2020.

[466] A. Karamullin, Knigi i Liudi. Kazan Tatar Book Publishing House 1985, p.245.

[467] O. de Lebedeff, *Abrégé de l'Histoire de Kazan*, Rome 1899, p. 90-91.

[468] O. de Lebedeff, *Abrégé de l'Histoire de Kazan*, Rome, 1899, p. 82

[469] A. Khalid, Representations of Russia in Central Asian Jadid Discourse; *Russia's Orient, Imperial Borderlands and Peoples 1700-1917*, Ed. Brower & Lazzerini, Indiana University Press, 1997, pp.197-201. Adeeb Khalid describes jadid literature which criticized Muslim society in Central Asia, saying it is hazardous to speak of a single Jadidism. In this case, the metaphor of the 'sleep of ignorance' matches the many references to 'ignorance' which pepper Olga's critique of Tatar fanaticism, a common thread amongst Jadid thinkers.

[470] R. Geraci, p. 156.

[471] A. Karamullin, *Knigi i Liudi*. Kazan Tatar Book Publishing House 1985, p.255.

[472] In 1872 Radloff had opened a secular girls' school in Kazan but it closed after a year due to low numbers.

ENDNOTES

[473] O. de Lebedeff, *De L'Emancipation de la Femme Musulmane*, Lisieux, 1900, p.15 The society is described in detail in Chapter 19, and in the translation of *On the New Rights of Muslim Women*.

[474] *Turkestanskie Vedomosti* No.33, 26 April 1901 (p.166).

[475] W. Dowler, Classroom and Empire, The Politics of Schooling Russia's Eastern Nationalities, McGill-Queen's Press, 2000, pp.10-14.

[476] This work is described by Ilmira Gafiyatullina in the online Russian article dated 3 March 2020: https://islam-today.ru/islam_v_rossii/tatarstan/znamenitye-zensiny-v-kazani-prosla-prezentacia-perevoda-knigi-rizaetdina-fahretdina/ Accessed 15 December 2021.

[477] https://tatarica.org/ru/razdely/sredstva-massovoj-informacii/periodicheskie-izdaniya/galyame-nisvan-zhenskij-mir Accessed 8 July 2023.

[478] G. Murat, Морат Г. *Кош хокукы: шигырьләр һәм поэмалар.* – К.: Татар.кит.нәшр., 2014. – Б. 152-153. Also published online: http://kazanutlary.ru/images/uploads/ckeditor/pdf/5f1dd19c11b8a_2014_7.pdf (accessed 2.1.21). Translation from Tatar into Russian by M. Nebolsina; into English by C.H. with help from T. Lukhnitskaya and J. Aliseyko.

[479] Dedication sent to De Gubernatis 1899 (without date) R. Biblioteca Nazionale Centrale di Firenze, De Gub,74, 48a, 6. Translation from the French by CH.

[480] Years previously, Karl Fuks published *The Kazan Tatars in Statistical and Ethnographic Terms* (1844). For more on this topic read: R. Geraci, Window on the East: National and Imperial Identities in Late Tsarist Russia, Cornell, 2001, Chapter 5 esp. pp. 163-164. In addition, Olga is identified as having written an article in a Brunswick illustrated journal : *Globus*, Nr 17 in October 1899 about the Volga Bulgars called the *Metal Mirror of Bulgar* (See TDV Encyclopedia), however, on close inspection of that paper, the author was Krahmer. The German article was taken from the *News* of Society of Archaeology, History and Ethnography, Kazan, 1898, Tape 14, Notebook 6.

[481] J. Strauss, Olga Lebedeva and her works in Ottoman Turkish, Simburg, Istanbul, 2002, p.297 on 25 March 1893 in an Ottoman periodical (Servet-ı Fünûn). It was entitled *Kazan Şehri*. See also T. Olcay www.researchgate.net/publication/317328324_Olga_Lebedeva_Madame_Gülnar_A_Russian_Orientalist_and_Translator_Enchants_the_Ottomans.

[482] Biblioteca Nazionale Central Firenze, Archive: de Gub. 74 / 48a / 4 & 27; dated 2/ 14 August 1899 and an undated letter damaged letter (no.27). This information is found in two letters sent in August 1899 from Olga in Lubiana to Count de Gubernatis, the organiser of the Congress.

[483] O.de Lebedeff, *Abrégé de l'histoire de Kazan*, Societa Editrice Dante Alighieri, 1899, excerpts translated by C. Hamilton pp.81-82.

[484] O.de Lebedeff, *Abrégé de l'histoire de Kazan*, Societa Editrice Dante Alighieri, 1899, pp. 7-13. (Reprint 2013 by Isha Books, New Delhi). Excerpts translated by C. Hamilton with Michael Atkinson.

[485] As above, pp.15-22.

[486] As above pp. 23-29.

[487] All photographs of the city are from the family collection.

[488] As above p. 79.

[489] Ibid. p. 81 This excerpt is my translation 'Quelques considérations sur la civilisation tatare'.

[490] O. de Lebedeff, as above p.82.

[491] In a letter to the organiser of the Congress, Count de Gubernatis, dated 2/14 August 1899 from Lubiana, Olga de Lebedeff amended this figure, citing the population of Tatars in Kazan as 30,000 as an error. The correct figure she cited was **45,000**. (Biblioteca Nazionale Central Firenze: de Gub. 74 / 48a / 4 & 27).

[492] O. de Lebedeff, as above: pp. 83-84.

[493] As above, p.73.

[494] As above, p. 78-79.

[495] As above, p.79. In the final siege, the city's chronicle reported 110,000 killed and more than 60,000 Russian slaves freed. M. Galleoti, A Short History of Russia, Penguin, 2021, p. 58.

[496] Suzerainty, quoting The Oxford Reference Dictionary, means a State having control of another State that is internally autonomous.

[497] E. Turnerelli, Russia on the Borders of Asia, Kazan The Ancient Capital of the Tatar Khans, London Richard Bentley 1854, Vol. 1, p. 134.

[498] P. Leigh Fermor, A Time of Gifts, p.219.

[499] This was a fear of the Russian government stoked at the beginning of the twentieth century by the Young Turks movement in Kazan. As a separate note, Queen Victoria ruled over more Muslims than the sultan over the Ottoman Empire.

[500] Norman Davies, Europe A History, OUP 1996, p. 560.

[501] G.R. Enikeev: 'Nasledie Tatar' Chapter 1, https://history.wikireading.ru/321211 / Accessed 8 September 2020. A proper assessment of the influence of Tatar-Turki language(s) on the Russian language would be interesting and there are many other loan words for instance the word coat (palto) and hat (shapka). However, I have not yet found such an assessment in English. Some of these may also be Arabic derivatives.

[502] C. Obolensky, p.4.

[503] M. Sixsmith, Russia, A 1000-year Chronicle of the Wild East, BBC Books, 2012, p.34.

[504] M Bassin, 'Russia between Europe and Asia: The Ideological Construction of Geographical Space', *Slavic Review*, 1991, p.5.

ENDNOTES

[505] R. Wortman, 'Russian Noble Officers and the Ethos of Exploration'. *Visual Texts, Ceremonial Texts, Texts of Exploration: Collected Articles on the Representation of Russian Monarchy.* Academic Studies Press. 2013. p.283. Brighton, MA, USA:. Accessed October 9, 2020, from www.jstor.org/stable/j.ctt21h4wkb.18.

[506] A. Karimullin, *Knigi i Liudi*, Kazan, 1985, p. 260.

[507] R. Wortman, 'Russian Noble Officers and the Ethos of Exploration'. *Visual Texts, Ceremonial Texts, Texts of Exploration: Collected Articles on the Representation of Russian Monarchy.* Academic Studies Press. 2013. p. 284. Brighton, MA, USA:. Accessed October 9, 2020, from www.jstor.org/stable/j.ctt21h4wkb.18.

[508] R. Wortman, p. 293

[509] M Bassin, pp. 8-11.

[510] V. Tolz, *Inventing the Nation, Russia*, Oxford University Press, 2001, p. 144

[511] M. Özgür Tuna, Pillars of the Nation, pp. 19-20

[512] O. de Lebedeff, *Abrégé de l'histoire de Kazan*, Rome, pp.82-83.

[513] Biblioteca Nazionale di Firenze, De gub 74 ins. 48 a (7). Letter to De Gubernatis, June 1899.

[514] Tolstoy's Letters, Vol. 2, Selected, edited, and translated by R.F. Christian 1880-1910, Faber Finds, 2010, pp.483-484 (+ p.411).

[515] Letters from Tolstoy to Olga de Lebedeff from 4 and 22 September 1894 are published In Collected Works of L. N. Tolstoy in 90 volumes. Extracts from these letters are published in the book «Lev Tolstoy i Vostok» (Moskva, 1971. – pages 364-367) by A. Shifman. Her letters to Tolstoy are kept in the Tolstoy Museum manuscript department: three letters (23 June, 1 August, 12 September 1894) and one letter dated (15/27 March 1895).

[516] C. Vaughn Findley, p. 22.

[517] Also 'The Death of Ivan Ilych, which was published on 16 April 1892'

[518] A. I. Shifman, Lev Tolstoy i Vostok, Moscow (1971) ('Lev Tolstoy and the Orient') pp. 367 This second letter to Tolstoy was included in an exhibition in Moscow in 2015 dedicated to the Year of Russian Literature and it related to the event 'Tolstoy is the whole world' on 22 April 2015 which focused on Tolstoy's relationship with Turkish culture and history.

[519] See Hülya Arslan.

[520] Mary Mills Patrick, *A Bosphorus Adventure*, Istanbul's Women's College 1871-1924.

[521] Hülya Arslan's Turkish article was kindly sent to me translated into English as: 'Olga Lebedeva, an Exemplary Translator in the Field of Intercultural Communication'. p.2. (The Paper was submitted to the "International Symposium of Issues Related to Translations and Translators" held on 11th - 12th October 2004 and organised by Sakarya University).

[522] A.I. Shifman, 'Lev Tolstoy I Vostok', *Nauka*, Moscow 1971, p. 364

[523] Quakers who travelled to Armenia saw the massacres as a 'Religious Crusade' for which the authorities were responsible. To some, such as British Quaker Helen Rendel, Pan-Islamism was becoming seen as state ideology. See: A. Falcetta, *The Biography of James Rendel Harris 1852-1941*, Bloomsbury 2018, p. 181.

[524] *Tolstoy's Letters* Vol. 02, Selected, edited and translated by R.F. Christian, Faber and Faber, 2010, p.507.

[525] A. I. Shifman, (1971) *Lev Tolstoy and the Orient*, pp. 364-367.

[526] R.F. Christian, *Tolstoy's War and Peace, A Study*, Clarenden Press Oxford, 1962, p.57.

[527] *The Memoirs of Count Witte*, Transl. & Edited by Sidney Harcave, pub. M.E. Sharpe, 1990, pp. 250-252.

[528] *Actes du dixième Congrès international des orientalistes* : session de Genève, 1894. Partie 1, p.28 https://gallica.bnf.fr/ark:/12148/bpt6k9691870g Accessed 23 February 2021.

[529] O.de Lebedeff, *De L'Emancipation de la Femme Musulmane*, Lisieux, 1900, p.14.

[530] *Fatat al-Sharq*, transl. Marilyn Booth. This reference is listed on the penultimate page of the article 'Famous Women'.

[531] See article: C. Van der Kooi, Towards an Abrahamic Ecumenism? Christian Faith and Violence 2, Studies in Reformed Theology, Vol. 11, Brill 2005, pp.34-35 and the work by Karl-Josef Kuschel Christmas and the Quran, Gingko, 2017.

[532] https://bahaiarc.org/bwns/44-research/1020-xix-history-r . Accessed 1 Nov. 2023. See: E. Lavisse & A. Rambaud, History of 19th Century, Vol. 6, Part II

[533] https://bahai-library.com/momen_ashkhabad. Accessed 1 Nov. 2023.

[534] Russian-Muslim Confrontation in the Caucasus Alternative visions of the conflict between Imam Shamil and the Russians, 1830–1859 Edited and translated by Thomas Sanders, Ernest Tucker and Gary Hamburg, Published by Routledge Curzon pp. 200-201.

[535] Tolstoy Museum, Moscow.

[536] L.N. Tolstoy, *Polnoe Sobranie Sochinenii*, Volume 52, Moscow 1952, p. 141.

[537] L.N. Tolstoy, 1952, pp. 223 & 224.

[538] According to the website https://bahaiteachings.org/happens-tolstoy-reviews-play/ (accessed 15.2.21) quote taken fromValentin Bulgakov, Count Leo Tolstoy's secretary, from a 1927 interview with Martha L. Root, *Star of the West*, Volume 10, pp. 303-304.

[539] *Tolstoy's Letters*, Vol. 2, Selected, edited, and translated by R.F. Christian 1880-1910, Faber Finds, 2010, p. 522. Tolstoy campaigned to help the Dukhobors leave Russia and settle in Canada and had the assistance of his son Sergei Lvovich Tolstoy as well as the support of British Quakers.

[540] See above reference to Hülya Arslan's paper where she references Tolstoy's article called "İzreçeniye Magometa, ne voşedşie v Quran". This pamphlet

ENDNOTES

of selected hadiths was published in Posrednik, No. 762, p. 31, Moscow, 1910 quoted in Leo Tolstoy and Islam, Some remarks on the theme by Dr Piotr Stawinski (published in The Quarterly Journal of Philosophical Meditations, Vol 2 No 5, Spring 2010, pp. 2-22).

[541] C. Vaughn Findley (see above), p. 35, note 90. Olga had doubtless seen him some years ago in Stockholm where A. Midhat is impressed with Max Muller.

[542] O.de Lebedeff, letter to Angelo de Gubernatis, R. Biblioteca Nazionale Centrale di Firenze, De Gub, 74, No. 48a, letters 1-27; In Cairo she stayed at the Hotel Continental or the *Hôtel d'Angleterre* where she continued with her Arabic studies during the winter of 1906.

[543] A. De Gubernatis/ Comes de Loup, *Dictionnaire international des écrivains du jour*, T2, p.788 https://gallica.bnf.fr/ark:/12148/bpt6k1079934/f125 /Accessed 24 April 2021.

[544] *The Journal of the Royal Asiatic Society of Great Britain and Ireland* (Jan. 1895), pp. 196-197, published by Cambridge University Press; www.jstor.org/stable/25197248.

[545] R. Biblioteca Nazionale Centrale di Firenze, De gub 74.

[546] Vladimir Pavlovich Bezobrazov (1828-1889).

[547] Dictionnaire international des écrivains du jour. T.2, p.788, Comes-Le Loup / A. De Gubernatis, Bibliothèque nationale de France. https://gallica.bnf.fr/ark:/12148/bpt6k1079934 Accessed 8 March 2021

[548] Les Femmes en Orient. I. La Péninsule orientale. II. La Russie (Zurich, Meyer et Zeller, 1859-1860, 2 volumes).

[549] Copies of this may be found here: http://digitale.bnc.roma.sbn.it/tecadigitale/giornale/MIL0530229/1934/unico Accessed 2 May 2023.

[550] https://italia.rastko.net/delo/12712 Accessed 26 July 2023.

[551] For more about the "Guru – Disciple" tradition in India see: https://en.wikipedia.org/wiki/Guru%E2%80%93shishya_tradition Accessed 10 April 2023.

[552] A quote from Contemporary Review 1878 (p. 598) reprinted in the *Atti dei IV Congresso internazionale degli orientalisti*, tenuto in Firenze nel settembre 1876, vol 2, Le Monnier, Florence, 1880, p. 192. https://catalog.hathitrust.org/Record/100349610. Accessed 3 May 2023

[553] Roma: Tip. Cooperativa Sociale, 1902.

[554] R. Biblioteca Nazionale Centrale di Firenze, De gub 74

[555] R. Biblioteca Nazionale Centrale di Firenze, De gub 74.

[556] Letter to de Gubernatis, dated 26 March 1909 (letter no.18). Photo credit: Biblioteca Nazionale Central Firenze.

[557] See *The Memoirs of Sir Ronald Storrs*. https://archive.org/stream/memoirsofsirrona001290mbp/memoirsofsirrona

001290mbp_djvu.txt p.96. She was a natural daughter of Prince Gagarin; her first husband was Count Beketoff.

[558] H. Watenpaugh, "The Harem as Biography: Domestic Architecture, Gender and Nostalgia in Modern Syria," in *Harem Histories: Lived Spaces and Envisioned Places*, ed. Marilyn Booth, Durham and London: Duke University Press, 2010. 211-236 (p.227).

[559] Memories of a shipwrecked world, being the memoirs of Countess Kleinmichel, Translated by Vivian Le Grand, Brentano's New York, 1923, p. 77
https://babel.hathitrust.org/cgi/pt?id=mdp.39015008813761&view=1up&seq=93&q1=77. Accessed 23 May 2023.

[560] Catherine Radziwill, *My Recollections*, New York, J. Pott & company, 1904. p. 277

[561] R. Allen *Journal of the American Research Center in Egypt*, Vol. 8 (1969-1970), pp. 79-84 (6 pages). www.jstor.org/stable/40000042 Accessed 21 March 2023.

[562] M. Booth May her Likes be Multiplied, Biography and Gender Politics in Egypt, University of California Press Ltd, 2001, p. xxxiii.

[563] M. Booth, Ibid, p. 3.

[564] M. Booth, Ibid, p. 23. The book was called: *Scattered Pearls on the Generations of the Mistresses of Seclusion*, or as Olga de Lebedeff cited it 'Les perles dispersées du sexe gracieux' in her *De L'Emancipation de la Femme Musulmane* (pp.11-12).

[565] M. Booth, 2001, p. 28.

[566] According to Isabella Grinevskaya's two-page biography, held in the Pushkinsky Dom archive of S.A. Vengerov Fond 377, op. 7, № 2101, it specifically states that the Olga translated Syed Ameer Ali's article from the English.

[567] M. Idris, Colonial hesitation, appropriation, and citation: Qasim Amin, empire, and saying 'no', *Colonial exchanges. Political theory and the agency of the colonized*. Manchester University Press, 2017, pp. 180-210.

[568] *Oxford Dictionary of Islam*, Oxford University Press, 2003, p. 41.

[569] Qasim Amin is referred to as 'Kassime Emine Bey' in the text.

[570] O de Lebedeff, *Abrégé de l'Histoire de Kazan*, 1899, (reprint 2013, Isha Books, New Delhi), pp. 93-97.

[571] O de Lebedeff, Ibid, p. 95 Tatar betrothals were described by Englishman Edward Turnerelli, how a Tatar must pay a price in roubles for his wife (a *kalym*), allowing the husband to separate from his wife whenever he might wish to do so, even on the very next day after the marriage, 'in case he may have found some reason to be dissatisfied with her'. (E. Turnerelli, Kazan the Ancient Capital of the Tatar Khans, Vol. 2, London 1854, p.49). Olga explains that if a *kalym* were thousand roubles, then five hundred would be given to the bride and the other half given later, in the case of divorce.

ENDNOTES

[572] O. de Lebedeff, *De L'Emancipation de la Femme Musulmane*, Lisieux, 1900, p. 11.

[573] For instance, to Tashkent: *Turkestanskie Vedomosti* No.33, 26 April 1901 (p. 166). See Russian copy online here: https://vivaldi.dspl.ru/bx0001950/view/?#page=1

[574] A. Karimullin, *O.S. Lebedeva – Gülnar Hanum*, Peoples of Asia and Africa (Narodi Asii i Afriki) 1977 n.3, pp146-152 under the chapter entitled: из историй востоковедения и африканистики. p. 151, footnote 15 (*Golnar Hanim (Lebedeva)*, Moslimeler horriate, Kazan 1907).

[575] *Le XIXe Siècle : journal quotidien politique et littéraire.* (p. 2) https://gallica.bnf.fr/ark:/12148/bpt6k7568000r / Accessed 26 February 2021.

[576] For more information, see K. Offen, Debating the Woman Question in the French Third Republic, 1870-1920, Cambridge University Press, 2018, pp.281-288. The event was called: Second Oeuvres et Institutions Féminines Congress.

[577] La Fronde, Paris, 23/11/1901, p. 1. https://gallica.bnf.fr/ark:/12148/bpt6k6705560f Accessed 5 January 2024.

[578] Emilie Hyacinth Loyson was President of the Alliance des Femmes Orientales et Occidentales, Parc de Neuilly. The motto of the society was this: To God through Science (Ad Deum Per Scientium).

[579] https://gallica.bnf.fr/ark:/12148/bpt6k579876b. Page 2. Accessed 26 February 2021.

[580] 'Improvement of the Condition of Muslim Women', *The French Association for the Advancement of the Sciences,* 1896, p.208. next Endnote for reference.

[581] La Fronde, Paris, 23/11/1901, p. 2 https://gallica.bnf.fr/ark:/12148/bpt6k6705560f/f2.item.r=congres%20international%20des%20femmes%20feministes / Accessed 15 Sept 2020.

[582] This source outlines the idea of Religious Progress and peace activism of the couple. https://fromthepage.com/digitalindy/may-wright-sewall-papers/letter-from-emilie-hyacinth-loyson-to-may-wright-sewall-bd525dce-c94d-47d7-81ed-fcdd2d0af7d0.

[583] Marie de Besneray was a novelist (*Nadine* (1884), *Vie Brisée (1884)*, *Les Grandes Époques de la peinture* (1898) and *La Veillée de Noel and Douleur d'aimer)*, was an active contributor to literary journals and literary reviews. She was an Officer of the Academy and a Member of the 'Society of People of Letters'. Born to French parents in Moscow in the same year as Olga; her maiden name was Boissonade (1852-1919), and her married name was Madame Léopold Bertre. Source : A. de Gubernatis, Dictionnaire international des écrivains du jour, vol. 1, p.289 Bibliothèque nationale de France https://gallica.bnf.fr/ark:/12148/bpt6k5568346c Accessed 8 March 2021.

584 Bibliothèque Nationale de France (Gallica) : https://gallica.bnf.fr/ark:/12148/bpt6k103796j /Accessed 6 June 2022 / Revue du monde musulmane, Paris, February 1907 p.594. To date the article has not yet been translated. He also published an article in Thessaloniki: [Abdullah Cevdet], "Gülnar Hanım. Madame Olga Dö Lebedef", Woman, nr. 16, Thessaloniki 26 Kanunusâni 1324 [transl. from Rumi calendar January 1906], pp. 7-9.

585 In the Revue du Monde Musulman 1 Nov 1906 published by E. Leroux Paris, there is a reference to this work : See Gallica, https://gallica.bnf.fr/ark:/12148/bpt6k103796j (p. 594) Accessed 16 January 2023.

586 J. Strauss, p. 314.

587 This copy was found at Princeton University Library.

588 The Guardian, London 18 Sept 1874; Newpapers.com. The Full speech can be read online on pp. 177-204 on this link. http://catalogue.bnf.fr/ark:/12148/cb303515983 accessed 1 Dec 2021

589 S. Whitman, p. 275 Letter from A. Vambery to S. Whitman

590 This society was all male until Miss Amy Yule joined in 1899 and Miss A.A. Smith in 1904. Members here were Protestant as Catholics did not go to university; women were excluded from university.

591 W. Lubenow, 'Only Connect' Learned Societies in Nineteenth Century Britain, The Boydell Press, 2015, p.98.

592 B. Brendemoen, 'The Eighth International Congress of Orientalists, Held in Stockholm/Uppsala, and Christiania (1-14 September 1889), and its Echo in Turkish Literature', *Turcologica Upsaliensia: An Illustrated Collection of Essays*, Brill, Leiden 2021, Chapter 10, p. 135.

593 C. Vaughn Findley, p. 35 Footnote 86.

594 Ibid, p. 37, Footnote 91.

595 *Actes du dixième Congrès international des orientalistes : session de Genève, 1894*. Partie 1, p. 28 https://gallica.bnf.fr/ark:/12148/bpt6k9691870g accessed 23 February 2021.

596 O.de Lebedeff, *De L'Emancipation de la Femme Musulmane*, Lisieux, 1900, p. 14.

597 Recorded in the online archives at the Library of Congress. The *Sun New York*, 27/11/1895 is one of three papers that published the same story, see example here: www.loc.gov/resource/sn83030272/1895-11-27/ed-1/?sp=6&q=Lebedeva&r=0.69,0.716,0.298,0.216,0 p.6 Accessed 13 February 2024.

598 Now known as Saiyid Amir Ali. For further reading on this see a review by H. Hirschfeld, in the Jewish Quarterly Review, Vol 5 1893 www.jstor.org/stable/1449861. Accessed 19 February 2024. Also see his obituary notice in the Journal of the Royal Asiatic Society of Great Britain

ENDNOTES

and Ireland, No 4, (Oct. 1928) pp. 986-989. www.jstor.org/stable/25221475. Accessed 19 February 2024.

[599] The biography of Olga written by Isabella Grinevskaya held in the archive of S.A. Vengerov at Pushkinsky Dom, Fond 377, op. 7, № 2101) lists this work as one of her translations.

[600] Archive of the Russian Academy of Sciences (SPbB ARAS) Fond 777, Inventory 2, Folder 243. Letter in German in cursive Gothic script. Translation by C. Hamilton.

[601] Translation from the French into Russian, *Istoria XIX Beka*, Moscow, 1939, Vol. 8, pp. 12-13

[602] A. Karimullin, *Knigi i Liudi*, Kazan, Tatarskoe Knizhnoe Izd. 1985, p.256

[603] T. Olcay, Olga Lebedeva (Madame Gülnar): A Russian Orientalist and Translator Enchants the Ottomans, *Slovo*, Vol. 29, No 2, (Summer 2017), p. 47. This anthology appears not yet to have been published by 1899, when Olga offered it to Count Angelo for the Rome International Congress of Orientalists (letter dated August 1899, Biblioteca Nazionale Central Firenze: de Gub. 74).

[604] I. Karaca.

[605] R. Biblioteca Nazionale Centrale di Firenze, De gub 74 ins. 48 a (13 & 14). The photographs are included in this volume in an earlier chapter.

[606] The photographs did not get published, neither was the note concerning the consulted authors: Ibn-Battuta, Prince Kurbsky, Professor Schpilevsky, Professor Zariansky and the Mullah Chinab-ud-dina.

[607] Dedication sent to De Gubernatis 1899 (without date) R. Biblioteca Nazionale Centrale di Firenze, De Gub,74, 48a, 6. Translation from the French by CH.

[608] R. Biblioteca Nazionale Centrale di Firenze, De gub 74 ins. 48 a (8 & 9). Meaning, that she was very anxious about delivering this address.

[609] https://gallica.bnf.fr/ark:/12148/bpt6k97609698 Accessed 23 Feb 2021. Vera Dlotovsky and Olga Lebedeva were with their mother at the Congress, their sister Nina and Ninette were at Hotel Regina Olga, Cernobbio, Lake Como (photo in the family collection).

[610] A Russian online article from Medina Publishing House entitled 'The Russian Muslim Movement for Women's Rights in 1917 - The First Shoots of Feminist Muslim Thought and Practice' outlines authors and names of women writers who were first inspired by Gülnar Khanum (O.S. Lebedeva). www.idmedina.ru/books/regions/?1562 / Line 3 / Accessed 15 Dec 2021.

[611] www.newspapers.com/image/392812159 / p.4 / Accessed 23 September 2021.

[612] From the collection of letters to De Gubernatis at Biblioteca Nazionale Central Firenze: De gub 74.

[613] Letter to Count de Gubernatis, R. Biblioteca Nazionale Centrale di Firenze, De Gub,74, 48a, 9.

[614] O.de Lebedeff : *De L'Emancipation de la Femme Musulmane* [transl. On the Emancipation of Muslim Women], 1900, p.14; finished in December 1899; 'Nous avons fait de la propagande pour cette idée, il y a trois ans, après un assez long séjour en Orient'. The letter to De Gubernatis quoting nearly five years in the epigraph is stored in the Biblioteca Nazionale Central Firenze: De gub 74 ins 48 a (19, 20) Karimullin mistakenly claims it had taken since 1887 to receive authorization for this.

[615] Archive of the Russian Academy of Sciences, SPbB ARAS, Fond 777, Inventory 2, Folder 243; the letter is dated Monday 26 February, and the reverse side says 1897; but 26th February was a Friday in the Julian calendar (the date of the meeting), not a Monday as specified on the letter.

[616] A. Karimullin, 1985, p.260; other orientalists mentioned are NI Konrad, KG Zaleman, PM Melioranksy, NF Katanov, NI Berezin.

[617] V. Tolz, 'European, National, and (Anti-)Imperial: The Formation of Academic Oriental Studies in Late Tsarist and Early Soviet Russia.' *Kritika: Explorations in Russian and Eurasian History*, vol. 9 no. 1, 2008, p. 53-81. *Project MUSE*, doi:10.1353/kri.2008.0004.

[618] D. Schimmelpennick van der Oye, 'The Curious Fate of Edward Said in Russia', *Études de lettres*, 2-3 | 2014, 81-94. There were also faculties established at Kharkov, Kiev and Moscow.

[619] V. Tolz, *Russia's Own Orient*, Oxford University Press 2011, p. 9.

[620] V. Tolz, 'European, National, and (Anti-)Imperial: The Formation of Academic Oriental Studies in Late Tsarist and Early Soviet Russia.' *Kritika: Explorations in Russian and Eurasian History*, vol. 9 no. 1, 2008, p. 53-81. *Project MUSE*, doi:10.1353/kri.2008.0004.

[621] *The Memoirs of Count Witte*, Edited by S. Harcave, M.E. Sharpe, Inc, London & Armonk, 1990, p.xvi.

[622] The Memoirs of Count Witte, pp. 186-286. The Foreign minister and Witte disagreed over Port Arthur.

[623] D. Brower, p. 132.

[624] O.de Lebedeff, *Ob emantsipatsii musulmanskikh zhenshin* (1900), p. 26; as it was published after 29 Feb 1900, this version of the essay lays out all the aims of the Society of Oriental Studies.

[625] A. Karamullin: 'OS Lebedeva – Gülnar Hanum', *Narodi Asii I Afriki* (1977), N.3 pp.149-150; Isabella Grinevskaya's biography clarifies that she began as President and later became Honorary President due to her absences from St Petersburg; Grinevskaya's account is held in the Pushkinsky Dom archive of S.A. Vengerov Fond 377, op. 7, № 2101.

[626] The Royal Asiatic Society had thirty original members. See: W.C. Lubenow, 'Only Connect' Learned Societies in Nineteenth Century Britain, The Boydell Press, 2015, p.96 For photographs of early British orientalists see: https://royalasiaticcollections.org/collection/film-photography/photo-collection/photo-24-portrait-photos-of-orientalists/ Accessed 25 June 2023.

ENDNOTES

[627] Letter to Angelo de Gubernatis, R. Biblioteca Nazionale Centrale di Firenze, De Gub, 74, 11.

[628] In Russian : 'практическая Восточная академия и курсы'.

[629] Entire St Petersburg register 1902, p. 356: *Ves Sankt-Peterburg* 1902 p.356.; (next door to where Pushkin's parents lived at no.5 in the 1820s). This venue is quoted in the 1910 Charter of the Practical Academy (held online at the Russian State Library).

[630] O.de Lebedeff, letter to Angelo de Gubernatis, R. Biblioteca Nazionale Centrale di Firenze, De Gub, 74, 11. The term enlightened is discussed by M. Özgür Tuna in his article Pillars of the Nation (p. 19).

[631] Spravochnik Nauchnich Obschchestv Rossii (Directory of Scientific Societies of Russia); www.snor.ru/?an=sc_249; State Historical Archive, St Petersburg, Fond 308.

[632] O. Pleshakova, *Knizhnie Znaki – v Sobrannii Politechnicheskoi Biblioteki*, Politechnicheski Muzei, Moscow 2015. Book 1, p.159 (Biblioteki rossiskikh organisatsii i uchrezhdenii, illiustrirovannii katalog).

[633] https://gallica.bnf.fr/ark:/12148/bpt6k6580276f Accessed 9 April 2021; the proceedings of the International Congress of Orientalists in Copenhagen in 1908 already lists the society as Société Impériale russe des Études Orientales.

[634] https://viewer.rsl.ru/ru/rsl01003771776?page=1&rotate=0&theme=white Accessed 23 May 2022. O.de Lebedeff's only contemporary biographer, I. Grinevskaya also referred to an Academy of Oriental Languages.

[635] Central State Historical Archive, St Petersburg: Fond 309. Op. 1. D. 27.

[636] V. Tolz, Russia's Own Orient (Oxford University Press 2011) p. 84.

[637] Turkestanskie Vedomosti, 26 April 1901 No.33, 26 April 1901.

[638] Spravochnik Nauchnich Obschchestv Rossii (Directory of Scientific Societies of Russia); www.snor.ru/?an=sc_249 Accessed 15 Oct 2016

[639] E. I. Campbell, 'The Muslim Question and Russian Imperial Governance', Indiana University Press, 2015 p. 171.

[640] O. Pleshakova, Book 1; p.158; no reference to the founder of the society.

[641] http://kpfu.ru/institutes/institut-vostokovedeniya-i-mezhdunarodnyh/obschestvo-vostokovedov-rossii; Accessed 11 January 2020.

[642] Correspondence to I. Krachkovsky from O. de Lebedeff is held at the Russian Academy of Sciences Archive SPbB ARAS, Fond 1026, Inventory 3, Folder 528.

[643] The nomination is stored in the French National Archive (F/17/40242); her name was put forward by General N.K. Schwedow.

[644] See Biography by Isabella Grinevskaya at Pushkinsky Dom, Fond 377, op. 7, № 2101. Also referenced in the article in *Fatat al-Sharq* in this volume.

[645] V. Dzevanovsky-Petrashevsky, Unknown Olga de Lebedev (1852-1928): Gülnar Hanım's life outside Turkey (Speaker at the Poznan conference on 16.2.21.

[646] Victor mentioned that she was the first to be employed by the university in 1913, however, I have only found a link which specifies that she was the first female employee at the Asiatic Museum in 1918 https://bioslovhist.spbu.ru/hist-pg-ld/3526-alekseeva-dakonova-natala-mihajlovna.html Accessed 5 July 2022.

[647] My grateful acknowledgements to Victor Dzevanovsky-Petrashevsky. See also article by A.A. Dolinina, Materiali V.A. Krachkovskoi v Sankt Peterburgskom Filiale Arkhiva RAN. https://dspace.spbu.ru/bitstream/11701/1867/1/64025-%D0%92%D0%BE%D1%81%D1%82%D0%BE%D0%BA%D0%BE%D0%B2%D0%B5%D0%B4%D0%B5%D0%BD%D0%B8%D0%B5%2830%29.pdf Accessed 6 April 2023.

[648] M.J. Hutton, p. 126

[649] A. Karimullin, 1985, p.252. Another translation: To spread amongst eastern peoples exact and accurate knowledge about Russia. To familiarize Russian society with the material needs and spiritual life of the East. To promote cultural exchange between Russia and eastern countries, and to act as a vehicle for Russian culture.

[650] M.J. Hutton, p. 62

[651] R. Irwin, pp. 217-219.

[652] R. Irwin, p. 196

[653] O.de Lebedeff, De L'Emancipation de la Femme Musulmane, Lisieux, 1900, pp. 13-14.

[654] Les Nouveaux Droits de la Femme Musulmane. Published in : Verhandlungen des XIII Internationalen Orientalisten-Kongresses, Hamburg September 1902, published by E.J. Brill, Leiden, 1904. pp. 314 – 319 https://gallica.bnf.fr/ark:/12148/bpt6k9681968g Accessed 23 February 2021.

[655] R. Irwin, p.196 A quote by Bernard Lewis, Islam in History: Ideas, People and Events in the Middle East, 2nd edition (Chicago and La Salle Illinois, 1993) p. 144.

[656] R. Allen *Journal of the American Research Center in Egypt*, Vol. 8 (1969-1970), p.80. www.jstor.org/stable/40000042 Accessed 22 March 2023.

[657] The German text says 'Schulrecht.'

[658] My Thanks to Carol Ermakova for her help translating the original German.

[659] L. Hawksley, March, Women, March, pub. By Andre Deutsch Ltd, 2013, pp. 12-13

[660] *Actes du XIV Congres international des orientalistes Algers 1905*, Ernest Leroux (ed.), Paris 1906, p.41. https://gallica.bnf.fr/ark:/12148/bpt6k6580445k

ENDNOTES

https://gallica.bnf.fr/ark:/12148/bpt6k6580445k / Accessed 1 Dec 2021. Transl. CH : Notre société m'a donné le mandate de transmettre aux membres éclairés de ce Congres tous ses voeux les plus sincères pour leur succès dans la voie du progrès des sciences et pour l'oeuvre entreprise en commun du rapprochement de l'Orient et de l'Occident.

[661] Histoire de la conversion des Georgiens au Christianisme : Codex 689 du Vatican / traduction de l'arabe par Olga De Lebedew, Rome : Tip. Casa Edit. Italiana. 1905. The Patriarch Macarius III Ibn Al Zaim was born in Aleppo and was bishop of Antioch between 1647 – 1672. He visited Russia as guest of Tsar Alexis and had a part in the religious reform of Russian Patriarch Nikon.

[662] Journal des travaux 1er trimestre 1905, société historique algérienne Langues musulmanes (de L'arabe). Another critique of ms arabe 689 du Vatican came out in the Revue critique d'histoire et de littérature / publiée sous la direction de MM. P. Meyer, Ch. Morel, G. The translation was also reviewed in *Revue des traditions populaires Société des traditions populaires* (Paris). April/ May 1906, which declared the text a precious document, never previously printed https://gallica.bnf.fr/ark:/12148/bpt6k6139943x/f45.item/ Accessed 23 September 2021.

[663] A copy is in the British Library.

[664] Advised by letters to an Orientalist seen by Victor Dzevanovsky.

[665] Arafate No 55 by Mahmoud Salem Bey. See: Idjtihad, January 1906 by Dr Abdullah Cevdet. http://isamveri.org/pdfosm/D00882/1906_10/1906_10_DJEVDETA3.pdf Accessed 3 May 2023.

[666] https://gallica.bnf.fr/ark:/12148/bpt6k6580276f accessed 9 April 2021.

[667] https://gallica.bnf.fr/ark:/12148/bpt6k6579584j Accessed 23 February 2021.

[668] Also Persian specialist Valentin Zhukovsky according to correspondence owned by Victor Dzevanovsky-Petrashevsky.

[669] Postcard to Isabella Grinevskaya postmarked from Athens, 18 April 1912. Fond 55, Op. 2 N 736.

[670] *Traité sur le Soufisme de l'imâm érudit Abou 'l-Kâsim Abd'Oul-kerim Ibn Hawazin el Kochâirî*, Casa Editrice Italiana, Rome, 1911. See : Actes du 16e Congrès international des Orientalistes. Session d'Athènes (6-14 avril 1912) https://gallica.bnf.fr/ark:/12148/bpt6k6580276f Accessed 23 February 2021.

[671] Translation by Professor Alexander D. Knysh, reviewed by Muhammed Eissa, Published by The Center for Muslim Contribution to Civilisation, 2020, p.76.

[672] R. Hartmann, *The Sufism of Al-Kushairi*, Kiel 1914; a university thesis https://archive.org/details/alkuschairisdars00hartuoft/page/n15/mode/2up? q Accessed 19 January 2023. Also see: Hamid Algar's Introduction to Al-Qushayri's Principles of Sufism, 1992 (Academia.com).

[673] C. Vaughn Findley, p.37, footnote 91. Another Russian Orientalist whose work encompassed Persian Sufism was Valentin A. Zhukovsky (1858-1918), professor of Persian literature at the Oriental Faculty of St Petersburg University, who was its Dean from 1905-1917.

[674] The Guardian, London 18 Sept 1874; Newpapers.com. The Full speech can be read online on pp. 177 204 on this link: http://catalogue.bnf.fr/ark:/12148/cb303515983. Accessed 1 Dec 2021.

[675] M. Carlson, *No Religion Higher than the Truth, A History of the Theosophical Movement in Russia 1875-1922*, Princeton University Press, copyright 1993, 2016. Princeton University Press, 2016, p. 30.

[676] S. Batchelor, The Awakening of the West, the Encounter of Buddhism and Western Culture, Parallax Press, California, 1994, pp. 252-253.

[677] M. Carlson, (1993). Theosophical Doctrine: An Outline. In *No Religion Higher Than Truth: A History of the Theosophical Movement in Russia, 1875-1922* (pp. 114–136). Princeton University Press. www.jstor.org/stable/j.ctt13x16r9.10 Accessed 24 Jan 2024

[678] M. Carlson p. 36.

[679] M. Carlson p. 205.

[680] M. Carlson p. 193.

[681] For further details of the society in Russia in that period, see the General Report of the Theosophical Society 1914, p.61. http://resources.theosophical.org/pdf/Series/Annual%20General%20Reports/General_Report_1914.pdf. Accessed 13 January 2024. Also of note, in 1925 Anna Kamenskaya published her translations of the Sanskrit text the *Bhagavad-Gita* into French and Russian.

[682] The lodge was founded on 7th May 1908 with the Swiss Leon Charles Oltramare (1884-1968), and Egizio Veronesi; the Italian for 'Egizio' means ancient Egyptian. There was a Veronesi family who specialized in famous watches in Cairo. The lodge in Cairo was described as 'non-sectionalised'.

[683] The Theosophist, 10 July 1908 (New York Public Library), viewed online: http://iapsop.com/archive/materials/theosophist/theosophist_v29_n10_jul_1908.pdf. Accessed 1 June 2023. This is the one of the few occasions that we read about Olga with the title of Countess, also, C.V. Findley, p. 31.

[684] My thanks to Marilyn Booth for this translation and the more modern wording 'al-hikma al-qadima'.

[685] General Report of the 42nd Anniversary and Convention of the Theosophical Society , Held at Calcutta, 1917. Published in Madras 1918. http://iapsop.com/ssoc/1917__anonymous___general_report_of_42nd_convention_of_theosophical_society.pdf Accessed 1 June 2023.

[686] The founder of Theosophy, Helena Blavatsky, had attempted to form a spiritual society there in 1871 without success. *International Theosophy Yearbook 1937*, p. 153.

ENDNOTES

[687] See Bahai.org A Tablet of 'Abdu'l-Baha, and IRLI RAN F. 55. Olga Lebedeva was registered at an address in St Petersburg, in the residential archive of St Petersburg dated 1913: Vasilievsky Island (opposite the Winter Palace), 11 Liniya 50 (where there is now a new, modern hotel). A 'liniya' is an 18th century name for a street; number 11 stretches from the embankment of Lieutenant Schmidt Embankment of the Smolenka River. Other times, according to a letter to Isabella Grinevskaya referred to by Victor Dzevanovsky, she stayed with her daughter Olga Gorlova (née Lebedeva) at 11 Moika Embankment.

[688] See the Appreciation of this text by Marilyn Booth in Book Two.

[689] *Récits de Voyages d'un Arabe*, published in St Petersburg, 1902 by Trenke i Fusnot / *Histoire de la Conversion des Georgiens au Christianisme*, Casa Editrice Italiana, Rome, 1905 / *Traité sur le Soufisme*, Casa Editrice Italiana, Rome, 1911.

[690] She paid 8,840.55 silver Austrian Florins (to the British Pound would have been in the region of £1= 10 Fl.) so £884; while this would be an approximate equivalent of £125,000, the British pound has lost 99% of its value since 1890. The closest exchange rate I could find was here: The Table of Foreign Monies listed in Bradshaw's 1853 Continental Railway Guide shows that the rate at that time was £1 to 10 Fl (Silver Florins of Austria). According to an inflation calculator, prices are 136 times higher than average prices in 1890.

[691] Aunt Princess Radziwill died in Paris on 29th July 1889. Being childless her estate was split between the seven Urusov nephews and nieces including Prascovia in 1891: Theodore and Vladimir Mikhailovich Ouroussov and Alexander and Serge Ivanovich Ouroussoff (sic). First mortgage and crippling debts had to be paid off by all the successors; the Ourousoff brothers were charged by the notary to pay all the expenses to settle the debts. https://gallica.bnf.fr/ark:/12148/bpt6k886054f Accessed 23 February 2021 and: https://gallica.bnf.fr/ark:/12148/bpt6k6341958n.

[692] S. Ioppi, *Di Villa in Villa*, pub. Il Sommolago, Arco 2004, pp. 53 -54

[693] La Vita del Kurort, ARCO: la memoria, i luoghi e le persone della città di cura nella fotografia (1866-1915), Il Sommolago, 1994, p. 115.

[694] E. von Salburg, *Erinnerungen einer Respektlosen*, Leipzig 1928, Volume II p. 83 & p. 108). A controversial memoirist according to Arco writer Paolo Boccafoglio.

[695] Letter to Count Gubernatis dated 28 February (NS). 'Jusqu'à présent je n'ai pas eu le coeur d'écrire. …le coup a été bien fort pour moi, d'autant plus qu'il était inattendu.'

[696] E. von Salburg.

[697] Newspaper *Novoe Vremya*, No. 8605 (10 February 1900) & No. 8607 (12 February 1900), preserved at the Russian National Library, St Petersburg.

[698] Including *The New Rights of Muslim Women*, a memoire in French presented to the XIII Congress of Orientalists in Hamburg in 1902. The booklet's full details are : 'Les nouveaux droits de la femme musulmane : mémoire présenté au 13.me Congrès international des orientalistes à Hambourg / par Mme Olga de Lébédew. Arco (TN): Emmert, C., 1902 ' Printed in Arco by Celestino Emmert (1849-1934); he was a well-known figure in the Kurort, the owner of a bookstore and a print shop. His son Bruno Emmert (1877-1959) was a bibliographer and bibliophile whose 50,000 volumes constitute the "Fondo Antico" of the Arco library.

[699] R. Biblioteca Nazionale Centrale di Firenze, De Gub, 74, 48a, 14.

[700] S. Ioppi, *Di Villa in Villa*, Il Sommolago, Arco 2004, pp. 53 &54. In October 1900.

[701] This was tested when in 1904 his name was linked to embezzlement of Red Cross funds; the Tsarina repaid these for him and she even continued to favour him by requesting his promotion in later years.

[702] Diary kept by Lucy Graves; Miss Clara Barton, Papers: Diaries and Journals, Library of Congress series: Diaries and Journals, 1849-1911 MSS11973, box: 8; Microfilm reel: 6, Image 100 dated November 30 1898 (Graves, L. (1898) *Clara Barton Papers: Diaries and Journals: Diarists other than Barton; Graves, Lucy, June 17-Dec. 30, Spanish-American War relief.*, June 17-Dec. 30. [Manuscript/Mixed Material] Retrieved from the Library of Congress, www.loc.gov/item/mss119730062/ Accessed 23 September 2021). Clara Barton was the President of the American Red Cross Society; she visited Constantinople in 1896 acc. to J. Rendel Harris & Helen B. Harris, *Letters from Armenia*, London, 1897, p. 1.

[703] Istanboul,01/1/1894 Bibliothèque Nationale de France, Gallica, p. 3 https://gallica.bnf.fr/ark:/12148/bd6t524492x/ Accessed 1 Jan 2023 They met at the Grand Hotel de Londres.

[704] St Petersburg Historical State Archive, Zapis' o kreshenii v MK tserkvi Departamenta udelov SPbB on 6 May 1905: TsGIA F.19. op.127. d.1675 kadr 274.) Tserkov dvorinskovo dvortsa. Granddaughter Irina arrived on 2 December 1904 Old Style (15 Dec NS). Both grandparents Alexander and Olga Lebedeff were godparents at the christening in the Tsar's Palace Church on 5 May 1905 in St Petersburg.

[705] Irina's other godparents were her paternal great aunt Ekaterina Alexandrovna Shamshina (Alexander's sister) and other grandfather Mikhail Pavlovich Gorloff. A year later in July they christened their second daughter Elena, born 31 May 1906. Elena was known as Olga.

[706] Yu. Manuilova, *Istoria Dinastii Lebedevikh*, Mozhginskie Vesti, Mozhga, 2019, p. 10.

[707] A. Izmorosin, *The Bridge of Tears – is a humpback*, (transl.) 24 Sept 2010 www.rt-online.ru/aticles/rubric-79/99740/ Accessed on 27 May 2015.

ENDNOTES

[708] *La Plume et l'épée*, edition 15 Sept-15 December 1910, p. 156 https://gallica.bnf.fr/ark:/12148/bpt6k1184632w Accessed 15 April 2021 Alexander Lebedeff, died in Kazan on 29 April 1910. The only other information found concerning Alexander is stored at the Kazan Federal University archive: Volzhskii Vestnik No.122 (Kazan), a socio-political and literary journal. These are dictated letters, appearing to have little relevance to the narrative.

[709] See Endnote 142.

[710] Letters to and from I. Grinevskaya are kept in literary archives in St Petersburg. Pushkinsky Dom Fond 55, Op. 2, № 100, N 736. A short biography of Olga written by Isabella Grinevskaya is held in the archive of S.A. Vengerov at Pushkinsky Dom, Fond 377, op. 7, No. 2101 Isabella survived the Russian Revolution and died in Istanbul.

[711] The outline literary biography of Olga de Lebedeff by Isabella Grinevskaya (2 pages) is kept at the Pushkinskii Dom Archive in St Petersburg in the archive of S.A. Vengerov F. 377, op. 7, No 2101.

[712] S. Safina, *Zhivite, Moi Lubyantsi !* Kazan, 2005, p.25. In Chistopolsky (where his great-grandfather had built the Pokrovsky Church) and Mamadishsky

[713] Kazan National Archive 'Dostoiny pamyati potomkov (Gorodskie golovi Kazani 1767-1917. Sbornik dokumentov i materialov', *Gasyr* , Compiled by A.M. Dimitrieva, P.P. Ismagilov, N. D. Neroznikova, N.A. Sharangina editor L.V. Gorokhova, academic editor D.R. Sharafutdinov. Kazan, 2002, p. 352.

[714] *Washington, Passenger and Crew Lists*, 1882-1965 for Michel Lebedef. Provided for Ancestry.com in association with National Archives and Records.

[715] *US World War I Draft Registration Cards,* 1917-1918 for Michael Lebedef, provided for Ancestry.com in association with National Archives and Records.

[716] Micha himself opted to become an American citizen in 1927, his name was Americanized to Michael Lebedev and he signed up for WWII. He died not too long after the war had ended in 1947, the same year that his sister and godmother Nina Dlotovsky-Bahache died far away in South America.

[717] S. Safina, *Lubiani, Rodina Lesovodov*. Kazan, 2011, p. 30 Apart from one wing, what had remained of the Lebedev's home was eventually destroyed in a fire in 1979.

[718] *New-York Tribune* (New York [N.Y.]), December 9, 1918, and 13 February 1921 Library of Congress, Washington, DC.

[719] C. Gousseff, *L'exile russe, La fabrique du refugie apatride*, CNRS Éditions, Paris 2008, p. 56.

[720] Online article by Medina Publishing House entitled *The Russian Muslim Movement for Women's Rights in 1917 - The First Shoots of Feminist Muslim Thought and Practice* outlines authors and names of women writers who

were first inspired by the activities of Gülnar Khanum (O.S. Lebedeva). This references a work published in Kazan by A. Kh. Makhmutova in 2003. www.idmedina.ru/books/regions/?1562. Accessed 14 Feb 2024.

[721] S. Safina, *Zhivite, Moi Lubyantsi* ! Kazan 2005, p.23 As for the sawmill, it was absorbed into state ownership and was to become known as the best in the newly formed Tatarstan; Lubiana became the location of a new forestry institute during the 1920s, which has continued to expand and grow to this day (Ibid. p. 30).

[722] *www.dlib.si/stream/URN:NBN:SI:doc-NB9F7X23/...cf8c... /PDF* Slovenec 18 May 1943, p.5 / Accessed 11 Sept 2016. Newspaper Slovenec p. 5.

[723] Acar, Atti 1926, XIV, 2deLebedeff, Arco Comune, Arco, Trentino.

[724] The house was sold to Mariangela Gigante, born Ferraris di Brindisi.

[725] Olga had helped support her daughters' finances, evidenced by postcards in which Vera tells Nina that *Maman* will be making the necessary financial arrangements.

[726] Registro della popolazione del Comune di Romarzolo [1923-1929], Arco

[727] J-C. Volpi, Menton, Une Exception Azuréenne ou 150 ans d'Histoire du Tourisme (1861-2011), p.10.

[728] Some 200,000 White Russians came to live in France after 1917, with Paris as the cultural and political centre of the émigré community. They became stateless as their Russian citizenship was revoked after the Revolution.

[729] Discovered by Victor Dzevanovsky-Petrashevsky in 2021 and very kindly shared with me.

[730] D. Smith, *Former People: The Last Days of the Russian Aristocracy*, Macmillan / Farrar, Strauss & Giroux, 2012.

[731] This information was kindly shared with me by Victor Dzevanovsky-Petrashevsky based on his research about Olga de Lebedeff in Russia.

[732] OFPRA historical archives, Paris: Dossier n°122118 Olga Gorloff, née Lebedeff 27/04/1881, Box G99. OFPRA historical archives, 201, rue Carnot 94120 FONTENAY-SOUS-BOIS.

[733] Olga Bobrovsky's birth record names her as Maria Magdalena Bobrovsky, she died in Japan aged two.

[734] Or 'which inspired his own writing in Russian' [CH].

[735] *Actes du douzième Congres international des orientalistes* : Rome 1899, Tome 1, p. CLXXXVI. https://gallica.bnf.fr/ark:/12148/bpt6k97609698. Accessed 23 Feb 2021.

[736] Harun al-Rashid ('Aaron the Rightly Guided') was Abbasid caliph who ruled in Baghdad from 786-809. He is also famous as a protagonist in One Thousand and One Nights.

[737] Thomas Moore published an Oriental romance in 1817, about the daughter of the seventeenth century Mughal emperor Aurangzeb.

[738] Customary laws are accepted traditional or moral norms which become unofficial laws, regarded as a legal practice.

ENDNOTES

[739] Louis-Aimé Martin (1782-1847) French man of letters and literary historian

[740] Edmond Groult was member of the Historical Society of Lisieux, advocate, Doctor of Law, founder of the regional museum of Lisieux (Calvados). He married Marie de Besneray in 1904.

[741] It was founded in St Petersburg on 29 February 1900, with Olga as honorary president.

[742] Madame Hyacinthe Loyson (Emilie) later published her travelogue *To Jerusalem through the lands of Islam among Jews, Christians, and Muslims* in 1905. She and her husband were engaged in ecumenical and interreligious encounters.

[743] Verhandlung, Sektion VI, pp. 314-319 (Congress Proceedings, Section 6).

[744] First Part, Section VI. Ernest Leroux, 1906 (pp. 41-42).

[745] 'Le rôle de compagne et de consolatrice de l'homme'. Perhaps this echoes Jean Jacques Rousseau, that women were supposed to conform to the ideal of helpers of men; yet a role that Olga de Lebedeff found difficult to square this ideal in her own marriages.

[746] Patriarche Macaire, *Histoire de la conversion des Géorgiens au Christianisme*, trans. Mme Olga de Lébédew (Roma : Casa Editrice Italiana, 1905). Codex 689 du Vatican. The Arabic text : *Nabdha fi akhbar al-Karj*.

[747] Marilyn Booth: I have given the French page numbers first and the Arabic second, even when I mention the Arabic before giving the French—for no reason, except that in the volume, the French precedes the Arabic; they are paginated separately.

[748] Instruction de sa majesté impérial Catherine II (St Petersburg : Academie des Sciences, 1769), 3. Taken from M Bassin, 'Russia between Europe and Asia : The Ideological Construction of Geographical Space', Slavic Review 1991, p.9. Translation [CH]: 'Russian is a European Power'.

[749] A contrasting example: In 1850 Queen Victoria was presented with an enslaved seven-year-old African, the daughter of a west African ruler given as a diplomatic gift by King Ghezo of Dahomey (now Benin). Originally known as Aina, she was renamed Sarah Forbes Bonetta. The queen paid for Aina /Sarah's education in Sierra Leone before she returned to England. Queen Victoria was her godmother.

[750] Kutaisi, an ancient city located in the southern Georgian lands of the Ottoman Empire was returned in 1770 to being the capital of the Imeretian Kingdom; today, Kutaisi, also known as 'city of roses', is in Georgia.

[751] Pending confirmation from the Georgian archives at Kutaisi.

[752] *Russkii Biograficheskii Slovar (Kn-Kiu)*, published by The Imperial Russian Historical Society, St Petersburg 1903, p. 617.

[753] Iu. A. Matiukhina, *Favoriti Pravitelei Rossii*, Moscow 2012, p. 217.

[754] The Morning Post (London, Greater London, England), Sat 1 April 1843, p.6. 'Houses of Counts of Russia' by order of creation, attrib. to Prince Dolgorouki.

[755] In The Atchison Weekly Patriot (Atchison, Kansas) on 28th May 1887; Newpapers.com.
[756] S. Sebag-Montefiore, *The Romanovs*, Weidenfeld & Nicholson, 2016, p.258.
[757] S. Sebag-Montefiore, p. 259.
[758] N. Davies, p. 739.
[759] Y Anisimov, *The Rulers of Russia*, Golden Lion Publishing House, St Petersburg 2012, pp. 138 - 139.
[760] S. Sebag-Montefiore, p. 278. See footnote.
[761] Y Anisimov, p. 141.
[762] W. Belsham, Memoirs of the Reign of George III, From his Accession to the Peace of Amiens, Volume 8, 1 January 1813, p. 177.
[763] S. Sebag-Montefiore, p. 271.
[764] http://ptzh.theatre.ru/1998/16/58/ website of the Peterburgskii Teatralniy Zhurnal, no 16, 1998, article by theatre critic Svetlana Melnikova (accessed 19 May 2020).
[765] L.E. Vigée-Lebrun, *Souvenirs de Madame Vigée Le Brun*. Tome 2, pp. 75 - 76, & Tome 3 p.13. (Bibliothèque nationale de France, 8-Ln27-11900 (3))
[766] Iu. A. Matiukhina, p. 218.
[767] C. Kelly, *A History of Russian Women's Writing 1820-1992*, Oxford University Press, 1994, p. 53; a quote from the memoirs of F. Vigel, Zapiski, 1. 110.
[768] The Standard (London) 21 February 1868, p. 6. (Newspapers.com) Accessed 3 July 2020.
[769] http://feb-web.ru/feb/rosarc/rad/Rad-061-.htm p. 62. Accessed 16 January 2023.
[770] According to Prascovia Nikolaevna Baranova, recorded 'Zapiski' Vol. 2, by Filip F. Vigel.
[771] Iu. A. Matiukhina, p. 218.
[772] N. Davies, pp. 652, 726, 739.
[773] Y Anisimov, p. 141.
[774] Omeljan Pritsak, 'The Pogroms of 1881', *Harvard Ukrainian Studies* Vol. XI June 1987. http://projects.iq.harvard.edu/files/huri/files/vxi_n1_2june1987.pdf.
[775] Professor Reginald Christian, my professor of Tolstoy at St Andrews University, recalled 'Princess Koutaissoff' when she was professor at Birmingham and Oxford universities.
[776] These many themes can be explored in the General Catalogue of the French Library by Otto Lorenz, French edition is called *Catalogue General de la Librairie Française* edited by D. Jordell, (Continuation de l'ouvrage d'Otto Lorenz), Paris, 1905, Vol. 16, pp. 403 - 406 https://gallica.bnf.fr/ark:/12148/bpt6k4880x Accessed 30 August 2023
[777] C. Vaughn Findley, p.45. This assertion was made by Ahmed Midhat in his travelogue.

ENDNOTES

[778] E. Said, *Orientalism*. Penguin Random House, 2003. First published 1978.
[779] R. Irwin, For Lust of Knowing. The Orientalists and their Enemies, published by Allan Lane, 2006, p. 197.
[780] R. Irwin, pp. 229 – 233.
[781] R. Irwin, p. 158.
[782] Turkestanskie Vedomosti, No.33, Tashkent, 26 April 1901 (p.166).
[783] T. Olcay, 'Olga Lebedeva (Madame Gülnar): A Russian Orientalist and Translator Enchants the Ottomans', *Slovo*, Vol. 29, 2 (Summer 2017).